Taste of Home Has Done It Again!

The world's **#1 cooking magazine** brings you an exciting, all-new collection packed from cover to cover with tasty favorites—**more than 500 recipes** your family is sure to love.

When a cookbook has the name *Taste of Home,* you know you can expect the very best. And that's just what you'll find inside this sensational, brand-new recipe collection!

The 19th edition in our best-selling cookbook series, *2012 Taste of Home Annual Recipes* is brimming with hundreds of scrumptious dishes published in *Taste of Home* magazine in 2011. Plus, we've included more than 100 bonus recipes never before seen in *Taste of Home.* That adds up to 509 recipes—all here in one convenient cookbook!

This can't-miss collection has everything you need to make every menu a success. Choose from irresistible appetizers, comforting soups, family-pleasing main dishes, delectable breads, standout sides and luscious desserts.

Here's more of what you'll find inside:

- **National Recipe Contest Winners**
  Enjoy all of the winning dishes from the following national recipe contests: Holiday Desserts, Garlic & Onions, Southwest, Summer Cookout and Five Ingredients.

- **Express Dishes Ready in 30 Minutes**
  You'll discover amazingly fast recipes you can fix in 30 minutes—or even less—scattered throughout the book. Turn to "Quick Fixes" (p. 230) for a whole chapter of them!

- **Holiday and Party Sensations**
  Celebrate special occasions with two festive chapters. "Holiday & Seasonal Celebrations" (p. 154) and "Tasteful Get-Togethers" (p. 288) offer showstoppers that are sure to impress.

- **Servings on the Lighter Side**
  Want to cut sodium, fat and calories? Rely on the guilt-free choices in "Cooking Lighter" (p. 250). These treats taste so good, your family and friends will never guess they're eating healthier.

- **Favorites from Family Cooks**
  We haven't forgotten the home-style chapters you've come to know and love. In "Mom's Best" (p. 190) and "Field Editor Favorites" (p. 208), fellow family cooks share their treasured recipes so you can enjoy them, too.

This must-have cookbook also includes gorgeous full-color photos, expert tips from the *Taste of Home* Test Kitchen and two handy indexes to help you find everything you need.

So go ahead—savor all of the great flavor there is to find inside *2012 Taste of Home Annual Recipes!*

TASTE-TEMPTING BEST

Whether you want a decadent cake, saucy entree, refreshing beverage or other dish, you just can't go wrong with the standouts inside *2012 Taste of Home Annual Recipes.* Indulge in scrumptious specialties such as (above, from top) Macadamia Toffee Snack Cake (p. 115), fruity Summertime Tea (p. 6) and delicious Orange-Pecan Salmon (p. 66).

taste of home 2012
ANNUAL RECIPES

Editor-in-Chief **Catherine Cassidy**
Vice President, Executive Editor/Books **Heidi Reuter Lloyd**
Creative Director **Howard Greenberg**
Senior Editor/Books **Mark Hagen**
Editor **Michelle Rozumalski**
Associate Creative Director **Edwin Robles, Jr.**
Art Director **Gretchen Trautman**
Content Production Manager **Julie Wagner**
Layout Designers **Nancy Novak, Kathy Crawford**
Copy Chief **Deb Warlaumont Mulvey**
Copy Editor **Susan Uphill**
Recipe Asset System Manager **Coleen Martin**
Administrative Assistant **Barb Czysz**

■ CONSUMER MARKETING
North American Chief Marketing Officer **Lisa Karpinski**
Vice President/Book Marketing **Dan Fink**
Creative Director/Creative Marketing **Jim Palmen**

■ TASTE OF HOME MAGAZINE
Executive Editor **Christian Millman**
Food Director **Diane Werner, RD**
Editor **Jeanne Ambrose**
Art Director **Erin Burns**
Senior Editor **Elizabeth Russell**
Recipe Editor **Irene Yeh**
Production Coordinator **Dena Ahlers**
Layout Designer **Dana Borremans**
Editorial Assistant **Jane Stasik**
Executive Assistant **Marie Brannon**

■ TEST KITCHEN
Test Kitchen Manager **Karen Scales**
Associate Food Editors **Alicia Bozewicz, RD; Marie Parker; Annie Rundle**
Recipe Specialists **Jenni Sharp, RD; Katie Bartnicki**
Test Kitchen Coordinator **Kristy Martin**
Test Kitchen Associates **Rita Krajcir, Wendy Herr, Jenny McCarthy**

■ PHOTOGRAPHY
Photo Studio Business Manager **Kimberly Gohr**
Photographers **Rob Hagen, Dan Roberts, Jim Wieland, Lori Foy**
Set Styling Manager **Stephanie Marchese**
Set Stylists **Melissa Haberman, Dee Dee Jacq, Deone Jahnke, Pam Stasney**
Food Styling Manager **Sarah Thompson**
Food Stylists **Kaitlyn Besasie, Alynna Malson, Shannon Roum, Diane Armstrong, Ronne Day, Kathryn Conrad**
Food Stylist Assistant **Leah Rekau**
Photo Studio Coordinator **Kathy Swaney**
Photo Coordinator **Trudi Bellin**
Assistant Photo Coordinator **Mary Ann Koebernik**

■ THE READER'S DIGEST ASSOCIATION, INC.
President and Chief Executive Officer **Tom Williams**
Executive Vice President, RDA, and President, North America **Dan Lagani**

Taste of Home Books
© 2011 Reiman Media Group, LLC
5400 S. 60th St., Greendale WI 53129

Taste of Home is a registered trademark of
The Reader's Digest Association, Inc.

International Standard Book Number (10): 0-89821-935-3
International Standard Book Number (13): 978-0-89821-935-7
International Standard Serial Number: 1094-3463

ON THE BACK COVER Jam-Topped Mini Cheesecakes (p. 129).

PICTURED AT LEFT Apple-Bacon Mini Loaves (p. 88), Finnish Cauliflower (p. 58) and Dutch Meatballs (Bitterballen) (p. 282).

contents

ON THE COVER Apricot-Glazed Turkey Breast (p. 264),
Herb Garden Vegetables (p. 151), Marmalade
Candied Carrots (p. 163) and Bluebarb Pie (p. 171).

Photographer: **Dan Roberts**
Set Stylist: **Stephanie Marchese**
Food Stylists: **Ronne Day, Shannon Roum**

FOR OTHER TASTE OF HOME BOOKS AND PRODUCTS, VISIT
ShopTasteofHome.com

Snacks & Beverages

For impressive party starters or just munchies to tide over the kids until dinner, look here. Everyone will love these satisfying bites and drinks, from Three-Pepper Bean Dip to Blueberry Thirst Quencher.

HOW REFRESHING. Clockwise from top left: Spiced Nuts (p. 13), Summertime Tea (p. 6), Lick-the-Bowl-Clean Hummus (p. 13) and Caramelized Fennel Tarts (p. 12).

reaches desired doneness (for medium-rare, a meat thermometer should read 145°; medium, 160°; well-done, 170°). Cut into thin slices.

Place bread on ungreased baking sheets. Bake at 400° for 4-6 minutes or until lightly browned.

Meanwhile, place the cream cheese, blue cheese, salt and pepper in a food processor; cover and process until blended. Spread each bread slice with 1 teaspoon cheese mixture; top with steak and onions. **Yield:** 4 dozen.

Summertime Tea

(Pictured below and on page 4)

PREP: 15 min. + chilling

You just can't have a summer gathering around here without this sweet tea to cool you down. It's wonderful for sipping while relaxing by the pool. —Angela Lively, Baxter, Tennessee

> 14 **cups water, *divided***
> 6 **individual black tea bags**
> 1-1/2 **cups sugar**
> 3/4 **cup thawed frozen orange juice concentrate**
> 3/4 **cup thawed frozen lemonade concentrate**
> 1 **cup tequila, optional**
> **Fresh mint leaves and lemon *or* lime slices, optional**

In a large saucepan, bring 4 cups water to a boil. Remove from heat; add tea bags. Cover and steep for 3-5 minutes. Discard tea bags.

Stir in the sugar, concentrates and remaining water. Add tequila if desired. Refrigerate until chilled. Garnish with mint and lemon slices if desired. **Yield:** 18 servings (3/4 cup each).

Blue Cheese-Onion Steak Bites

(Pictured above)

PREP: 15 min. **COOK:** 35 min.

I love the flavor pairing of blue cheese and steak. Adding garlic and onion makes it even better! This is a hearty appetizer for parties and can even be served as a light lunch or dinner.
—Jo-Ellen Neil, Arroyo Grande, California

> 3 **large onions, thinly sliced into rings**
> 12 **garlic cloves, minced**
> 3 **tablespoons butter**
> 4 **beef tenderloin steaks (6 ounces *each*)**
> 1/4 **teaspoon salt**
> 1/4 **teaspoon pepper**
> 1 **loaf (10-1/2 ounces) French bread baguette, cut into 1/4-inch slices**
> **SPREAD:**
> 4 **ounces cream cheese, softened**
> 1 **cup (4 ounces) crumbled blue cheese**
> 1/8 **teaspoon salt**
> 1/8 **teaspoon pepper**

In a large skillet, saute onions and garlic in butter until softened. Reduce heat to medium-low; cook, stirring occasionally, for 30 minutes or until golden brown.

Meanwhile, sprinkle beef with salt and pepper. Moisten a paper towel with cooking oil; using long-handled tongs, lightly coat the grill rack.

Grill steaks, covered, over medium heat or broil 4 in. from the heat for 5-7 minutes on each side or until meat

Grilled Prosciutto Asparagus

(Pictured above)

PREP/TOTAL TIME: 30 min.

After tasting a restaurant's asparagus appetizer, I wanted to create my own version of it to enjoy at home. This recipe was the yummy result. —Michele Merlino, Wakefield, Rhode Island

> 1/2 **pound thinly sliced prosciutto**
> 1 **log (4 ounces) fresh goat cheese**
> 1 **pound fresh asparagus, trimmed**

Cut prosciutto slices in half; spread with cheese. Wrap a piece around each asparagus spear; secure ends with toothpicks. Moisten a paper towel with cooking oil; using long-handled tongs, lightly coat the grill rack.

Grill, covered, over medium heat for 6-8 minutes or until the prosciutto is crisp, turning once. Discard the toothpicks. **Yield:** about 2 dozen.

Energizing Granola

PREP: 25 min. **BAKE:** 25 min. + cooling

This wholesome, fruit–filled snack combo packs a healthy punch of nutrition and can do double duty as breakfast, too.
—Nina Wiseman, Batavia, Ohio

> 2-1/2 **cups old-fashioned oats**
> 3/4 **cup chopped walnuts**
> 1/2 **cup unsalted sunflower kernels**
> 1/3 **cup packed brown sugar**
> 1/4 **cup flaked coconut**
> 1/4 **cup toasted wheat germ**
> 2 **tablespoons sesame seeds**
> 2 **tablespoons ground flaxseed**
> 1/3 **cup water**
> 2 **tablespoons honey**
> 2 **tablespoons molasses**
> 1 **tablespoon canola oil**
> 3/4 **teaspoon vanilla extract**
> 1/2 **teaspoon salt**
> 1/2 **teaspoon ground cinnamon**
> 1/3 **cup dried cranberries**
> 1/3 **cup golden raisins**
> 1/4 **cup dried banana chips**

In a large bowl, combine the first eight ingredients. In a small saucepan, combine the water, honey, molasses and oil. Heat for 3-4 minutes over medium until heated through. Remove from the heat; stir in the vanilla, salt and cinnamon. Pour over the oat mixture; stir to coat.

Transfer mixture to a 15-in. x 10-in. x 1-in. baking pan coated with cooking spray. Bake at 350° for 25-30 minutes or until lightly browned, stirring every 10 minutes. Cool completely on a wire rack. Stir in the dried cranberries, golden raisins and banana chips. Store in an airtight container. **Yield:** 6 cups.

Ensenada Shrimp Cocktail

(Pictured below)

PREP: 15 min. + chilling

Tomatoes, peppers, onions and cilantro replace cocktail sauce in this Southwestern makeover of the popular appetizer.
—*Teri Rasey, Cadillac, Michigan*

  1 **pound peeled and deveined cooked medium shrimp**
  2 **plum tomatoes, seeded and chopped**
  3 **jalapeno peppers, seeded and chopped**
  1 **serrano pepper, seeded and chopped**
1/4 **cup chopped red onion**
  2 **green onions, chopped**
  2 **tablespoons minced fresh cilantro**
  2 **tablespoons olive oil**
  1 **tablespoon rice vinegar**
  1 **tablespoon key lime juice** *or* **lime juice**
  1 **teaspoon adobo seasoning**
Lime wedges

In a large bowl, combine the shrimp, tomatoes, peppers, onions and cilantro. Combine the oil, vinegar, lime juice and adobo seasoning; drizzle over shrimp mixture and toss to coat.

Refrigerate for at least 1 hour. Using a slotted spoon, place shrimp mixture in cocktail glasses, about 1/2 cup in each. Garnish with lime wedges. **Yield:** 8 servings.

Editor's Note: We recommend wearing disposable gloves when cutting hot peppers. Avoid touching your face.

Peachy Keen Daiquiris

(Pictured above)

PREP/TOTAL TIME: 10 min.

You won't mind breaking out the blender for these frosty drinks. A little grenadine gives them an extra splash of color.
—*Joan Antonen, Arlington, South Dakota*

2-1/2 **cups ice cubes**
    3 **medium peaches, peeled and sliced**
  3/4 **cup thawed frozen limeade concentrate**
  1/4 **cup orange juice**
    2 **tablespoons confectioners' sugar**
  1/2 **cup rum, optional**
Grenadine syrup, optional

In a blender, combine ice, peaches, limeade concentrate, orange juice, confectioners' sugar and rum if desired; cover and process for 30 seconds or until smooth. Pour into chilled glasses; add grenadine, if desired. Serve immediately. **Yield:** 3 servings.

FESTIVE FINISHES. No-fuss garnishes, such as citrus slices, fruit skewers, and colorful straws and stirrers, add a touch of whimsy to your party beverages. For example, add a simple peach slice to Peachy Keen Daiquiris (recipe above) or a skewer of fresh blueberries to Blueberry Thirst Quencher (recipe on p. 17).

Strawberry Party Punch

PREP/TOTAL TIME: 15 min.

After munching something spicy or hot, cool your palate with this tangy thirst quencher. Let guests help themselves at the punch bowl or serve this beverage by the glass with fruit garnishes.
—*Deirdre Dee Cox, Milwaukee, Wisconsin*

- 6 **cups fresh** *or* **frozen unsweetened strawberries, thawed**
- 3/4 **cup thawed limeade concentrate**
- 1 **can (6 ounces) unsweetened pineapple juice**
- 4 **cups chilled lemon-lime soda**

Ice cubes, optional

Place strawberries in a food processor; cover and process until smooth. Stir in limeade concentrate and pineapple juice. Chill until serving.

Transfer to a punch bowl. Just before serving, stir in chilled lemon-lime soda. Serve over ice if desired. **Yield:** 13 servings (3/4 cup each).

Smokin' Hot Deviled Eggs

(Pictured below)

PREP/TOTAL TIME: 20 min.

Nearly everybody loves deviled eggs, and this variation has a nice kick. You can't go wrong bringing these to a party or potluck.
—*Jan Roberts, San Pedro, California*

- 12 **hard-cooked eggs**
- 1/2 **cup mayonnaise**
- 3 **chipotle peppers in adobo sauce, finely chopped**
- 1 **tablespoon capers, drained**

- 1 **tablespoon stone-ground mustard**
- 1/4 **teaspoon salt**
- 1/4 **teaspoon white pepper**

Minced fresh cilantro

Cut eggs in half lengthwise. Remove yolks; set whites aside. In a small bowl, mash yolks. Add the mayonnaise, chipotle peppers, capers, mustard, salt and white pepper; mix well. Stuff or pipe into egg whites. Refrigerate until serving. Sprinkle with cilantro. **Yield:** 2 dozen.

Sun-Dried Tomato Cheese Balls

(Pictured above)

PREP: 30 min. + chilling

Your get-together is sure to heat up once these bacon-coated miniature cheese balls are on the hors d'oeuvre table. Spiced with red pepper flakes, they're just the right size for nibbling.
—*Pamela Stepp, Dandridge, Tennessee*

- 12 **ounces cream cheese, softened**
- 2 **cups (8 ounces) shredded sharp cheddar cheese**
- 1/4 **cup finely chopped oil-packed sun-dried tomatoes**
- 1 **tablespoon finely chopped onion**
- 2 **teaspoons Worcestershire sauce**
- 1 **teaspoon lemon juice**
- 1/2 **teaspoon crushed red pepper flakes**
- 1/8 **teaspoon pepper**
- 1 **pound bacon strips, cooked and crumbled**

Assorted crackers

In a large bowl, beat the first eight ingredients until blended. Shape into 1-1/4-in. balls.

Place bacon into a small shallow dish; roll the cheese balls in bacon. Refrigerate for at least 1 hour. Serve with crackers. **Yield:** about 2-1/2 dozen.

Three-Pepper Bean Dip

(Pictured above)

PREP: 15 min. **BAKE:** 30 min.

My husband's great–grandmother and I developed this recipe together after trying a similar one from his aunt. So the dip is not only delicious, it also has a lot of sentimental value.
—*Amber Massey, Coppell, Texas*

   1 **can (16 ounces) refried beans**
1-1/2 **cups (12 ounces) reduced-fat sour cream**
   1 **cup salsa**
   4 **green onions, chopped**
   1 **can (4 ounces) chopped green chilies**
   3 **ounces reduced-fat cream cheese**
   1 **jalapeno pepper, seeded and chopped**
   2 **tablespoons chopped chipotle peppers
     in adobo sauce**
1-1/2 **teaspoons ground cumin**
 1/2 **teaspoon chili powder**
   1 **cup (4 ounces) shredded Colby-Monterey Jack
     cheese**
Tortilla chips *or* assorted fresh vegetables

In a large bowl, combine the first 10 ingredients. Transfer to a greased 1-1/2-qt. baking dish. Cover and bake at 325° for 25 minutes.

Sprinkle with cheese. Bake, uncovered, 5-10 minutes longer or until bubbly. Serve warm with tortilla chips. **Yield:** 5 cups.

Editor's Note: We recommend wearing disposable gloves when cutting hot peppers. Avoid touching your face.

Sweet Citrus Iced Tea

PREP: 15 min. + chilling

My family has been making iced tea this way—with lemon and orange juice—since I was a child. When I recently fixed some for an event at church, I received many requests for the recipe.
—*Diane Kirkpatrick, Terre Hill, Pennsylvania*

14-1/2 **cups water, *divided***
  10 **individual tea bags**
1-1/2 **cups sugar**
 2/3 **cup lemon juice**
 1/4 **cup thawed orange juice concentrate**
Ice cubes

In a large saucepan, bring 4 cups of water just to a boil. Remove from the heat. Add the tea bags; let stand for 10 minutes. Discard tea bags.

Pour tea into a large container. Stir in the sugar, lemon juice, orange juice concentrate and remaining water. Refrigerate until chilled. Serve over ice. **Yield:** 1 gallon.

Savory Cocktail Scones

PREP: 55 min. **BAKE:** 15 min.

Scones are comfort food to me, and I wanted to come up with a savory version featuring roasted garlic butter and pieces of bacon. The cocktail size of these bites makes them fun for parties, but they would also work for breakfast or brunch buffets.
—*Donna Marie Ryan, Topsfield, Massachusetts*

   1 **whole garlic bulb**
   2 **teaspoons olive oil**
 1/2 **cup butter, softened**
SCONES:
   2 **bacon strips, chopped**
 1/3 **cup chopped onion**
   2 **cups all-purpose flour**
   3 **teaspoons baking powder**
 1/2 **teaspoon baking soda**
 1/2 **teaspoon salt**
 1/2 **cup cold butter**
   1 **egg**
 1/2 **cup sherry**
 1/3 **cup heavy whipping cream**
 1/4 **cup 2% milk**

Remove papery outer skin from the garlic (do not peel or separate cloves). Cut top off of garlic bulb. Brush with oil. Wrap bulb in heavy-duty foil. Bake at 400° for 40-45 minutes or until softened. Cool for 10-15 minutes. Squeeze softened garlic into a small bowl; mash with fork. Stir in butter; set aside.

In a small skillet, cook the bacon over medium heat until crisp. Remove to paper towels with a slotted spoon; drain, reserving 1 tablespoon drippings. In the same skillet, cook and stir onion in the drippings until softened. Reduce heat to medium-low; cook, stirring occasionally, for 30 minutes or until deep golden brown. Set aside.

In a large bowl, combine flour, baking powder, baking soda and salt. Cut in butter until the mixture resembles coarse crumbs. Whisk the egg, sherry and cream; stir into the crumb mixture just until moistened. Fold in the onion and bacon.

Turn onto a floured surface; knead 10 times. Pat into a 10-in. x 5-in. rectangle. Using a floured knife, cut into eight 2-1/2-in. squares; cut each square diagonally in half.

Place on a parchment paper-lined baking sheet; brush with milk. Bake at 400° for 12-15 minutes or until golden brown. Serve warm with butter. **Yield:** 16 servings.

Sweet Chipotle Pretzels

(Pictured below)

PREP: 10 min. **BAKE:** 10 min. + cooling

It's hard to stop munching these sweet–spicy pretzels. I dressed them up with sugar, cinnamon, allspice and chipotle pepper.
—Geraldine Saucier, Albuquerque, New Mexico

    4 **cups miniature pretzels**
    1 **egg white**
    1 **tablespoon water**
  1/2 **cup packed brown sugar**
1-1/2 **teaspoons ground cinnamon**
  1/4 **teaspoon ground allspice**
  1/8 **teaspoon ground chipotle pepper**

Place the pretzels in a large bowl. Whisk the egg white and water until frothy; stir in the brown sugar, cinnamon, allspice and chipotle pepper. Pour over the pretzels; toss to coat.

Arrange in single layer on parchment paper-lined baking sheets. Bake at 350° for 10-12 minutes or until dry. Cool completely on a wire rack. Store in an airtight container. **Yield:** 4 cups.

Veggie Cheese People

(Pictured above)

PREP/TOTAL TIME: 30 min.

Make wholesome, nutritious snacks fun for kids. These edible characters from our Test Kitchen pros let little ones get creative at the table, encouraging them to nibble as they go.

Celery rib
Grape tomatoes
Small zucchini
Yellow summer squash
Fresh sugar snap peas
Pitted ripe olives
String cheese
Seeded quartered watermelon
Wooden skewers and toothpicks

Cut vegetables and cheese into desired shapes. To create people, thread shapes onto skewers; use toothpicks to attach arms and legs. Insert into melon. **Yield:** varies.

Sunny Asparagus Tapenade

(Pictured below)

PREP/TOTAL TIME: 30 min.

I use fresh asparagus from the farmers market for this healthy spread, which can also be served as a dip. I frequently make it for family gatherings. —Kathy Patalsky, New York, New York

- 3/4 **pound fresh asparagus, chopped**
- 3/4 **cup packed fresh parsley sprigs**
- 1/3 **cup unsalted sunflower kernels**
- 1/4 **cup lemon juice**
- 1/4 **cup orange juice**
- 1 **tablespoon olive oil**
- 2 **teaspoons maple syrup**
- 1 **small garlic clove, chopped**
- 1/2 **teaspoon salt**
- 1/2 **teaspoon crushed red pepper flakes**
- 1 **teaspoon pepper**

Additional sunflower kernels, optional
Assorted fresh vegetables, crackers *and/or* **toasted French bread baguette**

In a large saucepan, bring 1/2 in. of water to a boil. Add asparagus; cover and cook for 3-5 minutes or until tender. Drain and immediately place asparagus in ice water. Drain and pat dry.

Place in a food processor; add the parsley, sunflower kernels, lemon juice, orange juice, oil, syrup, garlic, salt, pepper flakes and pepper. Cover and process until desired consistency.

Transfer to a small bowl; sprinkle with additional sunflower kernels if desired. Serve at room temperature or chilled with the dippers of your choice. **Yield:** 2 cups.

Caramelized Fennel Tarts

(Pictured above and on page 4)

PREP: 45 min. **BAKE:** 15 min.

Fennel is a favorite of mine, no matter how it's cooked. I think it's really amazing sautéed until rich and golden, then baked on puff pastry for these tarts. —Lisa Speer, Palm Beach, Florida

- 2 **medium fennel bulbs, quartered and thinly sliced**
- 2 **tablespoons olive oil**
- 1-1/2 **teaspoons minced fresh thyme** *or* **1/2 teaspoon dried thyme**
- 1 **teaspoon balsamic vinegar**
- 1/4 **teaspoon salt**
- 1/8 **teaspoon pepper**
- 1 **package (17.3 ounces) frozen puff pastry, thawed**

In a large skillet, saute the fennel in oil until softened. Reduce the heat to medium-low; cook, uncovered, for 40 minutes or until deep golden brown, stirring occasionally. Stir in the thyme, vinegar, salt and pepper.

Unfold each puff pastry sheet onto an ungreased baking sheet. Using a knife, score 1 in. from the edges of each pastry sheet. Spread fennel mixture to within 1/2 in. of edges.

Bake at 400° for 12-15 minutes or until golden brown. Cut each tart into 12 pieces. **Yield:** 2 dozen.

FENNEL FACTS. An aromatic herb with a large pale green bulb and celery-like stems, fennel can be sauteed, braised, baked and added to soups or stews. The feathery leaves can be used in soups and salads or as a garnish.

Firecracker Float

PREP/TOTAL TIME: 5 min.

Our Test Kitchen pros came up with this fun-as-can-be yet simple float. Thanks to Pop Rocks candy, the frozen drink will literally make your taste buds tingle with flavor.

- **3 scoops vanilla ice cream**
- **1 envelope Pop Rocks candy, flavor of your choice**
- **1 cup chilled lemon-lime soda**

Place a scoop of ice cream in a tall glass; sprinkle with one-third of the candy. Repeat layers twice. Top with the soda. Serve immediately. **Yield:** 1 serving.

Lick-the-Bowl-Clean Hummus

(Pictured below and on page 4)

PREP: 10 min. **COOK:** 35 min.

Just about everyone loves hummus, but I enjoy the garlic and onion varieties so much that I decided to let them shine in this homemade version. I get so many compliments on it! Just add baked pita chips or fresh veggies for a terrific snack.
—*Sarah Gilbert, Beaverton, Oregon*

- **2 large sweet onions, thinly sliced**
- **1/4 cup plus 1/3 cup olive oil, *divided***
- **1 can (15 ounces) garbanzo beans *or* chickpeas, rinsed and drained**
- **1/4 cup plus 2 tablespoons lemon juice**
- **1/4 cup tahini**
- **4 garlic cloves, minced**
- **1/8 teaspoon salt**
- **1/8 teaspoon pepper**

Baked pita chips *or* assorted fresh vegetables

In a large skillet, saute the onions in 1/4 cup oil until softened. Reduce the heat to medium-low; cook, stirring occasionally, for 30 minutes or until deep golden brown.

Transfer to a food processor; add the beans, lemon juice, tahini, garlic, salt, pepper and remaining oil. Cover and process for 30 seconds or until smooth. Serve with chips. **Yield:** 2-1/2 cups.

Spiced Nuts

(Pictured above and on page 4)

PREP: 20 min. + cooling

These seasoned mixed nuts are great as a hostess gift or tucked in with a Christmas present for a yummy finishing touch. We like cardamom, so I often put another teaspoon in this recipe.
—*Judi Oudekerk, Buffalo, Minnesota*

- **1/4 cup butter, cubed**
- **1/2 cup plus 3 tablespoons sugar, *divided***
- **2 teaspoons ground cardamom**
- **1 cup salted cashews**
- **1 cup salted peanuts**
- **1 cup pecan halves**

In a large heavy skillet, melt butter. Add 1/2 cup sugar; cook and stir over high heat until sugar is dissolved. Meanwhile, place cardamom and remaining sugar in a large bowl; set aside.

Reduce heat to medium; add the cashews, peanuts and pecans to butter mixture. Cook and stir until nuts are toasted, about 3 minutes. Add hot nuts to reserved cardamom mixture; toss to coat. Spread on foil to cool. **Yield:** 3-1/2 cups.

Party Snacks on Sticks

TRY AS YOU MIGHT, it's difficult to mingle with the party crowd when you're juggling a plate of snacks in one hand and a beverage in the other. So the next time you host a get-together, put everyone at ease with these sweet and savory bites on skewers.

Your guests won't have to perform a balancing act when you serve hands-on morsels such as Caramel Apple & Brie Skewers, Ginger Tuna Kabobs, Cajun Shrimp Skewers and Caprese Appetizer Bites. With their built-in handles, these fun munchies are easy to grab when you're passing the buffet table. And they have another advantage as well—there are no messy fingers!

Caprese Appetizer Bites

(Pictured at top left in photo at left)

PREP/TOTAL TIME: 10 min.

This recipe is more creative than the usual vegetable platter and healthier than most chip-and-dip combinations. I often fix it as a snack to tide over my hungry family before dinner.
—*Christine Mitchell, Glendora, California*

- 24 **grape tomatoes**
- 12 **cherry-size fresh mozzarella cheese balls**
- 24 **fresh basil leaves**
- 2 **tablespoons olive oil**
- 2 **teaspoons balsamic vinegar**

On each of 12 wooden appetizer skewers, alternately thread two tomatoes, one mozzarella cheese ball and two basil leaves; place on a serving plate. In a small bowl, whisk the oil and vinegar; drizzle over kabobs just before serving. **Yield:** 12 kabobs.

Caramel Apple & Brie Skewers

(Pictured at top right in photo at left)

PREP/TOTAL TIME: 10 min.

I'm a caterer, and this is one of my best-selling appetizers. With store-bought caramel ice cream topping, apples and just three other basic ingredients, they're a breeze to assemble.
—*Camille Ellis, Tampa, Florida*

- 2 **medium apples, cubed**
- 1 **package (6 ounces) Brie cheese, cubed**
- 1/2 **cup hot caramel ice cream topping**
- 1/2 **cup macadamia nuts**
- 2 **tablespoons dried cranberries**

On each of six wooden appetizer skewers, alternately thread apple and Brie cheese cubes; place on a serving tray. Drizzle with caramel ice cream topping; sprinkle with macadamia nuts. Garnish with dried cranberries. **Yield:** 6 skewers.

Ginger-Tuna Kabobs

(Pictured at bottom right in photo at left)

PREP: 25 min. + marinating **COOK:** 5 min.

When you want something out of the ordinary, consider these distinctive kabobs. They feature pickled ginger, soy sauce, sesame seeds and wasabi mayonnaise to give your table a bit of Asian flair. To save time, prepare the dipping sauce a day in advance.
—*Mary Beth Harris-Murphree, Tyler, Texas*

- 1/4 **cup soy sauce**
- 2 **tablespoons rice vinegar**
- 1 **pound tuna steaks, cut into 16 cubes**
- 1 **tablespoon sesame seeds**
- 1 **tablespoon pepper**
- 2 **tablespoons canola oil**
- 16 **pickled ginger slices**
- 1 **bunch watercress, optional**
- 1/2 **cup wasabi mayonnaise**

In a large resealable plastic bag, combine the soy sauce and vinegar; add the tuna. Seal the bag and turn to coat; refrigerate for 30 minutes.

Drain tuna and pat dry; discard marinade. Sprinkle tuna with sesame seeds and pepper. In a large skillet, brown tuna in oil on all sides until medium rare or slightly pink in the center; remove from skillet.

On each of 16 wooden appetizer skewers, thread one ginger slice and one tuna cube. Arrange on a serving platter lined with watercress if desired. Serve kabobs with wasabi mayonnaise. **Yield:** 16 kabobs.

Cajun Shrimp Skewers

(Pictured at bottom left in photo at far left)

PREP: 20 min. + marinating **GRILL:** 5 min.

Give these skewers a try—you'll love them! Add some orange and red bell pepper rings on a bed of salad greens for a wholesome, elegant meal.
—*Bridget Coulter, San Diego, California*

- 2 **tablespoons olive oil**
- 1 **tablespoon onion powder**
- 1 **tablespoon paprika**
- 1 **tablespoon lemon juice**
- 1 **garlic clove, minced**
- 1/2 **teaspoon dried thyme**
- 1/4 **teaspoon crushed red pepper flakes**
- 1/4 **teaspoon coarsely ground pepper**
- 1/4 **teaspoon cayenne pepper**
- 1 **pound uncooked jumbo shrimp, peeled and deveined**
- 1 **medium lemon, cut into wedges**

In a large resealable plastic bag, combine the first nine ingredients. Add the shrimp; seal bag and turn to coat. Refrigerate for at least 30 minutes.

On eight metal or soaked wooden appetizer skewers, thread shrimp and lemon wedges. Grill, covered, over medium heat or broil 4 in. from the heat for 5-8 minutes or until shrimp turn pink, turning once. **Yield:** 8 skewers.

BRIE BASICS. Named after the French region of Brie, this soft cows' milk cheese is pale in color and has a grayish-white edible rind. The interior has a soft, spreadable consistency when served at room temperature.

Brie is ideal not only for Caramel Apple & Brie Skewers (recipe above left) but also for cheese trays, sandwiches, soups and fondues.

In a small bowl, combine the first eight ingredients; chill until serving.

In a large shallow bowl, combine the flour, salt and baking powder. In another shallow bowl, whisk the egg, milk, pepper sauce and minced garlic. In a third bowl, combine the bread crumbs, garlic powder and seasoned salt. Coat onions in flour mixture, dip in egg mixture, then roll in crumbs.

In a deep fryer or electric skillet, heat oil to 375°. Drop onion rings, a few at a time, into hot oil. Fry for 2-3 minutes or until golden brown. Drain on paper towels. Serve with sauce. **Yield:** 4 servings.

Make-Ahead Marinated Shrimp

(Pictured below)

PREP: 15 min. + marinating

Dress up your buffet table with this delicious shrimp. You'll have time to enjoy your party because this appetizer is so easy to make.
—*Phyllis Schmalz, Kansas City, Kansas*

  3/4 **cup water**
  1/2 **cup red wine vinegar**
  1/4 **cup olive oil**
  3/4 **teaspoon salt**
  3/4 **teaspoon minced fresh oregano *or*
       1/4 teaspoon dried oregano**
  3/4 **teaspoon minced fresh thyme *or* 1/4 teaspoon
       dried thyme**
    1 **garlic clove, minced**
  1/4 **teaspoon pepper**

Crispy Pub Rings

(Pictured above)

PREP: 40 min. **COOK:** 5 min./batch

I created these fried rings for a beer–tasting event we hosted, and they were a hit. Serve them when you entertain or on those nights when you have a craving for homemade "takeout."
—*Jennifer Rodriguez, West Jordan, Utah*

  1/2 **cup sour cream**
  1/2 **cup mayonnaise**
  1/2 **cup crumbled blue cheese**
    2 **green onions, finely chopped**
    1 **tablespoon dried parsley flakes**
    1 **garlic clove, minced**
  1/2 **teaspoon hot pepper sauce**
  1/4 **teaspoon garlic salt**
RINGS:
1-1/4 **cups all-purpose flour**
    1 **teaspoon salt**
    1 **teaspoon baking powder**
    1 **egg**
    1 **cup 2% milk**
1-1/2 **teaspoons hot pepper sauce**
    1 **garlic clove, minced**
  3/4 **cup dry bread crumbs**
    1 **teaspoon garlic powder**
    1 **teaspoon seasoned salt**
    1 **large sweet onion, sliced and separated into
       rings**
Oil for deep-fat frying

1-1/2 **pounds peeled and deveined cooked**
   jumbo shrimp
   1 **can (14 ounces) water-packed artichoke hearts,**
   rinsed, drained and halved
1/2 **pound small fresh mushrooms, halved**

In a large resealable plastic bag, combine the first eight ingredients. Add the shrimp, artichokes and mushrooms; seal and turn to coat. Refrigerate for eight hours or overnight, turning occasionally. **Yield:** 6 cups.

Blueberry Thirst Quencher

PREP/TOTAL TIME: 5 min.

I first sampled this cocktail at a Derby party and had to get the recipe. With beautiful color and a refreshing taste, it's perfect for a summer picnic or party. —Peggy Foster, Florence, Kentucky

   6 **cups chilled blueberry juice cocktail**
   3 **cups chilled lemon-lime soda**
   9 **ounces blueberry-flavored vodka, chilled**
Crushed ice
   1 **cup fresh blueberries**
Sliced peeled mango, optional

In a large pitcher, combine the juice, soda and vodka. Serve over ice; garnish with blueberries and mango if desired. **Yield:** 9 servings.

Bananas Foster Crunch Mix

PREP: 10 min. **COOK:** 5 min. + cooling

A classic dessert and ordinary snack mix come together in this delightfully different combo. It features plenty of banana chips and flavors everything with banana and rum extracts.
   —David Dahlman, Chatsworth, California

   3 **cups Honey Nut Chex**
   3 **cups Cinnamon Chex**
2-1/4 **cups pecan halves**
1-1/2 **cups dried banana chips**
 1/3 **cup butter, cubed**
 1/3 **cup packed brown sugar**
 1/2 **teaspoon ground cinnamon**
 1/2 **teaspoon banana extract**
 1/2 **teaspoon rum extract**

In a large microwave-safe bowl, combine the cereals, pecans and banana chips. In a small microwave-safe bowl, combine the butter, brown sugar and cinnamon. Microwave, uncovered, on high for 2 minutes, stirring once. Stir in extracts; pour over the cereal mixture and toss to coat.

   Cook, uncovered, on high for 3 minutes, stirring after each minute. Spread onto waxed paper to cool. Store in an airtight container. **Yield:** 2-1/2 quarts.

   Editor's Note: This recipe was tested in a 1,100-watt microwave.

Jungle Float

(Pictured above)

PREP/TOTAL TIME: 5 min.

This fun–filled beverage from our Test Kitchen staff lets children (and adults, too) be the masters of their own creations. What a yummy way to experiment with food!

   3 **tablespoons chocolate syrup**
   3 **scoops chocolate** *or* **vanilla ice cream**
   1 **cup chilled club soda**
Optional toppings: sliced banana, honey-roasted
   peanuts, cut-up peanut butter cups, animal crackers,
   whipped cream and maraschino cherries

Place 2 tablespoons chocolate syrup in a tall glass. Add ice cream and remaining chocolate syrup. Top with club soda. Garnish with toppings of your choice. Serve immediately. **Yield:** 1 serving.

CLEAN CUTS. Wash all fruit before eating, even those with a peel or rind. Microorganisms on the rind of a melon, for example, can be transferred to the flesh as you cut through with a knife. And what's on the skin of citrus fruits and bananas can be transferred to the fruit during peeling.

Salads & Dressings

As an elegant first course, potluck contribution or quick addition to a weekday menu, these fresh medleys just can't be beat. So take your pick from Easy Caesar Coleslaw, Buttermilk Salad Dressing, Grilled Romaine Toss and more.

IT'S A TOSS-UP. Clockwise from top left: Celery Root and Pear Slaw (p. 22), Candy Bar Apple Salad (p. 25), Roasted Pepper Salad with Balsamic Vinaigrette (p. 26) and Tossed Salad with Poppy Seed Dressing (p. 31).

1 tablespoon Dijon mustard
1/4 cup water
2 tablespoons olive oil
1/4 cup balsamic vinegar
1 tablespoon minced fresh basil
1/2 teaspoon pepper
Salad greens and vegetables of your choice

In a jar with a tight-fitting lid, combine the first six ingredients; shake well. Serve over salad. **Yield:** 2/3 cup.

Rhubarb Pear Gelatin

(Pictured below)

PREP: 25 min. + chilling

When I came up with this fruit–filled gelatin recipe, my family of 12 couldn't get enough. Rhubarb season always brings a bountiful crop, and this is one of our favorite ways to enjoy it.
—*Linda Strubhar, Cataldo, Idaho*

2 packages (6 ounces *each*) strawberry gelatin
2 cups miniature marshmallows, *divided*
4 cups sliced fresh *or* frozen rhubarb
2 cups water
2/3 cup sugar
2 cups cold water
1 can (15-1/4 ounces) sliced pears, drained and chopped

Place strawberry gelatin and 1 cup marshmallows in a large bowl; set aside.

In a large saucepan, combine the rhubarb, water and sugar. Bring to a boil. Reduce heat; cover and simmer for 3-4 minutes or until rhubarb is tender. Remove from the heat; pour over the marshmallow mixture, stirring to dissolve the gelatin. Stir in the cold water, pears and remaining marshmallows.

Transfer to a 13-in. x 9-in. dish. Refrigerate for at least 6 hours or until firm. **Yield:** 12 servings.

Special Occasion Salad

(Pictured above)

PREP/TOTAL TIME: 20 min.

This simple but sensational medley consistently gets rave reviews, no matter when I serve it. If you like, change the types of lettuce or dried fruit…or replace the almonds with candied pecans.
—*Jean Follmer, Lafayette, California*

1 package (6 ounces) fresh baby spinach
1 package (5 ounces) fresh arugula *or* additional baby spinach
1/2 cup dried cherries
1/3 cup sliced almonds, toasted
1/4 cup olive oil
1/4 cup balsamic vinegar
1/2 teaspoon salt
1/4 teaspoon pepper
1 cup crumbled goat cheese

In a salad bowl, combine the spinach, arugula, cherries and almonds. Combine the oil, balsamic vinegar, salt and pepper; drizzle over the salad and toss to coat. Sprinkle with goat cheese. Serve immediately. **Yield:** 16 servings (3/4 cup each).

Greens with Balsamic Vinaigrette

PREP/TOTAL TIME: 5 min.

I keep a bottle of this tangy vinaigrette in the refrigerator so we can have it anytime. All I need to do is combine the ingredients and shake! Store–bought versions just can't compare to this homemade blend. —*Sandy Hunt, Racine, Wisconsin*

Thai Steak Salad

(Pictured above)

PREP: 20 min. **COOK:** 15 min.

Thai food is popular in our house, so my husband and I created this fresh, fuss-free alternative to the usual meat-and-potatoes dinner. The spicy-sweet dressing is truly incredible!
—*Radelle Knappenberger, Oviedo, Florida*

- **1 tablespoon lime juice**
- **1 tablespoon soy sauce**
- **1 tablespoon honey**
- **1 teaspoon balsamic vinegar**
- **1/4 teaspoon hot pepper sauce**
- **1 small garlic clove, minced**

Dash salt
- **2 tablespoons olive oil, *divided***
- **1 boneless beef top loin steak (8 ounces)**
- **4 cups torn romaine**
- **2 tablespoons salted peanuts**
- **2 tablespoons fresh basil leaves, chopped**

For dressing, in a small bowl, combine the lime juice, soy sauce, honey, vinegar, pepper sauce, garlic and salt. Whisk in 1 tablespoon oil; set aside.

In a large skillet over medium heat, cook steak in remaining oil for 6-8 minutes on each side or until meat reaches desired doneness (for medium-rare, a meat thermometer should read 145°; medium, 160°; well-done, 170°). Remove from the pan and let stand for 5 minutes.

Divide romaine between two plates. Slice beef; arrange over romaine. Sprinkle with peanuts and basil; drizzle with dressing. **Yield:** 2 servings.

Editor's Note: Top loin steak may be labeled as strip steak, Kansas City steak, New York strip steak, ambassador steak or boneless club steak in your region.

LIVELY LETTUCE. Do you like extra-crispy salad greens? Consider romaine—a variety of lettuce that's naturally more crisp. Enjoy it in hearty Thai Steak Salad (recipe above).

Fresh as Summer Salad

(Pictured below)

PREP/TOTAL TIME: 25 min.

I wanted a light, refreshing salad to pair with my spicy Middle Eastern and Mediterranean dishes, and this one really fills the bill. Plus, it's easy to grow some of the herbs and veggies myself.
—Victor Finger, Sunbury, Ohio

- 2 romaine hearts, torn
- 2 tablespoons olive oil
- 3/4 cup chopped fresh cilantro, mint, sorrel *and/or* lemon balm
- 3 green onions, thinly sliced
- 1/2 cup plain Greek yogurt
- 1 teaspoon lemon juice
- 3/4 teaspoon salt
- 1/2 teaspoon ground nutmeg
- 1/4 teaspoon pepper
- 1 cup canned garbanzo beans *or* chickpeas
- 3 tablespoons pistachios
- 3 lemon wedges

Place romaine in a large bowl; drizzle with oil and toss to coat. Add herbs and onions; toss to combine. Whisk the yogurt, lemon juice, salt, nutmeg and pepper; add to romaine mixture and toss to coat.

Transfer to a serving platter. Top with garbanzo beans and pistachios. Squeeze lemon wedges over the top. Serve immediately. **Yield:** 8 servings.

Editor's Note: If Greek yogurt is not available in your area, line a strainer with a coffee filter and place over a bowl. Place 1 cup yogurt in prepared strainer; refrigerate overnight. Discard liquid from bowl; proceed as directed.

Celery Root and Pear Slaw

(Pictured above and on page 18)

PREP: 40 min.

Juicy pears, tangy blue cheese and sweet golden raisins make a tongue-tingling combination in this crunchy coleslaw. I think it's especially good served with pork roast or baked ham.
—Roxanne Chan, Albany, California

- 1 medium celery root, peeled and julienned
- 3 cups shredded red cabbage
- 3 medium pears, thinly sliced
- 1/3 cup golden raisins
- 1/4 cup chopped red onion
- 1/4 cup minced fresh parsley
- 1/4 cup sliced almonds
- 3/4 cup sour cream
- 1/3 cup mayonnaise
- 4-1/2 teaspoons poppy seeds
- 4-1/2 teaspoons lemon juice
- 4-1/2 teaspoons prepared horseradish
- 2 garlic cloves, minced
- 1-1/2 teaspoons honey
- 3/4 teaspoon grated lemon peel
- 3/4 teaspoon pepper
- 1/2 cup crumbled blue cheese

In a large bowl, combine the first seven ingredients. Combine sour cream, mayonnaise, poppy seeds, lemon juice, horseradish, garlic, honey, lemon peel and pepper; pour over coleslaw and toss to coat. Sprinkle with blue cheese. **Yield:** 16 servings (3/4 cup each).

Pizza Salad with Tomato Vinaigrette

PREP/TOTAL TIME: 25 min.

Many of the ingredients you find in a deluxe pizza pie go into this hearty, no-hassle medley. The dressing is great on other salads, too. Feel free to substitute pepperoni for the Canadian bacon.
—*Wendy Nickel, Kiester, Minnesota*

VINAIGRETTE:
    1 can (8 ounces) tomato sauce
    1/2 cup olive oil
    1/4 cup white wine vinegar
    1 teaspoon sugar
    1 teaspoon dried oregano
    1 garlic clove, minced
    1/2 teaspoon salt
SALAD:
    1 package (6 ounces) fresh baby spinach
    1/2 pound Canadian bacon, cut into thin strips
    1 cup (4 ounces) shredded part-skim mozzarella cheese
    1 cup (4 ounces) shredded reduced-fat cheddar cheese
    2 medium tomatoes, cut into wedges and seeded
    1 medium green pepper, finely chopped
    1 can (2-1/4 ounces) sliced ripe olives, drained
    3 fresh basil leaves, thinly sliced
    1 tablespoon minced chives

In a small bowl, whisk the vinaigrette ingredients. Chill until serving.

In a large salad bowl, combine the spinach, Canadian bacon, cheeses, tomatoes, green pepper, ripe olives, basil and chives. Just before serving, whisk the dressing and drizzle 1 cup over the salad; toss to coat. Save the remaining dressing for another use. **Yield:** 10-1/2 cups salad plus 3/4 cup leftover dressing.

Ranch Dressing and Dip Mix

PREP: 10 min.

Place this versatile mix in a decorative jar with instructions for making ranch dressing or dip. Then tuck the jar into a gift basket along with a pretty serving bowl and snack crackers or chips.
—*Joan Hallford, North Richland Hills, Texas*

4-1/2 teaspoons dried parsley flakes
    1 tablespoon minced chives
    1 tablespoon garlic powder
    2 teaspoons lemon-pepper seasoning
1-1/2 teaspoons dried tarragon
1-1/2 teaspoons dried oregano
    1 teaspoon salt
RANCH SALAD DRESSING:
    1/2 cup mayonnaise
    1/2 cup buttermilk

RANCH DIP:
    1 cup mayonnaise
    1 cup (8 ounces) sour cream

In a small bowl, combine the first seven ingredients. Transfer to a 4-ounce jar. Shake well before using. **Yield:** 1 jar (about 6 tablespoons).

For salad dressing: In a small bowl, whisk mayonnaise, buttermilk and 1 tablespoon mix. Refrigerate for at least 1 hour. **Yield:** 1 cup.

For dip: In a small bowl, combine the mayonnaise, sour cream and 2 tablespoons mix. Refrigerate for at least 2 hours. Serve with crackers and fresh vegetables or as a topping for baked potatoes. **Yield:** 2 cups.

Broccoli Raisin Salad

(Pictured below)

PREP: 10 min. + chilling

When I want a simple but sensational side dish, this is often my choice. I adjusted a friend's recipe to cut some of the calories. Golden raisins add sweetness, and bacon lends a nice crunch.
—*Angela Oelschlaeger, Tonganoxie, Kansas*

    4 cups fresh broccoli florets (1 medium bunch)
    3/4 cup golden raisins
    1 small red onion, chopped
    1/2 cup Miracle Whip
    1 tablespoon white vinegar
    2 teaspoons sugar
    3 bacon strips, cooked and crumbled

In a large bowl, combine the broccoli, raisins and onion. In a small bowl, combine the Miracle Whip, vinegar and sugar. Pour over broccoli mixture; toss to coat. Sprinkle with bacon. Refrigerate salad for at least 2 hours before serving. **Yield:** 6 servings.

Divide salad greens among four plates; top with cheese. Drizzle with dressing and sprinkle with honey pecans. **Yield:** 4 servings.

Grilled Romaine Toss

(Pictured below)

PREP: 25 min. **GRILL:** 10 min.

Even when I double this recipe, it's gone by the end of the night. During inclement weather, use your broiler instead of the grill.
—*Trisha Kruse, Eagle, Idaho*

- 1/4 cup olive oil
- 3 tablespoons sugar
- 1 teaspoon dried rosemary, crushed
- 1 teaspoon dried thyme
- 1/4 teaspoon salt
- 1/4 teaspoon pepper
- 8 plum tomatoes, quartered
- 2 large sweet onions, thinly sliced

GRILLED ROMAINE:
- 4 romaine hearts
- 2 tablespoons olive oil
- 1/4 teaspoon salt
- 1/4 teaspoon pepper

DRESSING:
- 1/4 cup olive oil
- 1/4 cup balsamic vinegar
- 3 garlic cloves, peeled and halved
- 2 tablespoons brown sugar
- 1/4 cup grated Parmesan cheese

In a large bowl, combine the first six ingredients. Add tomatoes and onions; toss to coat. Transfer to a grill wok or basket. Grill, covered, over medium heat for 8-12 minutes or until tender, stirring frequently. Set aside.

Honey Pecan & Goat Cheese Salad

(Pictured above)

PREP/TOTAL TIME: 25 min.

I tossed this together for my family once while our pizza was in the oven. My son is a fan of goat cheese, and one of my dreams is to own a herd of goats and make cheese. But whenever I talk about the idea with my wife, I get major eye rolls!
—*Greg Fontenot, The Woodlands, Texas*

- 1/2 cup chopped pecans
- 2 teaspoons plus 1 tablespoon honey, *divided*
- 1/3 cup plus 3 tablespoons olive oil, *divided*
- 2 tablespoons balsamic vinegar
- 1/2 teaspoon salt
- 1/8 teaspoon pepper
- 1/4 cup all-purpose flour
- 1 egg, beaten
- 3/4 cup seasoned bread crumbs
- 8 ounces fresh goat cheese
- 4 cups spring mix salad greens

In a shallow microwave-safe dish, combine the pecans and 2 teaspoons honey; microwave, uncovered, on high for 1-1/2 to 2 minutes or until toasted, stirring twice. Immediately transfer to waxed paper-lined baking sheet to cool. For dressing, in a small bowl, whisk 1/3 cup oil, vinegar, remaining honey, salt and pepper; set aside.

Place flour, egg and bread crumbs in separate shallow bowls. Shape the cheese into eight balls; flatten slightly. Coat cheese with flour, then dip in egg and coat with bread crumbs.

Heat remaining oil in a large skillet over medium-high heat. Fry the cheese for 1-2 minutes on each side or until golden brown. Drain on paper towels.

remove the seeds; stir into the pan. Discard the bean.

Bring to a boil. Reduce heat; simmer for 20 minutes or until reduced by half. Remove from the heat; cool for 10 minutes. Stir in lime juice and peel.

In a large bowl, combine pineapple, oranges, grapefruit and blueberries. Drizzle with vanilla-lime sauce and toss to coat. Refrigerate until chilled. **Yield:** 16 servings.

Candy Bar Apple Salad

(*Pictured below and on page 18*)

PREP/TOTAL TIME: 15 min.

This creamy, sweet salad is so yummy, it could be served as a dessert! With the crunch of crisp apples plus vanilla pudding, whipped topping and candy bars, it's a real people–pleaser and always goes fast. —*Cyndi Fynaardt, Oskaloosa, Iowa*

> 1-1/2 **cups cold 2% milk**
> 1 **package (3.4 ounces) instant vanilla pudding mix**
> 1 **carton (8 ounces) frozen whipped topping, thawed**
> 4 **large apples, chopped (about 6 cups)**
> 4 **Snickers candy bars (2.07 ounces *each*), cut into 1/2-inch pieces**

In a large bowl, whisk the milk and vanilla pudding mix for 2 minutes. Let stand for 2 minutes or until soft-set. Fold in the whipped topping. Fold in the apples and candy bars. Refrigerate until serving. **Yield:** 12 servings (3/4 cup each).

For the grilled romaine, cut the romaine hearts in half lengthwise, leaving ends intact. Brush with oil; sprinkle with salt and pepper. Place romaine halves cut sides down on grill. Grill, covered, over medium heat for 3-4 minutes on each side or until slightly charred and wilted.

For the dressing, place the oil, balsamic vinegar, garlic and brown sugar in a food processor; cover and process until smooth.

Coarsely chop romaine; divide among 10 salad plates. Top with tomato mixture; drizzle with dressing. Sprinkle with cheese. **Yield:** 10 servings.

Editor's Note: If you do not have a grill wok or basket, use a disposable foil pan. Poke holes in the bottom of the pan with a meat fork to allow liquid to drain.

Vanilla-Lime Fruit Salad

(*Pictured above*)

PREP: 40 min. + chilling

Feel free to be creative with the fruits you use in this medley. The dressing is also good on fresh strawberries and even pound cake. —*Kate Dampier, Quail Valley, California*

> 1/2 **cup sugar**
> 1/2 **cup water**
> 1-1/2 **teaspoons light corn syrup**
> 1/2 **vanilla bean**
> 2 **tablespoons lime juice**
> 1-1/2 **teaspoons grated lime peel**
> 3 **cups cubed fresh pineapple**
> 2 **large navel oranges, peeled and sectioned**
> 1 **large grapefruit, peeled and sectioned**
> 4 **cups fresh blueberries**

In a small saucepan, combine the sugar, water and corn syrup. With a sharp knife, scrape the vanilla bean to

turn. Broil and rotate until all sides are blistered and blackened. Immediately place peppers in a large bowl; cover and let stand for 20 minutes.

Peel off and discard charred skin. Remove stems and seeds. Cut peppers into thin strips; place in a large bowl. Add onion.

In a small bowl, whisk the oil, vinegar, herbs, garlic, garlic powder, cayenne, pepper and salt; pour over pepper mixture and toss to coat. Cover and refrigerate for up to 4 hours.

Before serving, allow the peppers to come to room temperature. Place on a serving plate; top with tomatoes, cheese and basil leaves. **Yield:** 5 servings.

Easy Caesar Coleslaw

(*Pictured below*)

PREP/TOTAL TIME: 10 min.

Add a refreshing side to just about any menu with this cool, crisp coleslaw. I adapted it from a more time-consuming recipe. This quicker version is easy to double or triple for potlucks, too.
 —Maryrose DeGroot, State College, Pennsylvania

   1 **package (14 ounces) coleslaw mix**
   1 **cup grape tomatoes**
1/4 **cup shredded Parmesan cheese**
3/4 **cup creamy Caesar salad dressing**
   1 **green onion, sliced**

In a salad bowl, combine the coleslaw mix, tomatoes and cheese. Add salad dressing; toss to coat. Chill until serving. Sprinkle with green onion. **Yield:** 6 servings.

Roasted Pepper Salad
With Balsamic Vinaigrette

(*Pictured above and on page 18*)

PREP: 20 min. + marinating **BROIL:** 20 min. + standing

I came up with this marinated dish for a 4-H project and took it all the way to the state competition, where I won first place. I'd love to have my own Italian restaurant someday.
 —Seth Murdoch, Red Rock, Texas

   2 *each* **large sweet yellow, red and green peppers**
   1 **small red onion, thinly sliced**
   6 **tablespoons olive oil**
   3 **tablespoons balsamic vinegar**
   1 **tablespoon** *each* **minced fresh oregano, rosemary, basil and parsley**
   1 **garlic clove, minced**
1/2 **teaspoon garlic powder**
1/2 **teaspoon cayenne pepper**
1/2 **teaspoon pepper**
1/4 **teaspoon salt**
   1 **cup cherry tomatoes, halved**
   1 **carton (8 ounces) fresh mozzarella cheese pearls**
   5 **fresh basil leaves**

Broil peppers 4 in. from the heat until skins blister, about 5 minutes. With tongs, rotate peppers a quarter

with tarragon. Serve warm or at room temperature. Refrigerate leftovers. **Yield:** 9 servings.

Editor's Note: If you do not have a grilling grid, use a disposable foil pan. Poke holes in the bottom of the pan with a meat fork to allow any liquid to drain.

Hearty Bean Salad

(*Pictured below*)

PREP: 20 min. + chilling

I discovered this medley years ago when I was a teenager. After I was married, I tried tossing in some different beans and water chestnuts for more crunch. The homemade dressing is so good and has just the right balance between sweet and sour.
—Jewell Dawson, Culver, Oregon

- 1 can (16 ounces) kidney beans, rinsed and drained
- 1 can (15-1/4 ounces) whole kernel corn, drained
- 1 can (14-1/2 ounces) cut wax beans, drained
- 1 can (14-1/2 ounces) cut green beans, drained
- 1 can (8 ounces) sliced water chestnuts, drained
- 1 small sweet red pepper, chopped

DRESSING:
- 2/3 cup sugar
- 1/2 cup cider vinegar
- 1 small onion, finely chopped
- 1 teaspoon salt
- 1/4 teaspoon pepper

In a large bowl, combine the first six ingredients. In a small bowl, whisk the dressing ingredients; pour over the bean mixture and toss to coat.

Cover and refrigerate for at least 1 hour. Stir before serving. Serve with a slotted spoon. **Yield:** 10 servings.

Backyard Red Potato Salad

(*Pictured above*)

PREP: 25 min. **GRILL:** 10 min.

This potato salad is one of my favorites because it's a nice change of pace. There's no mayo, so it's perfect for picnics. Plus, it looks as good as it tastes. —Holly Bauer, West Bend, Wisconsin

- 2-1/2 pounds small red potatoes
- 1 medium onion, cut into 1/2-inch slices
- 1/2 cup olive oil, *divided*
- 1 teaspoon salt, *divided*
- 1/2 teaspoon pepper, *divided*
- 3 tablespoons balsamic vinegar
- 2 tablespoons lemon juice
- 1 tablespoon Dijon mustard
- 2 teaspoons sugar
- 2 garlic cloves, minced
- 1/4 cup minced fresh tarragon

Place the red potatoes in a large saucepan and cover with water. Bring to a boil. Reduce heat; cover and cook for 10 minutes. Drain; cool slightly. Cut each in half.

In a large bowl, combine the potatoes, onion, 1/4 cup oil, 1/2 teaspoon salt and 1/4 teaspoon pepper; toss to coat. Arrange the cut sides down on a grilling grid; place on a grill rack. Grill, covered, over medium heat for 8-10 minutes or until vegetables are tender and lightly browned, turning occasionally. Chop onion. Place onion and potatoes in bowl.

In a small bowl, whisk the balsamic vinegar, lemon juice, mustard, sugar, garlic and remaining oil, salt and pepper. Add to potato mixture; toss to coat. Sprinkle

Strawberry Mango Salad

(Pictured above)

PREP/TOTAL TIME: 20 min.

I combined different ideas from several recipes to come up with this fruit-filled medley, and the result was a big hit.
—*Shawn Burcham, Jamestown, Indiana*

- **2 cups spring mix salad greens**
- **1/2 cup chopped peeled mango**
- **1/2 cup sliced fresh strawberries**
- **2 tablespoons dried cranberries**
- **3 tablespoons olive oil**
- **4 teaspoons sugar**
- **1 tablespoon balsamic vinegar**
- **Dash salt**
- **2 tablespoons slivered almonds, toasted**

In a serving bowl, combine the salad greens, mango, strawberries and cranberries. In a small bowl, whisk the oil, sugar, vinegar and salt. Pour over salad; toss to coat. Sprinkle with almonds. **Yield:** 2 servings.

MANGO METHOD. To prepare the mango for the Strawberry Mango Salad recipe (above), lay a washed mango on the counter and turn it so the top and bottom are the sides. With a sharp knife, make a lengthwise cut as close to the long seed as possible to remove each side of the fruit.

Trim the fruit away from the seed, then score each side of the fruit lengthwise and widthwise without cutting through the skin. Using your hand, push the skin up, turning the fruit out. Cut the fruit at the skin with a knife.

Texas Confetti Rice Salad

(Pictured below)

PREP: 30 min. + cooling

A spicy way to dress up rice, this Southwestern salad will impress at the dinner table or a potluck. Just bring a hearty appetite!
—*Linda Morten, Somerville, Texas*

- **2 cans (14-1/2 ounces *each*) chicken broth**
- **2 cups uncooked long grain rice**
- **1/2 cup water**
- **4 cups cubed cooked turkey**
- **4 medium tomatoes, seeded and chopped**
- **2 cups fresh *or* frozen corn, thawed**
- **1 large green pepper, chopped**
- **1 medium red onion, chopped**
- **1 cup olive oil**
- **1/2 cup minced fresh cilantro**
- **1 can (4 ounces) chopped green chilies**
- **3 tablespoons white wine vinegar**
- **3 tablespoons lime juice**
- **2 tablespoons Dijon mustard**
- **2-1/2 teaspoons ground cumin**
- **1 teaspoon garlic salt**
- **1/2 teaspoon crushed red pepper flakes**
- **1 medium ripe avocado, peeled and cubed**

In a large saucepan, bring the broth, rice and water to a boil. Reduce heat; cover and simmer for 15-18 minutes or until liquid is absorbed and rice is tender. Transfer to a large bowl; cool completely.

Stir in the turkey, tomatoes, corn, green pepper and red onion. In a small bowl, whisk the oil, cilantro, green chilies, vinegar, lime juice, mustard, cumin, garlic salt and red pepper flakes. Pour over the salad; toss to coat. Chill until serving. Just before serving, stir in avocado. **Yield:** 12 servings (1-1/3 cups each).

Black-Eyed Pea Pasta Salad

(Pictured above)

PREP: 30 min. + chilling

Grilling out? Consider adding this refreshing, make-ahead dish to the menu. A jazzed-up Italian dressing enhances the chopped vegetables, pepperoni, provolone cheese and spiral pasta.
—Joan Huggins, Waynesboro, Mississippi

- **1 jar (7-1/2 ounces) marinated quartered artichoke hearts**
- **1 cup uncooked tricolor spiral pasta**
- **1 can (15-1/2 ounces) black-eyed peas, rinsed and drained**
- **4 slices provolone cheese, cut into thin strips**
- **1/2 cup chopped green pepper**
- **1/2 cup chopped sweet red pepper**
- **1/2 cup thinly sliced red onion**
- **1/2 cup sliced pepperoni, cut into thin strips**
- **1/2 cup mayonnaise**
- **1/4 cup prepared Italian salad dressing**

Drain artichokes, reserving 1/4 cup liquid; chop and set aside. Cook pasta according to package directions.

Meanwhile, in a large bowl combine the artichokes, peas, cheese, peppers, onion and pepperoni. Drain pasta; add to artichoke mixture.

In a small bowl, combine mayonnaise, salad dressing and reserved artichoke liquid. Pour over pasta mixture; toss to coat. Cover and refrigerate for at least 1 hour. **Yield:** 8 servings.

Buttermilk Salad Dressing

PREP: 10 min. + chilling

This thick, creamy mixture has the flavor of ranch dressing and is a breeze to prepare. All I have to do is blend three ingredients! Use it to top mixed greens or as a dip for fresh veggies.
—Vicki Floden, Story City, Iowa

- **3/4 cup buttermilk**
- **2 cups (16 ounces) 2% cottage cheese**
- **1 envelope ranch salad dressing mix**
- **Salad greens and vegetables of your choice**

In a blender, combine the buttermilk, cottage cheese and salad dressing mix; cover and process for 20 seconds or until smooth.

Pour the salad dressing into a small pitcher or bowl. Cover and refrigerate for 1 hour. Stir before serving with salad. **Yield:** 2-3/4 cups.

Swiss Spinach Salad

(Pictured above)

PREP/TOTAL TIME: 10 min.

My garden provides a treasure trove of vegetables to spark my imagination. When I toss my spinach with bacon and Swiss, the combo tastes like quiche Lorraine—without all the effort!
—Nella Parker, Hersey, Michigan

- 1 package (6 ounces) fresh baby spinach
- 1 cup (4 ounces) shredded Swiss cheese
- 3 tablespoons crumbled cooked bacon
- 1/2 cup creamy Caesar salad dressing

Salad croutons

In a salad bowl, combine the spinach, cheese and bacon. Drizzle with dressing and toss to coat. Top with croutons. Serve immediately. **Yield:** 4 servings.

Roasted Red Potato Salad

PREP: 55 min.

I'm a fan of Southwestern flavors, which led me to create this party-perfect dish. I'd been experimenting with smoked paprika for a while and found it makes a great addition to this recipe.
—Kelly Faust, Louisville, Kentucky

- 2 pounds small red potatoes, quartered
- 1/4 cup olive oil
- 3/4 teaspoon salt, *divided*
- 1/2 teaspoon pepper, *divided*
- 1 package (3 ounces) cream cheese, softened
- 1/2 cup sour cream
- 1 can (4 ounces) chopped green chilies
- 1 teaspoon smoked paprika
- 1/2 teaspoon garlic powder
- 1 can (15-1/4 ounces) whole kernel corn, drained
- 1 small red onion, finely chopped
- 1 small sweet red pepper, finely chopped
- 1/3 cup minced fresh cilantro

Toss the red potatoes with oil, 1/2 teaspoon salt and 1/4 teaspoon pepper; place in a greased 15-in. x 10-in. x 1-in. baking pan. Bake at 400° for 30-35 minutes or until tender, stirring once. Cool slightly.

For dressing, in a small bowl, beat cream cheese and sour cream until smooth. Stir in the chilies, paprika, garlic powder and remaining salt and pepper.

In a large bowl, combine the corn, onion, red pepper and potatoes. Add 1 cup dressing and cilantro; toss to coat (save remaining dressing for another use). Serve immediately. **Yield:** 8 servings.

Christmas Cranberry Salad

(Pictured below)

PREP: 30 min. + chilling

With a sprinkling of pecans on top, this ruby-red holiday salad is popular in my family and has been requested every year since I first brought it to Christmas Eve dinner. The not-too-sweet flavor is the perfect accompaniment to just about any meat.
—Jennifer Mastnick-Cook, Hartville, Ohio

- 2 packages (3 ounces *each*) raspberry gelatin
- 2 cups boiling water, *divided*
- 1 can (14 ounces) whole-berry cranberry sauce
- 2 tablespoons lemon juice
- 1 cup heavy whipping cream
- 1 package (8 ounces) cream cheese, softened
- 1/2 cup chopped pecans

Place the romaine, tomato, cucumber and carrot in a salad bowl. Drizzle desired amount of dressing over the salad; toss to coat. Refrigerate leftover dressing. **Yield:** 6 servings.

Watercress with Fennel & Berries

(Pictured below)

PREP/TOTAL TIME: 20 min.

When I'm in the kitchen, I enjoy experimenting. This different, fresh-tasting summer medley is one of my favorite successes.
—*Jim Rude, Janesville, Wisconsin*

- **4 cups watercress**
- **1 cup thinly sliced fennel bulb**
- **1/2 cup fresh blueberries**
- **1/4 cup chopped fennel fronds**
- **1/4 cup pistachios, toasted**
- **1/3 cup refrigerated spinach salad dressing with bacon**
- **1 tablespoon orange juice**
- **1 teaspoon grated orange peel**
- **1 teaspoon teriyaki sauce**

In a salad bowl, combine the first five ingredients. In a small bowl, whisk the remaining ingredients. Drizzle over salad; toss to coat. Serve immediately. **Yield:** 6 servings.

Editor's Note: This recipe was tested with Marie's brand salad dressing.

In a small bowl, dissolve gelatin in 1 cup boiling water. In another bowl, combine cranberry sauce and remaining water; add gelatin mixture and lemon juice. Pour into a 13-in. x 9-in. dish coated with cooking spray; refrigerate until firm, about 1 hour.

In a large bowl, beat cream until stiff peaks form. In another bowl, beat cream cheese until smooth. Stir in 1/2 cup whipped cream; fold in remaining whipped cream. Spread over gelatin mixture; sprinkle with pecans. Refrigerate for at least 2 hours. **Yield:** 12 servings.

Tossed Salad with Poppy Seed Dressing

(Pictured above and on page 18)

PREP/TOTAL TIME: 20 min.

Give your lettuce a boost with this refreshing and tangy dressing. It's the finishing touch that will make guests say wow!
—*Jennifer Kauffman Figueroa, Greenville, South Carolina*

- **1/3 cup white vinegar**
- **3/4 cup sugar**
- **2 tablespoons chopped onion**
- **1 teaspoon salt**
- **1 teaspoon ground mustard**
- **1 cup canola oil**
- **5 teaspoons poppy seeds**
- **6 cups torn romaine**
- **1 large tomato, sliced**
- **1 small cucumber, sliced**
- **1/4 cup shredded carrot**

In a blender, combine the first five ingredients; cover and process until smooth. While processing, gradually add oil in a steady stream. Stir in poppy seeds.

Soups & Sandwiches

Roasted Poblano Beef Stew...Bistro Apple Panini...Creamy Vegetable Chowder...Toasty Deli Hoagies...the comforting creations in this chapter will make any lunch or dinner extra special. Just try them and see!

BOWLED OVER. Clockwise from top left: Sweet & Spicy Fusion Burgers (p. 43), Best-Ever Chicken Fajita Chowder (p. 36), Authentic Cajun Gumbo (p. 34) and Fig-a-licious Pork Burgers (p. 42).

In the same pan, cook and stir the oil and flour over medium heat until caramel-colored, about 14 minutes (do not burn). Add the finely chopped onion; cook and stir 2 minutes longer. Gradually stir in broth. Bring to a boil.

Carefully stir in the sausage and reserved chicken. Reduce the heat; simmer, uncovered, for 10 minutes. Stir in the okra and oysters. Simmer, uncovered, 10-15 minutes longer or just until the okra is tender. Stir in the gumbo file powder. Serve with rice. **Yield:** 20 servings (1-1/4 cups each).

Editor's Note: Gumbo file powder, used to thicken and flavor Creole recipes, is available in spice shops. If you don't want to use gumbo file powder, combine 2 tablespoons each cornstarch and cold water until smooth. Gradually stir into gumbo. Bring to a boil; cook and stir for 2 minutes or until thickened.

Authentic Cajun Gumbo

(Pictured above)

PREP: 1 hour + simmering **COOK:** 45 min.

I learned to cook in Louisiana and love Cajun food. This hearty chicken-oyster gumbo is one of my all-time favorite dishes.
—*Paul Morris, Kelso, Washington*

- 6 quarts water
- 1 chicken (5 pounds), cut up
- 2 large onions, quartered
- 4 celery ribs, cut into 3-inch pieces
- 6 garlic cloves, coarsely chopped
- 2 tablespoons salt
- 1 teaspoon garlic powder
- 1/2 teaspoon poultry seasoning
- 1/2 teaspoon cayenne pepper
- 1/2 teaspoon pepper
- 1/4 teaspoon white pepper
- 1 cup canola oil
- 1-1/2 cups all-purpose flour
- 1 large onion, finely chopped
- 1 pound fully cooked andouille sausage links, chopped
- 2 pounds sliced okra
- 2 pints shucked oysters
- 3 tablespoons gumbo file powder

Hot cooked rice

Place the first 11 ingredients in a stockpot; bring to a boil. Reduce heat; cover and simmer for 1-1/2 hours.

Remove the chicken and allow to cool. Strain the broth, discarding the vegetables; skim fat. Remove meat from the bones; cut chicken into bite-size pieces and set aside. Discard bones.

Bistro Apple Panini

(Pictured below)

PREP: 20 min. **COOK:** 5 min./batch

The bacon, apple and tarragon in these hot Italian sandwiches go together so well. If you don't have a panini maker or indoor grill, you can easily pan-fry or broil them instead.
—*Noelle Myers, Grand Forks, North Dakota*

- 12 thick-sliced bacon strips, cut in half
- 1 medium apple, thinly sliced
- 1 tablespoon ginger ale
- 1 teaspoon lemon juice
- 1/4 cup apple jelly
- 4 teaspoons minced fresh tarragon
- 12 slices sourdough bread
- 6 slices Havarti cheese
- 2 tablespoons Dijon mustard
- 3 tablespoons butter, softened

In a large skillet, cook bacon over medium heat until crisp. Remove to paper towels to drain. In a small bowl, toss apple with ginger ale and lemon juice; set aside.

Place the apple jelly in a small microwave-safe bowl; microwave on high for 20-30 seconds or until softened. Stir in tarragon.

Spread the jelly mixture over six bread slices. Top with cheese, apple and bacon. Spread mustard over remaining bread; place over bacon. Spread outsides of sandwiches with butter.

Cook on a panini maker or indoor grill for 3-4 minutes or until the bread is browned and the cheese is melted. **Yield:** 6 servings.

Easy Egg Drop Soup

PREP/TOTAL TIME: 15 min.

We start many stir-fry dinners with this Asian classic, which requires just five ingredients and is table-ready in 15 minutes flat. There are many variations, but we prefer the addition of cornstarch to thicken the soup and give it a rich, golden color.
—Amy Corlew-Sherlock, Lapeer, Michigan

> 3 cups chicken broth
> 1 tablespoon cornstarch
> 2 tablespoons cold water
> 1 egg, lightly beaten
> 1 green onion, sliced

In a large saucepan, bring broth to a boil over medium heat. Combine the cornstarch and water until smooth; gradually stir into broth. Bring to a boil; cook and stir for 2 minutes or until thickened.

Reduce heat. Drizzle beaten egg into the hot broth, stirring constantly. Remove from the heat; stir in green onion. **Yield:** 4 servings.

Family-Friendly Stuffed Cheeseburgers

PREP: 30 min. **GRILL:** 10 min.

We were experimenting in the kitchen one evening and came up with the recipe for these mouthwatering cheese-stuffed burgers. Our children, friends and neighbors all fell in love with them. They're so good, we often don't use any condiments.
—Alethea Osborne, Florence, Kentucky

> 1 cup chopped sweet onion
> 1/2 cup crushed saltines (about 15 crackers)
> 1 egg
> 1 jalapeno pepper, seeded and minced
> 1 envelope ranch salad dressing mix
> 1 tablespoon Worcestershire sauce
> 1 garlic clove, minced
> 1 teaspoon pepper
> 2 pounds ground beef
> 1-1/2 cups (6 ounces) shredded cheddar cheese
> 1 jar (4-1/2 ounces) sliced mushrooms, drained
> 3 tablespoons cream cheese, softened
> 6 kaiser rolls, split

In a large bowl, combine the first eight ingredients. Crumble beef over mixture and mix well. Shape into twelve thin patties.

Combine the cheddar cheese, mushrooms and cream cheese; spoon onto centers of six patties. Top with remaining patties; press edges firmly to seal.

Grill burgers, covered, over medium heat or broil 4 in. from heat for 5-7 minutes on each side or until a meat thermometer reads 160° and juices run clear. Serve on rolls. **Yield:** 6 servings.

Sweet & Tangy Pulled Pork

(Pictured above)

PREP: 15 min. **COOK:** 8 hours

The slow cooker makes this zippy shredded pork a snap to serve on even the busiest weeknights—just add hamburger buns.
—Megan Klimkewicz, Kaiser, Missouri

> 1 boneless pork shoulder butt roast
>   (3 to 4 pounds)
> 1 jar (18 ounces) apricot preserves
> 1 large onion, chopped
> 2 tablespoons reduced-sodium soy sauce
> 2 tablespoons Dijon mustard
> Hamburger buns, split, optional

Cut pork roast in half; place in a 4- or 5-qt. slow cooker. Combine the preserves, onion, soy sauce and mustard; pour over roast. Cover and cook on low for 8-10 hours or until meat is tender.

Remove meat; cool slightly. Skim fat from the cooking juices. Shred pork with two forks and return to the slow cooker; heat through. Serve pork on hamburger buns, if desired. **Yield:** 12 servings.

Tangy Asparagus Soup

(Pictured below)

PREP: 40 min. **COOK:** 15 min.

A dollop of creme fraiche makes this pretty asparagus soup the ideal starter for an elegant springtime dinner party. Serve a Parmesan cheese crisp on the side for the perfect finishing touch.
—*Jamie Concannon, Plymouth, California*

- 1/4 **cup butter, cubed**
- 1 **cup sliced shallots**
- 2 **pounds fresh asparagus, cut into 1-inch pieces**
- 2-1/2 **cups chicken broth**
- 1/2 **cup white wine *or* additional chicken broth**
- 2 **teaspoons ground coriander**
- 1/4 **teaspoon pepper**
- 1 **cup shredded Parmesan cheese**
- 1/4 **cup creme fraiche *or* sour cream**
- 1/2 **teaspoon lemon juice**
- 1/4 **teaspoon grated lemon peel**

In a large skillet over medium heat, melt the butter. Add shallots; cook and stir until tender. Add asparagus; cook 1 minute longer. Stir in the broth, wine and coriander. Bring to a boil. Reduce heat; cover and simmer for 3-5 minutes or until asparagus is tender. Do not drain. Cool slightly. Place in blender; cover and process until pureed. Stir in pepper. Keep warm.

To make crisps, heat a lightly greased small skillet over medium heat. Add about 2 tablespoons cheese; cook for 1-2 minutes or until golden brown and cheese is bubbly. Carefully flip the Parmesan crisp; cook 30 seconds longer. Remove to waxed paper to cool. Repeat.

In a small bowl, combine the creme fraiche, lemon juice and lemon peel.

Ladle the soup into cups; dollop with the creme fraiche mixture. Serve with Parmesan crisps. **Yield:** 7 servings.

Best-Ever Chicken Fajita Chowder

(Pictured above and on page 32)

PREP: 15 min. **COOK:** 45 min.

On cool evenings, warm up your family with this thick, cheesy chowder. It captures the zippy flavors of the Southwest.
—*Beverly Matthews, Pasco, Washington*

- 1 **pound boneless skinless chicken breasts, chopped**
- 1 *each* **medium green, sweet red and yellow peppers, chopped**
- 1 **medium onion, chopped**
- 2 **tablespoons olive oil**
- 3 **cups water**
- 2 **cups frozen corn**
- 1 **cup uncooked brown rice**
- 1 **cup green enchilada sauce**
- 1/4 **cup canned chopped green chilies**
- 1/4 **teaspoon salt**
- 1 **cup (4 ounces) shredded Mexican cheese blend**
- 1 **cup (8 ounces) sour cream**

Tortilla chips and minced fresh chives, optional

In a Dutch oven over medium-high heat, cook and stir the chicken, peppers and onion in oil until vegetables are crisp-tender. Stir in the water, corn, rice, enchilada sauce, green chilies and salt. Bring to a boil. Reduce heat; cover and simmer for 35-40 minutes or until rice is tender.

Remove from the heat. Stir in cheese and sour cream until cheese is melted. Serve with chips and chives if desired. **Yield:** 6 servings.

Ultimate Panini

PREP: 40 min. **COOK:** 5 min./batch

The aroma of onions cooking at country fairs and street vendor carts gets me craving caramelized onions. I wanted to add them to something special, and this sandwich is just that.
—Charlene Brogan, Falmouth, Maine

    2 large onions, sliced
    2 tablespoons canola oil
    4 slices provolone cheese
1/2 pound thinly sliced deli ham
    1 large tomato, sliced
    8 garlic-flavored sandwich pickle slices
    8 slices Italian bread (1/2 inch thick)
    2 tablespoons butter, softened

In a large skillet, saute the onions in oil until softened. Reduce heat to medium-low; cook, stirring occasionally, for 30 minutes or until deep golden brown.

Layer the provolone cheese, ham, tomato, pickles and caramelized onions on four bread slices; top with the remaining bread. Spread the outsides of sandwiches with butter.

Cook on a panini maker or indoor grill for 3-4 minutes or until the bread is browned and the cheese is melted. **Yield:** 4 servings.

Squash Apple Soup

PREP: 20 min. **COOK:** 25 min.

Bowls of this rich, creamy blend are worthy of being on a holiday menu. Try croutons and grated Parmesan as garnishes.
—Holly Wilhelm, Sioux Falls, South Dakota

    3 celery ribs, chopped
    1 large apple, peeled and chopped
    1 small onion, chopped
    1 tablespoon olive oil
    1 tablespoon butter
    1 garlic clove, minced
1/2 teaspoon poultry seasoning
1/4 teaspoon salt
1/4 teaspoon pepper
    2 cans (14-1/2 ounces *each*) chicken broth, *divided*
    2 packages (12 ounces *each*) frozen cooked winter squash, thawed
Salad croutons and grated Parmesan cheese, optional

In a large saucepan, saute the celery, apple and onion in oil and butter until tender. Stir in the garlic, poultry seasoning, salt and pepper; cook 1 minute longer.

In a blender, combine 1 cup broth and the vegetable mixture; cover and process until smooth. Return to the pan; add the squash and remaining broth. Heat through. Serve with croutons and Parmesan cheese if desired. **Yield:** 7 servings.

Toasty Deli Hoagies

(Pictured below)

PREP: 35 min. **BROIL:** 5 min.

These deluxe broiled hoagies are generously stacked with deli meats, guacamole, cheese, veggies and a homemade spread.
—Staci Hoard, Bronston, Kentucky

    1 loaf (1 pound) French bread
    2 tablespoons mayonnaise
    1 tablespoon lemon juice
    2 garlic cloves, minced
1/2 pound thinly sliced deli smoked turkey
1/2 pound thinly sliced deli ham
    6 slices hard salami
    1 medium sweet yellow pepper, julienned
    1 small red onion, thinly sliced
1/2 pound sliced provolone cheese
1-1/2 cups guacamole

Cut French bread in half lengthwise; place cut side up on a baking sheet. Bake at 350° for 4-5 minutes or until toasted.

In a small bowl, combine the mayonnaise, lemon juice and garlic; spread over bread bottom. Layer with turkey, ham, salami, yellow pepper, onion and provolone cheese. Bake for 7-8 minutes or until the meat is heated through; broil 3-4 in. from the heat for 3 minutes or until cheese is lightly browned.

Spread guacamole over bread top; place over cheese. Cut into six slices. **Yield:** 6 servings.

Chicken Chorizo Posole

(Pictured above)

PREP: 40 min. **COOK:** 40 min.

I first sampled posole in Santa Fe. It was a revelation! I began experimenting with different versions, and this one has become a favorite. —Jennifer Beckman, Falls Church, Virginia

- 1 **pound tomatillos, husks removed, cut in half**
- 1 **large onion, quartered**
- 2 **jalapeno peppers, halved and seeded**
- 4 **garlic cloves, peeled**
- 4 **cups water**
- 1 **cup reduced-sodium chicken broth**
- 1 **whole garlic bulb, loose paper removed, cut in half**
- 5 **whole cloves**
- 2 **bay leaves**
- 2 **boneless skinless chicken breast halves (6 ounces *each*)**
- 1 **pound uncooked chorizo *or* bulk spicy pork sausage**
- 2 **cans (15 ounces *each*) hominy, rinsed and drained**
- 3 **teaspoons lime juice, *divided***
- 1 **teaspoon dried oregano**
- 1 **teaspoon ground cumin**
- 1/2 **teaspoon salt, *divided***

SALSA:
- 1 **cup minced fresh cilantro, *divided***
- 1 **medium mango, peeled and cubed**
- 1 **medium ripe avocado, peeled and cubed**
- 5 **radishes, chopped**

GARNISH:
- 6 **cups tortilla chips**

Place the tomatillos, onion, jalapenos and garlic cloves on a greased baking sheet. Bake at 425° for 25-30 minutes or until tomatillos are tender. Cool slightly. Transfer to a food processor; cover and process until blended.

In a Dutch oven, bring the water, broth, garlic bulb, cloves and bay leaves to a boil. Reduce heat; add chicken breasts and poach, uncovered, for 15-20 minutes or until no longer pink.

Remove the chicken from the broth and shred. Strain broth, discarding the seasonings. Crumble the chorizo into Dutch oven; cook over medium heat for 6-8 minutes or until fully cooked. Drain. Return the broth to Dutch oven. Stir in the hominy, 2 teaspoons lime juice, oregano, cumin, 1/4 teaspoon salt, tomatillo mixture and shredded chicken; heat through. Stir in 1/2 cup cilantro.

For salsa, in a small bowl, combine mango, avocado, radishes and remaining cilantro, lime juice and salt. Serve with soup. Garnish with chips. **Yield:** 9 servings.

Editor's Note: We recommend wearing disposable gloves when cutting hot peppers. Avoid touching your face.

CHOOSING CHORIZO. A coarsely ground fresh or smoked pork sausage, chorizo has Portuguese, Mexican and Spanish origins and is traditionally flavored with paprika or chili powder. Try it in egg dishes, soups, casseroles and Mexican fare.

Ham and Brie Melts

PREP/TOTAL TIME: 20 min.

Tired of the usual BLTs, tuna salad or grilled cheese? Try these special, quick and crispy sandwiches for a scrumptious change of pace. It's hard to believe that just ham, Brie, apricot preserves and two other ingredients can add up to such great taste.
—*Bonnie Bahler, Ellington, Connecticut*

   8 slices multigrain bread
1/4 cup apricot preserves
1/2 pound sliced deli ham
   1 round (8 ounces) Brie cheese, rind removed, sliced
   3 tablespoons butter, softened

Spread four of the bread slices with half of the apricot preserves. Layer with the deli ham and Brie cheese. Spread the remaining bread slices with the remaining apricot preserves; place on top. Butter the outsides of the sandwiches.

   In a large skillet over medium heat, toast sandwiches for 2-3 minutes on each side or until the bread is lightly browned and the cheese is melted. **Yield:** 4 servings.

Stephanie's Slow Cooker Stew

PREP: 20 min. **COOK:** 7-1/2 hours

Start this heartwarming one-pot meal before you head out in the morning for work or errands. By the time you get home, the well-seasoned meat will be tender and mouthwatering. Pair big bowlfuls with a loaf of fresh-baked bread or rolls.
—*Stephanie Rabbitt-Schapp, Cincinnati, Ohio*

   1 pound beef stew meat
   2 medium potatoes, peeled and cubed
   1 can (14-1/2 ounces) beef broth
   1 can (11-1/2 ounces) V8 juice
   2 celery ribs, chopped
   2 medium carrots, chopped
   1 medium sweet onion, chopped
   3 bay leaves
1/2 teaspoon salt
1/2 teaspoon dried thyme
1/2 teaspoon chili powder
1/4 teaspoon pepper
   2 tablespoons cornstarch
   1 tablespoon cold water
1/2 cup frozen corn
1/2 cup frozen peas

In a 3-qt. slow cooker, combine the first 12 ingredients. Cover and cook on low for 7-8 hours or until the meat is tender. Discard bay leaves.

   In a small bowl, combine the cornstarch and water until smooth; stir into the stew. Add the corn and peas. Cover and cook on high for 30 minutes or until thickened. **Yield:** 5 servings.

Cool as a Cucumber Soup

(Pictured below)

PREP: 15 min. + standing

This creamy chilled soup can make a wonderful appetizer or side on a hot summer's afternoon. Bursts of fresh dill provide a pleasant contrast to the milder flavor of cucumber.
—*Deirdre Dee Cox, Milwaukee, Wisconsin*

   1 pound cucumbers, peeled, seeded and sliced
1/2 teaspoon salt
1-1/2 cups fat-free plain yogurt
   1 green onion, coarsely chopped
   1 garlic clove, minced
4-1/2 teaspoons snipped fresh dill
Additional chopped green onion and snipped fresh dill

In a colander set over a bowl, toss cucumbers with salt. Let stand for 30 minutes. Squeeze and pat dry.

   Place cucumbers, yogurt, onion and garlic in a food processor; cover and process until smooth. Stir in the dill. Serve immediately in chilled bowls. Garnish with additional onion and dill. **Yield:** 7 servings.

Roasted Poblano Beef Stew

(Pictured below)

PREP: 40 min. + standing **COOK:** 2 hours

I like to keep my son's heritage alive through cooking, and this stew reflects my wife's Hispanic background. The first time I fixed it, she gave me high praise. Try serving it in flour tortillas.
—Greg Fontenot, The Woodlands, Texas

- 5 poblano peppers
- 1 boneless beef chuck roast (2 to 3 pounds), cut into 1-inch cubes
- 2 tablespoons olive oil
- 1 medium onion, chopped
- 3 garlic cloves, minced
- 1 carton (32 ounces) beef broth
- 2 medium tomatoes, chopped
- 1/3 cup minced fresh cilantro
- 1 tablespoon chili powder
- 1 teaspoon salt
- 1 teaspoon ground cumin
- 1/2 teaspoon pepper
- 2 large potatoes, peeled and cut into 1-inch cubes

Broil poblano peppers 4 in. from the heat until the skins blister, about 5 minutes. With tongs, rotate peppers a quarter turn. Broil and rotate until all sides are blistered and blackened. Immediately place poblanos in a small bowl; cover and let stand for 20 minutes.

Peel off and discard charred skins. Remove stems and seeds. Coarsely chop poblanos.

In a Dutch oven, brown beef in oil in batches. Remove and keep warm. In the same pan, saute the onion until tender. Add garlic; cook 1 minute longer.

Gradually add the beef broth; stir in the tomatoes, cilantro, chili powder, salt, cumin, pepper, poblanos and beef. Bring to a boil. Reduce heat; cover and simmer

1-1/2 hours or until beef is tender. Add potatoes; cook 10-15 minutes longer or until potatoes are tender. Skim fat. **Yield:** 8 servings (3 quarts).

Crouton-Topped Garlic Soup

(Pictured above)

PREP: 20 min. **COOK:** 1 hour

Pan roasting the garlic gives this special soup rich flavor, while a touch of heavy cream lends body. Each bowlful gets an extra kick from the toppings—grated Gruyere or Swiss cheese, crunchy herbed croutons made from scratch and fresh parsley.
—Carolyn Kumpe, El Dorado, California

- 20 garlic cloves, peeled
- 1 tablespoon olive oil
- 2 large onions, halved and sliced
- 2 tablespoons butter
- 2-1/2 cups reduced-sodium chicken broth
- 1 tablespoon minced fresh thyme *or* 1 teaspoon dried thyme
- 1 bay leaf
- 1 cup heavy whipping cream

CROUTONS:
- 2 cups cubed sourdough bread, crusts removed
- 2 tablespoons olive oil
- 1 teaspoon minced fresh rosemary *or* 1/4 teaspoon dried rosemary, crushed
- 1/4 teaspoon salt
- 1/8 teaspoon pepper

TOPPINGS:
- 1/2 cup shredded Gruyere *or* Swiss cheese
- 2 tablespoons minced fresh parsley

In a small skillet, cook the garlic in oil over low heat for 3-5 minutes or until golden brown. Remove from the heat; set aside.

In a Dutch oven over medium-high heat, cook onions in butter until softened. Reduce the heat to medium-low; cook, stirring occasionally, for 30 minutes or until deep golden brown.

Add chicken broth, thyme, bay leaf and reserved garlic. Bring to a boil. Reduce heat; cover and simmer for 20 minutes to allow flavors to blend. Stir in the heavy whipping cream; heat through. Discard bay leaf.

For croutons, place bread in a small bowl. Combine the oil, rosemary, salt and pepper; drizzle over bread and toss to coat. Place in an ungreased 15-in. x 10-in. x 1-in. baking pan. Bake at 400° for 15-20 minutes or until golden brown, stirring occasionally.

Divide the soup among four bowls. Top with croutons, cheese and parsley. **Yield:** 4 servings.

Cajun Beef Burgers

PREP: 30 min. **GRILL:** 10 min.

Big appetites are no match for these hefty sandwiches boasting bits of veggies and Cajun seasoning. A homemade sauce of mayo and Creole mustard adds even more Louisana–style flair.
— *Rebecca Baird, Salt Lake City, Utah*

- 1/4 **cup mayonnaise**
- 1 **green onion, thinly sliced**
- 1-1/2 **teaspoons Creole mustard**
- 1/2 **teaspoon minced garlic**
- 1/2 **teaspoon grated lime peel**
- 1/2 **teaspoon lime juice**
- 1/4 **teaspoon pepper**
- 1/8 **teaspoon salt**
Dash hot pepper sauce
Dash Worcestershire sauce
BURGERS:
- 1/4 **cup *each* finely chopped onion, celery and carrot**
- 2 **tablespoons minced fresh parsley**
- 1 **tablespoon butter**
- 1 **tablespoon Cajun seasoning**
- 1/4 **teaspoon salt**
- 1/4 **teaspoon hot pepper sauce**
- 1 **pound lean ground beef (90% lean)**
- 4 **onion rolls, split**

In a small bowl, combine the first 10 ingredients until blended; chill until serving.

In a large skillet, saute onion, celery, carrot and parsley in butter for 6-8 minutes or until tender; cool slightly.

In a large bowl, combine the vegetable mixture, Cajun seasoning, salt and pepper sauce. Crumble beef over the mixture and mix well. Shape into four patties.

Grill the burgers, covered, over medium heat or broil 4 in. from the heat for 5-7 minutes on each side or until a meat thermometer reads 160° and juices run clear. Grill rolls, cut side down, over medium heat for 30-60 seconds or until toasted. Serve burgers on onion rolls with sauce. **Yield:** 4 servings.

Champion Lamb Burgers

(Pictured below)

PREP/TOTAL TIME: 25 min.

This recipe is a fantastic alternative to beef burgers. I think the sauteed onions with rosemary make it especially delicious.
— *Charlene Chambers, Ormond Beach, Florida*

- 2 **large red onions, thinly sliced**
- 2 **teaspoons olive oil**
- 1 **tablespoon red wine vinegar**
- 2 **teaspoons minced fresh rosemary**
- 1-1/2 **teaspoons sugar**
- 1 **teaspoon stone-ground mustard**
- 1/4 **teaspoon salt**
- 1/4 **teaspoon pepper**
BURGERS:
- 2 **pounds ground lamb**
- 2 **garlic cloves, minced**
- 1 **teaspoon salt**
- 1/4 **teaspoon pepper**
- 6 **pita pocket halves**
- 2 **tablespoons olive oil**
- 1-1/2 **cups spring mix salad greens**

In a large skillet, saute onions in oil until tender. Add the vinegar, rosemary, sugar, mustard, salt and pepper; cook 5 minutes longer. Keep warm.

Crumble ground lamb into a large bowl; sprinkle with the garlic, salt and pepper and mix well. Shape into six patties. Grill burgers, covered, over medium heat or broil 4 in. from the heat for 4-6 minutes on each side or until a meat thermometer reads 160° and juices run clear.

Brush pita pockets with oil; lightly grill on both sides. Serve burgers in pita pockets with lettuce and onions. **Yield:** 6 servings.

Golden Clam Chowder

(Pictured above)

PREP: 20 min. **COOK:** 20 min.

Yes, you and your family can enjoy bowls of homemade clam chowder for dinner tonight. This version is perfectly seasoned and packed with veggies. It's comfort food at its best!
—Amanda Bowyer, Caldwell, Idaho

- 2 **celery ribs**
- 2 **medium carrots**
- 1 **medium onion**
- 2 **teaspoons olive oil**
- 4 **garlic cloves, minced**
- 4 **medium potatoes, peeled and diced**
- 2 **cans (6-1/2 ounces *each*) minced clams, undrained**
- 1 **bottle (8 ounces) clam juice**
- 1 **cup plus 1 tablespoon water, *divided***
- 1 **teaspoon dried thyme**
- 1/2 **teaspoon salt**
- 1/2 **teaspoon pepper**
- 1 **can (12 ounces) evaporated milk**
- 2 **teaspoons cornstarch**
- 2 **bacon strips, cooked and crumbled**

Finely chop celery, carrots and onion. In a Dutch oven, saute the vegetables in oil until tender. Add the garlic; cook 1 minute longer. Stir in the potatoes, clams, clam juice, 1 cup water, thyme, salt and pepper. Bring to a boil. Reduce heat; cover and simmer for 12-15 minutes or until potatoes are tender.

Gradually stir in the milk; heat through. Combine the cornstarch and remaining water until smooth; stir into chowder. Bring to a boil; cook and stir for 2 minutes or until thickened. Stir in bacon. **Yield:** 7 servings.

Fig-a-licious Pork Burgers

(Pictured below and on page 32)

PREP: 40 min. **GRILL:** 10 min.

The ingredients in these pork patties may seem unusual, but give them a try—you'll be glad you did! With fig puree and melted Gorgonzola cheese, they taste like a gourmet meal.
—Mary Cannataro, Chicago, Illinois

- 2 **cups dry red wine**
- 1 **medium onion, finely chopped**
- 10 **ounces dried figs, quartered**
- 2 **cups white wine**
- 3/4 **cup chopped walnuts**
- 1/3 **cup dry bread crumbs**
- 6 **fresh sage leaves, thinly sliced**
- 1-1/2 **teaspoons salt**
- 1 **teaspoon pepper**
- 1-1/2 **pounds ground pork**
- 3/4 **cup crumbled Gorgonzola cheese**
- 6 **hard rolls, split**
- 2 **cups fresh arugula or baby spinach**

In a large saucepan, bring red wine and onion to a boil; cook until the liquid is reduced to 2 tablespoons, about 20 minutes. Set aside to cool.

In another large saucepan, bring figs and white wine to a boil. Reduce heat; simmer, uncovered, for 20 minutes or until figs are plumped and tender. Cool slightly. Transfer to a food processor; cover and process until blended. Stir in walnuts.

In a large bowl, combine the bread crumbs, sage, salt, pepper and red wine mixture. Crumble pork over mixture and mix well. Shape into six patties.

Grill burgers, covered, over medium heat or broil 4 in. from heat for 5-6 minutes on each side or until a meat thermometer reads 160° and juices run clear. Top with Gorgonzola cheese; cover and grill 1-2 minutes longer or until cheese is melted.

Grill the rolls, cut side down, on medium heat for 30-60 seconds or until toasted. Spread each roll with 1 tablespoon fig mixture; top with a burger and arugula. (Save remaining mixture for another use.) **Yield:** 6 servings.

Creamy Vegetable Chowder

PREP: 30 min. **COOK:** 1 hour

It's easy to double or triple the recipe for this rich, creamy soup loaded with potatoes, carrots, onions and more. To lower the fat content, use turkey bacon, vegetable broth and skim milk.
—*Suzanna VandeBrake, Peyton, Colorado*

- 3/4 **pound sliced bacon, chopped**
- 2 **large onions**
- 2 **medium carrots**
- 2 **celery ribs**
- 2 **medium parsnips**
- 2 **small turnips**
- 3/4 **cup all-purpose flour**
- 1/2 **teaspoon salt**
- 1/2 **teaspoon cayenne pepper**
- 2 **cartons (32 ounces *each*) chicken broth**
- 1 **medium sweet potato, peeled and chopped**
- 3 **small red potatoes, chopped**
- 2 **bay leaves**
- 1 **tablespoon Worcestershire sauce**
- 1/4 **teaspoon hot pepper sauce**
- 1 **cup half-and-half cream**
- 1/2 **cup minced fresh parsley**

In a Dutch oven, cook the bacon over medium heat until crisp. Remove to paper towels; drain, reserving 3 tablespoons drippings. Chop the onions, carrots, celery, parsnips and turnips; add to the pan. Cook and stir for 6-8 minutes or until fragrant.

Sprinkle vegetables with flour, salt and cayenne; stir until blended. Gradually add broth. Bring to a boil; cook and stir for 2 minutes or until thickened. Stir in the sweet potato, potatoes, bay leaves, Worcestershire sauce and pepper sauce.

Reduce heat; cover and simmer for 15-20 minutes or until potatoes are tender. Stir in cream and parsley; heat through. Discard bay leaves. **Yield:** 12 servings (3 quarts).

Sweet & Spicy Fusion Burgers

(Pictured above right and on page 32)

PREP: 25 min. **GRILL:** 10 min.

These deliciously different turkey burgers combine some of my favorite flavors and textures. Plus, you can do most of the prep work ahead of time. You'll find naan, an Indian flatbread, in the international or bread section of your grocery store.
—*Jamie Brown-Miller, Napa, California*

- 2 **cups shredded cabbage**
- 2 **teaspoons sesame seeds**
- 2 **teaspoons lemon juice**
- 2 **teaspoons Dijon mustard**
- 2 **teaspoons sesame oil**
- 2 **tablespoons sriracha Asian hot chili sauce**
- 2 **tablespoons soy sauce**

- 2 **tablespoons honey**
- 1 **tablespoon red wine vinegar**
- 1/4 **teaspoon salt**
- 1/4 **teaspoon pepper**
- 1 **pound ground turkey**
- 4 **naan flatbreads, warmed**
- 1 **package (5.3 ounces) fresh goat cheese**
- 1/2 **medium cucumber, thinly sliced**
- 1/2 **cup julienned sweet red pepper**

Place the cabbage in a small bowl. In another small bowl, combine the sesame seeds, lemon juice, mustard and oil; pour over cabbage and toss to coat.

In a large bowl, combine chili sauce, soy sauce, honey, vinegar, salt and pepper. Crumble turkey over mixture and mix well. Shape into four patties.

Moisten a paper towel with cooking oil; using long-handled tongs, lightly coat the grill rack. Grill burgers, covered, over medium heat or broil 4 in. from the heat for 5-7 minutes on each side or until a meat thermometer reads 165° and juices run clear.

Spread four flatbread halves with goat cheese. Top with the burgers, cucumber, red pepper and cabbage mixture. **Yield:** 4 servings.

IT'S DONE. To test Sweet & Spicy Fusion Burgers (recipe above) or other burgers for doneness, hold the burger with tongs while inserting an instant-read thermometer horizontally from a side. Make sure the thermometer is far enough in to read the temperature in the center.

Side Dishes & Condiments

After choosing an outstanding entree, look here to round out your menu in an equally impressive way. Enjoy Make-Ahead Mashed Potatoes, Gingered Carrot Chutney, Basil Baked Tomatoes and many more accompaniments.

PERFECT PLATE-FILLERS. Clockwise from top left: Over-the-Top Cherry Jam (p. 56), Mango Cuke Relish (p. 55), Finnish Cauliflower (p. 58) and Chipotle Lime Corn on the Cob (p. 47).

Transfer the potato mixture to a greased 13-in. x 9-in. baking dish; sprinkle with the cheese, onions and bacon. Cover and refrigerate until ready to use.

Remove from refrigerator 30 minutes before baking. Bake, uncovered, at 350° for 40-50 minutes or until heated through. **Yield:** 10 servings.

Pecan Stuffed Butternut Squash

(Pictured below)

PREP: 10 min. **BAKE:** 1-1/4 hours

I love autumn, when butternut squash is at its peak. Here, it bakes up tender and has a fabulous, creamy pecan filling.
—*Sheryl Little, Sherwood, Arkansas*

>   2 medium butternut squash (about 3 pounds *each*)
>   3/4 teaspoon salt
> Pepper, optional
>   4 ounces cream cheese, softened
>   1/4 cup butter, softened
>   3 tablespoons brown sugar
>   1/2 cup chopped pecans

Cut each squash in half lengthwise; discard seeds. Place squash cut side down in two 13-in. x 9-in. baking dishes; add 1/2-in. water. Bake, uncovered, at 350° for 1 hour.

Turn the squash over; sprinkle with salt and pepper if desired. In a small bowl, beat the cream cheese, butter and brown sugar until light and fluffy; stir in the pecans. Spoon into squash cavities.

Bake 15-20 minutes longer or until the filling is lightly browned and squash is tender. **Yield:** 8 servings.

Make-Ahead Mashed Potatoes

(Pictured above)

PREP: 25 min. **BAKE:** 40 min.

Mashed potatoes are even better when smothered with a savory trio of cheddar cheese, green onions and bacon. Plus, my recipe provides the make–ahead convenience busy cooks appreciate.
—*Amanda Sauer, University City, Missouri*

>   3 pounds potatoes (about 9 medium), peeled and cubed
>   1 package (8 ounces) cream cheese, softened
>   1/2 cup sour cream
>   1/2 cup butter, cubed
>   1/4 cup 2% milk
> 1-1/2 teaspoons onion powder
>   1 teaspoon salt
>   1 teaspoon garlic powder
>   1/2 teaspoon pepper
>   6 bacon strips, chopped
>   1 cup (4 ounces) shredded cheddar cheese
>   3 green onions, chopped

Place the potatoes in a Dutch oven and cover with water. Bring to a boil. Reduce the heat; cover and cook for 10-15 minutes or until tender. Drain; mash the potatoes with the cream cheese, sour cream and butter. Stir in the milk and seasonings.

In a small skillet, cook the bacon over medium heat until crisp. Remove bacon to paper towels with a slotted spoon; drain.

Chipotle Lime Corn on the Cob

(Pictured above and on page 44)

PREP: 25 min. **GRILL:** 25 min.

In Mexico, grilled corn sometimes gets slathered in mayo, rolled in grated cheese and served with lime and chili powder. Here is my family's version. —Carolyn Kumpe, El Dorado, California

- 6 large ears sweet corn in husks
- 1/2 cup mayonnaise
- 1 chipotle pepper in adobo sauce, finely chopped
- 2 tablespoons minced fresh cilantro
- 2 tablespoons lime juice
- 1-1/2 teaspoons grated lime peel
- 1 garlic clove, minced
- 1/2 cup grated Asiago cheese

Carefully peel back the corn husks to within 1 in. of the bottoms; remove silk. Rewrap corn in husks and secure with kitchen string. Place in a stockpot; cover with cold water. Soak for 20 minutes; drain.

Grill corn, covered, over medium heat for 25-30 minutes or until tender, turning often.

In a small bowl, combine the mayonnaise, chipotle pepper, cilantro, lime juice, lime peel and garlic; spread one heaping tablespoon over each ear of corn. Sprinkle with Asiago cheese. **Yield:** 6 servings.

DRIED HERB DO'S. Dried herbs don't spoil but do lose flavor and potency over time, so you may want to replace herbs that are over a year old. Store dried herbs in airtight containers and keep them away from heat and light.

Herbed Dipping Oil

(Pictured below)

PREP/TOTAL TIME: 5 min.

Our Test Kitchen experts combined a blend of herbs to create this mouthwatering mix. Plumping the herbs in water before stirring them into the olive oil enhances the flavor.

- 1 tablespoon dried minced garlic
- 1 tablespoon dried rosemary, crushed
- 1 tablespoon dried oregano
- 2 teaspoons dried basil
- 1 teaspoon crushed red pepper flakes
- 1/2 teaspoon salt
- 1/2 teaspoon coarsely ground pepper

ADDITIONAL INGREDIENTS (for each batch):
- 1 tablespoon water
- 1/2 cup olive oil
- 1 French bread baguette (10-1/2 ounces)

In a small bowl, combine the first seven ingredients. Store in an airtight container in a cool dry place for up to 6 months. **Yield:** 3 batches (1/4 cup total).

To prepare dipping oil: In a small microwave-safe bowl, combine 4 teaspoons herb mix with the water. Microwave, uncovered, on high for 10-15 seconds. Drain excess water. Transfer to a shallow serving plate; add oil and stir. Serve with bread. **Yield:** 1/2 cup per batch.

Bacon, Cremini & Brie Potatoes

(Pictured below)

PREP: 10 min. **BAKE:** 50 min.

This is my version of an ultimate baked potato. Rich Brie cheese, crispy bacon and cremini mushrooms transform the humble spud into something really special. It's almost a meal in itself.
—Jan Valdez, Chicago, Illinois

    4 medium potatoes
    4 teaspoons olive oil
1/2 teaspoon salt
    6 bacon strips, chopped
1/2 pound sliced baby portobello (cremini)
      mushrooms
    4 ounces Brie cheese, sliced
Chopped fresh chives, optional

Scrub and pierce the potatoes. Rub the potato skins with oil; sprinkle with salt. Bake at 400° for 50-60 minutes or until tender.

In a large skillet, cook the bacon over medium heat until crisp. Remove to paper towels with a slotted spoon; drain, reserving 2 tablespoons bacon drippings. Saute mushrooms in the drippings.

Cut a 2-in. "X" in tops of potatoes; insert cheese slices. Top with mushrooms, bacon and chives. **Yield:** 4 servings.

Maple Horseradish Beets

(Pictured above)

PREP: 50 min. **COOK:** 10 min.

Even folks who don't care for beets think my simple treatment is a winner. An easy glaze gives them terrific taste and a little zip.
—Leslie Palmer, Swampscott, Massachusetts

1-3/4 pounds fresh beets
    1 tablespoon canola oil
    2 tablespoons butter
1/4 cup maple syrup
    3 tablespoons prepared horseradish
    2 tablespoons cider vinegar
1/4 teaspoon salt
1/4 teaspoon pepper

Peel beets and cut into wedges. Place in a 15-in. x 10-in. x 1-in. baking pan; drizzle with oil and toss to coat. Bake at 400° for 40-50 minutes or until tender.

In a small saucepan, melt the butter. Stir in the maple syrup, horseradish, vinegar, salt and pepper. Bring to a boil. Carefully stir in beets; cook for 5-6 minutes or until liquid is slightly thickened, gently stirring occasionally. **Yield:** 6 servings.

PORTOBELLO POINTERS. With a large size and meaty texture, portobello mushrooms are well suited for grilling and broiling and are popular in vegetarian recipes. Baby portobellos, also known as cremini mushrooms, can be used instead of white mushrooms for a flavor boost.

Curry Butter

PREP/TOTAL TIME: 5 min.

You'll love the earthy flavor that corn gets from this curry butter, but it's also good with potatoes and other vegetables.
—*Elke Rose, Waukesha, Wisconsin*

- 1/2 cup butter, softened
- 1-1/2 teaspoons curry powder
- 1/2 teaspoon ground cumin
- 1/4 teaspoon crushed red pepper flakes

In a small bowl, beat all ingredients. Chill until serving.
Yield: 1/2 cup.

All-Around Seasoning Mix

(Pictured below)

PREP/TOTAL TIME: 10 min.

I always keep this tongue-tingling mixture on hand because it's great on just about anything, especially grilled pork, chicken and veggies. The cayenne pepper gives it even more of a kick.
—*Greg Fontenot, The Woodlands, Texas*

- 1/2 cup paprika
- 3 tablespoons onion powder
- 3 tablespoons garlic powder
- 3 tablespoons cayenne pepper
- 2 tablespoons white pepper
- 2 tablespoons pepper
- 4 teaspoons salt
- 4 teaspoons dried thyme
- 4 teaspoons dried oregano
- 4 teaspoons ground cumin
- 4 teaspoons chili powder

In a small bowl, combine all ingredients. Store in an airtight container in a cool dry place for up to 6 months.
Yield: 1-2/3 cups.

Rustic Fig, Onion & Pear Tart

(Pictured above)

PREP: 50 min. **BAKE:** 15 min.

This recipe was one of my first creations. The fig preserves, pears and sweet onions work together well and are perfectly suited for the rustic crust. I've served this as a side dish and even dessert.
—*Tina MacKissock, Manchester, New Hampshire*

- 3 large sweet onions, halved and thinly sliced
- 3 medium pears, peeled and sliced
- 4-1/2 teaspoons olive oil
- 4-1/2 teaspoons butter
- 1 cup fig preserves
- 1 tablespoon plus 1 teaspoon cider vinegar
- 1/8 teaspoon salt
- 1 sheet refrigerated pie pastry
- 1/8 teaspoon pepper
- 1 egg, beaten

In a large skillet, saute onions and pears in oil and butter until softened. Reduce heat to medium-low; cook, stirring occasionally, for 30 minutes or until deep golden brown.

Add the fig preserves, vinegar and salt. Bring to a boil; cook for 5 minutes or until thickened. Cool slightly.

Place half of the onion mixture in a food processor; cover and process until pureed. Set the remaining onion mixture aside.

Place pie pastry on a greased 12-in. pizza pan. Spoon pureed onion mixture over the pastry to within 2 in. of edges; sprinkle with pepper. Top with the reserved onion mixture. Fold up the edges of pastry over filling, leaving center uncovered. Brush edges of tart with egg.

Bake at 450° for 15-20 minutes or until crust is golden and filling is bubbly. **Yield:** 12 servings.

Discard the spice bag. Stir in the coconut, ginger and hot pepper sauce.

Carefully ladle the hot chutney into hot half-pint jars, leaving 1/2-in. headspace. Remove air bubbles; wipe rims and adjust lids. Process for 10 minutes in a boiling-water canner. **Yield:** 9 half-pints.

Editor's Note: The processing time listed is for altitudes of 1,000 feet or less. For altitudes up to 3,000 feet, add 5 minutes; 6,000 feet, add 10 minutes; 8,000 feet, add 15 minutes; 10,000 feet, add 20 minutes.

Two-Tone Potato Wedges

(Pictured below)

PREP: 10 min. **BAKE:** 40 min.

These two-tone baked potato wedges are cheesy, zippy and a real crowd-pleaser. Plus, they're on the dinner table in no time.
—*Maria Nicolau Schumacher, Larchmont, New York*

- 2 **medium potatoes**
- 1 **medium sweet potato**
- 1 **tablespoon olive oil**
- 1/4 **teaspoon salt**
- 1/4 **teaspoon pepper**
- 1 **tablespoon grated Parmesan cheese**
- 2 **garlic cloves, minced**

Cut each potato and the sweet potato into eight wedges; place in a large resealable plastic bag. Add the oil, salt and pepper; seal the bag and shake to coat. Arrange in a single layer in a 15-in. x 10-in. x 1-in. baking pan coated with cooking spray.

Bake, uncovered, at 425° for 20 minutes. Turn potatoes; sprinkle with Parmesan cheese and garlic. Bake 20-25 minutes longer or until golden brown, turning once. **Yield:** 4 servings.

Gingered Carrot Chutney

(Pictured above)

PREP: 1 hour **PROCESS:** 10 min.

Tangy and bright, this delicious condiment is so versatile. It can top your favorite cheese spread on crackers or be spooned on a dinner plate alongside nearly any type of meat. Give a jar of the chutney as a gift for a friend or neighbor for the holidays.
—*Deb Darr, Falls City, Oregon*

- 4 **pounds carrots, sliced**
- 2 **medium oranges**
- 1 **medium lemon**
- 2 **tablespoons mixed pickling spices**
- 2-1/2 **cups sugar**
- 1-1/3 **cups cider vinegar**
- 1 **cup flaked coconut**
- 1 **tablespoon minced fresh gingerroot**
- 1/2 **teaspoon hot pepper sauce**

Place the carrots in a Dutch oven and cover with water. Bring to a boil. Reduce heat; cover and cook for 20-25 minutes until very tender. Drain the carrots; puree in a food processor.

Using a vegetable peeler, remove peel from oranges and half of the lemon; cut peel into long narrow strips. Remove remaining peel from lemon and white pith from lemon and oranges; thinly slice fruit, discarding seeds.

Place the pickling spices on a double thickness of cheesecloth; bring up the corners of cloth and tie with string to form a bag. Place in a Dutch oven. Add the sugar, vinegar and citrus peels; bring to a boil.

Reduce heat; simmer, uncovered, for 5 minutes. Stir in the carrots and sliced fruit. Return to a boil. Reduce heat; simmer, uncovered, for 30 minutes, stirring frequently.

Root for Winter Vegetables

(Pictured above)

PREP: 30 min. **BAKE:** 55 min.

Here's an updated version of a recipe my mom grew up with. The medley of parsnips, turnips, carrots and more is my favorite way to prepare veggies and is wonderful with fresh–baked rolls.
—Julie Butler, Puyallup, Washington

- 1 whole garlic bulb
- 3 tablespoons olive oil, *divided*
- 1 pound fresh beets
- 3 medium parsnips
- 2 small rutabagas
- 2 medium turnips
- 4 medium carrots
- 2 large red onions, cut into wedges
- 1 teaspoon salt
- 15 whole peppercorns
- 3 bay leaves
- 1/2 cup white wine *or* vegetable broth
- 1/2 cup vegetable broth
- 2 tablespoons butter

Remove the papery outer skin from garlic (do not peel or separate cloves). Cut the top off of garlic bulb. Brush with 1/2 teaspoon oil. Wrap bulb in heavy-duty foil.

Peel beets, parsnips, rutabagas, turnips and carrots; cut into 2-in. pieces. Place in a large bowl; add the red onions, salt, peppercorns, bay leaves and remaining oil. Toss to coat.

Transfer to three greased 15-in. x 10-in. x 1-in. baking pans. Place garlic on one of the pans.

Bake at 400° for 35 minutes or until garlic is softened, stirring once. Remove garlic; set aside to cool. Drizzle the wine and vegetable broth over vegetables. Bake 20-30 minutes longer or until vegetables are tender. Squeeze softened garlic over vegetables; dot with butter. Transfer to a serving platter. **Yield:** 13 servings (3/4 cup each).

Wasabi Butter

PREP/TOTAL TIME: 5 min.

A hint of wasabi's mustard–horseradish flavor makes the sweet taste of corn pop. The butter is just as good on corn bread.
—Nila Grahl, Gurnee, Illinois

- 1/2 cup butter, softened
- 1 tablespoon chopped green onion (green part only)
- 1-1/2 teaspoons prepared wasabi
- 1/4 teaspoon reduced-sodium soy sauce

In a small bowl, beat all ingredients. Chill until serving. **Yield:** 1/2 cup.

Cuban Chimichurri

(Pictured below)

PREP/TOTAL TIME: 20 min.

This fresh Cuban sauce wonderfully complements steak, but pour it over a burger, too. Your taste buds will thank you!
—*Elaine Sweet, Dallas, Texas*

    7 garlic cloves, peeled
1-1/4 cups packed fresh cilantro leaves
  3/4 cup packed fresh parsley sprigs
    1 teaspoon crushed red pepper flakes
    1 teaspoon coarsely ground pepper
  1/4 cup white balsamic vinegar
    2 tablespoons lime juice
    1 tablespoon soy sauce
  1/2 teaspoon grated lime peel
  1/3 cup olive oil
Grilled steak

Place the garlic in a small food processor; cover and chop. Add the cilantro, parsley, pepper flakes and pepper; cover and process until finely chopped.

Add vinegar, lime juice, soy sauce and lime peel. While processing, gradually add oil in a steady stream. Serve with steak. **Yield:** 1 cup.

Herbed Veggie Mix-Up

(Pictured above)

PREP/TOTAL TIME: 25 min.

The simple addition of herbs and seasonings brings out the best in a colorful medley of beans, carrots, mushrooms and onion.
—*Marie Forte, Raritan, New Jersey*

  1/2 pound fresh green beans, cut into
       1-inch pieces
    2 medium carrots, julienned
  1/4 cup butter, cubed
  1/2 pound sliced fresh mushrooms
    1 medium onion, sliced
    2 tablespoons minced fresh parsley
  1/2 teaspoon salt
  1/2 teaspoon dried oregano
  1/2 teaspoon dried basil
  1/8 teaspoon white pepper

Place beans and carrots in a steamer basket; place in a large saucepan over 1 in. of water. Bring to a boil; cover and steam for 7-10 minutes or until crisp-tender.

Meanwhile, in a large skillet, melt the butter. Add the mushrooms and onion; saute until tender. Stir in the parsley, salt, oregano, basil, pepper, beans and carrots; heat through. **Yield:** 5 servings.

SAVORING CILANTRO. Have fresh cilantro left over after preparing Cuban Chimichurri (recipe above left)? Use this herb to make salsa or jazz up store-bought salsa...or add it to Mexican fare, scrambled eggs or traditional lettuce salads.

Microwave Mac 'n' Cheese

(Pictured below)

PREP/TOTAL TIME: 30 min.

My family really loves homemade macaroni and cheese, and this 30-minute recipe is an easy way to keep them happy. Whenever we have a family get-together, I bring this comforting microwave version. Its made-from-scratch goodness can't be beat.
—Linda Gingrich, Freeburg, Pennsylvania

- 2 **cups uncooked elbow macaroni**
- 2 **cups hot water**
- 1/3 **cup butter, cubed**
- 1/4 **cup chopped onion**
- 3/4 **teaspoon salt**
- 1/4 **teaspoon pepper**
- 1/4 **teaspoon ground mustard**
- 1/3 **cup all-purpose flour**
- 1-1/4 **cups milk**
- 8 **ounces process cheese (Velveeta), cubed**

In a 2-qt. microwave-safe dish, combine the first seven ingredients. Cover and microwave on high for 3 minutes; stir. Cover and cook at 50% power for 3 minutes or until mixture comes to a boil.

Combine the flour and milk until smooth; gradually stir into the macaroni mixture. Add the cheese. Cover and cook on high for 6-8 minutes or until the macaroni is tender and the sauce is bubbly, stirring every 3 minutes. **Yield:** 4 servings.

Editor's Note: This recipe was tested in a 1,100-watt microwave.

Maple Butter

(Pictured above)

PREP/TOTAL TIME: 5 min.

The sweet aroma of maple syrup draws you in, but after one bite of corn that's slathered in this butter, you'll be hooked for life!
—Kevin Varble, Harrisville, Utah

- 1/2 **cup butter, softened**
- 2 **tablespoons maple syrup**
- 1 **teaspoon minced fresh parsley**

Dash pepper

In a small bowl, beat all ingredients. Chill until serving. **Yield:** 1/2 cup.

Easy Grilled Squash

PREP/TOTAL TIME: 20 min.

I love butternut squash not just for its flavor, but also because it's a great source of vitamin A. This dish is one of my favorite sides. I usually make it when I'm grilling steak or chicken.
—Esther Horst, Monterey, Tennessee

- 3 **tablespoons olive oil**
- 2 **garlic cloves, minced**
- 1/4 **teaspoon salt**
- 1/4 **teaspoon pepper**
- 1 **small butternut squash, peeled and cut lengthwise into 1/2-inch slices**

In a small bowl, combine the oil, garlic, salt and pepper. Brush over squash slices.

Grill the squash, covered, over medium heat or broil 4 in. from the heat for 4-5 minutes on each side or until tender. **Yield:** 4 servings.

Sausage Toppings to Relish

THE BEST PART of the summer season just might be the wurst—bratwurst and other sausages, that is! And when you add a generous amount of the flavor-packed relishes here, you'll have pure bliss on a bun.

Created with everyday ingredients, each tempting topping offers a hint of the unexpected and a taste of the sensational to give any sausage four-star appeal. So skip store-bought relishes and treat your guests to these homemade varieties.

All that's left to do is rustle up some stellar side dishes and plenty of ice-cold beverages. You'll soon have a summertime menu that's top dog!

Raspberry Onion Relish

(Pictured below)

PREP/TOTAL TIME: 15 min.

I don't remember where I got this recipe, but it's a nice change from barbecue sauce. Try it on chicken and turkey, too.
—Sylvia Muir, Toronto, Ontario

- **2 cups fresh raspberries**
- **4 green onions, thinly sliced**
- **1/2 cup chopped red onion**
- **2 tablespoons white wine vinegar**
- **2 tablespoons olive oil**
- **3 garlic cloves, minced**
- **1 tablespoon minced fresh mint**
- **1/8 teaspoon salt**
- **1/8 teaspoon coarsely ground pepper**

In a small bowl, combine all ingredients. Serve relish immediately. **Yield:** 2-1/2 cups.

Happy Hot Dog Relish

PREP/TOTAL TIME: 25 min.

This sweet–tart combination of cranberry sauce and sauerkraut is so good! It also goes well with hamburgers, pork and ham.
—Elizabeth Carlson, Corvallis, Oregon

- **1 medium onion, chopped**
- **1 tablespoon olive oil**
- **1 cup whole-berry cranberry sauce**
- **1 tablespoon Dijon mustard**
- **1 teaspoon sugar**
- **1/2 teaspoon garlic powder**
- **1/4 teaspoon hot pepper sauce**
- **1/2 cup sauerkraut, rinsed and drained**

In a small saucepan, saute the onion in oil until tender. Add the cranberry sauce, mustard, sugar, garlic powder and hot pepper sauce. Cook and stir for 5-10 minutes or until cranberry sauce is melted. Add sauerkraut; heat through. **Yield:** 1-1/2 cups.

Mango Cuke Relish

(Pictured below and on page 44)

PREP/TOTAL TIME: 20 min.

Colorful and crunchy, this unusual take on Thai green curry has a subtly spicy kick that just about everyone will enjoy.
—Suzanna Vicheinrut, Long Beach, California

- 1 medium mango, peeled and finely chopped
- 1/2 cup chopped peeled cucumber
- 1/4 cup chopped cashews
- 1/4 cup finely chopped sweet red pepper
- 1 green onion, thinly sliced
- 1 tablespoon minced fresh basil
- 1 tablespoon minced fresh cilantro
- 1 tablespoon seasoned rice vinegar
- 1 garlic clove, minced
- 1 teaspoon green curry paste
- 1/2 teaspoon grated lime peel
- 1/4 teaspoon crushed red pepper flakes

In a small bowl, combine all ingredients. Chill relish until serving. **Yield:** 2 cups.

Spicy Olive Relish

(Pictured above)

PREP/TOTAL TIME: 10 min.

With just four simple ingredients and 10 minutes, you can whip up this zippy condiment that olive-lovers will line up for.
—James MacGillivray, San Marcos, California

- 1 jar (16 ounces) pickled hot cherry peppers, drained
- 1 jar (7 ounces) pimiento-stuffed olives, drained
- 1 small onion, quartered
- 1 tablespoon yellow mustard

Place the peppers, olives and onion in a food processor; cover and process until finely chopped. Transfer to a bowl; stir in mustard. **Yield:** 2 cups.

SAUSAGE SUCCESS. Grill fully cooked sausages over direct medium heat, turning occasionally, until they are browned and heated through, about 7-10 minutes.

Using fresh (uncooked) sausages? Grill them over medium-low heat for 20-30 minutes until a meat thermometer reads 165°. You can also simmer them first in water or beer, seasoned with sauerkraut or sliced veggies, then remove the sausages from the liquid and grill them over medium heat until they reach 165°.

Baked Parmesan Broccoli

PREP: 30 min. **BAKE:** 15 min.

I began fixing this years ago as a way to get my children to eat nutritious broccoli, and they gobbled it up. They're now adults and still ask me to make this creamy bake. Garlic, Parmesan cheese and buttery seasoned bread crumbs make it yummy.
—*Barbara Uhl, Wesley Chapel, Florida*

    4 bunches broccoli, cut into florets
    6 tablespoons butter, *divided*
    1 small onion, finely chopped
    1 garlic clove, minced
  1/4 cup all-purpose flour
    2 cups 2% milk
    1 egg yolk, beaten
    1 cup grated Parmesan cheese
  1/2 teaspoon salt
  1/8 teaspoon pepper
  1/2 cup seasoned bread crumbs

Place half of the broccoli in a steamer basket; place in a large saucepan over 1 in. of water. Bring to a boil; cover and steam for 3-4 minutes or until broccoli is crisp-tender. Place in a greased 13-in. x 9-in. baking dish; repeat with the remaining broccoli.

Meanwhile, in a small saucepan over medium heat, melt 4 tablespoons butter. Add onion; cook and stir until tender. Add garlic; cook 1 minute longer.

Stir in the flour until blended; gradually add the milk. Bring to a boil; cook and stir for 2 minutes or until thickened. Stir a small amount of the hot mixture into the egg yolk; return all to the pan, stirring constantly. Cook and stir 1 minute longer. Remove from the heat; stir in cheese, salt and pepper.

Pour over the broccoli. In a small skillet, cook the bread crumbs in remaining butter until golden brown; sprinkle over the top.

Bake, uncovered, at 400° for 15-18 minutes or until heated through. **Yield:** 12 servings (3/4 cup each).

Over-the-Top Cherry Jam

(Pictured above and on page 44)

PREP: 35 min. **PROCESS:** 5 min.

We live in Door County, an area known for its wonderful tart cherries. This ruby–red, sweet jam makes a lovely gift.
—*Karen Haen, Sturgeon Bay, Wisconsin*

  2-1/2 pounds fresh tart cherries, pitted
      1 package (1-3/4 ounces) powdered fruit pectin
    1/2 teaspoon butter
  4-3/4 cups sugar

In a food processor, cover and process the cherries in batches until finely chopped. Transfer to a Dutch oven; stir in pectin and butter. Bring to a full rolling boil over high heat, stirring constantly. Stir in the sugar; return to a full rolling boil. Boil for 1 minute, stirring constantly.

Remove from the heat; skim off foam. Ladle the hot mixture into hot sterilized half-pint jars, leaving 1/4-in. headspace. Remove air bubbles; wipe the rims and adjust the lids. Process for 5 minutes in a boiling-water canner. **Yield:** 6 half-pints.

Editor's Note: The processing time listed is for altitudes of 1,000 feet or less. Add 1 minute to the processing time for each 1,000 feet of additional altitude.

BROCCOLI VS. BROCCOLINI. Broccoli (featured in the Baked Parmesan Broccoli recipe above) comes from the Latin word *brachium*, which means branch or arm. When purchasing this popular vegetable fresh, look for bunches that have a deep green color, tightly closed buds and crisp leaves.

Also called baby broccoli, Broccolini (used in the Broccolini with Shallots recipe at right) is a cross between broccoli and Chinese kale. Broccolini has broccoli-like florets on slim, individual, asparagus-like stalks. It has a sweet, mild flavor with a peppery bite. The entire stalk is edible and does not need to be peeled.

Broccolini with Shallots

PREP/TOTAL TIME: 15 min.

Shallots, garlic and lemon juice are nice complements to the peppery bite of the Broccolini in this side dish from our Test Kitchen staff. If you can't find that vegetable at your grocery store, simply use broccoli spears instead. (See the tip box below left to find out more about Broccolini.)

- **1/2** **pound Broccolini *or* broccoli spears**
- **1** **shallot, sliced**
- **1** **tablespoon olive oil**
- **2** **garlic cloves, minced**
- **1** **to 2 teaspoons lemon juice *or* white balsamic vinegar**
- **1/4** **teaspoon salt**
- **1/4** **teaspoon pepper**

Place the Broccolini in a large skillet; cover with water. Bring to a boil. Reduce the heat; cover and simmer for 5-7 minutes or until tender. Drain well. Remove Broccolini and keep warm.

In the same skillet, saute shallot in oil until tender. Add garlic; cook 1 minute longer. Add Broccolini, lemon juice, salt and pepper. Saute for 1-2 minutes or until heated through. **Yield:** 3 servings.

Glazed Pearl Onions

(*Pictured above*)

PREP/TOTAL TIME: 15 min.

These delicious onions were served at a restaurant I visited in Florida. They were so good, I had to ask for the recipe. The chef's assistant shared it with me, and I was pleasantly surprised to see that it's very easy. Now I whip these up in my own kitchen.
—Dixie Terry, Goreville, Illinois

- **1** **package (16 ounces) frozen pearl onions, thawed**
- **2** **tablespoons butter**
- **2** **tablespoons plus 1-1/2 teaspoons brown sugar**
- **1** **tablespoon Dijon mustard**
- **2** **tablespoons minced fresh parsley**

In a large skillet, saute the pearl onions in butter until tender. Add the brown sugar and Dijon mustard; cook 2 minutes longer. Sprinkle with minced fresh parsley. **Yield:** 6 servings.

Finnish Cauliflower

(Pictured below and on page 44)

PREP: 20 min. **BAKE:** 30 min.

After my Finnish grandmother passed away, I discovered a large index card in a box of her trinkets. I had the writing translated, and it turned out to be this delicious cauliflower casserole.
—*Judy Batson, Tampa, Florida*

- 2 **cups cubed day-old rye bread**
- 1 **small head cauliflower, cut into florets**
- 2 **tablespoons butter**
- 1 **teaspoon caraway seeds**
- 3 **cups (12 ounces) shredded sharp cheddar cheese**
- 4 **eggs, beaten**
- 1 **cup flat beer *or* nonalcoholic beer**
- 1 **teaspoon ground mustard**
- 1/2 **teaspoon ground coriander**
- 1/4 **teaspoon pepper**

Place the bread in a 15-in. x 10-in. x 1-in. baking pan; bake at 300° for 15-20 minutes or until crisp. In a large skillet, saute cauliflower in butter with the caraway seeds until tender. Remove from the heat; stir in bread and cheese. Transfer to a greased 11-in. x 7-in. baking dish.

In a small bowl, whisk eggs, beer, mustard, coriander and pepper. Pour over bread mixture. Bake at 350° for 30-35 minutes or until a knife inserted near the center comes out clean. **Yield:** 8 servings.

Glazed Baby Carrots

(Pictured above)

PREP/TOTAL TIME: 20 min.

With only two ingredients, these little carrots glazed with orange marmalade are ideal for nights when you need something quick.
—*Linda Hoffman, Logansport, Indiana*

- 2 **packages (16 ounces *each*) baby carrots**
- 1 **jar (12 ounces) orange marmalade**

Place 1 in. of water in a large saucepan; add the carrots. Bring to a boil. Reduce heat; cover and simmer for 12-15 minutes or until crisp-tender.

Drain carrots and place in a large serving bowl; stir in marmalade. Serve with a slotted spoon. **Yield:** 8 servings.

Broccoli with Almonds

PREP/TOTAL TIME: 15 min.

Everyone enjoys this tasty, dressed-up side. Plus, preparation is a breeze! Feel free to pair it with a variety of main courses.
—*Verna Puntigan, Pasadena, Maryland*

- 1-1/2 **pounds fresh broccoli, cut into spears**
- 1 **cup water**
- 1 **teaspoon chicken bouillon granules**
- 1/4 **cup sliced almonds**
- 3 **tablespoon stick margarine**
- 1/2 **cup finely chopped onion**
- 1 **teaspoon salt**

In a large saucepan, bring broccoli, water and bouillon to a boil. Reduce heat; cover and simmer for 5-8 minutes or until broccoli is crisp-tender. Drain and place in a serving dish; keep warm. In a skillet, saute almonds in margarine until browned. Add onion and salt; saute until onion is tender. Pour over broccoli; toss to coat. **Yield:** 6 servings.

Mediterranean Couscous

PREP/TOTAL TIME: 15 min.

With plenty of garlic and Parmesan cheese, this is a terrific dish and relies on a convenient packaged item to get started.
—*Beth Tomlinson, Streetsboro, Ohio*

  2 tablespoons chopped onion
  2 tablespoons olive oil, *divided*
  3 teaspoons minced garlic
1-1/4 cups water
  1 package (5.6 ounces) couscous with **toasted pine nuts**
1-1/2 teaspoons chicken bouillon granules
1/2 cup cherry tomatoes, halved
  2 tablespoons grated Parmesan cheese

In a small skillet, saute onion in 1 tablespoon oil for 3-4 minutes or until tender. Add garlic; cook 1 minute longer.

Meanwhile, in a large saucepan, combine the water, contents of seasoning packet from the couscous mix, bouillon and remaining oil. Bring to a boil.

Stir in the onion mixture and couscous. Cover and remove from the heat; let stand for 5 minutes. Fluff with a fork. Stir in the tomatoes and cheese. **Yield:** 4 servings.

Basil Baked Tomatoes

(Pictured below)

PREP/TOTAL TIME: 25 min.

This recipe has been in our family for many years—my mother brought it with her when she came to the United States from Italy. When you have an abundance of ready-to-pick tomatoes in the garden, this is a wonderful way to use them up.
—*Mary Detzi, Wind Gap, Pennsylvania*

1 garlic clove, minced
1 tablespoon olive oil
1/2 cup soft bread crumbs
2 large tomatoes

4 fresh basil leaves, chopped
1/8 teaspoon coarsely ground pepper

In a small skillet, saute the garlic in oil for 1 minute. Add bread crumbs; cook and stir until lightly browned. Remove from the heat.

Cut the tomatoes in half widthwise. Place cut side up in an 8-in. square baking dish. Sprinkle with the basil and pepper; top with the bread crumb mixture. Bake at 325° for 15-20 minutes or until the tomatoes are slightly softened. **Yield:** 4 servings.

Early-Bird Asparagus Supreme

(Pictured above)

PREP/TOTAL TIME: 10 min.

If you love savoring spring's crop of fresh asparagus, you'll want to try this! Onion soup and mozzarella enhance the great flavor.
—*Joyce Speckman, Holt, California*

3 pounds fresh asparagus, cut into 1-inch pieces
3 tablespoons butter, melted
1 envelope onion soup mix
1 cup (4 ounces) shredded mozzarella *or* Monterey Jack cheese

In a large saucepan, bring 1/2 in. of water to a boil. Add the asparagus; cover and boil for 3 minutes. Drain and immediately place the asparagus in ice water. Drain and pat dry.

Place in a 13-in. x 9-in. baking dish coated with cooking spray. Combine butter and onion soup mix; drizzle over asparagus. Sprinkle with mozzarella cheese.

Bake, uncovered, at 425° for 10-12 minutes or until the asparagus is tender and mozzarella cheese is melted. **Yield:** 6 servings.

Main Dishes

Whether you want a special dinner entree, such as Merlot Filet Mignon, or a quick family-pleaser, such as Savory Sausage Penne Supper, the rave-winning recipes in this chapter are sure to become mainstays on your menus.

MAIN ATTRACTION. Clockwise from top left: Mexican Skillet Rice (p. 74), Orange-Pecan Salmon (p. 66), Fiesta Chicken Bundles (p. 74) and Martha's Fish Tacos (p. 76).

Chipotle Beef Tenderloins

(Pictured below)

PREP: 40 min. **GRILL:** 10 min.

Head outside for dinner and grill this Southwestern steak—you'll be glad you did! A smoky homemade picante sauce gives it zip.
—*Gene Peters, Edwardsville, Illinois*

    3/4 cup chopped sweet onion
    3/4 cup chopped green pepper
      1 jalapeno pepper, seeded and minced
      1 chipotle pepper in adobo sauce, minced
      2 tablespoons olive oil
      3 cups seeded chopped tomatoes
      1 tablespoon chipotle hot pepper sauce
      2 teaspoons sugar
      1 teaspoon salt
      1 teaspoon chili powder
    1/2 teaspoon ground cumin
      2 tablespoons minced fresh cilantro
      1 teaspoon Liquid Smoke, optional
      6 beef tenderloin steaks (1-1/2 inches thick
        and 6 ounces *each*)
      2 teaspoons steak seasoning

In a Dutch oven, saute the onion, green pepper, jalapeno and chipotle pepper in oil until tender. Add the tomatoes, pepper sauce, sugar, salt, chili powder and cumin. Bring to a boil. Reduce heat; simmer, uncovered, for 30 minutes or until thickened, stirring frequently.

Remove from the heat; stir in cilantro and Liquid Smoke if desired.

Meanwhile, sprinkle steaks with steak seasoning. Grill, over medium heat for 7-8 minutes on each side or until meat reaches desired doneness (for medium-rare, a meat thermometer should read 145°; medium, 160°; well-done, 170°). Serve with sauce. **Yield:** 6 servings.

Four-Cheese Baked Ziti

(Pictured above)

PREP: 20 min. **BAKE:** 30 min.

Made with prepared Alfredo sauce, this baked ziti is deliciously different from typical tomato-based pasta dishes. Extra cheesy, it comes together quickly and always goes over well at potlucks.
—*Lisa Varner, Charleston, South Carolina*

      1 package (16 ounces) ziti *or* small tube pasta
      2 cartons (10 ounces *each*) refrigerated Alfredo
        sauce
      1 cup (8 ounces) sour cream
      2 eggs, lightly beaten
      1 carton (15 ounces) ricotta cheese
    1/2 cup grated Parmesan cheese, *divided*
    1/4 cup grated Romano cheese
    1/4 cup minced fresh parsley
    1-3/4 cups shredded part-skim mozzarella cheese

Cook the ziti according to package directions; drain and return to the pan. Stir in Alfredo sauce and sour cream. Spoon half into a lightly greased 3-qt. baking dish.

In a small bowl, combine eggs, ricotta cheese, 1/4 cup Parmesan cheese, Romano cheese and parsley; spread over pasta. Top with remaining pasta mixture; sprinkle with mozzarella and remaining Parmesan.

Cover and bake at 350° for 25 minutes or until a thermometer reads 160°. Uncover; bake 5-10 minutes longer or until bubbly. **Yield:** 8 servings.

Heavenly Greek Tacos

PREP: 30 min. + marinating **GRILL:** 10 min.

The name of these Greek fish tacos says it all. I first fixed them as a special meal for my fiance and me, and we were in heaven!
—*Meagan Jensen, Reno, Nevada*

- 1/3 cup lemon juice
- 2 tablespoons olive oil
- 4 teaspoons grated lemon peel
- 3 garlic cloves, minced, *divided*
- 1 teaspoon dried oregano
- 1/4 teaspoon salt
- 1/4 teaspoon pepper
- 2 pounds mahi mahi
- 1-1/2 cups shredded red cabbage
- 1/2 medium red onion, thinly sliced
- 1/2 medium sweet red pepper, julienned
- 1/2 cup crumbled feta cheese
- 6 tablespoons chopped pitted Greek olives, *divided*
- 1/4 cup minced fresh parsley
- 1-1/2 cups plain Greek yogurt
- 1/2 medium English cucumber, cut into 1-inch pieces
- 1 teaspoon dill weed
- 1/2 teaspoon ground coriander
- 12 whole wheat tortillas (8 inches), warmed

In a large resealable plastic bag, combine lemon juice, oil, lemon peel, 2 garlic cloves, oregano, salt and pepper. Add the mahi mahi; seal bag and turn to coat. Refrigerate for up to 30 minutes.

In a bowl, combine cabbage, onion, red pepper, cheese, 3 tablespoons olives and parsley; set aside.

Place yogurt, cucumber, dill, coriander and remaining garlic and olives in a food processor; cover and process until blended.

Drain fish and discard marinade. Moisten a paper towel with cooking oil; using long-handled tongs, lightly coat the grill rack. Grill mahi mahi, covered, over medium heat or broil 4 in. from the heat for 3-4 minutes on each side or until fish flakes easily with a fork.

Place a portion of the fish on each tortilla; top with the cabbage mixture and sauce. **Yield:** 6 servings.

FETA FACTS. Although feta cheese is mostly associated with Greek cooking, "feta" comes from the Italian word *fette*, meaning slice of food. Feta is a white, salty, semi-firm cheese. Traditionally made from sheep or goat's milk, it's now also made with cow's milk. Enjoy feta in seafood dishes such as Heavenly Greek Tacos (recipe above) or use it with chicken, olives, pasta salads, green salads or vegetables .

Dad's Best Pork Chops

(Pictured below)

PREP/TOTAL TIME: 25 min.

My son has liked pork chops since he was little. This is one of his favorite recipes because we pick the fresh mint from our garden. A little jalapeno pepper gives the meat a bit of a kick.
—*Greg Fontenot, The Woodlands, Texas*

- 2 medium tomatoes, chopped
- 1/4 cup chopped onion
- 3 tablespoons minced fresh mint
- 1 jalapeno pepper, chopped
- 2 tablespoons key lime juice
- 1-1/2 teaspoons minced fresh rosemary
- 4 bone-in pork loin chops (3/4 inch thick)
- 1/4 teaspoon salt
- 1/4 teaspoon pepper

In a small bowl, combine the first six ingredients. Chill until serving.

Sprinkle pork chops with salt and pepper. Grill chops, covered, over medium heat or broil 4 in. from the heat for 4-5 minutes on each side or until a meat thermometer reads 160°. Serve with salsa. **Yield:** 4 servings.

Editor's Note: We recommend wearing disposable gloves when cutting hot peppers. Avoid touching your face.

In a large resealable plastic bag, combine the broth, lime juice, 1 tablespoon oil, garlic, Worcestershire sauce, salt, 1 teaspoon soup mix, Dijon mustard, pepper, cayenne and Liquid Smoke if desired. Add the steaks; seal bag and turn to coat. Refrigerate for 8 hours or overnight.

In a large bowl, combine onions, green pepper, yellow pepper and remaining oil and soup mix. Place half of the mixture on each of two double thicknesses of heavy-duty foil (about 12 in. square). Fold foil around vegetables and seal tightly.

Drain the beef and discard marinade. Grill steaks and vegetable packets, covered, over medium heat for 10-13 minutes or until meat reaches the desired doneness (for medium-rare, a meat thermometer should read 145°; medium, 160°; well-done, 170°) and vegetables are tender, turning steaks once.

Open foil packets carefully to allow steam to escape. Thinly slice steaks; place beef and vegetables on tortillas. Serve with salsa, cheese, guacamole and sour cream if desired. **Yield:** 6 servings.

Sizzling Tex-Mex Fajitas

(Pictured above)

PREP: 30 min. + marinating **GRILL:** 10 min.

My family likes garlic, so I came up with a delicious homemade marinade to flavor the beef in our fajita dinners. It needs only 8 hours to work its magic, but it's even better left overnight.
—*Karyn Power, Arlington, Texas*

- 1/3 **cup beef broth**
- 1/4 **cup lime juice**
- 3 **tablespoons olive oil,** *divided*
- 4 **garlic cloves, minced**
- 2 **teaspoons Worcestershire sauce**
- 1 **teaspoon salt**
- 1 **envelope savory herb with garlic soup mix,** *divided*
- 1 **teaspoon Dijon mustard**
- 1/2 **teaspoon pepper**
- 1/2 **teaspoon cayenne pepper**
- 1/2 **teaspoon Liquid Smoke, optional**
- 2 **pounds beef skirt steak, cut into 4 to 6-inch portions**
- 2 **large onions, sliced**
- 1 **medium green pepper, sliced**
- 1 **medium sweet yellow pepper, sliced**
- 12 **flour tortillas (8 inches)**

Salsa, shredded cheese, guacamole and sour cream, optional

Andalusian Pork Tenderloin

(Pictured below)

PREP: 20 min. + chilling **BAKE:** 20 min.

I'm a fan of the complex tastes and textures in Spanish cuisine, and the olive topping in this main course really complements the seasoned pork. Plus, I can start preparing it a day ahead.
—*Patterson Watkins, Philadelphia, Pennsylvania*

- 2 **pork tenderloins (3/4 pound** *each***)**
- 3 **tablespoons olive oil**
- 3 **garlic cloves, minced**
- 2 **teaspoons paprika**
- 1/2 **teaspoon salt**
- 1/4 **teaspoon ground cinnamon**
- 1/8 **teaspoon cayenne pepper**
- 1/8 **teaspoon ground nutmeg**

GREEN OLIVE SALAD:
- 3/4 cup pimiento-stuffed olives, quartered
- 1/2 cup cherry tomatoes, quartered
- 1/4 cup chopped red onion
- 1-1/2 teaspoons capers, drained
- 1 tablespoon olive oil
- 1 tablespoon red wine vinegar
- 1 garlic clove, minced

Rub tenderloins with oil. Combine garlic, paprika, salt, cinnamon, cayenne and nutmeg; rub over tenderloins. Refrigerate for 8 hours or overnight.

Place tenderloins in a 13-in. x 9-in. baking pan. Bake, uncovered, at 450° for 20-25 minutes or until a meat thermometer reads 160°. Let pork stand for 5 minutes before slicing.

In a small bowl, combine remaining ingredients. Serve with pork. **Yield:** 4 servings.

Rice-Stuffed Pork Chops

PREP: 20 min. **BAKE:** 35 min.

Seasoned coating and rice mixes speed up these delicious chops. They really impressed my husband when we were dating.
—*Becky Aderman, Niagara, Wisconsin*

- 2-1/4 cups water
- 1 tablespoon butter
- 1 package (5.6 ounces) instant chicken-flavored rice and sauce mix
- 4 bone-in pork loin chops (1-inch thick and 8 ounces *each*)
- 1 envelope seasoned coating mix

In a large saucepan, combine the water, butter and rice with contents of sauce mix. Bring to a boil; stir. Reduce heat; cover and simmer for 4 minutes or until the rice is almost tender. Let stand for 5 minutes.

Meanwhile, moisten the pork chops with water; dip in the coating mix. Cut a pocket in each chop; fill with rice mixture. Place in an ungreased 13-in. x 9-in. baking dish. Spoon remaining rice around chops. Bake, uncovered, at 425° for 35-40 minutes or until the meat juices run clear. **Yield:** 4 servings.

Editor's Note: This recipe was tested with Lipton risotto mix and Shake 'n' Bake seasoned coating mix.

Fresh and Spicy Cioppino

(*Pictured above right*)

PREP: 25 min. **COOK:** 25 min.

With clams, mussels, shrimp and scallops, this one-pot dinner is a dream for seafood lovers. Just add a side of fresh bread.
—*Doris Mancini, Port Orchard, Washington*

- 5 garlic cloves, minced
- 2 tablespoons olive oil
- 1 jar (24 ounces) tomato basil pasta sauce

- 1 bottle (8 ounces) clam juice
- 1 cup dry white wine *or* chicken broth
- 1/4 cup water
- 1 teaspoon salt
- 1 teaspoon sugar
- 1 teaspoon crushed red pepper flakes
- 1 teaspoon minced fresh basil
- 1 teaspoon minced fresh thyme
- 1 pound fresh littleneck clams
- 1 pound fresh mussels, scrubbed and beards removed
- 1 pound uncooked medium shrimp, peeled and deveined
- 1 pound bay scallops
- 1 package (6 ounces) fresh baby spinach

In a Dutch oven, saute the garlic in oil until tender. Add the pasta sauce, clam juice, wine, water and seasonings. Bring to a boil. Reduce the heat; simmer, uncovered, for 10 minutes.

Add the clams, mussels and shrimp. Bring to a boil. Reduce heat; simmer, uncovered, for 10 minutes, stirring occasionally.

Stir in the scallops and spinach; cook 5 to 7 minutes longer or until clams and mussels open, shrimp turn pink and scallops are opaque. Discard any unopened clams or mussels. **Yield:** 8 servings (3 quarts).

Nacho Cheese Beef Bake

(Pictured below)

PREP: 25 min. **BAKE:** 15 min.

My daughter came up with this yummy Southwestern casserole when she was visiting her fiancé's family. After taking a bite, her future father–in–law declared that she was a pretty good cook!
—*Kendra McIntyre, Webster, South Dakota*

- 2 **cups uncooked egg noodles**
- 1 **pound ground beef**
- 1 **can (14-1/2 ounces) diced tomatoes, undrained**
- 1 **can (10-3/4 ounces) condensed nacho cheese soup, undiluted**
- 1 **jar (5-3/4 ounces) sliced pimiento-stuffed olives, drained**
- 1 **can (4 ounces) chopped green chilies**
- 1-1/2 **cups (6 ounces) shredded cheddar cheese**
- 2 **cups crushed tortilla chips**
- 1/3 **cup prepared ranch salad dressing**

Shredded lettuce, sour cream *and/or* salsa, optional

Cook the noodles according to package directions; drain. Meanwhile, in a large saucepan, cook beef over medium heat until no longer pink; drain. Stir in tomatoes, soup, olives and chilies. Bring to a boil. Reduce heat; simmer, uncovered, for 10 minutes. Stir in noodles.

Transfer to a greased 11-in. x 7-in. baking dish. Sprinkle with the cheese. Bake at 350° for 15-20 minutes or until heated through. Top with tortilla chips; drizzle with salad dressing. Serve with lettuce, sour cream and/or salsa if desired. **Yield:** 4 servings.

Orange-Pecan Salmon

(Pictured above and on page 60)

PREP: 10 min. + marinating **BAKE:** 20 min.

I first prepared this nutty, citrusy baked salmon for a girlfriends' luncheon, and it received rave reviews. I really liked the fact that I could pop the fish fillets in the oven just before my guests arrived and could still have lunch on the table in 20 minutes.
—*Pat Neaves, Lees Summit, Missouri*

- 1 **cup chopped pecans, toasted**
- 1 **cup orange marmalade**
- 1/2 **cup reduced-sodium soy sauce**
- 1/4 **teaspoon salt**
- 1/4 **teaspoon pepper**
- 4 **salmon fillets (6 ounces *each* and 1 inch thick)**

In a small bowl, combine the first five ingredients. Pour 1 cup marinade into a large resealable plastic bag. Add the salmon; seal the bag and turn to coat. Refrigerate for up to 30 minutes. Set aside remaining marinade.

Drain and discard the marinade from the salmon. Place salmon in a greased 11-in. x 7-in. baking dish. Bake, uncovered, at 350° for 20-25 minutes or until the fish flakes easily with a fork.

In a small saucepan, bring the reserved marinade to a boil; cook until liquid is reduced to 3/4 cup. Serve with salmon. **Yield:** 4 servings.

Lemon-Sage Chicken

PREP: 30 min. **BAKE:** 15 min.

I've had this recipe from my mother for years, but I only recently began making it. When I tasted the nicely coated chicken and the rich wine sauce, I wished I'd rediscovered it sooner!
—Denise Kleffman, Gardena, California

- 4 boneless skinless chicken breast halves (6 ounces *each*)
- 3 eggs, beaten
- 1/4 cup grated Parmesan and Romano cheese blend
- 1 tablespoon minced fresh parsley
- 1 teaspoon dried basil
- 1/2 teaspoon salt
- 1/8 teaspoon pepper
- 1/2 cup all-purpose flour
- 2 tablespoons olive oil

SAUCE:

- 2 tablespoons chopped shallot
- 3 garlic cloves, minced
- 1/4 cup white wine
- 4-1/2 teaspoons lemon juice
- 1 tablespoon minced fresh parsley
- 1 teaspoon dried sage leaves
- 1 teaspoon grated lemon peel
- 1/2 cup heavy whipping cream
- 3 tablespoons cold butter, cubed

Flatten the chicken to 1/2-in. thickness. In a shallow bowl, combine the eggs, cheese and seasonings. Place flour in another shallow bowl. Coat chicken with flour, then dip in egg mixture.

In a large skillet, brown the chicken in oil in batches. Transfer to a greased 15-in. x 10-in. x 1-in. baking pan. Bake, uncovered, at 375° for 15-20 minutes or until a meat thermometer reads 170°.

In the drippings, saute the shallot until tender. Add the garlic; cook 1 minute longer. Add the white wine, lemon juice, herbs and lemon peel; cook over medium heat until the liquid is reduced by half. Add heavy whipping cream; cook until thickened, stirring occasionally. Stir in the cold butter until melted. Serve the sauce with the chicken. **Yield:** 4 servings.

CHIP TIP. Have leftover tortilla chips that are going stale? Try these solutions:
• Crush chips and sprinkle them on casseroles before baking as a tasty topping.
• Add coarsely crushed chips to spicy Mexican-style soups or chowders....or use them in place of croutons on a salad.
• Use finely crushed chips in place of dry bread crumbs as a coating for poultry or fish.

Migas, My Way

(Pictured below)

PREP/TOTAL TIME: 25 min.

This Mexican egg scramble gets a big thumbs–up from my family. Sometimes I replace the chips with fresh corn tortillas—I just cut them into strips and saute them with the onion and pepper.
—Joan Hallford, North Richland Hills, Texas

- 1/4 cup chopped onion
- 1/4 cup chopped green pepper
- 1 tablespoon bacon drippings *or* canola oil
- 4 eggs
- 1 tablespoon water
- 1 tablespoon salsa
- 1/2 cup crushed tortilla chips
- 1/2 cup shredded cheddar cheese, *divided*

Chopped green onions, additional salsa and warm flour tortillas, optional

In a large skillet, saute the onion and green pepper in the bacon drippings until tender. In a small bowl, whisk the eggs, water and salsa. Add to the skillet; cook and stir until set. Stir in the crushed tortilla chips and 1/4 cup cheddar cheese.

Sprinkle with the remaining cheese. Top with green onions and additional salsa and serve with tortillas if desired. **Yield:** 2 servings.

and stir for 1-2 minutes or until thickened. Stir in 2 cups cheese, nutmeg and remaining salt and pepper. Transfer to a blender; squeeze softened garlic into blender. Cover and process until smooth. Pour mixture over chicken.

Cover and bake at 425° for 30-35 minutes or until a meat thermometer reads 170° and sauce is bubbly. Uncover; sprinkle with remaining cheese. Bake 5 minutes longer. Serve with pasta. Sprinkle with tomato and parsley if desired. **Yield:** 6 servings.

Slow and Easy BBQ Ribs

(Pictured below)

PREP: 15 min.   **COOK:** 5-1/2 hours

Let your slow cooker do the cooking for you! Take advantage of that convenient appliance with these saucy, lip-smacking ribs.
—*Kimi Short, Prior Lake, Minnesota*

- 2 **pounds boneless country-style pork ribs**
- 1 **can (6 ounces) unsweetened pineapple juice**
- 1 **medium onion, thinly sliced**
- 1 **garlic clove, minced**
- 2/3 **cup barbecue sauce**
- 1/3 **cup plum jam**

In a large skillet coated with cooking spray, brown ribs on all sides. Transfer to a 3-qt. slow cooker; top with the pineapple juice, onion and garlic. Cover and cook on low for 5-6 hours or until meat is tender.

Remove the ribs; drain and discard cooking juices and onion. Return ribs to the slow cooker. Combine barbecue sauce and jam; pour over ribs. Cover and cook on high for 30 minutes. **Yield:** 4 servings.

Saucy Garlic Chicken

(Pictured above)

PREP: 40 min. + cooling   **BAKE:** 35 min.

Roasted garlic lends rich flavor to this chicken and complements the spinach nicely. Ideal for entertaining, the entree can be put together in advance and baked shortly before dinnertime.
—*Joanna Johnson, Flower Mound, Texas*

- 4 **whole garlic bulbs**
- 2 **tablespoons olive oil,** *divided*
- 1 **package (9 ounces) fresh baby spinach**
- 3/4 **teaspoon salt,** *divided*
- 1/2 **teaspoon coarsely ground pepper,** *divided*
- 6 **boneless skinless chicken breast halves (6 ounces** *each***)**
- 6 **tablespoons butter, cubed**
- 6 **tablespoons all-purpose flour**
- 3 **cups 2% milk**
- 2-1/2 **cups grated Parmesan cheese,** *divided*
- 1/8 **teaspoon nutmeg**

Hot cooked pasta

Chopped tomato and minced fresh parsley, optional

Remove the papery outer skin from garlic (do not peel or separate cloves). Cut tops off of garlic bulbs; brush bulbs with 1 tablespoon oil. Wrap each bulb in heavy-duty foil. Bake at 425° for 30-35 minutes or until softened. Cool for 10-15 minutes.

Meanwhile, place the spinach in a greased 13-in. x 9-in. baking dish; sprinkle with 1/4 teaspoon each of salt and pepper. In a large skillet, brown chicken in remaining oil on both sides; place over spinach.

In a large saucepan, melt the butter. Stir in the flour until smooth; gradually add the milk. Bring to a boil; cook

Southwest Frito Pie

PREP: 20 min. **COOK:** 25 min.

I got a real culture shock when we moved to New Mexico several years ago, and we fell in love with the food. Now back in South Carolina, we still enjoy Southwest taste with this beefy pie.
—*Janet Scoggins, North Augusta, South Carolina*

- 2 **pounds lean ground beef (90% lean)**
- 3 **tablespoons chili powder**
- 2 **tablespoons all-purpose flour**
- 1 **teaspoon salt**
- 1 **teaspoon garlic powder**
- 2 **cups water**
- 1 **can (15 ounces) pinto beans, rinsed and drained, optional**
- 4-1/2 **cups corn chips**
- 2 **cups shredded lettuce**
- 1-1/2 **cups (6 ounces) shredded cheddar cheese**
- 3/4 **cup chopped tomatoes**
- 6 **tablespoons finely chopped onion**

Sour cream and minced fresh cilantro, optional

In a Dutch oven, cook beef over medium heat until no longer pink; drain. Stir in the chili powder, flour, salt and garlic powder until blended; gradually stir in water.

Add the beans, if desired. Bring to a boil. Reduce heat; simmer, uncovered, for 12-15 minutes or until thickened, stirring occasionally.

To serve, divide corn chips among six serving bowls. Top with the beef mixture, lettuce, cheese, tomatoes and onion; garnish with sour cream and cilantro, if desired. **Yield:** 6 servings.

Lance's Own French Toast

PREP: 10 min. **COOK:** 10 min./ batch

When my young son, Lance, helps me prepare this for breakfast, he knows when to add each ingredient and even how much to measure out. To make the French toast even more appealing for kids, use large cookie cutters to cut the slices into fun shapes.
—*Janna Steele, Magee, Mississippi*

- 4 **eggs**
- 1 **cup 2% milk**
- 1 **tablespoon honey**
- 1/2 **teaspoon ground cinnamon**
- 1/8 **teaspoon pepper**
- 12 **slices whole wheat bread**

Sugar and additional ground cinnamon, optional

In a large bowl, whisk the eggs, milk, honey, cinnamon and pepper. Dip the bread in the egg mixture; cook on a greased hot griddle for 3-4 minutes on each side or until golden brown.

Cut slices of French toast into decorative shapes and sprinkle with sugar and additional cinnamon if desired. **Yield:** 6 servings.

Mediterranean Shrimp Skillet

(Pictured above)

PREP/TOTAL TIME: 30 min.

Tender shrimp, fresh spinach and minced basil combine with feta cheese and tangy lemon in this wonderful pasta dinner.
—*Heidi Farnworth, Riverton, Utah*

- 8 **ounces uncooked angel hair pasta**
- 1-1/2 **pounds uncooked medium shrimp, peeled and deveined**
- 1-1/2 **teaspoons olive oil**
- 3 **garlic cloves, minced**
- 1/4 **teaspoon salt**
- 1/4 **teaspoon pepper**
- 1-1/2 **cups chicken broth, *divided***
- 2 **tablespoons lemon juice**
- 1/2 **teaspoon dried basil**
- 2 **teaspoons cornstarch**
- 4 **cups chopped fresh spinach**
- 1/2 **cup crumbled feta cheese**
- 1/4 **cup minced fresh basil**

Cook pasta according to package directions. Meanwhile, in a large skillet, saute the shrimp in oil until the shrimp turn pink. Add the garlic, salt and pepper; cook 1 minute longer. Remove and set aside.

In the same skillet, heat 1 cup broth, lemon juice and dried basil. In a small bowl, combine the cornstarch and remaining broth until smooth; stir into the pan. Bring to a boil; cook and stir for 2 minutes or until thickened. Stir in spinach and shrimp; cook until spinach is wilted.

Drain pasta; serve with shrimp mixture. Sprinkle with cheese and fresh basil. **Yield:** 4 servings.

Marsala Pork Chops

(Pictured above)

PREP: 15 min. **COOK:** 20 min.

Knowing that my husband and I like onions and garlic, a friend prepared these delicious chops for us. We couldn't stop raving about them, and she was kind enough to share the recipe.
—Jan Huntington, Painesville, Ohio

   1/2 **cup seasoned bread crumbs**
     4 **bone-in center-cut pork loin chops**
       (6 ounces *each***)**
     3 **tablespoons olive oil,** *divided*
     3 **medium onions, thinly sliced**
     6 **garlic cloves, minced**
   1/2 **cup white wine** *or* **chicken broth**
     1 **tablespoon marsala wine** *or* **chicken broth**
   1/4 **teaspoon pepper**
   1/8 **teaspoon salt**
   1/4 **cup cold butter, cubed**
Hot cooked egg noodles

Place bread crumbs in a large resealable plastic bag. Add pork chops, one at a time, and shake to coat. In a large skillet, cook chops in 2 tablespoons oil over medium heat for 4-6 minutes on each side or until a meat thermometer reads 160°. Remove and keep warm.

   In the same skillet, saute the onions in remaining oil until tender. Add garlic; cook 2 minutes longer. Add the white wine, marsala, pepper and salt, stirring to loosen browned bits from pan. Cook, stirring occasionally, until liquid is nearly evaporated. Stir in butter until melted. Serve with pork chops and noodles. **Yield:** 4 servings.

Italian Stuffed Portobellos

PREP: 1 hour **BAKE:** 10 min.

Here, big portobello mushrooms become mini specialty pizzas thanks to a savory stuffing and cheeses sprinkled on top. Eating one is like being transported to a ristorante in Rome!
—Jeanne Holt, Mendota Heights, Minnesota

     4 **ounces sliced pancetta** *or* **bacon strips, finely chopped**
     1 **tablespoon plus 1 teaspoon olive oil,** *divided*
     4 **cups sliced onions**
     2 **tablespoons finely chopped oil-packed sun-dried tomatoes**
   1/4 **teaspoon salt**
   1/8 **teaspoon pepper**
     1 **whole garlic bulb**
     3 **tablespoons crumbled goat cheese**
PIZZAS:
     4 **large portobello mushrooms**
     2 **tablespoons olive oil**
   1/3 **cup shredded part-skim mozzarella cheese**
     3 **tablespoons shredded Parmesan cheese**
     1 **tablespoon minced fresh basil** *or* **1 teaspoon dried basil**

In a large skillet over medium heat, cook the pancetta in 1 tablespoon oil until crisp. Remove to paper towels with a slotted spoon; set aside.

   In the same skillet, cook and stir onions until softened. Reduce heat to medium-low; cook, stirring occasionally, for 30 minutes or until deep golden brown. Stir in the sun-dried tomatoes, salt, pepper and pancetta. Remove from the heat; keep warm.

   Remove the papery outer skin from the garlic (do not peel or separate the garlic cloves). Cut the top off of the garlic bulb. Brush with the remaining oil. Wrap the garlic bulb in heavy-duty foil. Bake at 425° for 30-35 minutes or until softened. Cool for 10-15 minutes. Squeeze the softened garlic into a small bowl; stir in the goat cheese and onion mixture.

   Brush portobello mushrooms with oil. Grill, covered, over medium heat or broil 4 in. from the heat for 6-8 minutes on each side or until tender. Fill mushrooms with the onion mixture. Sprinkle with the mozzarella and Parmesan cheeses.

   Place on a greased baking sheet. Bake at 375° for 8-10 minutes or until cheese is melted. Sprinkle with basil. **Yield:** 4 servings.

Spicy Beef Brisket

PREP: 30 min. **COOK:** 2-1/2 hours

This fork-tender brisket is a convenient entree choice because it's just as good when cooked a day ahead of time, refrigerated and reheated. I like to pair it with mashed potatoes, rice or noodles to take advantage of every last drop of flavorful sauce.
—Wendy Kiehn, Sebring, Florida

1 fresh beef brisket (3 pounds)
1/2 teaspoon seasoned salt
1/4 teaspoon pepper
2 tablespoons olive oil
2 large onions, sliced
3 garlic cloves, minced
1 cup beef broth
1 cup chili sauce
1/3 cup packed brown sugar
1/3 cup cider vinegar
2 to 3 tablespoons chili powder
2 bay leaves
3 tablespoons all-purpose flour
1/4 cup cold water

Sprinkle the brisket with seasoned salt and pepper. In a Dutch oven, brown meat in oil on both sides. Remove and keep warm. In the same pan, saute onions and garlic until tender. Return brisket to pan.

Combine broth, chili sauce, brown sugar, vinegar, chili powder and bay leaves; pour over meat. Bring to a boil. Reduce the heat; cover and simmer for 2-1/2 to 3 hours or until meat is tender.

Remove the brisket to a serving platter. Skim fat from the cooking juices; discard bay leaves. Combine the flour and cold water until smooth; stir into the pan. Bring to a boil; cook and stir for 2 minutes or until thickened.

Thinly slice meat across the grain; serve with sauce. **Yield:** 8 servings.

Editor's Note: This is a fresh beef brisket, not corned beef.

Curried Coconut Chicken

PREP: 10 min. **BAKE:** 30 min.

Bored with your usual chicken dinners? Consider the no-fuss option here. It's a nice change of pace from the ordinary because it's sweet, savory and a little exotic. Serve it over rice or couscous and add a green salad or vegetable for a complete meal.
—Becky Walch, Manteca, California

3 tablespoons butter, melted
1 cup flaked coconut
2 teaspoons curry powder
4 boneless skinless chicken breast halves (6 ounces *each*)
1/4 teaspoon salt
1 cup apricot preserves, warmed

Place the butter in a shallow bowl. In another shallow bowl, combine the coconut and curry powder. Dip the chicken breast halves in the butter, then coat with the coconut mixture.

Place in a greased 13-in. x 9-in. baking dish; sprinkle with salt. Bake, uncovered, at 350° for 30-35 minutes or until a meat thermometer reads 170°. Serve with apricot preserves. **Yield:** 4 servings.

Savory Sausage Penne Supper

(Pictured below)

PREP/TOTAL TIME: 30 min.

I enjoyed a similar pasta dish at a restaurant and decided to try fixing it at home, with a few changes to suit my family. If I have extra sauce, I freeze it and use it as a base for soup later.
—Noelle Myers, Grand Forks, North Dakota

1 package (16 ounces) penne pasta
1 can (15 ounces) tomato sauce
1 jar (7 ounces) roasted sweet red peppers, drained
1 medium onion, cut into wedges
1 tablespoon olive oil
2 garlic cloves, peeled
2 teaspoons balsamic vinegar
1 teaspoon sugar
1 teaspoon Italian seasoning
1/2 teaspoon ground coriander
1/2 teaspoon fennel seed
1/4 teaspoon garlic salt
1 pound bulk Italian sausage
1/3 cup shredded Parmesan cheese
1/4 cup minced fresh basil

Cook pasta according to package directions. Meanwhile, place the tomato sauce, red peppers, onion, oil, garlic, vinegar, sugar, Italian seasoning, coriander, fennel seed and garlic salt in a food processor; cover and process until blended. Set aside.

In a large skillet, cook sausage over medium heat until no longer pink; drain. Add tomato mixture. Bring to a boil. Reduce the heat; simmer, uncovered, for 10-15 minutes or until slightly thickened.

Drain pasta; toss with sauce. Sprinkle with cheese and basil. **Yield:** 6 servings.

A Catch of Crab Cakes

WHEN YOU have a taste for seafood, is crab the king of them all? You can have your crab cakes and eat them, too, thanks to the delectable recipes here.

Whether you want a casual summer meal on the patio for your family or a special dinner for guests, try any of these popular patties representing different regions of the United States. Choose from a cornmeal-coated creation, sweet potato variety and traditional Eastern shore version.

They're sure to please and easier to make than you might think. In fact, all of these cakes are either ready to eat or ready to cook in 30 minutes or less!

Eastern Shore Crab Cakes

(Pictured below)

PREP/TOTAL TIME: 25 min.

Here in Delaware, we're surrounded by an abundance of fresh seafood, and I take advantage of it in my cooking with recipes like this one. My secret to great crab cakes is using fresh meat and not too much filler. Also, I don't break up the crab too much.
—*Cynthia Bent, Newark, Delaware*

- 1 egg, beaten
- 1/2 cup dry bread crumbs
- 1/2 cup mayonnaise
- 3/4 teaspoon seafood seasoning
- 1/2 teaspoon lemon juice
- 1/2 teaspoon Worcestershire sauce
- 1/8 teaspoon white pepper
- 1 pound fresh lump crabmeat
- 2 tablespoons canola oil

In a large bowl, combine egg, bread crumbs, mayonnaise, seafood seasoning, lemon juice, Worcestershire sauce and white pepper. Fold in the crab. Shape the mixture into six patties.

In a large skillet, cook crab cakes in oil for 4-5 minutes on each side or until browned. **Yield:** 3 servings.

Sweet Potato Crab Cakes

(Pictured above)

PREP: 20 min. **COOK:** 10 min./batch

Mild sweet potato flavor and a chipotle kick really enhance these patties. Serve them with your favorite mayo or aioli sauce.
—*Robert Bosley, Pacific, Washington*

- 1 egg plus 1 egg yolk, beaten
- 1 medium green pepper, finely chopped
- 1/2 cup dry bread crumbs
- 1/4 cup cornmeal
- 1/4 cup mashed sweet potato
- 1 green onion (white part only), chopped
- 2 tablespoons minced fresh parsley
- 2 tablespoons lemon juice
- 2 tablespoons mayonnaise
- 2 teaspoons seafood seasoning
- 2 teaspoons ground mustard
- 1-1/2 teaspoons salt-free Southwest chipotle seasoning blend
- 4 cans (6 ounces *each*) lump crabmeat, drained
- 1/2 teaspoon salt
- 1/4 cup canola oil

In a large bowl, combine the egg, egg yolk, green pepper, bread crumbs, cornmeal, sweet potato, onion, parsley, lemon juice, mayonnaise, seafood seasoning, mustard and seasoning blend. Fold in crab. Form into 12 patties; sprinkle with salt.

In a large skillet over medium heat, cook crab cakes in oil in batches for 3-4 minutes on each side or until golden brown. **Yield:** 6 servings.

Herbed Cornmeal Crab Cakes

(Pictured below)

PREP/TOTAL TIME: 30 min.

I grow a variety of herbs in my garden and am always looking for ways to incorporate them into meals. These crispy crab cakes featuring chives, parsley and thyme are one of my creations. My husband fell in love with them and requests them often.
—*Audrey Collins, Columbus, Georgia*

- **2 tablespoons cornmeal**
- **2 tablespoons dry bread crumbs**
- **1 tablespoon all-purpose flour**
- **1/4 teaspoon garlic powder**
- **1/8 teaspoon onion powder**
- **1/8 teaspoon salt**

CRAB CAKES:
- **1 egg, beaten**
- **1/4 cup dry bread crumbs**
- **2 tablespoons minced chives**
- **1 tablespoon minced fresh parsley**
- **1-1/2 teaspoons minced fresh thyme**
- **1 tablespoon mayonnaise**
- **1 tablespoon tartar sauce**
- **2 teaspoons spicy brown mustard**
- **1/2 teaspoon lemon juice**
- **1/2 teaspoon Worcestershire sauce**
- **1/4 teaspoon celery salt**
- **1 can (6 ounces) crabmeat, drained, flaked and cartilage removed**
- **2 tablespoons canola oil**

In a shallow bowl, combine the first six ingredients; set aside. In a large bowl, combine egg, bread crumbs, chives, parsley, thyme, mayonnaise, tartar sauce, spicy brown mustard, lemon juice, Worcestershire sauce and celery salt. Fold in crab. Shape into four patties; coat with cornmeal mixture.

In a large skillet over medium heat, cook the crab cakes in oil for 3-4 minutes on each side or until golden brown. **Yield:** 2 servings.

Mexican Skillet Rice

(Pictured above and on page 60)

PREP/TOTAL TIME. 30 min.

I never come home with leftovers when I take my Mexican rice to potlucks and parties. But I do get quite a few compliments!
—Mary Ann Dell, Phoenixville, Pennsylvania

- 1 **egg, beaten**
- 1 **pound chicken tenderloins, chopped**
- 1 **small onion, chopped**
- 1 **tablespoon olive oil**
- 2 **garlic cloves, minced**
- 2 **cups cooked jasmine *or* long grain rice**
- 1 **can (15 ounces) black beans, rinsed and drained**
- 1 **can (11 ounces) Mexicorn, drained**
- 1 **jar (7 ounces) roasted sweet red peppers, drained and sliced**
- 1 **jar (8 ounces) taco sauce**
- 2 **green onions, chopped**
- 1/4 **cup minced fresh cilantro**

In a large skillet coated with cooking spray, cook and stir egg over medium-high heat until set. Remove and set aside.

In the same skillet, stir-fry the chicken and onion in oil until chicken is no longer pink. Add garlic; cook 1 minute longer. Stir in the rice, beans, Mexicorn, peppers, taco sauce and green onions; heat through. Stir in reserved egg. Sprinkle rice with cilantro. **Yield:** 6 servings.

Chicken with Shallot Sauce

PREP: 10 min. **COOK:** 50 min.

This special chicken requires just 10 minutes of prep but tastes like it simmered all day. It's wonderful with mashed potatoes and a green vegetable. —*Kathy Anderson, Rockford, Illinois*

- 6 **bacon strips, chopped**
- 1 **broiler/fryer chicken (3 to 4 pounds), cut up**
- 1/2 **teaspoon salt**
- 1/2 **teaspoon pepper**
- 10 **shallots, thinly sliced**
- 1 **cup water**
- 1 **whole garlic bulb, cloves separated and peeled**
- 1/2 **cup balsamic vinegar**

In a large skillet, cook the bacon over medium heat until crisp. Remove to paper towels with a slotted spoon; drain, reserving 2 tablespoons drippings.

Sprinkle the chicken with the salt and pepper; brown in the bacon drippings. Remove and keep warm. Add the shallots; cook and stir until tender. Stir in water and garlic. Return the chicken to the pan. Bring to a boil. Reduce the heat; cover and simmer for 30-35 minutes or until a meat thermometer reads 180°.

Remove the chicken to a serving platter; keep warm. Skim the fat from cooking juices. Mash the garlic; add the vinegar. Bring the liquid to a boil; cook until slightly thickened. Spoon over chicken; sprinkle with reserved bacon. **Yield:** 4 servings.

Fiesta Chicken Bundles

(Pictured below and on page 60)

PREP: 25 min. **COOK:** 20 min.

I dreamed up these little bundles when I was on vacation and had limited ingredients to use. We love the Southwestern flavor.
—Merry Graham, Newhall, California

- 4 **boneless skinless chicken breasts (6 ounces each)**
- 4 **corn tortillas (6 inches), chopped**
- 1 **cup (4 ounces) shredded pepper Jack cheese**
- 1-1/4 **cups salsa verde, *divided***
- 1/2 **cup cornmeal**
- 1 **teaspoon garlic salt**

2 tablespoons canola oil
1/2 cup water
3 tablespoons orange marmalade
1 teaspoon chili powder
1/4 cup sour cream
1/3 cup minced fresh cilantro
2 cans (15 ounces *each*) Southwestern black beans, warmed

Flatten chicken breasts to 1/4-in. thickness; set aside. In a small bowl, combine the tortillas, cheese and 1/2 cup salsa verde. Spoon tortilla mixture down the center of each chicken breast; roll up and secure with toothpicks.

Combine cornmeal and garlic salt in a shallow bowl; coat chicken with cornmeal mixture.

In a large skillet, brown chicken in oil. Add the water, marmalade, chili powder and remaining salsa to the pan. Bring to a boil. Reduce heat; cover and cook for 15-20 minutes or until a meat thermometer reads 170°. Discard the toothpicks.

Top chicken with sour cream and cilantro. Serve with beans. **Yield:** 4 servings.

Smoky Cranberry Ribs

PREP: 25 min. + chilling **GRILL:** 2 hours

Living near New Jersey's cranberry bogs inspires me to develop new and delicious ways to use those tangy berries. One of my favorite creations is this lip–smacking rib recipe.
—*Christine Wendland, Browns Mills, New Jersey*

4-1/2 teaspoons paprika
4 teaspoons salt
2 teaspoons fennel seed
1-1/2 teaspoons pepper
1 teaspoon onion powder
1 teaspoon caraway seeds
1 teaspoon ground allspice
1/2 teaspoon garlic powder
1/2 teaspoon rubbed sage
6 pounds pork baby back ribs

SAUCE:
1-1/2 cups fresh *or* frozen cranberries, thawed
1-1/2 cups packed dark brown sugar
1 cup cider vinegar
1 small sweet onion, chopped
1/4 cup ketchup

In a spice grinder or with a mortar and pestle, combine the first nine ingredients; grind until fennel and caraway seeds are crushed. Set aside 4 teaspoons for sauce.

Rub the remaining spice mixture over ribs. Cover and refrigerate for at least 1 hour.

Wrap the ribs in a large piece of heavy-duty foil (about 28 in. x 18 in.); seal tightly. Prepare the grill for indirect heat, using a drip pan. Place the ribs over the drip pan and grill, covered, over indirect medium heat for 1-1/2 to 2 hours or until tender.

In a small saucepan, combine the cranberries, brown sugar, cider vinegar, onion and reserved spice mixture. Cook over medium heat until the cranberries pop, about 15 minutes; cool slightly. Transfer to a blender; add the ketchup. Cover and process until smooth. Set aside 1 cup sauce for serving.

Moisten a paper towel with cooking oil; using long-handled tongs, lightly coat the grill rack. Carefully remove the ribs from foil. Place over direct heat; baste with some of the sauce. Grill, covered, over medium heat for 20-30 minutes or until browned, turning and basting occasionally. Serve with reserved sauce. **Yield:** 6 servings.

Sizzling Ancho Ribeyes

(Pictured above)

PREP/TOTAL TIME: 25 min.

Here in New Mexico, we like chipotle chili on nearly everything. This entree proves that chipotle pairs perfectly with grilled steak.
—*Angela Spengler, Clovis, New Mexico*

4 teaspoons salt
4 teaspoons ground ancho chili pepper
1 teaspoon pepper
6 beef ribeye steaks (3/4 pound *each*)
6 tablespoons butter, softened
6 chipotle peppers in adobo sauce

In a small bowl, combine salt, chili pepper and pepper; rub over steaks.

In another small bowl, beat the butter and chipotle peppers until blended.

Grill steaks, covered, over medium heat or broil 3-4 in. from the heat for 5-7 minutes on each side or until meat reaches the desired doneness (for medium-rare, a meat thermometer should read 145°; medium, 160°; well-done, 170°). Serve with chipotle butter. **Yield:** 6 servings.

Cool the corn slightly; remove kernels from cobs. Place in a large bowl. Add the lettuce, tomatoes, red pepper, avocado, taco sauce, 1 tablespoon lime juice, cilantro, lime peel and remaining chili powder.

Drizzle remaining lime juice over fish; cut into 1/2-in. cubes. Add to corn mixture. Spoon 1/2 cup mixture over each tortilla. Serve immediately. **Yield:** 6 servings.

Crispy Onion Chicken

(Pictured below)

PREP: 10 min. **BAKE:** 30 min.

My family loves chicken, and I'm always on the lookout for delicious new ways to make it. This golden–brown entree with a crunchy french–fried onion coating is great with rice, baked potatoes, macaroni salad or potato salad for a complete meal.
—*Charlotte Smith, McDonald, Pennsylvania*

- 1/2 **cup butter, melted**
- 1 **tablespoon Worcestershire sauce**
- 1 **teaspoon ground mustard**
- 1/2 **teaspoon garlic salt**
- 1/4 **teaspoon pepper**
- 1 **can (6 ounces) cheddar *or* original french-fried onions, crushed, *divided***
- 4 **boneless skinless chicken breast halves**

In a shallow bowl, combine butter, Worcestershire sauce, mustard, garlic salt and pepper. In another shallow bowl, add 1/2 cup french-fried onions. Dip chicken in the butter mixture, then coat with onions.

Place in a greased 9-in. square baking pan. Top with the remaining onions; drizzle with any remaining butter mixture. Bake, uncovered, at 350° for 30-35 minutes or until chicken juices run clear. **Yield:** 4 servings.

Martha's Fish Tacos

(Pictured above and on page 60)

PREP: 25 min. **GRILL:** 10 min.

We can't get enough barbecued fish at our house. Here's a main dish that can be eaten right off the grill or prepared in advance and enjoyed cold. Either way, these tacos are fantastic!
—*Martha Benoit, Proctorsville, Vermont*

- 2 **large ears sweet corn**
- 1 **teaspoon butter, softened**
- 1/8 **teaspoon salt**
- 1/8 **teaspoon pepper**
- 1 **haddock fillet (8 ounces)**
- 2 **teaspoons chili powder, *divided***
- 2 **cups shredded lettuce**
- 2 **medium tomatoes, seeded and chopped**
- 1 **medium sweet red pepper, chopped**
- 1 **medium ripe avocado, peeled and chopped**
- 3 **tablespoons taco sauce**
- 2 **tablespoons lime juice, *divided***
- 1 **tablespoon minced fresh cilantro**
- 1-1/2 **teaspoons grated lime peel**
- 12 **flour tortillas (8 inches)**

Spread the corn with the butter and sprinkle with salt and pepper. Grill, covered, over medium heat for 10-12 minutes or until tender, turning occasionally.

Meanwhile, sprinkle the fish with 1 teaspoon chili powder. Moisten a paper towel with cooking oil; using long-handled tongs, lightly coat the grill rack. Grill fish, covered, over medium heat for 7-9 minutes or until fish flakes easily with a fork.

Merlot Filet Mignon

PREP/TOTAL TIME: 20 min.

Although this filet is simple to prepare and comes together in just 20 minutes, you can feel confident and proud serving it to guests. The rich wine sauce adds a touch of elegance to the tender steaks. Round out the menu with mixed greens and rolls.
—*Jauneen Hosking, Wind Lake, Wisconsin*

- 2 **beef tenderloin steaks (8 ounces *each*)**
- 3 **tablespoons butter, *divided***
- 1 **tablespoon olive oil**
- 1 **cup merlot**
- 2 **tablespoons heavy whipping cream**
- 1/8 **teaspoon salt**

In a small skillet, cook steaks in 1 tablespoon butter and oil over medium heat for 4-6 minutes on each side or until meat reaches desired doneness (for medium-rare, a meat thermometer should read 145°; medium, 160°; well-done, 170°). Remove and keep warm.

In the same skillet, add the wine, stirring to loosen the browned bits from pan. Bring to a boil; cook until liquid is reduced to 1/4 cup. Add the cream, salt and remaining butter; bring to a boil. Cook and stir for 1-2 minutes or until slightly thickened and butter is melted. Serve with steaks. **Yield:** 2 servings.

Herbed Italian Rib Roast

PREP: 30 min. **BAKE:** 1-3/4 hours + standing

This amazing recipe is a longtime favorite. I like to roast twice as many vegetables so I can fix a quick hash with the leftovers.
—*Lily Julow, Gainesville, Florida*

- 1 **bone-in beef rib roast (4 to 5 pounds)**
- 2 **pounds Yukon gold potatoes, peeled and quartered**
- 1 **pound parsnips, quartered**
- 1 **pound carrots, quartered**
- 2 **large onions, cut into wedges**
- 1/2 **cup butter, melted**
- 2 **tablespoons dried rosemary, crushed**
- 2 **tablespoons dried oregano**
- 1 **teaspoon salt**
- 1/4 **teaspoon pepper**

Place the roast in a large shallow roasting pan. Bake, uncovered, at 350° for 45 minutes.

In a large bowl, combine the potatoes, parsnips, carrots and onions. Drizzle with butter; toss to coat. Spoon the vegetables around the roast; sprinkle with the rosemary, oregano, salt and pepper.

Bake 1 to 1-1/4 hours longer or until meat reaches desired doneness (for medium-rare, a meat thermometer should read 145°; medium, 160°; well-done, 170°), stirring vegetables occasionally. Let stand for 10 minutes before slicing. **Yield:** 10 servings.

Bravo Italian Chicken

(*Pictured above*)

PREP: 20 min. + standing **BAKE:** 35 min.

I use a handful of Italian–style pantry staples to assemble this hearty entree. Just pair it with breadsticks, and dinner's done!
—*Kristin Miller, Carmel, Indiana*

- 1 **medium eggplant, peeled and cut into 1-inch cubes**
- 1 **teaspoon salt**
- 4 **boneless skinless chicken breast halves (5 ounces *each*)**
- 1/4 **teaspoon Italian seasoning**
- 1/4 **teaspoon pepper**
- 1-1/2 **cups (6 ounces) shredded part-skim mozzarella cheese, *divided***
- 1 **jar (24 ounces) tomato basil pasta sauce**

Place eggplant in a colander over a plate; sprinkle with salt and toss. Let stand for 30 minutes.

Meanwhile, sprinkle chicken with Italian seasoning and pepper. In a large nonstick skillet coated with cooking spray, brown chicken on both sides. Transfer chicken to a greased 13-in. x 9-in. baking dish; sprinkle with 3/4 cup mozzarella cheese.

Rinse eggplant; pat dry with paper towels. Transfer to a large bowl; add pasta sauce and toss to coat. Spoon over chicken; top with remaining cheese.

Cover and bake at 350° for 35-40 minutes or until a meat thermometer inserted into the chicken reads 170°. **Yield:** 4 servings.

Breads, Rolls & Muffins

Mmm! From Rhubarb-Buttermilk Coffee Cake and Green Onion Drop Biscuits to Three-Cheese Garlic Bread and German Sour Cream Twists, these warm-from-the-oven goodies are guaranteed to draw a crowd.

FRESH-BAKED FAVORITES. Clockwise from top left: Apple-Bacon Mini Loaves (p. 88), Dilled Wheat Bread (p. 88), Blueberry Yogurt Muffins (p. 85) and Cinnamon Zucchini Bread (p. 89).

Apple Cream Cheese Kuchen

(Pictured above)

PREP: 40 min. + rising **BAKE:** 30 min. + cooling

This is an old recipe my mother prepared as our Sunday dessert when I was a child in Germany. If you prefer, replace the apples with a different fruit such as plums, fresh peaches or apricots.
—Trudy Wolbert, Maryville, Missouri

- 1-1/4 teaspoons active dry yeast
- 2 tablespoons warm water (110° to 115°)
- 1 egg
- 1/4 cup warm milk (110° to 115°)
- 2 tablespoons butter, softened
- 2 tablespoons sugar
- 1 teaspoon grated lemon peel
- 1/4 teaspoon salt
- 1-1/4 to 1-1/2 cups all-purpose flour
TOPPING:
- 4 ounces cream cheese, softened
- 1 tablespoon sugar
- 1 large tart apple, peeled and sliced
- 2 teaspoons butter, melted
Confectioners' sugar

In a small bowl, dissolve yeast in warm water. Add the egg, milk, butter, sugar, lemon peel, salt and 3/4 cup flour. Beat until smooth. Stir in enough remaining flour to form a soft dough (dough will be sticky).

Turn onto a floured surface. With floured hands, knead until smooth and elastic, about 6-8 minutes. Press into a greased 8-in. square baking dish; build up edges slightly.

For topping, in a small bowl, combine cream cheese and sugar. Gently spread over the dough. Arrange apple slices over the top; brush with butter. Cover and let rise in a warm place until doubled, about 1 hour.

Bake at 350° for 30-40 minutes or until golden brown and the apple slices are tender. Cool on a wire rack. Dust with confectioners' sugar. Refrigerate leftovers. **Yield:** 6 servings.

Easy Yeast Rolls

(Pictured below)

PREP: 45 min. + rising **BAKE:** 15 min. + cooling

If you've never baked with yeast before, these simple rolls are the perfect starting point. They always come out of the oven golden brown and delicious. *—Wilma Harter, Witten, South Dakota*

- 2 packages (1/4 ounce *each*) active dry yeast
- 2 cups warm water (110° to 115°)
- 1/2 cup sugar
- 1 egg
- 1/4 cup canola oil
- 2 teaspoons salt
- 6 to 6-1/2 cups all-purpose flour

In a large bowl, dissolve yeast in warm water. Add the sugar, egg, oil, salt and 4 cups flour. Beat until smooth. Stir in enough remaining flour to form a firm dough.

Turn onto a floured surface; knead until smooth and elastic, about 6-8 minutes. Place in a greased bowl, turning once to grease the top. Cover and let rise in a warm place until doubled, about 1 hour.

Punch dough down; turn onto a lightly floured surface. Divide dough into four portions. Shape each portion into 12 balls. To form knots, roll each ball into an 8-in. rope; tie into a knot. Tuck ends under. Place rolls 2 in. apart on greased baking sheets. Cover and let rise until doubled, about 30 minutes.

Bake at 350° for 15-20 minutes or until golden brown. Remove from pans to wire racks to cool. **Yield:** 4 dozen.

Rosemary Cheddar Muffins

PREP/TOTAL TIME: 25 min.

My 96-year-old stepmother shared this recipe with me many years ago, and my family has been gobbling up the biscuitlike muffins ever since. Rosemary and cheddar cheese give them such scrumptious flavor, you may not want to spread on butter!
—*Bonnie Stallings, Martinsburg, West Virginia*

- 2 cups self-rising flour
- 1/2 cup shredded sharp cheddar cheese
- 1 tablespoon minced fresh rosemary *or*
  1 teaspoon dried rosemary, crushed
- 1-1/4 cups 2% milk
- 3 tablespoons mayonnaise

In a large bowl, combine the flour, cheese and rosemary. In another bowl, combine the milk and mayonnaise; stir into the dry ingredients just until moistened. Spoon into 12 greased muffin cups.

Bake at 400° for 8-10 minutes or until lightly browned and toothpick inserted in muffin comes out clean. Cool for 5 minutes before removing from pan to a wire rack. Serve warm. **Yield:** 1 dozen.

Three-Cheese Garlic Bread

PREP: 20 min. BAKE: 15 min.

This tempting loaf is smothered not only with mozzarella, feta and Parmesan cheeses, but also with pesto, artichoke hearts, spaghetti sauce, tomatoes and olives. Try serving the rich slices as an appetizer or an as accompaniment to your favorite pasta.
—*Sarah Sparks, Elgin, Illinois*

- 1 loaf (1 pound) unsliced French bread
- 1/4 cup butter, melted
- 3 garlic cloves, minced
- 1/3 cup prepared pesto
- 3/4 cup spaghetti sauce
- 1 cup (4 ounces) shredded part-skim mozzarella cheese
- 1/3 cup water-packed artichoke hearts, rinsed, drained and chopped
- 1/2 cup chopped ripe olives
- 1/4 cup oil-packed sun-dried tomatoes, finely chopped
- 4 medium tomatoes, sliced
- 1/2 cup crumbled feta cheese
- 1/4 cup grated Parmesan cheese

Cut the loaf of French bread in half lengthwise and then in half widthwise. Combine the butter and garlic; brush over the cut sides of the bread. Place on two ungreased baking sheets.

Spread the cut sides of bread with prepared pesto and spaghetti sauce; sprinkle with mozzarella. Top with the remaining ingredients.

Bake at 400° for 14-16 minutes or until golden brown. Cut into slices. **Yield:** 16 appetizer servings.

Cran-Orange Streusel Muffins

(Pictured above)

PREP: 20 min. BAKE: 20 min.

In less than 45 minutes, you can have a dozen of these tender, fruity, streusel-topped muffins on your breakfast table or brunch buffet. Serving a crowd? It's easy to make a double batch.
—*Hannah Barringer, Loudon, Tennessee*

- 1/4 cup butter, softened
- 1/2 cup sugar
- 1 egg
- 1 cup fat-free milk
- 1/4 cup unsweetened applesauce
- 1/2 teaspoon vanilla extract
- 2 cups all-purpose flour
- 2 teaspoons baking powder
- 1/2 teaspoon salt
- 1 cup fresh *or* frozen cranberries, coarsely chopped
- 2-1/2 teaspoons grated orange peel

STREUSEL TOPPING:
- 2 tablespoons all-purpose flour
- 2 tablespoons brown sugar
- 1/4 teaspoon ground cinnamon
- 2 tablespoons cold butter

In a large bowl, beat the butter and sugar until crumbly, about 2 minutes. Beat in egg. Beat in the milk, applesauce and vanilla. Combine the flour, baking powder and salt; stir into butter mixture just until moistened. Fold in the cranberries and orange peel.

Coat muffin cups with cooking spray; fill three-fourths full with batter. For topping, combine the flour, brown sugar and cinnamon in a small bowl. Cut in butter until crumbly. Sprinkle over batter.

Bake at 400° for 18-22 minutes or until a toothpick inserted near the center comes out clean. Cool muffins for 5 minutes before removing from pan to a wire rack. **Yield:** 1 dozen.

Green Onion Drop Biscuits

(Pictured above)

PREP/TOTAL TIME: 30 min.

From the pros in our Test Kitchen, these golden gems are beyond scrumptious—crunchy on the outside yet moist and tender inside. Feel free to substitute chives for the green onions.

    2 cups all-purpose flour
  1/2 cup thinly sliced green onions
    2 teaspoons sugar
    2 teaspoons baking powder
  1/2 teaspoon salt
  1/4 teaspoon baking soda
    6 tablespoons cold butter, cubed
    1 egg
  3/4 cup buttermilk

In a small bowl, combine the flour, green onions, sugar, baking powder, salt and baking soda. Cut in the butter until the mixture resembles coarse crumbs. Combine the egg and buttermilk; stir into the crumb mixture just until moistened.

Drop by 1/4 cupfuls 2 in. apart onto a greased baking sheet. Bake at 400° for 12-15 minutes or until golden brown. Serve warm. **Yield:** 10 servings.

Sesame Breadsticks

PREP/TOTAL TIME: 20 min.

Thanks to the convenience of refrigerated dough and just two other ingredients, these irresistible sticks come together in a jiffy. They make an easy and yummy addition to any meal.
—Dee Drew, Aliso Viejo, California

    1 tube (11 ounces) refrigerated breadsticks
    1 tablespoon butter, melted
    2 tablespoons sesame seeds

Unroll and separate breadsticks; place on an ungreased baking sheet. Brush with butter and sprinkle with sesame seeds. Bake at 400° for 12-14 minutes or until golden brown. Serve warm. **Yield:** 1 dozen.

Tomato-Herb Focaccia

(Pictured below)

PREP: 30 min. + rising   **BAKE:** 20 min.

With its medley of herbs and tomatoes, this rustic bread will liven up everything from a family dinner to a game day get-together.
—Janet Miller, Indianapolis, Indiana

      1 package (1/4 ounce) active dry yeast
      1 cup warm water (110° to 115°)
      2 tablespoons olive oil, *divided*
  1-1/2 teaspoons salt
      1 teaspoon sugar
      1 teaspoon garlic powder
      1 teaspoon *each* dried oregano, thyme and rosemary, crushed
    1/2 teaspoon dried basil
        Dash pepper
      2 to 2-1/2 cups all-purpose flour
      2 plum tomatoes, thinly sliced
    1/4 cup shredded part-skim mozzarella cheese
      1 tablespoon grated Parmesan cheese

In a large bowl, dissolve the yeast in warm water. Add 1 tablespoon oil, salt, sugar, garlic powder, herbs, pepper and 1-1/2 cups flour. Beat until smooth. Stir in enough remaining flour to form a soft dough (the dough will be sticky).

Turn onto a floured surface; knead until smooth and elastic, about 6-8 minutes. Place in a greased bowl, turning once to grease the top. Cover and let rise in a warm place until doubled, about 1 hour.

Punch dough down. Cover and let rest for 10 minutes. Shape dough into a 13-in. x 9-in. rectangle; place on a greased baking sheet. Cover and let rise until doubled,

about 30 minutes. With fingertips, make several dimples over top of dough.

Brush dough with the remaining oil; arrange tomatoes over the top. Sprinkle with cheeses. Bake at 400° for 20-25 minutes or until golden brown. Remove to a wire rack. **Yield:** 1 loaf (12 pieces).

Lemon Currant Loaves

(Pictured above)

PREP: 30 min. + rising **BAKE:** 50 min. + cooling

My grandmother baked these loaves often when I was growing up. I can still remember the tantalizing aroma of lemon as they came out of the oven.　　　*—Loraine Meyer, Bend, Oregon*

> 1 **package (10 ounces) dried currants**
> 1/2 **cup sugar**
> 2 **teaspoons grated lemon peel**
> **DOUGH:**
> 2 **packages (1/4 ounce *each*) active dry yeast**
> 1/2 **cup sugar, *divided***
> 1/2 **cup warm water (110° to 115°)**
> 2 **cups warm 2% milk (110° to 115°)**
> 3/4 **cup butter, softened, *divided***
> 3 **eggs, lightly beaten**
> 5 **tablespoons lemon juice**
> 2 **teaspoons grated lemon peel**
> 1-1/2 **teaspoons salt**
> 8 **to 9 cups all-purpose flour**

ICING:
> 1 **cup confectioners' sugar**
> 1 **tablespoon lemon juice**

For the filling, in a small bowl, combine dried currants, sugar and lemon peel; set aside. In a large bowl, dissolve yeast and 1 tablespoon sugar in warm water; let stand for 5 minutes. Add the milk, 1/2 cup butter, eggs, lemon juice, lemon peel, salt, remaining sugar and enough flour to form a soft dough.

Turn onto a floured surface; knead until smooth and elastic, about 6-8 minutes. Place in a greased bowl, turning once to grease the top. Cover and let rise in a warm place until doubled, about 1 hour.

Punch dough down. Divide into six portions; roll each portion into a 10-in. x 4-in. rectangle. Melt remaining butter; brush over dough. Sprinkle filling to within 1/2 in. of edges. Roll up jelly-roll style, starting with a long side, to form a rope; pinch seams to seal.

Place three ropes of dough on a floured surface and braid; pinch the ends to seal and tuck under. Transfer to a greased 9-in. x 5-in. loaf pan. Repeat with the remaining ropes. Cover and let rise in a warm place until doubled, about 45 minutes.

Bake at 375° for 50-55 minutes or until golden brown, covering loosely with foil during the last 15 minutes. Cool for 10 minutes before removing from pans to wire racks to cool completely.

Combine icing ingredients; drizzle over loaves. **Yield:** 2 loaves (16 slices each).

Ribbon Nut Bread

(Pictured below)

PREP: 25 min. **BAKE:** 55 min. + cooling

With lemon, walnuts and a center of sweetened cream cheese, this pretty loaf is a tempting treat. At holiday time, I like to bake one for us and one to wrap up as a gift for a friend or neighbor.
—Linda Evancoe–Coble, Leola, Pennsylvania

    1 package (8 ounces) cream cheese, softened
    1/3 cup sugar
    1 egg
BATTER:
    2 cups all-purpose flour
    1/3 cup sugar
    1/3 cup packed brown sugar
    1 teaspoon baking soda
    1/2 teaspoon salt
    2 eggs
    1/2 cup milk
    1/2 cup canola oil
    1 teaspoon grated lemon peel
    1 cup chopped walnuts

For filling, in a small bowl, beat cream cheese and sugar. Beat in egg; set aside.

In a large bowl, combine flour, sugars, baking soda and salt. Whisk the eggs, milk, oil and lemon peel; stir into dry ingredients just until moistened. Fold in walnuts.

Spoon 1 cup batter into a greased 9-in. x 5-in. loaf pan. Spread filling evenly over batter. Top with remaining batter, carefully spreading to cover.

Bake at 350° for 55-60 minutes or until a toothpick inserted near the center comes out clean. Cool bread for 10 minutes before removing from pan to a wire rack. Store in the refrigerator. **Yield:** 1 loaf (16 slices).

Confetti Fiesta Braids

PREP: 1 hour + rising **BAKE:** 25 min. + cooling

This special bread is a twist on a recipe that won a local contest I judged. For my version, I created a double braid and added more peppers. Don't let the number of ingredients or steps fool you—it's not difficult to make. Plus, it smells glorious!
—Fancheon Resler, Bluffton, Indiana

    5-1/2 to 6-1/2 cups all-purpose flour
    1 cup cornmeal
    2 packages (1/4 ounce *each*) active dry yeast
    1 tablespoon sugar
    2 teaspoons salt
    1 cup buttermilk
    1/2 cup butter, cubed
    1/2 cup finely chopped onion
    2 eggs
    1-1/2 cups (6 ounces) shredded cheddar cheese
    1 can (8-1/4 ounces) cream-style corn
    1/2 cup finely chopped sweet red, yellow *and/or* orange peppers
    1/4 cup chopped seeded jalapeno peppers
    1/4 cup butter, melted

In a large bowl, combine 4 cups flour, cornmeal, yeast, sugar and salt. In a small saucepan, heat the buttermilk, butter and onion to 120°-130°. Add to the dry ingredients; beat just until moistened. Add eggs; beat until smooth. Stir in cheddar cheese, corn and peppers. Stir in enough remaining flour to form a stiff dough.

Turn dough onto a floured surface; knead until smooth and elastic, about 6-8 minutes. Place in a greased bowl, turning once to grease the top. Cover and let rise in a warm place until doubled, about 1 hour.

Punch the dough down. Turn onto a lightly floured surface; divide dough in half. Divide half of dough into two portions so that one portion is twice the size of the other; shape larger portion into three 16-in. ropes. Place on a greased baking sheet and braid; pinch ends to seal and tuck under.

Shape smaller portion into three 10-in. ropes. Braid on a lightly floured surface; tuck ends under. Brush bottom of braid with water and place over larger braid. Cover loaf and let rise until doubled, about 45 minutes. Repeat with remaining dough.

Bake at 350° for 25-30 minutes or until golden brown. Brush with melted butter. Cool on a wire rack. Refrigerate leftovers. **Yield:** 2 loaves (20 slices each).

Editor's Note: We recommend wearing disposable gloves when cutting hot peppers. Avoid touching your face.

Overnight Refrigerator Rolls

(Pictured above)

PREP: 25 min. + chilling **BAKE:** 15 min.

Homemade dinner rolls don't get any tastier than these buttery, make–ahead goodies. They're a heartwarming accompaniment to a wide variety of soups, salads and main courses.
—*Jennifer Kauffman Figueroa, Greenville, South Carolina*

- 1 package (1/4 ounce) active dry yeast
- 1/2 cup warm water (110° to 115°)
- 1/2 cup warm 2% milk (110° to 115°)
- 1/4 cup butter-flavored shortening
- 1 tablespoon sugar
- 1 teaspoon salt
- 1 egg
- 3 cups all-purpose flour

In a large bowl, dissolve yeast in warm water. Add the milk, shortening, sugar, salt, egg and 2 cups flour. Beat on medium speed for 2 minutes. Stir in enough remaining flour to form a soft dough (do not knead). Place in a greased bowl, turning once to grease the top. Cover and refrigerate overnight.

Punch dough down. Turn onto a lightly floured surface; divide into 12 pieces. Shape each into a ball. Place 2 in. apart on greased baking sheets. Cover and let rise in a warm place until doubled, about 1-1/2 hours.

Bake at 400° for 15-20 minutes or until golden brown. Remove from pans to wire racks. **Yield:** 1 dozen.

BLUEBERRY BASICS. Look for fresh blueberries that are firm, dry, plump, smooth-skinned and relatively free from leaves and stems. Blueberries should be deep purple-blue to blue-black in color. Use them within 5 days.

Blueberry Yogurt Muffins

(Pictured below and on page 78)

PREP: 15 min. **BAKE:** 20 min.

With the addition of vanilla yogurt, these quick and easy muffins always turn out moist and tender. My husband loves to grab one for breakfast on mornings when he's rushing out the door.
—*Cindi Budreau, Neenah, Wisconsin*

- 1 cup all-purpose flour
- 6 tablespoons sugar
- 1/4 teaspoon salt
- 1/4 teaspoon baking powder
- 1/4 teaspoon baking soda
- 1 egg
- 1/2 cup vanilla yogurt
- 3 tablespoons canola oil
- 2 tablespoons 2% milk
- 1/2 cup fresh *or* frozen blueberries

In a small bowl, combine the flour, sugar, salt, baking powder and baking soda. In another bowl, combine the egg, yogurt, oil and milk. Stir into dry ingredients just until moistened. Fold in blueberries.

Fill greased or paper-lined muffin cups three-fourths full. Bake at 350° for 20-22 minutes or until a toothpick inserted near the center comes out clean. Cool muffins for 5 minutes before removing from pan to a wire rack. Serve warm. **Yield:** 6 muffins.

Editor's Note: If using frozen blueberries, use without thawing to avoid discoloring the batter.

Favorite Swedish Rye

(Pictured above)

PREP: 45 min. + rising **BAKE:** 25 min. + cooling

I came up with this bread years ago while I was experimenting, and it's still a staple in my home. Sometimes I serve thick slices with cheese and deli cold cuts for a hearty snack or meal.
—Lorraine Caland, Thunder Bay, Ontario

 2 **cups golden raisins**
 1 **tablespoon active dry yeast**
2-1/2 **cups warm water (110° to 115°)**
 3/4 **cup packed brown sugar**
 1/2 **cup molasses**
 1/4 **cup shortening**
 1 **teaspoon salt**
 2 **cups rye flour**
 7 **to 8 cups all-purpose flour**

Place raisins in a small bowl. Cover with boiling water; let stand for 5 minutes. Drain and set aside.

In a large bowl, dissolve the yeast in warm water. Add the brown sugar, molasses, shortening, salt, rye flour and 4 cups all-purpose flour. Beat on medium speed for 3 minutes. Stir in enough remaining flour to form a soft dough (dough will be sticky).

Turn dough onto a floured surface; knead until smooth and elastic, about 6-8 minutes. Place in a greased bowl, turning once to grease the top. Cover and let rise in a warm place until doubled, about 1 hour.

Punch the dough down; shape into three round loaves. Place on greased baking sheets. Cover and let rise until doubled, about 45 minutes. Bake at 375° for 25-30 minutes or until bread sounds hollow when tapped. Remove to wire racks to cool. **Yield:** 3 loaves (8 wedges each).

Coffee-Klatch Kolaches

(Pictured below)

PREP: 45 min. + rising **BAKE:** 10 min.

These pastries are easy to make with canned cherry pie filling. Or, try the homemade prune filling (see the directions at the end of the recipe). —Carol Houdek, Minneapolis, Minnesota

 1 **package (1/4 ounce) active dry yeast**
1/4 **cup warm water (110° to 115°)**
3/4 **cup warm 2% milk (110° to 115°)**
1/3 **cup sugar**
1/3 **cup shortening**
 1 **teaspoon salt**
1/8 **teaspoon ground nutmeg**
 2 **eggs**
 4 **cups all-purpose flour**
 1 **can (21 ounces) cherry pie filling**
 3 **tablespoons butter, melted**
GLAZE:
 1 **cup confectioners' sugar**
 1 **tablespoon butter, melted**
 5 **teaspoons 2% milk**

In a large bowl, dissolve yeast in warm water. Add warm milk, sugar, shortening, salt, nutmeg, eggs and 2 cups flour; beat until smooth. Add enough remaining flour to form a soft dough. Turn onto a floured surface; knead until smooth and elastic, about 6-8 minutes.

Place in a greased bowl, turning once to grease the top. Cover and let rise in a warm place until doubled, about 1 hour.

Punch the dough down. Divide in half; shape each half into 12 balls. Place 3 in. apart on greased baking sheets. Flatten each ball to a 3-in. circle. Cover and let rise in a

warm place until doubled, about 30 minutes.

Make a depression in the center of each roll; add a rounded tablespoonful of filling. Bake at 350° for 10-15 minutes or until golden brown.

Brush rolls with butter. Remove from the pans to wire racks to cool. Combine the glaze ingredients; drizzle over tops. **Yield:** 2 dozen.

Prune Kolaches: For prune filling, in a small saucepan, bring an 18 oz. package of pitted dried plums and 2 cups water to a boil. Reduce heat; simmer, uncovered, for 15 minutes or until plums are tender. Drain. Transfer to blender; add 1/4 cup sugar and 1/2 teaspoon ground cinnamon. Cover and process until pureed; cool. Proceed as directed.

Thin Crust Pizza Dough

PREP: 10 min.+ standing

Our family loves thin pizza crust, and this is our go-to version. It's less expensive than delivery and tastes so much better.
—*Theresa Rohde, Scottville, Michigan*

  3-1/2 **cups bread flour**
     1 **cup whole wheat flour**
     5 **teaspoons quick-rise yeast**
  1-1/2 **teaspoons kosher salt**
     1 **teaspoon honey**
  1-1/2 to 1-2/3 **cups warm water (120° to 130°)**

Place the flours, yeast and salt in a food processor; pulse until blended. Add honey. While processing, gradually add warm water until a ball forms. Continue processing 60 seconds to knead dough.

Turn dough onto floured surface; shape into a ball. Cover and let rest 10 minutes. Divide dough into quarters. Use immediately or freeze for later use. **Yield:** 2 pounds (enough for 4 pizzas).

To make pizza: Grease a 12-in. pizza pan; sprinkle with cornmeal. On a lightly floured surface, stretch and shape one portion of dough to form a 12-in. crust; transfer to the prepared pizza pan. Top crust as desired. Bake at 450° for 15-20 minutes or until crust is lightly browned. If using frozen dough, thaw in refrigerator overnight. Proceed as directed.

German Sour Cream Twists

(Pictured at right)

PREP: 45 min. + chilling **BAKE:** 15 min./batch + cooling

With a subtle sweetness, these pretty glazed twists are perfect for breakfast or afternoon tea. Wrap up extras as a gift for a friend.
—*Sally Gregg, Twinsburg, Ohio*

     1 **package (1/4 ounce) active dry yeast**
   1/4 **cup warm water (110° to 115°)**
  3-1/2 **cups all-purpose flour**
     1 **teaspoon salt**
   2/3 **cup shortening**

   1/3 **cup cold butter**
     1 **egg**
     2 **egg yolks**
   3/4 **cup sour cream**
     1 **teaspoon vanilla extract**
  1-1/2 **cups sugar,** *divided*
     4 **cups confectioners' sugar**
   1/3 **cup half-and-half cream**

In a small bowl, dissolve yeast in warm water. In a large bowl, combine the flour and salt. Cut in shortening and butter until mixture resembles coarse crumbs. Beat in the egg, yolks, sour cream, vanilla and yeast mixture. Cover and refrigerate for at least 2 hours. Place three ungreased baking sheets in the refrigerator.

Sprinkle 1/2 cup sugar over a clean work surface. On the sugared surface, roll half of dough into a 12-in. x 8-in. rectangle (refrigerate remaining dough until ready to use). Sprinkle rectangle with 4 teaspoons sugar; fold into thirds.

Give dough a quarter turn and repeat rolling, sugaring and folding two more times. Roll dough into a 12-in. x 8-in. rectangle. Cut into twelve 1-in.-wide strips; twist. Place on chilled baking sheets. Repeat with remaining sugar and dough.

Bake at 375° for 15-20 minutes or until lightly browned. Immediately remove from pans to wire racks to cool.

For icing, combine confectioners' sugar and cream. Dip twists into icing or drizzle icing over twists. **Yield:** 2 dozen.

Dilled Wheat Bread

(Pictured above and on page 78)

PREP: 25 min. + rising **BAKE:** 30 min.

My house smells so good when I'm baking this loaf, which makes a terrific meal served with soup. I love to cut thick slices with an electric knife and eat them while they're still warm.
—*Beverly Preston, Fond du Lac, Wisconsin*

   2 **cups all-purpose flour**
   1 **cup whole wheat flour**
   2 **tablespoons sugar**
   1 **tablespoon dried minced onion**
   1 **package (1/4 ounce) active dry yeast**
   2 **teaspoons dill weed**
   1 **teaspoon salt**
   1 **cup (8 ounces) cream-style cottage cheese**
1/2 **cup water**
   1 **tablespoon butter**
   1 **egg**
   2 **teaspoons butter, melted**
Coarse salt, optional

In a large bowl, combine 3/4 cup all-purpose flour, whole wheat flour, sugar, onion, yeast, dill and salt. In a small saucepan, heat cottage cheese, water and 1 tablespoon butter to 120°-130°. Add to the dry ingredients; beat just until moistened. Add the egg; beat until smooth. Stir in enough remaining all-purpose flour to form a soft dough (dough will be sticky).

Turn dough onto a floured surface; knead until smooth and elastic, about 6-8 minutes. Place in a greased bowl, turning once to grease the top. Cover and let rise in a warm place until doubled, about 1 hour.

Punch the dough down. Shape into a loaf. Place in a greased 8-in. x 4-in. loaf pan. Cover and let rise in a warm place until doubled, about 45 minutes.

Bake at 350° for 25-30 minutes or until golden brown. Remove to a wire rack. Brush with melted butter; sprinkle with coarse salt if desired. **Yield:** 1 loaf (12 slices).

Apple-Bacon Mini Loaves

(Pictured below and on page 78)

PREP: 15 min. **BAKE:** 25 min. + cooling

I created these yummy miniature goodies for a tailgate party at a University of Tennessee football game. The school colors are orange and white, so cheddar cheese was the perfect touch.
—*Jay Davis, Knoxville, Tennessee*

   1 **cup all-purpose flour**
   2 **tablespoons sugar**
   1 **teaspoon baking powder**
1/4 **teaspoon salt**
   1 **egg**
1/2 **cup 2% milk**
   2 **tablespoons butter, melted**
   1 **cup (4 ounces) shredded sharp cheddar cheese**
1/3 **cup crumbled cooked bacon**
1/4 **cup finely chopped apple**

In a large bowl, combine the flour, sugar, baking powder and salt. In another bowl, whisk the egg, milk and butter. Stir into dry ingredients just until moistened. Fold in the cheese, bacon and apple.

Transfer to two greased 5-3/4-in. x 3-in. x 2-in. loaf pans. Bake at 350° for 25-30 minutes or until a toothpick

inserted near the center comes out clean. Cool bread for 10 minutes before removing from the pans to wire racks. **Yield:** 2 mini loaves (6 slices each).

Rhubarb-Buttermilk Coffee Cake

(Pictured above)

PREP: 30 min. **BAKE:** 25 min.

Take advantage of rhubarb season and surprise your family with this moist coffee cake. It has a nice balance of tart and sweet.
—*Cindy Ashley, Gregory, Michigan*

- 2 cups diced fresh *or* frozen rhubarb
- 1/4 cup plus 2/3 cup sugar, *divided*
- 1/2 cup butter, softened
- 2 eggs
- 1-1/2 teaspoons vanilla extract
- 1-1/2 cups all-purpose flour
- 1 teaspoon baking powder
- 1/2 teaspoon salt
- 1/8 teaspoon baking soda
- 3/4 cup buttermilk
- 2 tablespoons brown sugar
- 1/2 teaspoon ground cinnamon

In a small bowl, combine the rhubarb and 1/4 cup sugar; set aside.

In a large bowl, cream butter and remaining sugar until light and fluffy. Add the eggs, one at a time, beating well after each addition. Stir in the vanilla. Combine the flour, baking powder, salt and baking soda; add to the creamed mixture alternately with buttermilk, beating well after each addition. Fold in rhubarb.

Pour into a greased 9-in. square baking pan. Combine brown sugar and cinnamon; sprinkle over batter.

Bake at 350° for 25-30 minutes or until a toothpick inserted near the center comes out clean. Serve warm or at room temperature. **Yield:** 9 servings.

Editor's Note: If using frozen rhubarb, measure the rhubarb while still frozen, then thaw completely. Drain in a colander, but do not press liquid out.

Cinnamon Zucchini Bread

(Pictured below and on page 78)

PREP: 25 min. **BAKE:** 50 min. + cooling

When I was a kid, the only way Mom could get me to eat veggies was to bake zucchini bread. This is a lighter version of her recipe.
—*Kathie Meyer, Round Rock, Texas*

- 3/4 cup sugar
- 1/4 cup unsweetened applesauce
- 1/4 cup canola oil
- 2 egg whites
- 1 teaspoon vanilla extract
- 1-1/2 cups all-purpose flour
- 1-1/2 teaspoons ground cinnamon
- 1 teaspoon baking powder
- 1/2 teaspoon salt
- 1/2 teaspoon ground nutmeg
- 1/4 teaspoon baking soda
- 1-1/4 cups shredded peeled zucchini
- 1/2 cup raisins

In a small bowl, beat sugar, applesauce, oil, egg whites and vanilla until well blended. Combine flour, cinnamon, baking powder, salt, nutmeg and baking soda; gradually beat into sugar mixture. Fold in zucchini and raisins.

Transfer to an 8-in. x 4-in. loaf pan coated with cooking spray. Bake at 350° for 50-60 minutes or until a toothpick inserted near the center comes out clean. Cool bread for 10 minutes before removing from pan to a wire rack to cool completely. **Yield:** 1 loaf (12 slices).

Cookies, Bars & Candies

One just isn't enough when you taste the yummy goodies here. So fill your cookie jar, treat tray or candy dish to the brim with delights such as Orange Cocoa Sandies, Delectable Maple Nut Chocolates and Frosted Nutmeg Logs.

DELIGHTS BY THE DOZEN. Clockwise from top left: Caramel-Nut Candy Bars (p. 100), Diamond Almond Bars (p. 96), Lemon Cream Bonbons (p. 98) and Tumbleweeds (p. 92).

Vanilla Walnut Crescents

(Pictured above)

PREP: 30 min. + chilling **BAKE:** 20 min./batch

My friends look forward to receiving gifts of these fancy-looking crescents sprinkled with nuts, cinnamon and sugar. The pastry is tender and flaky, and the vanilla comes through beautifully.
—*Betty Lawton, Pennington, New Jersey*

- 2 **cups all-purpose flour**
- 1/8 **teaspoon salt**
- 1 **cup cold butter, cubed**
- 1 **egg,** *separated*
- 2/3 **cup sour cream**
- 1/2 **teaspoon vanilla extract**
- 2/3 **cup finely chopped walnuts**
- 2/3 **cup sugar**
- 1 **teaspoon ground cinnamon**

In a large bowl, combine the flour and salt; cut in butter until mixture resembles coarse crumbs. In a small bowl, whisk the egg yolk, sour cream and vanilla; add to crumb mixture and mix well. Cover and refrigerate for 4 hours or overnight.

Divide dough into thirds. On a lightly floured surface, roll each portion into a 10-in. circle. Combine the walnuts, sugar and cinnamon; sprinkle 1/4 cup over each circle. Cut each circle into 12 wedges.

Roll up each wedge from the wide end and place point side down 1 in. apart on greased baking sheets. Curve the ends to form crescents. Whisk the egg white until foamy; brush over the crescents. Sprinkle with the remaining nut mixture.

Bake at 350° for 18-20 minutes or until lightly browned. Remove to wire racks to cool. Store cookies in an airtight container. **Yield:** 3 dozen.

Apple Oatmeal Cookies

PREP: 10 min. **BAKE:** 15 min./batch

I brought dozens of these yummy cookies to work, and they were gone in seconds flat. A convenient cake mix cuts prep time.
—*Nicki Woods, Springfield, Missouri*

- 1 **package (18-1/4 ounces) yellow cake mix**
- 1-1/2 **cups quick-cooking oats**
- 1/2 **cup packed brown sugar**
- 2 **teaspoons ground cinnamon**
- 1 **egg**
- 3/4 **cup unsweetened applesauce**
- 1 **cup finely chopped peeled apple**
- 1/2 **cup raisins**

In a large bowl, combine yellow cake mix, oats, brown sugar and cinnamon. In a small bowl, combine the egg, applesauce, apple and raisins. Stir into the oats mixture and mix well.

Drop dough by heaping teaspoonfuls 2 in. apart onto baking sheets coated with cooking spray. Bake at 350° for 12-14 minutes or until golden brown. Let stand for 2 minutes before removing to wire racks to cool. **Yield:** about 5 dozen.

Tumbleweeds

(Pictured below and on page 90)

PREP: 25 min. + chilling

With just four everyday ingredients, these sweet-salty clusters delight children and adults alike. I simply coat the peanuts and potato sticks with melted butterscotch chips and peanut butter. After you've had one, it's hard to resist grabbing another!
—*Peggy Gray, Savannah, Tennessee*

1 package (11 ounces) butterscotch chips
2 tablespoons creamy peanut butter
1 jar (12 ounces) dry roasted peanuts
1 can (4 ounces) potato sticks

In a microwave-safe bowl, melt butterscotch chips and peanut butter; stir until smooth. Stir in the peanuts and potato sticks.

Drop by tablespoonfuls onto waxed paper-lined pans. Refrigerate until set. Store in an airtight container. **Yield:** 5 dozen.

Coconut Chocolate-Covered Cherries

(Pictured above)

PREP: 25 min. + chilling

I have a weakness for chocolate–covered cherries. The coconut and crunchy walnuts in this version make it absolutely divine.
—Sylvia Chiappone, San Ardo, California

1/2 cup butter, softened
3-3/4 cups confectioners' sugar

1/2 cup sweetened condensed milk
1 teaspoon vanilla extract
2 cups flaked coconut
2 cups finely chopped walnuts
2 jars (16 ounces *each*) maraschino cherries with stems, well drained and patted dry
2 packages (11-1/2 ounces *each*) milk chocolate chips
1 tablespoon shortening

In a large bowl, beat the butter and confectioners' sugar until smooth. Beat in the sweetened condensed milk and vanilla extract until the mixture is well blended and looks like softened butter. Fold in the flaked coconut and walnuts.

With moist hands, shape 2 teaspoonfuls of coconut mixture around each cherry, forming a ball. Place on a waxed paper-lined baking sheet. Cover and refrigerate for 1 hour or until chilled.

In a microwave, melt chocolate chips and shortening; stir until smooth. Dip the coated cherries into melted chocolate. Place on waxed paper; let stand until set. Store in an airtight container at room temperature for up to 1 month. **Yield:** about 5 dozen.

Swedish Raspberry Almond Bars

(Pictured below)

PREP: 35 min. **BAKE:** 20 min. + cooling

When I was a single mother with a young daughter and little money, my Swedish neighbor brought me a batch of these nutty raspberry bars at Christmastime. My daughter is now grown, and I've been preparing these memorable favorites for years.
—*Marina Castle, North Hollywood, California*

- 3/4 cup butter, softened
- 3/4 cup confectioners' sugar
- 1-1/2 cups all-purpose flour
- 3/4 cup seedless raspberry jam
- 3 egg whites
- 6 tablespoons sugar
- 1/2 cup flaked coconut
- 1 cup sliced almonds, *divided*

Additional confectioners' sugar

In a large bowl, cream the butter and confectioners' sugar until light and fluffy. Gradually add the flour and mix well. Press onto the bottom of a greased 13-in. x 9-in. baking pan. Bake at 350° for 18-20 minutes or until lightly browned.

Spread the jam over the crust. In a large bowl, beat the egg whites until soft peaks form. Gradually beat in sugar, 1 tablespoon at a time, on high until stiff peaks form. Fold in coconut and 1/2 cup almonds. Spread over jam. Sprinkle with remaining almonds. Bake at 350° for 18-22 minutes or until golden brown. **Yield:** 2 dozen.

Iced Cinnamon Chip Cookies

(Pictured above)

PREP: 30 min. **BAKE:** 10 min./batch + cooling

My mom helped me make my first batch of cookies when I was 8 years old, and I still enjoy baking. I like taking these to family gatherings and giving them as gifts. With cinnamon chips and a soft vanilla frosting spread on top, they're extra special.
—*Katie Jean Boyd, Roachdale, Indiana*

- 1 cup butter, softened
- 3/4 cup sugar
- 3/4 cup packed brown sugar
- 2 eggs
- 1 teaspoon vanilla extract
- 3 cups all-purpose flour
- 1 teaspoon baking soda
- 1 teaspoon salt
- 1 package (10 ounces) cinnamon baking chips

ICING:
- 1/4 cup butter, melted
- 1/4 cup shortening
- 1-1/4 cups confectioners' sugar
- 1 tablespoon milk
- 3/4 teaspoon vanilla extract

In a large bowl, cream butter and sugars until light and fluffy. Beat in eggs and vanilla. Combine the flour, baking soda and salt; gradually add to creamed mixture and mix well. Fold in cinnamon chips.

Drop the cookie dough by rounded tablespoonfuls 2 in. apart onto ungreased baking sheets. Bake at 350° for 10-12 minutes or until golden brown. Remove to wire racks to cool.

In a small bowl, combine the icing ingredients; beat on high speed for 1-2 minutes or until fluffy. Spread icing over cooled cookies. **Yield:** about 3-1/2 dozen.

Carrot Cake Bars

PREP: 35 min. **BAKE:** 20 min. + cooling

A friend served a big panful of these moist, cakelike goodies at an outdoor party, and everyone raved about the classic taste.
—Agnes Ward, Stratford, Ontario

         3 **eggs**
  1-1/4 **cups canola oil**
       2 **cups all-purpose flour**
       2 **cups sugar**
       2 **teaspoons ground cinnamon**
       1 **teaspoon baking powder**
    1/2 **teaspoon baking soda**
    1/4 to 1/2 **teaspoon salt**
       1 **jar (6 ounces) carrot baby food**
       1 **container (3-1/2 ounces) applesauce baby food**
       1 **container (3-1/2 ounces) apricot baby food**
    1/2 **cup chopped walnuts, optional**
FROSTING:
       1 **package (8 ounces) cream cheese, softened**
    1/2 **cup butter, softened**
       1 **teaspoon vanilla extract**
  3-3/4 **cups confectioners' sugar**

In a large bowl, beat eggs and oil for 2 minutes. Combine the flour, sugar, cinnamon, baking powder, baking soda and salt; add to egg mixture. Add baby foods; mix well. Stir in walnuts if desired.

Transfer the mixture to a greased 15-in. x 10-in. x 1-in. baking pan. Bake at 350° for 20-25 minutes or until a toothpick inserted near the center comes out clean. Cool on a wire rack.

For frosting, in a small bowl, beat cream cheese and butter until light and fluffy. Beat in vanilla. Gradually beat in confectioners' sugar. Frost; cut into bars. Store in the refrigerator. **Yield:** 3 dozen.

TREAT TIPS. When making Peanut Butter Ice Cream Sandwiches (recipe above right), gently press the cookies together until the ice cream is even with the edges. For added fun, roll the edges of the sandwich in toppings such as mini chocolate chips, chopped nuts or chocolate jimmies. Serve the sandwiches immediately or wrap them in plastic wrap and freeze for later.

Peanut Butter Ice Cream Sandwiches

(Pictured below)

PREP: 45 min. **BAKE:** 10 min. + freezing

Store-bought ice cream treats just can't compare to homemade ones. These frozen peanut butter sandwiches are irresistible.
—Teresa Gaetzke, North Freedom, Wisconsin

    1/2 **cup shortening**
    1/2 **cup creamy peanut butter**
    3/4 **cup sugar, *divided***
    1/2 **cup packed brown sugar**
       1 **egg**
    1/2 **teaspoon vanilla extract**
  1-1/2 **cups all-purpose flour**
       1 **teaspoon baking soda**
    1/2 **teaspoon salt**
     12 **ounces dark chocolate candy coating, chopped**
       1 **quart vanilla ice cream, softened**

In a large bowl, cream the shortening, peanut butter, 1/2 cup sugar and brown sugar until light and fluffy. Beat in egg and vanilla. Combine the flour, baking soda and salt; gradually add to creamed mixture and mix well.

Roll dough into 1-in. balls; roll in the remaining sugar. Place 1 in. apart on ungreased baking sheets. Flatten with a fork, forming a crisscross pattern.

Bake at 350° for 9-11 minutes or until set (do not overbake). Remove to wire racks to cool completely.

In a microwave, melt candy coating; stir until smooth. Spread a heaping teaspoonful on the bottom of each cookie; place chocolate side up on waxed paper until set.

To make sandwiches, place 1/4 cup ice cream on the bottom of half of the cookies; top with remaining cookies. Wrap in plastic wrap; freeze. **Yield:** 16 servings.

Diamond Almond Bars

(Pictured above and on page 90)

PREP: 20 min.   **BAKE:** 25 min. + cooling

Baking these has been a tradition in our family for generations. The chewy bars with crunchy sliced almonds on top are always popular. I like to freeze several dozen to enjoy later.
—Liz Green, Tamworth, Ontario

> 1 cup butter, softened
> 1 cup plus 1 tablespoon sugar, *divided*
> 1 egg, *separated*
> 1 teaspoon almond extract
> 2 cups all-purpose flour
> 1/2 cup blanched sliced almonds
> 1/4 teaspoon ground cinnamon

In a large bowl, cream butter and 1 cup sugar until light and fluffy. Add the egg yolk; beat well. Stir in extract. Add flour, beating until combined.

Press into a greased 15-in. x 10-in. x 1-in. baking pan. Beat the egg white until foamy; brush over dough. Top with almonds. Combine cinnamon and remaining sugar; sprinkle over the top.

Bake at 350° for 25-30 minutes or until lightly browned (do not overbake). Cool on a wire rack for 10 minutes. Cut into diamond-shaped bars. Cool bars completely. **Yield:** 5 dozen.

Molasses Fudge

(Pictured below)

PREP: 25 min.   **COOK:** 20 min. + cooling

The blend of molasses and spices in this fudge reminds people of gingerbread. The little squares are loaded with old-fashioned flavor and are sure to please at Christmastime or any time.
—Becky Burch, Marceline, Missouri

> 1 teaspoon plus 2 tablespoons butter, *divided*
> 1 cup sugar
> 1 cup packed brown sugar
> 1/2 cup half-and-half cream
> 2 tablespoons molasses
> 1/2 teaspoon ground cinnamon
> 1/4 teaspoon ground nutmeg
> 1/8 teaspoon ground cloves
> 1-1/2 teaspoons vanilla extract
> 1/2 cup coarsely chopped walnuts

Line a 9-in. x 5-in. loaf pan with foil. Grease the foil with 1/2 teaspoon butter; set aside.

Grease the sides of a large heavy saucepan with 1/2 teaspoon butter. Add sugars, cream, molasses and spices. Cook and stir over medium heat until the sugar is dissolved and the mixture comes to a boil. Cook over medium-low heat until a candy thermometer reads 240° (soft-ball stage), stirring often.

Remove from the heat. Add the vanilla and remaining butter (do not stir). Cool, without stirring, to 110°, about 55 minutes.

Remove thermometer; beat vigorously with a wooden spoon until mixture begins to thicken; add walnuts. Beat until fudge is very thick and mixture begins to lose its gloss, about 10 minutes.

Quickly pour into the prepared pan. While warm, score into 1-in. squares. When the fudge is firm, use the foil to lift the candy out of the pan; cut candy into squares.

Store in an airtight container. **Yield:** about 4 dozen.

Editor's Note: We recommend that you test your candy thermometer before each use by bringing water to a boil; the thermometer should read 212°. Adjust your recipe temperature up or down based on your test.

Peanut Butter Candy

PREP: 10 min. + cooling

During the holiday season, I make a lot of candy to give friends. With a decadent combination of white chocolate and chunky peanut butter, this simple recipe is an annual favorite.
—Deloris Morrow, Lake City, Iowa

    1/2   teaspoon butter
    1-1/4 pounds white candy coating, coarsely chopped
    1-1/2 cups chunky peanut butter

Line a 9-in. square pan with foil; butter the foil with 1/2 teaspoon butter and set aside.

In a microwave-safe bowl, melt the candy coating; stir until smooth. Stir in peanut butter until melted. Transfer to the prepared pan. Cool to room temperature. Cut into squares. **Yield:** about 1-1/2 pounds.

Editor's Note: This recipe was tested in a 1,100-watt microwave.

Cranberry-Cashew Drop Cookies

PREP: 20 min.   BAKE: 10 min./batch

A great change of pace from the usual chocolate chip version, this exceptional cookie is packed with yummy ingredients—dried cranberries, chopped cashews and white baking chips. You'll want to whip up plenty because they disappear quickly!
—Monica McGilvray, Mukwonago, Wisconsin

    1   cup butter, softened
    1   cup packed brown sugar
    1/2   cup sugar
    2   eggs
    1   teaspoon vanilla extract
    2-1/4 cups all-purpose flour
    1   teaspoon baking soda
    1   teaspoon salt
    1   package (10 to 12 ounces) white baking chips
    1   cup chopped cashews
    1   cup dried cranberries

In a large bowl, cream butter and sugars until light and fluffy. Beat in eggs and vanilla.

Combine the flour, baking soda and salt; gradually add to the creamed mixture and mix well. Stir in the chips, cashews and cranberries.

Drop dough by rounded tablespoonfuls 2 in. apart onto ungreased baking sheets. Bake at 350° for 9-11 minutes or until golden brown. Remove to wire racks to cool. **Yield:** 4-1/2 dozen.

Pastel Tea Cookies

(Pictured above)

PREP: 1 hour + chilling BAKE: 10 min./batch + standing

These glazed cutouts spread with a pretty pastel glaze are perfect for nibbling between sips at a tea party, graduation or shower.
—Lori Henry, Elkhart, Indiana

    1   cup butter, softened
    2/3   cup sugar
    1   egg
    1   teaspoon vanilla extract
    2-1/2 cups all-purpose flour
    1/2   teaspoon salt
    1-1/4 cups confectioners' sugar
    2   teaspoons meringue powder
    5   teaspoons water
Pastel food coloring

In a large bowl, cream the butter and sugar until light and fluffy. Beat in the egg and vanilla. Combine flour and salt; gradually add to the creamed mixture. Cover and refrigerate for 1-2 hours until dough is easy to handle.

On a lightly floured surface, roll out the cookie dough to 1/8-in. thickness. Cut with floured 2-1/2-in. butterfly or flower cookie cutters. Place 1 in. apart on ungreased baking sheets.

Bake at 350° for 8-10 minutes or until edges are lightly browned. Remove to wire racks to cool.

For glaze, in a small bowl, combine the confectioners' sugar and meringue powder; stir in water until smooth. Divide among small bowls; tint pastel colors. Spread over cookies; let stand until set. **Yield:** 4 dozen.

Editor's Note: Meringue powder is available from Wilton Industries. Call 800-794-5866 or visit *wilton.com*.

Treats with a Citrus Twist

COMBINE the sugary sweetness of cookies and candy with a burst of tangy citrus, and what do you get? Especially yummy creations your family and friends simply won't be able to resist.

The popular recipes featured here give you a twist of tongue-tingling fruit flavor in every bite. Indulge in old-fashioned Soft Orange Marmalade Cookies, Orange Cocoa Sandies, Lemon Poppy Seed Cookies and chocolaty Lemon Cream Bonbons.

Whether you want goodies to put on a holiday tray or just to keep around the house for the kids, you can't go wrong with these refreshing sweets.

Orange Cocoa Sandies

(Pictured below)

PREP: 15 min. **BAKE:** 15 min./batch + cooling

When I was growing up, I loved to help my mother cut out the dessert recipes from newspapers and magazines and paste them into a big book. These chocolaty bites are in our collection.
—*Nella Parker, Hersey, Michigan*

1/2 cup butter, softened
1/2 cup plus 2 tablespoons confectioners' sugar, divided
1/2 teaspoon orange extract
1 cup all-purpose flour
2 tablespoons baking cocoa
1/2 cup finely chopped pecans

In a large bowl, cream butter and 1/2 cup confectioners' sugar until light and fluffy; beat in the extract. Combine flour and cocoa; gradually add to creamed mixture. Stir in pecans.

Roll the dough into 1-in. balls. Place balls 1 in. apart on ungreased baking sheets. Bake at 350° for 12-14 minutes or until set. Cool for 1-2 minutes before removing to wire racks. Dust with remaining confectioner's sugar. **Yield:** about 2 dozen.

Lemon Cream Bonbons

(Pictured above and on page 90)

PREP: 30 min. + freezing

I used to save these special treats for Christmastime, but they're in such demand that I now keep them on hand year–round.
—*Ann Barber, Creola, Ohio*

2 packages (8 ounces *each*) cream cheese, softened
3 tablespoons lemon juice
2 tablespoons grated lemon peel
1 teaspoon lemon extract
1 cup confectioners' sugar
1 pound dark chocolate candy coating, melted
4 ounces white candy coating, melted

In a large bowl, beat the cream cheese, lemon juice, peel and extract. Gradually beat in confectioners' sugar. Cover and freeze for 2 hours.

Using a small ice cream scoop, drop the mixture by 1-in. balls onto waxed paper-lined baking sheets. Cover and freeze for 1 hour.

Working with a few frozen balls at a time, dip into the melted chocolate; allow the excess to drip off. Place on waxed paper-lined baking sheets. Let stand until set.

Spoon melted white candy coating into a heavy-duty

resealable plastic bag. Cut a small hole in the corner of the bag; drizzle the coating over the candies. Store in the refrigerator. Remove from the refrigerator just before serving. **Yield:** about 4 dozen.

Soft Orange Marmalade Cookies

(Pictured below)

PREP: 40 min. **BAKE:** 10 min./batch

We prefer soft cookies to crispy ones, and these are among our favorites. The orange marmalade makes them tender and adds yummy flavor. I spread a simple homemade frosting on top.
—Margaret Peterson, Forest City, Iowa

- 1/2 cup shortening
- 1 cup sugar
- 2 eggs
- 1 cup (8 ounces) sour cream
- 1/2 cup orange marmalade
- 4 cups all-purpose flour
- 2 teaspoons baking powder
- 1 teaspoon baking soda
- 1/2 teaspoon salt

FROSTING:
- 1/2 cup butter, softened
- 1/4 cup orange marmalade
- 3 cups confectioners' sugar

In a large bowl, cream shortening and sugar. Add eggs, one at a time, beating well after each addition. Combine sour cream and orange marmalade; set aside. Combine the flour, baking powder, baking soda and salt; add to creamed mixture alternately with sour cream mixture.

Drop by tablespoonfuls 2 in. apart onto greased baking sheets. Bake at 375° for 10-12 minutes or until lightly browned. Remove to wire racks to cool completely.

For the frosting, in a small bowl, combine butter and marmalade. Gradually beat in confectioners' sugar until blended. Frost cookies. **Yield:** 6-1/2 dozen.

Lemon Poppy Seed Cookies

(Pictured above)

PREP: 35 min. + chilling **BAKE:** 10 min./batch

My family of lemon lovers just can't get enough of these cutouts. Enjoy a few as an afternoon pick-me-up with coffee or tea.
—Carol Owen, Salina, Kansas

- 1-1/4 cups sugar
- 1 cup butter-flavored shortening
- 2 eggs
- 1/4 cup light corn syrup
- 1 tablespoon grated lemon peel
- 1-1/2 teaspoons lemon extract
- 1 teaspoon vanilla extract
- 3 cups all-purpose flour
- 2 tablespoons poppy seeds
- 1 teaspoon ground ginger
- 3/4 teaspoon baking powder
- 1/2 teaspoon salt
- 1/2 teaspoon baking soda

In a large bowl, cream sugar and shortening until light and fluffy. Beat in the eggs, corn syrup, lemon peel and extracts. Combine the remaining ingredients; gradually add to creamed mixture and mix well.

Shape into three balls, then flatten into disks. Wrap in plastic wrap and refrigerate for 1 hour or until firm.

Roll each portion of cookie dough between two sheets of waxed paper to 1/8-in. thickness. Cut with a floured 2-1/2-in. fluted round cookie cutter. Using a floured spatula, place 1 in. apart on greased baking sheets. Reroll scraps if desired.

Bake at 375° for 6-8 minutes or until edges are golden brown. Cool for 2 minutes before removing from pans to wire racks. **Yield:** about 4-1/2 dozen.

Caramel-Nut Candy Bars

(Pictured below and on page 90)

PREP: 25 min. + chilling

As a busy mother of six, I look for treats that are quick, easy and family-pleasing. These Snickers-like bars are all of the above!
—Sheralyn Ylioja, Lethbridge, Alberta

> 1-1/2 **teaspoons plus 1/4 cup butter, softened,** *divided*
>   2 **packages (11-1/2 ounces** *each***) milk chocolate chips**
> 1/4 **cup shortening**
>   1 **package (14 ounces) caramels**
>   5 **teaspoons water**
>   1 **cup chopped pecans**

Line a 13-in. x 9-in. pan with foil and grease the foil with 1-1/2 teaspoons butter; set aside. In a microwave, melt milk chocolate chips and shortening at 70% power for 1 minute; stir. Microwave at additional 10- to 20-second intervals, stirring until smooth.

Spread half of mixture into prepared pan. Refrigerate for 15 minutes or until firm. Set the remaining chocolate mixture aside.

In a large microwave-safe bowl, melt caramels, water and remaining butter; stir until smooth. Stir in pecans. Spread over chocolate layer.

Heat the reserved chocolate mixture if necessary to achieve spreading consistency; spread over the caramel layer. Cover and refrigerate for 1 hour or until firm.

Using the foil, lift the candy out of the pan. Gently peel off foil; cut candy into 1-1/2-in. x 1-in. bars. Store in the refrigerator. **Yield:** 2-1/4 pounds.

Editor's Note: This recipe was tested in a 1,100-watt microwave.

Cookout Brownies

(Pictured above)

PREP: 2 hours + cooling

For extra fun at a barbecue, transform brownie cupcakes into these grill-themed delights. Hot Tamale candies form the tiny hot dogs on top. You could also use caramel cream candies for steaks...or gumdrops on toothpicks for colorful kabobs.
—Jenny Sturma, Milwaukee, Wisconsin

Brownie cupcakes *or* **chocolate cupcakes**
Orange colored sugar
**   1 tube (4-1/4 ounces) black decorating icing**
Caramel cream candies, gumdrops and Hot Tamales
Colored toothpicks

Sprinkle brownies with colored sugar to resemble hot coals. Pipe grill grates onto brownies using icing.

Cut caramel candies into slices; indent slightly to form steaks. Cut the gumdrops in half and cut a caramel candy into small pieces; thread alternately onto toothpicks to form kabobs.

Arrange the hot dogs (Hot Tamales), steaks and kabobs on brownies. Pipe grill marks over the tops using icing. **Yield:** varies.

Ginger Creme Sandwich Cookies

PREP: 25 min. + chilling **BAKE:** 10 min./batch + cooling

These spiced goodies with a lemony cream-cheese filling have all of the old-fashioned, comfort-food appeal people love. Be warned—a fresh-baked batch will get snatched up in no time! Pack a few in a lunch box to surprise someone special.
—Carol Walston, Granbury, Texas

3/4 cup shortening
1 cup packed light brown sugar
1 egg
1/4 cup molasses
2-1/4 cups all-purpose flour
3 teaspoons ground ginger
2 teaspoons baking soda
1 teaspoon ground cinnamon
1/2 teaspoon salt
1/4 cup sugar
FILLING:
1 package (3 ounces) cream cheese, softened
1/3 cup butter, softened
2 teaspoons lemon extract
2 cups confectioners' sugar
1 teaspoon vanilla extract

In a large bowl, cream shortening and brown sugar until light and fluffy. Beat in egg and molasses. Combine the flour, ginger, baking soda, cinnamon and salt; gradually add to the creamed mixture and mix well. Cover and refrigerate overnight.

Shape into 1-in. balls; roll in sugar. Place 2 in. apart on ungreased baking sheets. Flatten with a fork, forming a crisscross pattern. Bake at 375° for 8-10 minutes or until set (do not overbake). Remove to wire racks to cool.

In a small bowl, combine the filling ingredients until smooth. Spread the filling over the bottoms of half of the cookies; top with the remaining cookies. Store in the refrigerator. **Yield:** 2-1/2 dozen.

Honey Maple Cookies

PREP: 20 min. **BAKE:** 10 min./batch

With honey and maple syrup, these chocolate chip cookies are deliciously different. The chopped pecans add a nice crunch.
—Barbara Kuder, Tribune, Kansas

1 cup shortening
3/4 cup honey
3/4 cup maple syrup
2 eggs
1 teaspoon vanilla extract
2-1/2 cups all-purpose flour
1 teaspoon baking soda
1 teaspoon salt
2 cups (12 ounces) semisweet chocolate chips
1 cup chopped pecans

In a large bowl, beat shortening until light and fluffy. Add honey and syrup, a little at a time, beating well after each addition. Add eggs, one at a time, beating well after each addition (mixture will appear curdled). Beat in the vanilla. Combine the flour, baking soda and salt. Gradually add to honey mixture and mix just until moistened. Stir in the chocolate chips and pecans.

Drop cookie dough by rounded tablespoonfuls onto greased baking sheets. Bake at 350° for 8-10 minutes or until golden brown. Remove to wire racks. **Yield:** 5 dozen.

Delectable Maple Nut Chocolates

(Pictured below)

PREP: 1 hour + chilling

My father liked just about anything that had the flavor of maple, so my mother tweaked a brownie recipe to suit his tastes. It's now 40 years later, and this yummy candy is still a winner.
—Elizabeth King, Duluth, Minnesota

1 can (14 ounces) sweetened condensed milk
1/2 cup butter, cubed
7-1/2 cups confectioners' sugar
2 cups chopped walnuts
2 teaspoons maple flavoring
1 teaspoon vanilla extract
4 cups (24 ounces) semisweet chocolate chips
2 ounces bittersweet chocolate, chopped
2 teaspoons shortening

In a small saucepan, combine sweetened condensed milk and butter. Cook and stir over low heat until the butter is melted. Place the confectioners' sugar in a large bowl; add the milk mixture and beat until smooth. Stir in the walnuts, maple flavoring and vanilla.

Roll the mixture into 3/4-in. balls; place on waxed paper-lined baking sheets. Refrigerate balls until firm, about 1 hour.

In a microwave, melt the chocolate chips, bittersweet chocolate and shortening; stir until smooth. Dip the balls into chocolate; allow excess to drip off. Place on waxed paper; let stand until set. Store the candy in an airtight container. **Yield:** about 13 dozen.

Editor's Note: Shape and freeze the balls of maple candy for up to 2 months if desired. Thaw candy before dipping into melted chocolate mixture.

Chocolate Macadamia Macaroons

(Pictured above)

PREP: 20 min. **BAKE:** 15 min. + cooling

I love coconut, chocolate and macadamia nuts. For a special indulgence, I combined them all into these dipped macaroons.
—*Darlene Brenden, Salem, Oregon*

    2 cups flaked coconut
    1/2 cup finely chopped macadamia nuts
    1/3 cup sugar
    3 tablespoons baking cocoa
    2 tablespoons all-purpose flour
Pinch salt
    2 egg whites, beaten
    1 tablespoon light corn syrup
    1 teaspoon vanilla extract
    4 ounces semisweet chocolate, chopped

In a large bowl, combine the coconut, macadamia nuts, sugar, cocoa, flour and salt. Add egg whites, corn syrup and vanilla and mix well.

Drop by rounded tablespoonfuls onto greased baking sheets. Bake at 325° for 15-20 minutes or until set and dry to the touch. Cool for 5 minutes before removing from pans to wire racks to cool completely.

In a microwave, melt chocolate; stir until smooth. Dip the bottom of each cookie in chocolate; allow excess to drip off. Place on waxed paper; let stand until set. **Yield:** 1-1/2 dozen.

Chocolate Peanut Cookies

PREP: 20 min. **BAKE:** 10 min./batch

Instead of preparing the usual chocolate chip cookies, I bake this variation, which is loaded with peanut flavor. The goodies are crisp on the outside yet moist and tender on the inside.
—*Clara Coulson Minney, Washington Court House, Ohio*

    1/4 cup butter, softened
    1/4 cup peanut butter
    1/4 cup packed brown sugar
    2 tablespoons sugar
    2 tablespoons beaten egg
    2 tablespoons 2% milk
    1/2 teaspoon vanilla extract
    1 cup all-purpose flour
    1/2 teaspoon baking soda
    1/8 teaspoon salt
    1/3 cup honey-roasted peanuts
    1/3 cup semisweet chocolate chips
    1/3 cup coarsely chopped miniature
        peanut butter cups

In a large bowl, cream butter, peanut butter and sugars until light and fluffy. Beat in the egg, milk and vanilla. Combine the flour, baking soda and salt; gradually add to the creamed mixture and mix well. Stir in the peanuts, chocolate chips and peanut butter cups.

Drop cookie dough by tablespoonfuls 2 in. apart onto ungreased baking sheets. Bake at 350° for 10-12 minutes or until golden brown. Remove to wire racks. Store in an airtight container. **Yield:** about 2 dozen.

Frosted Nutmeg Logs

(Pictured below)

PREP: 30 min. **BAKE:** 15 min./batch + cooling

This is my son's favorite Christmas cookie. The log–shaped treats have wonderful nutmeg flavor and are perfect for the holidays.
—Janie Colle, Hutchinson, Kansas

- 1 **cup butter, softened**
- 3/4 **cup sugar**
- 1 **egg**
- 2 **teaspoons rum extract**
- 2-1/2 **cups all-purpose flour**
- 1-1/4 **teaspoons ground nutmeg**

Dash salt
FROSTING:
- 1/4 **cup butter, softened**
- 3 **cups confectioners' sugar**
- 2 **teaspoons rum extract**
- 2 to 3 **tablespoons 2% milk**

Ground nutmeg

In a large bowl, cream butter and sugar until light and fluffy. Beat in egg and extract. Combine the flour, nutmeg and salt; gradually add to creamed mixture and mix well.

Divide dough into three portions. Roll each portion into 3/4-in.-thick logs; cut into 2-in. pieces. Place on ungreased baking sheets; flatten slightly.

Bake at 350°, for 12-16 minutes or until the bottoms are lightly browned. Cool for 2 minutes before removing to wire racks to cool completely.

For the frosting, in a large bowl, beat the butter until fluffy. Beat in the confectioners' sugar, extract and enough milk to achieve the desired consistency. Frost the cookies. Press down with tines of a fork, making lines down frosting to resemble tree bark. Sprinkle with nutmeg. **Yield:** 3 dozen.

Chocolate Brownie Cookies

(Pictured above)

PREP: 20 min. + chilling **BAKE:** 10 min./batch

Kids like the crackled sugar coating on these chocolaty goodies. They taste like brownies but are easier to hold and transport.
—Ruth Cain, Hartselle, Alabama

- 1/2 **cup sugar**
- 1 **egg**
- 2 **tablespoons canola oil**
- 1 **ounce unsweetened chocolate, melted and cooled**
- 1/2 **teaspoon vanilla extract**
- 1/2 **cup all-purpose flour**
- 1/2 **teaspoon baking powder**
- 1/8 **teaspoon salt**

Confectioners' sugar

In a bowl, beat the sugar, egg, oil, chocolate and vanilla. Combine the flour, baking powder and salt; gradually add to creamed mixture. Chill for at least 2 hours.

Shape dough into 1-in. balls; roll in confectioners' sugar. Place 2 in. apart on lightly greased baking sheets. Bake at 350° for 10-12 minutes or until set. Remove to wire racks. **Yield:** about 1 dozen.

Editor's Note: Dough will be sticky. Dip hands in confectioners' sugar when shaping dough into balls.

NUTMEG KNOW-HOW. Nutmeg complements cookies, cider, sweet potatoes, custard, soups, sauces and more. It tastes best when freshly grated (as shown in the photo at left). One whole nutmeg equals 2-3 teaspoons grated.

Cakes & Pies

Treat your family to a little slice of heaven! Peachy Gingerbread Cake Roll, Orange Coconut Meringue Pie, Cherry Cola Chocolate Cake, Vanilla Custard Pie and the other recipes in this chapter will make any meal one to remember.

SWEET SENSATIONS. Clockwise from top left: Macadamia Toffee Snack Cake (p. 115), Fresh Blueberry Pie (p. 111), Grandma's Lemon Poppy Seed Cake (p. 111) and Spiced Pear Upside-Down Cake (p. 108).

Strawberry Pineapple Pie

(Pictured above)

PREP: 30 min. + chilling

Hosting a springtime party, baby shower, ladies' luncheon or other get-together? Consider this sweet-tangy, pretty pink pie.
—*Irene Caron, Loudon, New Hampshire*

    1 can (20 ounces) crushed pineapple, undrained
   10 frozen unsweetened whole strawberries, thawed
    3 tablespoons quick-cooking tapioca
    2 egg yolks
  3/4 cup plus 1 tablespoon sugar, *divided*
  3/4 teaspoon lemon extract, *divided*
    5 drops red food coloring, optional
    1 pastry shell (9 inches), baked
    1 cup heavy whipping cream

Place pineapple and strawberries in a food processor; cover and process until smooth. Transfer to a saucepan. Stir in the tapioca, egg yolks and 3/4 cup sugar; let stand for 5 minutes.

Cook and stir over medium heat until mixture comes to a full boil. Remove from the heat; stir in 1/2 teaspoon extract and food coloring if desired. Pour into the pastry shell; refrigerate for 1 hour.

In a small bowl, beat cream until it begins to thicken. Add remaining sugar and extract; beat until stiff peaks form. Spread over the top of pie. Refrigerate for at least 4 hours or until set. **Yield:** 8 servings.

Dark Chocolate Cream Pie

(Pictured below)

PREP: 30 min. + chilling

You just can't go wrong when you finish a meal with this smooth, old-fashioned delight. Topped with a dollop of fluffy whipped cream, it will be a hit with children and adults alike.
—*Kezia Sullivan, Sackets Harbor, New York*

  1-1/4 cups sugar
    1/4 cup cornstarch
    1/4 teaspoon salt
      3 cups milk
      3 ounces unsweetened chocolate, chopped
      4 egg yolks, lightly beaten
      3 tablespoons butter
  1-1/2 teaspoons vanilla extract
      1 pastry shell (9 inches), baked

In a large saucepan, combine the sugar, cornstarch and salt. Stir in the milk and unsweetened chocolate. Cook and stir over medium-high heat until thickened and bubbly. Reduce the heat; cook and stir 2 minutes longer. Remove from the heat.

Stir a small amount of hot filling into egg yolks; return all to the pan, stirring constantly. Bring to a gentle boil; cook and stir 2 minutes longer. Remove from the heat.

Gently stir in the butter and vanilla. Spoon into the pastry shell. Cool on a wire rack. Cover and chill for at least 3 hours. **Yield:** 8 servings.

Marvelous Cannoli Cake

PREP: 30 min. + chilling **BAKE:** 25 min. + cooling

A luscious, chocolate-studded cannoli filling separates the tender vanilla layers of this rich cake, which is best served well chilled. It's hard to believe that such a special dessert is made with a mix!
—Antoinette Owens, Ridgefield, Connecticut

- 1 package (18-1/4 ounces) French vanilla cake mix

FILLING:
- 1 carton (16 ounces) ricotta cheese
- 1/2 cup confectioners' sugar
- 2 teaspoons ground cinnamon
- 1 teaspoon almond extract
- 1 teaspoon rum extract
- 1 teaspoon vanilla extract
- 2 ounces semisweet chocolate, finely chopped

FROSTING:
- 2 cartons (8 ounces *each*) Mascarpone cheese
- 3/4 cup confectioners' sugar
- 1/4 cup whole milk
- 2 teaspoons almond extract
- 1 teaspoon vanilla extract
- 1 cup sliced almonds
- 2 tablespoons miniature semisweet chocolate chips

Prepare and bake the cake mix according to the package directions, using two greased and floured 9-in. round baking pans. Cool for 10 minutes before removing from pans to wire racks to cool completely.

In a large bowl, combine ricotta cheese, confectioners' sugar, cinnamon and extracts; stir in the semisweet chocolate. In another bowl, beat the Mascarpone cheese, confectioners' sugar, milk and extracts until smooth; cover and refrigerate filling and frosting until frosting reaches spreading consistency.

Place one cake layer on a serving plate; spread with 1 cup filling. Top with the second cake layer. Spread the remaining filling over top of cake to within 1 in. of edges. Frost sides and top edge of cake with 2 cups frosting.

Press almonds into the sides of cake; pipe remaining frosting around edges. Sprinkle chocolate chips over top. Refrigerate until serving. **Yield:** 12 servings.

PRETTY PRESENTATION. When frosting a layer cake such as Marvelous Cannoli Cake (recipe above), the serving plate can get a bit messy. To help keep it clean, try this trick:

Cut several 3-inch strips of waxed paper and tuck them slightly under the cake, covering the edge of the cake plate. Frost the cake as desired, then carefully remove the waxed paper.

Cherry Cream Pie

(Pictured above)

PREP: 40 min. + chilling

A popular vacation destination in the Midwest—Door County, Wisconsin (in the "thumb" of the state)—is known not only for its beautiful shorelines, but also for its abundance of cherry orchards. That's where I got this recipe, which features a nutty crumb crust, cream cheese and, of course, cherry pie filling.
—Carol Wencka, Greenfield, Wisconsin

CRUST:
- 1 cup all-purpose flour
- 1 cup finely chopped walnuts
- 1/2 cup butter, softened
- 1/4 cup packed brown sugar

FILLING:
- 1 package (8 ounces) cream cheese, softened
- 1 cup confectioners' sugar
- 1/4 teaspoon almond extract
- 1/2 cup heavy whipping cream, whipped
- 1 can (21 ounces) cherry pie filling

In a small bowl, combine the flour, walnuts, butter and brown sugar. Transfer to a 13-in. x 9-in. baking pan. Bake at 375° for 15 minutes, stirring once. Set aside 1 cup of crumbs. While warm, press the remaining crumbs into a greased 9-in. pie plate, firmly pressing onto the bottom and up the sides. Chill for 30 minutes.

In a small bowl, beat the cream cheese, confectioners' sugar and almond extract until smooth. Spread over bottom of crust. Gently fold whipped cream into the pie filling; spread over cream cheese layer. Sprinkle with reserved crumbs. Chill for at least 4 hours before serving. **Yield:** 6-8 servings.

Spiced Pear Upside-Down Cake

(Pictured below and on page 104)

PREP: 25 min. **BAKE:** 35 min. + cooling

The flavors of fresh-picked pears and spicy gingerbread blend beautifully in this autumn twist on pineapple upside-down cake. Topped with vanilla ice cream, it's a wonderful treat. Leftovers are just as good the next day—but don't count on having any!
—*Lisa Varner, Charleston, South Carolina*

        1/2 cup butter, melted
        1/2 cup coarsely chopped walnuts
        1/4 cup packed brown sugar
          2 large pears, peeled and sliced
        1/2 cup butter, softened
        1/3 cup sugar
          1 egg
        1/3 cup molasses
      1-1/2 cups all-purpose flour
        3/4 teaspoon ground ginger
        3/4 teaspoon ground cinnamon
        1/2 teaspoon salt
        1/4 teaspoon baking powder
        1/4 teaspoon baking soda
        1/2 cup warm water
    Ice cream, optional

Pour the melted butter into a 9-in. square baking pan; sprinkle with the walnuts and brown sugar. Arrange the pears over the walnuts.

In a large bowl, cream softened butter and sugar until light and fluffy. Beat in egg and molasses. Combine the flour, ginger, cinnamon, salt, baking powder and baking soda; add to the creamed mixture alternately with water, beating well after each addition.

Spread the cake batter over the pears. Bake at 350° for 35-40 minutes or until a toothpick inserted near the center comes out clean. Cool for 10 minutes before inverting onto a serving plate. Serve warm with ice cream if desired. **Yield:** 9 servings.

Orange Coconut Meringue Pie

PREP: 35 min. **BAKE:** 15 min. + chilling

I have won first place in two cream pie competitions with this yummy, fruity recipe. It's one of my all-time favorites.
—*Daisy Duncan, Stillwater, Oklahoma*

          1 cup sugar
          3 tablespoons cornstarch
          3 tablespoons all-purpose flour
        1/4 teaspoon salt
      1-1/2 cups water
        3/4 cup orange juice
          3 egg yolks, lightly beaten
        3/4 cup flaked coconut
          2 tablespoons butter
          1 tablespoon grated orange peel
          2 tablespoons lemon juice
          1 pastry shell (9 inches), baked
    MERINGUE:
          3 egg whites
        1/2 teaspoon vanilla extract
        1/4 teaspoon cream of tartar
          6 tablespoons sugar

In a large saucepan, combine sugar, cornstarch, flour and salt. Gradually stir in water and orange juice until smooth. Cook and stir over medium-high heat until thickened and bubbly. Reduce the heat; cook and stir 2 minutes longer. Remove from the heat.

Stir a small amount of hot filling into egg yolks; return all to the pan, stirring constantly. Bring to a gentle boil; cook and stir 2 minutes longer. Remove from the heat. Stir in the coconut, butter and orange peel. Gently stir in lemon juice. Pour into pastry shell.

In a small bowl, beat egg whites, vanilla and cream of tartar on medium speed until soft peaks form. Gradually beat in sugar, 1 tablespoon at a time, on high until stiff glossy peaks form and sugar is dissolved. Spread evenly over hot filling, sealing edges to crust.

Bake at 350° for 12-15 minutes or until the meringue is golden brown. Cool on a wire rack for 1 hour. Refrigerate for at least 3 hours before serving. Refrigerate leftovers. **Yield:** 6-8 servings.

Pear Praline Pie

PREP: 30 min. **BAKE:** 35 min. + cooling

Looking for a new way to finish off a holiday meal? Try this! Big slices are heavenly served warm or at room temperature.
—Diane Halferty, Corpus Christi, Texas

- 1/4 cup all-purpose flour
- 1/2 teaspoon grated lemon peel
- 1/2 teaspoon ground ginger
- 4 medium pears, peeled and sliced
- Pastry for double-crust pie (9 inches)
- 1 cup packed brown sugar
- 1/2 cup chopped pecans, toasted
- 1/4 cup butter, melted

In a large bowl, combine the flour, lemon peel and ginger. Add pears; toss gently to coat.

Line a 9-in. pie plate with the bottom pastry; trim even with edge of plate. Add pear mixture. Combine the brown sugar, pecans and butter; sprinkle over pears.

Roll out the remaining pastry to fit the top of the pie; cut a decorative design in the center if desired. Place over the filling; trim, seal and flute the edges. (If using the whole pastry on top without a decorative design, cut slits in pastry.)

Bake at 400° for 35-45 minutes or until the filling is bubbly and the pears are tender (cover edges with foil during the last 15 minutes to prevent overbrowning if necessary). Cool completely on a wire rack. Store in the refrigerator. **Yield:** 6-8 servings.

Susan's Favorite Mocha Cake

(Pictured above right)

PREP: 30 min. **BAKE:** 25 min. + chilling

My family members always request "the best cake in the world" for Christmas dinner. I know they mean this luscious dessert.
—Susan Bazan, Sequim, Washington

- 1 package (18-1/4 ounces) chocolate cake mix
- 1-3/4 cups sour cream
- 2 eggs
- 1/2 cup coffee liqueur
- 1/4 cup canola oil
- 2 cups (12 ounces) semisweet chocolate chips, *divided*
- 1 package (10 to 12 ounces) white baking chips
- 1/3 cup butter, cubed
- 1 tablespoon instant coffee granules
- 1 teaspoon rum extract
- 1 envelope unflavored gelatin
- 1-1/2 cups heavy whipping cream, *divided*
- **WHIPPED CREAM:**
- 2 cups heavy whipping cream
- 1/2 cup sugar
- 1 teaspoon vanilla extract

In a large bowl, combine the cake mix, sour cream, eggs, coffee liqueur and oil; beat on low speed for 30 seconds. Beat on medium for 2 minutes. Stir in 1 cup chocolate chips. Transfer to three greased and floured 9-in. round baking pans.

Bake at 350° for 24-28 minutes or until a toothpick inserted near the center comes out clean. Cool cakes for 10 minutes before removing from pans to wire racks to cool completely.

In a microwave, melt the white baking chips, butter and remaining chocolate chips; stir until smooth. Stir in coffee granules and extract. Cool to room temperature.

In a small saucepan, sprinkle the gelatin over 1/4 cup cream; let stand for 1 minute. Heat over low heat, stirring until gelatin is completely dissolved. Stir into the cooled chocolate mixture. In a large bowl, beat the remaining 1-1/4 cups cream until soft peaks form. Add to the cooled chocolate mixture; beat until stiff peaks form.

For whipped cream, in a small bowl, beat cream until it begins to thicken. Add sugar and vanilla; beat until stiff peaks form.

Place the bottom cake layer on a serving plate; top with half of the chocolate mixture. Repeat layers. Top with the remaining cake layer. Frost the top and sides of cake with whipped cream. Refrigerate for at least 2 hours before serving. **Yield:** 16 servings.

Poteca Cake

(Pictured above)

PREP: 25 min. + chilling **BAKE:** 1 hour + cooling

Our city of Rock Springs is home to 56 nationalities, and this delightful holiday dessert showcases its Slavic heritage.
—*Rachelle Strattoin, Rock Springs, Wyoming*

- **1 cup butter, cubed**
- **1/2 cup 2% milk**
- **3 egg yolks, beaten**
- **2 packages (1/4 ounce *each*) active dry yeast**
- **1/4 cup warm water (110° to 115°)**
- **2-1/2 cups all-purpose flour**
- **1 tablespoon sugar**
- **1/4 teaspoon salt**

FILLING:
- **2 cups ground walnuts**
- **2 cups chopped dates**
- **1/4 cup 2% milk**
- **3 tablespoons plus 1 cup sugar, *divided***
- **1/2 teaspoon ground cinnamon**
- **3 egg whites**

Confectioners' sugar, optional

In a small saucepan, melt butter with the milk; cool. Stir in egg yolks until blended. In a small bowl, dissolve yeast in warm water.

In a large bowl, combine the flour, sugar and salt; add the butter mixture and yeast mixture. Beat on medium speed for 3 minutes (the dough will be sticky). Cover and refrigerate overnight.

In a small saucepan over medium heat, combine the walnuts, dates, milk, 3 tablespoons sugar and cinnamon. Cook and stir until mixture forms a paste. Transfer to a large bowl.

In a small bowl, beat the egg whites until soft peaks form. Gradually beat in remaining sugar, 1 tablespoon at a time, on high until stiff peaks form. Fold into the walnut mixture.

Cut the dough in half; on a floured surface, roll one portion of dough into a 20-inch square. Spread with half of the filling. Roll up tightly jelly-roll style. Place, seam side up, in a greased 10-in. tube pan. Repeat with the second portion of dough; place, seam side down, over the first roll-up in tube pan (the layered roll-ups will bake as one loaf).

Bake at 350° for 60-70 minutes or until golden brown. Cool for 10 minutes before removing from pan to a wire rack to cool completely. Sprinkle with confectioners' sugar if desired. **Yield:** 12 servings.

Almond Snack Cake

PREP: 10 min. **BAKE:** 25 min. + cooling

My oldest son was allergic to chocolate, so I needed to find treats I could fix without it. With this cake's yummy flavor, he never felt deprived. —Mary Lou Crabill, Peyton, Colorado

- **4 eggs**
- **2-1/4 cups sugar,** *divided*
- **1 cup butter, melted**
- **2 cups all-purpose flour**
- **1/4 teaspoon salt**
- **1-1/2 teaspoons almond extract**
- **1/2 cup sliced almonds**

In a large bowl, beat eggs until light and lemon-colored. Gradually add 2 cups sugar, beating until combined. Stir in the butter, flour, salt and extract.

Spread into a greased 13-in. x 9-in. baking pan. Sprinkle with almonds and remaining sugar. Bake at 350° for 25-30 minutes or until a toothpick inserted near the center comes out clean. Cool on a wire rack. **Yield:** 24 servings.

Fresh Blueberry Pie

(Pictured below and on page 104)

PREP: 20 min. + chilling

We live in blueberry country, and here is one of my favorite ways to use the bountiful crop. We've been enjoying this berry–filled pie ever since a neighbor introduced us to it years ago.
—R. Ricks, Kalamazoo, Michigan

- **3/4 cup sugar**
- **3 tablespoons cornstarch**
- **1/8 teaspoon salt**
- **1/4 cup water**
- **4 cups fresh blueberries,** *divided*
- **1 graham cracker crust (9 inches)**
Whipped cream

In a large saucepan, combine the sugar, cornstarch and salt. Gradually add the water, stirring until smooth. Stir in 2 cups of blueberries. Bring to a boil; cook and stir for 1-2 minutes or until thickened. Remove from the heat; cool to room temperature.

Spoon remaining blueberries into the crust; top with cooled blueberry mixture. Cover and refrigerate for 1-2 hours or until chilled. Serve with whipped cream. **Yield:** 6-8 servings.

Grandma's Lemon Poppy Seed Cake

(Pictured above and on page 104)

PREP: 20 min. **BAKE:** 30 min. + cooling

This moist cake comes from a collection of family recipes. My granddaughter, Riley, likes that it tastes like lemons but is sweet.
—Phyllis Harmon, Nelson, Wisconsin

- **1 package (18-1/4 ounces) lemon cake mix**
- **1 package (3.4 ounces) instant vanilla pudding mix**
- **4 eggs**
- **1 cup water**
- **1/2 cup canola oil**
- **1/4 cup poppy seeds**
DRIZZLE:
- **2 cups confectioners' sugar**
- **2 tablespoons water**
- **2 tablespoons lemon juice**

In a large bowl, combine cake mix, pudding mix, eggs, water and oil; beat on low speed for 30 seconds. Beat on medium for 2 minutes. Fold in poppy seeds. Transfer to a greased and floured 13-in. x 9-in. baking pan. Bake at 350° for 30-35 minutes or until a toothpick inserted near center comes out clean. Cool on a wire rack.

For drizzle, in a small bowl, combine the confectioners' sugar, water and lemon juice; drizzle over the cake. **Yield:** 15 servings.

Cherry Cola Chocolate Cake

(Pictured below)

PREP: 30 min. + standing **COOK:** 2 hours + standing

For a truly different chocolate cake, think outside the box—boxed mix, that is—and inside your slow cooker! This crowd-pleasing dessert always comes out warm, moist, fudgy and wonderful.
—Elaine Sweet, Dallas, Texas

- 1/2 cup cola
- 1/2 cup dried tart cherries
- 1-1/2 cups all-purpose flour
- 1/2 cup sugar
- 2 ounces semisweet chocolate, chopped
- 2-1/2 teaspoons baking powder
- 1/2 teaspoon salt
- 1 cup chocolate milk
- 1/2 cup butter, melted
- 2 teaspoons vanilla extract

TOPPING:

- 1-1/4 cups cola
- 1/2 cup sugar
- 1/2 cup packed brown sugar
- 2 ounces semisweet chocolate, chopped
- 1/4 cup dark rum

Vanilla ice cream and maraschino cherries, optional

In a small saucepan, bring the cola and dried cherries to a boil. Remove from the heat; let stand for 30 minutes.

In a large bowl, combine the flour, sugar, chocolate, baking powder and salt. Combine the chocolate milk, butter and vanilla; stir into the dry ingredients just until moistened. Fold in the cherry mixture. Pour into a 3-qt.

slow cooker coated with cooking spray.

For topping, in a small saucepan, combine the cola, sugar and brown sugar. Cook and stir until the sugar is dissolved. Remove from the heat; stir in chocolate and rum until smooth. Pour over cherry mixture; do not stir.

Cover and cook on high for 2 to 2-1/2 hours or until set. Turn off heat; let stand, covered, for 30 minutes. Serve warm with ice cream and maraschino cherries if desired. **Yield:** 8 servings.

Editor's Note: This recipe does not use eggs.

Raspberry Apple Cake

(Pictured above)

PREP: 15 min. **BAKE:** 30 min. + chilling

This was the first-place recipe at the Apple Festival in Lincoln County, North Carolina. I spread raspberry jam over the crust, then cover that with pie filling and a sour cream topping.
—Pinkie Mosteller, Lincolnton, North Carolina

- 1/3 cup butter, softened
- 1/3 cup packed brown sugar
- 1 egg
- 1 cup all-purpose flour
- 1/2 teaspoon baking powder
- 1/4 teaspoon salt
- 1/4 cup seedless raspberry jam
- 1 can (21 ounces) apple pie filling
- 4 tablespoons sugar, *divided*
- 1/2 teaspoon ground cinnamon
- 1 cup (8 ounces) sour cream
- 1 teaspoon vanilla extract

In a small bowl, cream the butter and brown sugar until light and fluffy. Beat in egg. Combine the flour, baking powder and salt; gradually add to the creamed mixture and mix well.

Spread into a greased 9-in. square baking pan. Bake at 350° for 20-25 minutes or until lightly browned.

Remove the cake. Spread with jam and top with pie filling. Combine 1 tablespoon sugar and the cinnamon; sprinkle over filling. Combine the sour cream, vanilla and remaining sugar; spread over top.

Bake 10 minutes longer or until the topping is set. Cool on a wire rack for 1 hour. Refrigerate for 3 hours or until chilled. **Yield:** 6 servings.

Sweet Potato Praline Pie

PREP: 30 min. **BAKE:** 50 min. + cooling

Here's a new, delicious twist on a holiday classic. Macadamia nuts are popular in our family, and the praline accent is what makes this treat extra special. Garnish it with whipped cream.
—*Marie Rizzio, Interlochen, Michigan*

Pastry for single-crust pie (9 inches)
- 2 eggs
- 2 cups mashed sweet potatoes
- 1 can (12 ounces) evaporated milk
- 3/4 cup sugar
- 1 teaspoon ground cinnamon
- 1 teaspoon vanilla extract
- 1/2 teaspoon ground ginger
- 1/2 teaspoon ground nutmeg
- 1/4 teaspoon salt

TOPPING:
- 3 tablespoons brown sugar
- 3 tablespoons light corn syrup
- 1 tablespoon butter
- 1/2 teaspoon vanilla extract
- 1 jar (3 ounces) macadamia nuts, coarsely chopped
- 1/2 cup heavy whipping cream, whipped

Line a 9-in. pie plate with pastry. Trim the pastry to 1/2 in. beyond edge of plate; flute edges.

In a large bowl, combine eggs, sweet potatoes, milk, sugar, cinnamon, vanilla, ginger, nutmeg and salt. Pour into pastry. Bake at 425° for 15 minutes. Reduce heat to 350°; bake 25 minutes longer.

Meanwhile, in a small saucepan, bring the brown sugar, corn syrup and butter to a boil. Reduce the heat; simmer, uncovered, for 2 minutes. Remove from the heat; stir in the vanilla.

Sprinkle the nuts over the pie; drizzle with the caramel. Place a foil-lined baking sheet on a rack below the pie to catch any spills. Bake pie 10-15 minutes longer or until caramel starts to bubble. Cover edges with foil to prevent overbrowning if necessary. Cool on a wire rack.

Garnish pie with whipped cream. Refrigerate leftovers.
Yield: 8 servings.

Frozen Peach Pies

(Pictured below)

PREP: 20 min. **BAKE:** 10 min. + freezing

Mellow peaches and crunchy graham crackers combine perfectly in these fluffy favorites. I freeze them for up to 3 days.
—*Athena Russell, Florence, South Carolina*

- 2-1/2 cups graham cracker crumbs
- 1/2 cup plus 2 tablespoons butter, melted
- 1/4 cup sugar
- 1 can (14 ounces) sweetened condensed milk
- 1/4 cup lemon juice
- 1/4 cup orange juice
- 1 package (16 ounces) frozen unsweetened sliced peaches
- 1 tablespoon grated lemon peel
- 1-1/2 cups heavy whipping cream

In a small bowl, combine graham cracker crumbs, butter and sugar; press onto the bottom and up the sides of two greased 9-in. pie plates. Bake at 350° for 10-12 minutes or until lightly browned. Cool on wire racks.

In a blender, combine milk, lemon juice, orange juice, peaches and lemon peel; cover and process until smooth. Transfer to a large bowl. In a large bowl, beat cream until stiff peaks form; fold into peach mixture.

Spoon into crusts. Cover and freeze for at least 4 hours or until firm. Remove from the freezer 15 minutes before serving. **Yield:** 2 pies (8 servings each).

With clean beaters, beat egg whites on medium speed until soft peaks form. Gradually fold into batter. Spread into a greased 13-in. x 9-in. baking pan.

Bake at 350° for 40-45 minutes or until the cake springs back when lightly touched. Place the pan on a wire rack.

Poke holes in cake with a skewer, about 1/2 in. apart. Combine the syrup ingredients; slowly pour over the cake, allowing the mixture to absorb into cake. Let stand for 30 minutes. Cover and refrigerate for 2 hours.

In a large bowl, beat the whipping cream until it begins to thicken. Add the confectioners' sugar and vanilla; beat until soft peaks form. Spread over the cake; sprinkle with coconut. **Yield:** 15 servings.

Fluffy Key Lime Pie

(Pictured below)

PREP: 20 min. + chilling

For a taste of the tropics, try this creamy lime creation. It's on the lighter side and calls for only five simple ingredients.
—*Frances VanFossan, Warren, Michigan*

- 1 package (.3 ounce) sugar-free lime gelatin
- 1/4 cup boiling water
- 2 cartons (6 ounces *each*) key lime yogurt
- 1 carton (8 ounces) frozen fat-free whipped topping, thawed
- 1 reduced-fat graham cracker crust (8 inches)

In a large bowl, dissolve gelatin in boiling water. Whisk in yogurt. Fold in whipped topping. Pour into crust.

Cover and refrigerate pie for at least 2 hours or until set. **Yield:** 8 servings.

Coconut Cream Yummy Cake

(Pictured above)

PREP: 30 min. **BAKE:** 40 min. + chilling

I saw this in one of Mom's cookbooks when I was a kid. I baked the cake years later, and now I get requests for it each Christmas. Sometimes I tint the coconut red and green for the holiday.
—*Angela Renae Fox, Gober, Texas*

- 6 egg whites
- 3/4 cup butter, softened
- 1-1/3 cups sugar
- 1 cup coconut milk
- 1/2 cup 2% milk
- 2 teaspoons vanilla extract
- 2-1/4 cups cake flour
- 2-1/2 teaspoons baking powder
- 1 teaspoon salt

SYRUP:
- 1 can (13.66 ounces) coconut milk
- 1 can (14 ounces) sweetened condensed milk

TOPPING:
- 1-1/2 cups heavy whipping cream
- 3 tablespoons confectioners' sugar
- 1/4 teaspoon vanilla extract

Flaked coconut

Place the egg whites in a large bowl; let stand at room temperature for 30 minutes.

Meanwhile, in another large bowl, cream the butter and sugar until light and fluffy. Combine the coconut milk, milk and vanilla. Combine the flour, baking powder and salt; add to the creamed mixture alternately with the milk mixture.

Southern Honey-Pecan Pie

PREP: 15 min. **BAKE:** 45 min. + cooling

Packed with pecans, this recipe makes a classic even sweeter with the addition of honey. I like a piece with a hot cup of coffee.
—*Allie Smith, New Orleans, Louisiana*

- 1/4 cup sugar
- 3 tablespoons all-purpose flour
- 3 eggs, lightly beaten
- 1 cup honey
- 1/3 cup butter, melted
- 1 teaspoon vanilla extract
- 1/4 teaspoon salt
- 1 cup chopped pecans
- 1 unbaked pastry shell (9 inches)
- 1/2 cup pecan halves

In a small bowl, combine the sugar and flour. Stir in the eggs, honey, butter, vanilla and salt. Add chopped pecans and mix well. Pour into the pastry shell. Arrange pecan halves around edge and center of pie.

Cover the edges loosely with foil. Bake at 350° for 25 minutes. Remove the foil; bake 20-25 minutes longer or until a knife inserted near the center comes out clean. Cool pie on a wire rack. Store in the refrigerator. **Yield:** 6-8 servings.

Red Raspberry Pie

PREP: 20 min. + standing **BAKE:** 45 min. + cooling

This ruby-red raspberry pie bursts with the fresh-picked flavor of summer...and is a breeze to prepare using a refrigerated crust.
—*Patricia Morrow, Mapleton, Minnesota*

- 1-1/2 cups plus 1/2 teaspoon sugar, *divided*
- 1/3 cup quick-cooking tapioca
- 1/4 teaspoon salt
- 6 cups fresh raspberries
- 1 teaspoon lime juice
- Pastry for double-crust pie (9 inches)
- 1 tablespoon butter
- 1 teaspoon 2% milk

In a large bowl, combine 1-1/2 cups sugar, tapioca and salt. Add raspberries and lime juice; toss gently to coat. Let stand for 15 minutes.

Line a 9-in. pie plate with the bottom pastry; trim even with edge of plate. Add filling; dot with butter. Roll out remaining pastry to fit top of pie; place over filling. Trim, seal and flute the edges. Cut slits in top. Brush with milk; sprinkle with remaining sugar.

Bake at 450° for 10 minutes. Reduce heat to 350°; bake 35-40 minutes longer or until the crust is golden brown and the filling is bubbly. Cover the edges with foil during the last 15 minutes to prevent overbrowning if necessary. Cool on a wire rack. Store pie in the refrigerator. **Yield:** 6-8 servings.

Macadamia Toffee Snack Cake

(Pictured above and on page 104)

PREP: 15 min. **BAKE:** 30 min. + cooling

I worked in a restaurant preparing desserts and love serving them to family and friends. This crowd-pleasing favorite is loaded with white chocolate chips, macadamia nuts and coconut.
—*Marie Zajdowicz, Riva, Maryland*

- 2 cups all-purpose flour
- 1-1/2 cups packed brown sugar
- 1/2 cup cold butter
- 1 teaspoon baking powder
- 1/2 teaspoon salt
- 1 egg
- 1 cup milk
- 1 teaspoon vanilla extract
- 1 cup vanilla *or* white chips
- 1/2 cup chopped macadamia nuts
- 1/4 cup flaked coconut

In a large bowl, combine the flour and brown sugar. Cut in the butter until the mixture resembles coarse crumbs. Set aside 1 cup for the topping. Add baking powder and salt to remaining crumb mixture. In another bowl, whisk the egg, milk and vanilla. Stir into the crumb mixture just until moistened.

Transfer to a greased 13-in. x 9-in. baking pan; sprinkle with the reserved topping mixture, vanilla chips, nuts and coconut. Bake at 350° for 30-35 minutes or until golden brown and the edges pull away from the sides of the pan. Cool completely on a wire rack before cutting. **Yield:** 20 servings.

Peachy Gingerbread Cake Roll

(Pictured below)

PREP: 25 min. **BAKE:** 15 min. + cooling

My dad loved gingerbread, so I combined a few dessert ideas to create this one for him. It gets kudos every time I serve it.
—Dawn DePew, Blacklick, Ohio

    4 eggs
  1/2 cup sugar
  1/2 cup packed dark brown sugar
  1/4 cup water
    3 tablespoons butter, melted
    3 tablespoons molasses
    1 teaspoon vanilla extract
1-1/3 cups all-purpose flour
    2 teaspoons pumpkin pie spice
    1 teaspoon ground cinnamon
  1/2 teaspoon baking powder
  1/2 teaspoon baking soda
  1/4 teaspoon salt
       Confectioners' sugar
FILLING:
    3 packages (two 8 ounces, one 3 ounces) cream
       cheese, softened
1-1/4 cups peach preserves
1-1/4 teaspoons ground ginger
1-1/4 teaspoons ground cinnamon
  1/4 teaspoon ground nutmeg
       Confectioners' sugar and sliced peaches, optional

Line a greased 15-in. x 10-in. x 1-in. baking pan with waxed paper; grease the paper and set aside.

In a large bowl, beat the eggs for 3 minutes. Gradually add the sugars, beating until the mixture is thickened. Beat in the water, butter, molasses and vanilla. Combine the flour, pumpkin pie spice, cinnamon, baking powder, baking soda and salt; fold into egg mixture. Spread batter into prepared pan.

Bake at 350° for 12-15 minutes or until cake springs back when lightly touched. Cool for 5 minutes. Invert onto a kitchen towel dusted with confectioners' sugar. Gently peel off waxed paper. Roll up cake in the towel jelly-roll style, starting with a short side. Cool completely on a wire rack.

For filling, in a small bowl, beat the cream cheese, preserves, ginger, cinnamon and nutmeg until smooth. Unroll cake; spread filling over cake to within 1/2 in. of edges. Roll up again. Place seam side down on a serving platter. Dust with confectioners' sugar and garnish with sliced peaches if desired. **Yield:** 12 servings.

Blueberry Citrus Cake

PREP: 40 min. **BAKE:** 20 min. + cooling

This treat is my favorite way to use the blueberries my husband and I grow for market. Both the cake and cream cheese frosting are accented with the flavors of orange and lemon.
—Shirley Cooper, Salemburg, North Carolina

    1 package (18-1/4 ounces) yellow cake mix
    3 eggs
    1 cup orange juice
  1/3 cup canola oil
1-1/2 cups fresh blueberries
    1 tablespoon grated lemon peel
    1 tablespoon grated orange peel
CITRUS FROSTING:
    1 package (3 ounces) cream cheese, softened
  1/4 cup butter, softened
    3 cups confectioners' sugar
    2 tablespoons orange juice
    2 teaspoons grated orange peel
    1 teaspoon grated lemon peel
    2 cups whipped topping

In a large bowl, combine the cake mix, eggs, orange juice and oil; beat on low speed for 30 seconds. Beat on medium for 2 minutes. Fold in the blueberries, lemon peel and orange peel. Pour into two greased and floured 9-in. round baking pans.

Bake at 350° for 20-25 minutes or until a toothpick inserted near the center comes out clean. Cool cakes for 10 minutes before removing from pans to wire racks to cool completely.

For the frosting, in a small bowl, combine the cream cheese and butter until fluffy. Add the confectioners' sugar, orange juice and peels; beat until blended. Fold in the whipped topping.

Spread the frosting between the cake layers and over the top and sides of cake. Refrigerate until serving. **Yield:** 12 servings.

Vanilla Custard Pie

(Pictured above)

PREP: 30 min. **BAKE:** 15 min. + chilling

My grandmother passed down this recipe to my mother, who in turn passed it down to me. Now, my daughter is preparing it for her own family. —*Bernard Parys, Ixonia, Wisconsin*

1-1/4 **cups graham cracker crumbs**
    3 **tablespoons brown sugar**
  1/3 **cup butter, melted**
FILLING:
  1/2 **cup sugar**
  1/4 **cup all-purpose flour**
  1/2 **teaspoon salt**
    2 **cups milk**
    2 **egg yolks, lightly beaten**
    2 **teaspoons vanilla extract**
MERINGUE:
    2 **egg whites**
  1/4 **teaspoon vanilla extract**
  1/8 **teaspoon cream of tartar**
  1/4 **cup sugar**
  1/4 **cup graham cracker crumbs**

Combine the graham cracker crumbs, brown sugar and butter; press onto the bottom and up the sides of an ungreased 9-in. pie plate. Bake at 350° for 8-10 minutes or until lightly browned. Cool on a wire rack.

  In a small saucepan, combine the sugar, flour and salt. Stir in milk until smooth. Cook and stir over medium-high heat until thickened and bubbly. Reduce the heat; cook and stir 2 minutes longer. Remove from the heat. Stir a small amount of hot filling into the egg yolks; return all to the pan. Bring to a gentle boil, stirring constantly; cook and stir 2 minutes longer. Remove from the heat. Gently stir in vanilla. Pour into crust.

  In a small bowl, beat the egg whites, vanilla and cream of tartar on medium speed until soft peaks form. Gradually beat in the sugar, 1 tablespoon at a time, on high until stiff peaks form. Spread over the hot filling, sealing the edges to the crust. Sprinkle with the graham cracker crumbs.

  Bake at 350° for 15 minutes or until golden brown. Cool on a wire rack for 1 hour. Refrigerate for at least 3 hours before serving. **Yield:** 8 servings.

Chunky Fresh Mango Cake

(Pictured below)

PREP: 20 min. **BAKE:** 30 min. + cooling

Sweet, moist and nutty with slightly crisp edges, this after-dinner delight is scrumptious. It originated years ago with a great-aunt who lived in Florida and had her own mango tree.
      —*Allene Bary-Cooper, Wichita Falls, Texas*

  1/2 **cup sugar**
  1/3 **cup canola oil**
    1 **egg**
  1/2 **cup plus 2 tablespoons all-purpose flour**
  3/4 **teaspoon baking powder**
  1/4 **teaspoon salt**
  1/4 **teaspoon ground cinnamon**
  1/8 **teaspoon ground nutmeg**
  3/4 **cup chopped peeled mango**
  1/4 **cup chopped pecans**
Confectioners' sugar and whipped topping, optional

In a small bowl, beat the sugar, oil and egg until well blended. In another bowl, combine flour, baking powder, salt, cinnamon and nutmeg; gradually beat into the sugar mixture and mix well. Fold in mango and pecans.

  Transfer to a greased 6-in. round baking pan. Bake at 375° for 25-30 minutes or until a toothpick inserted near the center comes out clean. Cool for 10 minutes before removing from pan to a wire rack to cool completely.

  Garnish cake with confectioners' sugar and whipped topping if desired. **Yield:** 4 servings.

Just Desserts

It's easy to save room for a sweet treat when these after-dinner delights are on the menu. Indulge in Blackberry-Basil Panna Cotta, Baked Cherry Pudding, White Chocolate Brie Cups, Cool Coffee Gels and much more.

SIMPLY IRRESISTIBLE. Clockwise from top left: Apple Raspberry Crisp (p. 129), Tropical Rainbow Dessert (p. 126), Peach Cobbler (p. 123) and Jam-Topped Mini Cheesecakes (p. 129).

In a small saucepan, sprinkle the gelatin over lime juice and cold water; let stand for 1 minute. Stir in the sugar, eggs and lime peel. Cook and stir over medium heat until mixture reaches 160°. Remove from the heat.

In a large bowl, beat the cream cheese and butter until fluffy. Gradually beat in the gelatin mixture. Cover and refrigerate for 45 minutes or until partially set, stirring occasionally.

In a small bowl, beat the heavy whipping cream until stiff peaks form; fold into the lime mixture. Spoon into the crust. Cover and refrigerate for 3-4 hours or until set. Just before serving, remove the sides of pan. Refrigerate leftovers. **Yield:** 12 servings.

White Chocolate Brie Cups

(Pictured below)

PREP/TOTAL TIME: 25 min.

Try these unique little tarts as a delightfully different treat after dinner…or serve them as sweet appetizers before a special meal.
—*Angela Vitale, Delaware, Ohio*

- 1 package (9 ounces) frozen miniature phyllo tart shells
- 1-1/2 ounces white baking chocolate, chopped
- 2 ounces Brie cheese, chopped
- 1/3 cup orange marmalade

Fill each tart shell with chocolate, then cheese. Place on an ungreased baking sheet. Top with marmalade.

Bake at 350° for 6-8 minutes or until golden brown. Serve warm. **Yield:** 15 appetizers.

No-Bake Lime Cheesecake

(Pictured above)

PREP: 30 min. + chilling

Being from the Sunshine State, I'm a fan of recipes that contain citrus. This one goes together quickly—and disappears almost as fast! I complete each slice with a dollop of whipped cream. For another great cheesecake, substitute orange juice, zest and slices.
—*Robin Spires, Tampa, Florida*

- 3 cups graham cracker crumbs
- 2/3 cup sugar
- 2/3 cup butter, melted

FILLING:

- 2 envelopes unflavored gelatin
- 1 cup lime juice
- 1/4 cup cold water
- 1-1/2 cups sugar
- 5 eggs, lightly beaten
- 2 teaspoons grated lime peel
- 2 packages (8 ounces *each*) cream cheese, softened
- 1/2 cup butter, softened
- 1/2 cup heavy whipping cream

In a large bowl, combine graham cracker crumbs, sugar and butter. Press onto the bottom and 2 in. up the sides of a greased 9-in. springform pan. Cover and refrigerate for at least 30 minutes.

On a lightly floured surface, roll one sheet of puff pastry into an 11-in. x 8-in. rectangle. Combine the sugar and cinnamon; sprinkle half of mixture over pastry.

Working from the short sides, roll up dough jelly-roll style toward the center. With a sharp knife, cut the roll into 1/2-in. slices. Place on parchment paper-lined baking sheets. Repeat with remaining pastry and sugar mixture.

Bake at 375° for 12-15 minutes or until crisp and golden brown. Remove from the pans to wire racks. **Yield:** about 2-1/2 dozen.

Chocolate Banana Bundles

(*Pictured below*)

PREP/TOTAL TIME: 30 min.

Bananas and chocolate make such an irresistible combination that I fix this dessert often. Sometimes, I sprinkle on a dash of sea salt. If you have any of the butter–sugar mixture left over, you could add that, too. —Thomas Faglon, Somerset, New Jersey

  2 **tablespoons butter**
1/4 **cup packed brown sugar**
  2 **medium ripe bananas, halved lengthwise**
  1 **sheet frozen puff pastry, thawed**
  4 **ounces semisweet chocolate, melted**
Vanilla ice cream, optional

In a large skillet, melt butter over medium heat. Stir in brown sugar until blended. Add bananas; stir to coat. Remove from the heat; set aside.

Unfold puff pastry. Cut into four rectangles. Place a halved banana in the center of each square. Overlap two opposite corners of pastry over banana; pinch tightly to seal. Place on parchment paper-lined baking sheets.

Bake at 400° for 20-25 minutes or until golden brown. Drizzle with the chocolate. Serve warm with ice cream if desired. **Yield:** 4 servings.

Molded Margaritas

(*Pictured above*)

PREP: 15 min. + chilling

With a refreshing burst of lime and a fun, festive look, these cool margaritas are perfect for parties. For a non–alcoholic version, simply replace the tequila with an equal amount of water.
—Barbara Gersitz, Philadelphia, Pennsylvania

  2 **packages (3 ounces** *each***) lime gelatin**
  2 **cups boiling water**
1/2 **cup thawed non-alcoholic margarita mix** *or* **limeade concentrate**
1/2 **cup tequila**

In a small bowl, dissolve the gelatin in boiling water. Stir in margarita mix and tequila. Pour into four margarita glasses. Refrigerate for 4 hours or until set. Gently stir with a fork before serving if desired. **Yield:** 4 servings.

Easy Elephant Ears

PREP: 20 min. **BAKE:** 15 min./batch

You'll love the classic cinnamon–sugar flavor of these crispy, bite–size goodies. Even more, you'll love that they require just three ingredients and are so simple to assemble.
—Bob Rose, Waukesha, Wisconsin

  1 **package (17.3 ounces) frozen puff pastry, thawed**
1/2 **cup sugar**
  2 **teaspoons ground cinnamon**

Caramel Pumpkin Tiramisu

(Pictured below)

PREP: 35 min. + chilling

I'm not particularly fond of traditional Italian tiramisu, so I tried adding pumpkin and substituting bourbon for the coffee. It was fabulous! Now, I always prepare more sauce than I'll need and save it to eat over scoops of vanilla ice cream.
—Mary Filipiak, Fort Wayne, Indiana

  18 crisp ladyfinger cookies
1/4 cup maple syrup
  2 tablespoons bourbon
  1 cup heavy whipping cream, *divided*
1/4 cup sugar
3/4 cup solid-pack pumpkin
  1 teaspoon ground cinnamon
1/2 teaspoon ground ginger
1/4 teaspoon salt
  4 ounces cream cheese, softened
  3 tablespoons confectioners' sugar
SAUCE:
3/4 cup caramel ice cream topping
  2 teaspoons bourbon

Using a serrated knife, cut six ladyfinger cookies in half widthwise. In a shallow bowl, combine maple syrup and bourbon. Dip six whole ladyfingers and six halves into mixture; arrange in a single layer in an 8-in. square dish.

In a small bowl, beat 1/2 cup cream until it begins to thicken. Gradually add sugar; beat until soft peaks form. In a large bowl, combine the pumpkin, cinnamon, ginger and salt; fold in whipped cream. In another bowl, beat the cream cheese, confectioners' sugar and remaining cream until thickened.

Spread half of pumpkin mixture over ladyfingers in the dish. Dip remaining ladyfingers; arrange over the top. Top

with the remaining pumpkin mixture and cream cheese mixture. Cover and refrigerate for 8 hours or overnight.

In a microwave, heat caramel sauce; stir in bourbon. Serve warm with tiramisu. **Yield:** 9 servings.

Editor's Note: This recipe was prepared with Alessi brand ladyfinger cookies.

Spiced Tea Delight

(Pictured above)

PREP: 25 min. + chilling

I created this as the finale for an Asian-themed dinner I was serving. The treat has a delicate chai flavor and lovely color.
—Maria Barnet, Elkins Park, Pennsylvania

  3 cups water
  4 ginger-flavored herbal tea bags
  4 green tea bags
  3 envelopes unflavored gelatin
3/4 cup cold water
  1 cup heavy whipping cream
1/2 cup honey
  2 tablespoons brown sugar
1/2 teaspoon ground cinnamon
1/4 teaspoon ground cloves
Additional ground cinnamon, optional

Bring 3 cups water to a boil in a large saucepan; add the tea bags. Cover and steep for 3-5 minutes.

Meanwhile, in a small saucepan, sprinkle gelatin over the cold water; let stand for 1 minute. Heat over low heat, stirring until gelatin is completely dissolved. Stir into tea mixture. Discard tea bags.

Stir in the heavy whipping cream, honey, brown sugar, cinnamon and cloves. Pour into a 5-cup mold coated with cooking spray or divide among six dessert dishes. Cover and refrigerate until set. Sprinkle with additional cinnamon if desired. **Yield:** 6 servings.

Chocolate-Almond Banana Splits

(Pictured below)

PREP/TOTAL TIME: 10 min.

When the weather's warm and your kids are craving something cool and sweet, whip up these speedy banana splits. It's fun to experiment with different kinds of ice cream and toppings.
—*Candace McMenamin, Lexington, South Carolina*

- **2 milk chocolate candy bars with almonds (1.45 ounces *each*), chopped**
- **3 tablespoons heavy whipping cream**
- **2 medium bananas**
- **1 cup chocolate ice cream**
- **2 tablespoons chopped almonds, toasted**

In a microwave, melt the candy bars with the cream. Stir until blended; keep warm.

Halve the bananas lengthwise; arrange in two dessert dishes. Add the ice cream; drizzle with warm chocolate sauce. Sprinkle with almonds. **Yield:** 2 servings.

Peach Cobbler

(Pictured above and on page 118)

PREP: 20 min. **BAKE:** 40 min.

This comforting dessert is heavenly prepared with fresh-picked fruit. I grew up in Oklahoma, and we used Elberta peaches right off our trees when we made this outstanding cobbler.
—*Virginia Crowell, Lyons, Oregon*

- **1 cup all-purpose flour**
- **1/2 cup sugar**
- **2 teaspoons baking powder**
- **1/2 teaspoon salt**
- **1/2 cup milk**
- **3 cups sliced peeled fresh *or* frozen peaches**

TOPPING:
- **2 cups water**
- **1/2 cup sugar**
- **1/2 cup packed brown sugar**
- **1 tablespoon butter**
- **1/4 teaspoon ground nutmeg**

Ground cinnamon, optional
Half-and-half cream

In a large bowl, combine the flour, sugar, baking powder and salt. Stir in milk just until combined; fold in peaches. Spread into a greased 8-in. square baking dish.

In a large saucepan, combine the water, sugars, butter and nutmeg and cinnamon if desired. Bring to a boil, stirring until the sugars are dissolved. Pour over top.

Bake at 400° for 40-50 minutes or until filling is bubbly and a toothpick inserted in topping comes out clean. Serve warm or cold with cream. **Yield:** 8 servings.

Fresh from the Freezer

SUMMERTIME always conjures up images of people enjoying a classic seasonal treat—frozen pops. This year, why not try something deliciously different?

Myrna Campbell, of Philomath, Oregon, shares her delightful new twists on four ice pops here. They showcase fresh herbs for a tongue-tingling flavor sensation your family and friends are sure to love.

Combine blackberry with mint, strawberry with cilantro, lemon with rosemary or peach with thyme. Each fruit-and-herb combo is a breeze to make.

Chances are, after trying these yummy creations, you'll never see frozen pops the same way again!

Blackberry Mint Pops

(Pictured at bottom in the photo below left)

PREP: 20 min. + freezing

Mint is always so refreshing. On a summer's day when you need to cool off, it's hard to resist a minty treat like this one.
—*Myrna Campbell, Philomath, Oregon*

- **2 cups water**
- **1 cup packed brown sugar**
- **2 cups strained blackberry puree (from 4 cups fresh blackberries)**
- **1/4 cup minced fresh mint**
- **16 Popsicle molds *or* paper cups (3 ounces *each*) and Popsicle sticks**

In a small saucepan, bring the water and brown sugar to a boil. Cook and stir until the sugar is dissolved. Stir in the blackberry puree and mint.

Fill the molds or cups with 1/4 cup fruit mixture. Freeze for 1 hour or until slushy.

Insert a stick into each mold or cup and gently stir to distribute the mint; freeze the pops until firm. **Yield:** 16 pops.

Strawberry Cilantro Pops

(Pictured at top in the photo at left)

PREP: 20 min. + freezing

People are drawn to these pops because of the sweet strawberries, which just about everyone likes. The cilantro is the bonus!
—*Myrna Campbell, Philomath, Oregon*

- **2 cups water**
- **1 cup packed brown sugar**
- **2 cups strawberry puree**
- **3 tablespoons minced fresh cilantro**
- **2 tablespoons lime juice**
- **16 Popsicle molds *or* paper cups (3 ounces *each*) and Popsicle sticks**

In a small saucepan, bring the water and brown sugar to a boil. Cook and stir until the sugar is dissolved. Stir in the strawberry puree, cilantro and lime juice.

Fill molds or cups with 1/4 cup fruit mixture. Freeze for 1 hour or until slushy.

Insert a stick into each mold or cup and gently stir to distribute the cilantro; freeze the pops until firm. **Yield:** 16 pops.

Rosemary Lemonade Pops

(Pictured at right in the photo at left)

PREP: 20 min. + freezing

Lemonade on a hot afternoon? It's a no-brainer...and these fun sweets take that classic taste up a notch with fresh rosemary.
—*Myrna Campbell, Philomath, Oregon*

- **2 cups water**
- **1 cup packed brown sugar**
- **3/4 cup lemon juice**
- **1 teaspoon minced fresh rosemary**
- **12 Popsicle molds *or* paper cups (3 ounces *each*) and Popsicle sticks**

In a small saucepan, bring the water and brown sugar to a boil. Cook and stir until the sugar is dissolved. Stir in the lemon juice and rosemary.

Fill molds or cups with 1/4 cup lemon mixture. Freeze for 1 hour or until slushy.

Insert a stick into each mold or cup and gently stir to distribute the rosemary; freeze the pops until firm. **Yield:** 12 pops.

Peach Thyme Pops

(Pictured at left in the photo at far left)

PREP: 20 min. + freezing

These treats really are peachy keen! The combination of that mellow fruit and the thyme in these pops is simply wonderful.
—*Myrna Campbell, Philomath, Oregon*

- **2 cups water**
- **1 cup packed brown sugar**
- **2 cups peach puree**
- **1 teaspoon minced fresh thyme**
- **16 Popsicle molds *or* paper cups (3 ounces *each*) and Popsicle sticks**

In a small saucepan, bring the water and brown sugar to a boil. Cook and stir until the sugar is dissolved. Stir in the peach puree and thyme.

Fill the molds or cups with 1/4 cup fruit mixture. Freeze for 1 hour or until slushy.

Insert a stick into each mold or cup and gently stir to distribute the thyme; freeze the pops until firm. **Yield:** 16 pops.

HERB APPEAL. Fresh herbs give delightful flair to the recipes on this page. Here are two easy ways to store your fresh herbs to better preserve their flavor and nutrients:
- Dry Them—Simply snip off healthy branches and remove the leaves from the bottom inch of the stem. Bundle several stems together with a string or rubber band, then hang them upside down in a warm, airy room. Check them weekly until they are completely dry, them crumble the leaves into spice jars.
- Freeze Them—Chop herbs and fill the sections of an ice cube tray with them. Then carefully pour water into each herb-filled compartment and freeze them until needed.

Blackberry-Basil Panna Cotta

(Pictured above)

PREP: 35 min. + chilling

I love the simple taste and texture of panna cotta. I decided to try preparing it with fresh blackberries and basil from our local farmers market, and my family really enjoyed the results.
—Karen Shelton, Collierville, Tennessee

> 2 **cups heavy whipping cream**
> 2 **cups half-and-half cream**
> 3/4 **cup sugar**
> 2 **envelopes unflavored gelatin**
> 2 **teaspoons grated lemon peel**
> 1-1/2 **teaspoons vanilla extract**

SAUCE:

> 2 **cups fresh blackberries *or* frozen blackberries**
> 1 **cup sugar**
> 1 **cup blackberry wine *or* ruby port wine**
> 1/4 **cup minced fresh basil**
> 2 **tablespoons cold butter**

Additional blackberries and fresh basil, optional

In a small saucepan, combine the heavy whipping cream, half-and-half cream and sugar. Sprinkle with the gelatin; let stand for 1 minute. Heat over low heat, stirring until sugar and gelatin are completely dissolved. Remove from the heat; stir in lemon peel and vanilla.

Pour into six 6-oz. ramekins or custard cups coated with cooking spray. Cover and refrigerate for at least 4 hours or until set.

For sauce, in a small saucepan, combine blackberries, sugar and blackberry wine. Bring to a boil; cook until mixture is thickened and reduced to about 1-1/4 cups. Remove from the heat; stir in basil and butter. Cool to room temperature.

Unmold panna cotta onto dessert plates; serve with sauce. Garnish with additional blackberries and basil if desired. **Yield:** 6 servings.

Tropical Rainbow Dessert

(Pictured below and on page 118)

PREP: 30 min. + chilling

Classic ribbon gelatin salad gets a makeover with this tropical treatment. Cream of coconut creates the creamy layers.
—Dan Kelmenson, West Bloomfield, Michigan

> 2 **packages (3 ounces *each*) strawberry gelatin, *divided***
> 5 **cups boiling water, *divided***
> 5 **cups cold water, *divided***
> 1 **can (15 ounces) cream of coconut, *divided***
> 2 **packages (3 ounces *each*) orange gelatin, *divided***
> 2 **packages (3 ounces *each*) pineapple gelatin, *divided***
> 2 **packages (3 ounces *each*) lime gelatin, *divided***

In a small bowl, dissolve one package of strawberry gelatin in 3/4 cup boiling water. Stir in 3/4 cup cold water. Divide among 12 dessert dishes and refrigerate until set, or pour into a 3-qt. gelatin mold coated with cooking spray and refrigerate until set but not firm, 20-25 minutes.

In a small bowl, dissolve the remaining package of strawberry gelatin in 1/2 cup boiling water. Add 1/2 cup cold water and scant 1/2 cup cream of coconut; stir. Spoon over the first layer. Chill until set but not firm, 20-25 minutes.

Repeat six times, alternating plain gelatin layers with creamy gelatin layers. Chill each layer until set but not firm before spooning the next layer on top. Refrigerate for 4 hours or overnight. Unmold onto a serving platter. **Yield:** 12 servings.

Editor's Note: This recipe takes time to prepare since each layer must be set before the next layer is added.

Cool Coffee Gels

PREP/TOTAL TIME: 20 min.

If you like coffee, you'll really like this! It's a yummy java dessert served in mugs or custard cups and eaten with a spoon.
—Lily Julow, Gainesville, Florida

> 1 **envelope unflavored gelatin**
> 1/4 **cup cold water**
> 1-1/2 **cups hot brewed coffee**
> 1/4 **cup plus 2 tablespoons sugar,** *divided*
> 1/2 **cup heavy whipping cream**
> **Instant espresso powder and chocolate-covered coffee beans, optional**

In a small saucepan, sprinkle the gelatin over the cold water; let stand for 1 minute. Stir in the hot coffee and 1/4 cup sugar. Heat over low heat, stirring until gelatin is completely dissolved.

Pour into four Irish coffee mugs or 4-oz. custard cups. Cover and refrigerate until set.

In a large bowl, beat cream until it begins to thicken. Add remaining sugar; beat until stiff peaks form. Serve with gelatin. Garnish with espresso powder and coffee beans if desired. **Yield:** 4 servings.

Lemonade Cheesecake Parfaits

PREP: 40 min. + chilling

My friends rave about the contrasting tart lemonade and sweet cheesecake layers in these parfaits. For an elegant presentation, I top them with crushed pomegranate seeds and lemon zest.
—Teena Petrus, Johnstown, Pennsylvania

> 2 **whole graham crackers, crushed**
> 1 **cup half-and-half cream**
> 1-3/4 **cups sugar,** *divided*
> 2 **tablespoons lemon juice,** *divided*
> 2 **envelopes unflavored gelatin**
> 1 **package (8 ounces) cream cheese, softened**
> 3 **teaspoons grated lemon peel,** *divided*
> 1 **teaspoon vanilla extract**
> 1-1/4 **cups cold water**
> 1 **tablespoon grenadine syrup**
> **Dash salt**

Divide the graham crackers among six dessert dishes. In a small saucepan, combine cream, 1 cup sugar and 1 tablespoon lemon juice. Sprinkle 1 envelope of gelatin over the cream mixture; let stand for 1 minute or until softened. Heat over low heat, stirring until gelatin and sugar are completely dissolved.

In a large bowl, beat the cream cheese until smooth. Beat in gelatin mixture. Stir in 1 teaspoon lemon peel and vanilla. Pour into glasses over the graham crackers, about 1/2 cup in each. Cover and refrigerate until firm.

In a small saucepan, combine the water, grenadine, salt and remaining sugar and lemon juice. Sprinkle remaining

gelatin over the water mixture; let stand for 1 minute. Heat over low heat, stirring until gelatin and sugar are completely dissolved. Pour 2 tablespoons mixture into each parfait glass. Cover and refrigerate until firm.

Refrigerate remaining grenadine mixture until syrupy, about 30 minutes. With a hand mixer, beat until frothy. Divide among glasses. Cover and refrigerate until firm. Garnish with remaining lemon peel. **Yield:** 6 parfaits.

Instant Chocolate Pastries

(Pictured above)

PREP/TOTAL TIME: 20 min.

My sister and I became "addicted" to Nutella while traveling in Europe. Now, we're always thinking of ways to incorporate that rich spread into recipes. This one came about after making puff pastries with apples. We thought, "Why not try chocolate?"
—Dee Wolf, Syracuse, Utah

> 1 **sheet frozen puff pastry, thawed**
> 6 **tablespoons Nutella (chocolate hazelnut spread)**
> 1 **egg, beaten**
> **Confectioners' sugar, optional**

Unfold puff pastry; cut into six rectangles. Place on a greased baking sheet. Spread 1 tablespoon Nutella over half of a rectangle; fold dough over filling. Press edges with a fork to seal. Repeat for remaining pastries. Brush with egg; prick tops with a fork.

Bake at 400° for 10-14 minutes or until puffy and golden brown. Sprinkle with confectioners' sugar if desired. Serve warm. **Yield:** 6 servings.

Editor's Note: Look for Nutella in the peanut butter section of your grocery store.

Buttery Rhubarb Baklava

(Pictured above)

PREP: 45 min. **BAKE:** 35 min. + standing

I like to bring goodies for my coworkers at the nursery/gift shop where I work. When rhubarb season arrives, I make this rich, sweet baklava so I can share the fruits of my garden.
—*Sue Bolsinger, Anchorage, Alaska*

     1 cup butter, melted
    20 sheets phyllo dough (14 inches x 9 inches)
     3 cups finely chopped walnuts
 1-1/2 cups finely chopped fresh *or* frozen rhubarb
     1 cup sugar
 1-1/2 teaspoons ground cinnamon
 1-1/2 cups honey

Brush a 13-in. x 9-in. baking pan with some of the butter. Unroll phyllo dough; trim to fit into pan. In a large bowl, combine the walnuts, rhubarb, sugar and cinnamon.

Layer five sheets of phyllo dough in the prepared pan, brushing each with butter. (Keep remaining phyllo covered with plastic wrap and a damp towel to prevent it from drying out.) Sprinkle with a third of the nut mixture. Repeat layers twice. Top with remaining phyllo dough, brushing each sheet with butter.

Using a sharp knife, cut baklava into 1-1/2-in. diamond shapes. Bake at 350° for 35-40 minutes or until golden brown. In a small saucepan, heat honey over low heat until thinned. Pour over warm baklava. Cool completely on a wire rack. Cover and let stand for several hours or overnight. **Yield:** 2-1/2 dozen.

Editor's Note: If using frozen rhubarb, measure the rhubarb while still frozen, then thaw completely. Drain in a colander, but do not press liquid out.

Baked Cherry Pudding

PREP: 10 min. **BAKE:** 30 min.

Our mother managed to please all six of her children with her great cooking. One of my brothers was especially fond of her cherry pudding. Every time he came home, Mom would fix this cakelike dessert. Now, I surprise him with it when he visits me.
—*Loretta Broderick, Plattsburg, Missouri*

 1-2/3 cups sugar, *divided*
     1 cup all-purpose flour
     2 teaspoons baking powder
   1/8 teaspoon salt
   2/3 cup milk
     1 can (14-1/2 ounces) pitted tart cherries, undrained
     1 tablespoon butter

In a small bowl, combine 2/3 cup sugar, flour, baking powder and salt. Stir in milk. Spread into a greased 11-in. x 7-in. baking dish; set aside.

In a small saucepan, combine the cherries, butter and remaining sugar. Bring to a boil; cook and stir for 1-2 minutes or until the sugar is dissolved. Spoon over crust. Bake at 350° for 30-35 minutes or until golden brown. Serve warm. **Yield:** 6 servings.

Lemony Gingerbread Whoopie Pies

PREP: 25 min. + chilling **BAKE:** 10 min./batch + cooling

These yummy whoopie pies combine two popular flavors in one treat. The moist ginger cookies are rolled in sugar before baking for a bit of crunch. A lemony filling is the finishing touch.
—*Jamie Jones, Madison, Georgia*

   3/4 cup butter, softened
   3/4 cup packed brown sugar
   1/2 cup molasses
     1 egg
     3 cups all-purpose flour
     2 teaspoons ground ginger
     1 teaspoon ground cinnamon
     1 teaspoon baking soda
   1/4 teaspoon salt
   1/2 cup sugar
FILLING:
   3/4 cup butter, softened
   3/4 cup marshmallow creme
 1-1/2 cups confectioners' sugar
   3/4 teaspoon lemon extract

In a large bowl, cream butter and brown sugar until light and fluffy. Beat in molasses and egg. Combine the flour, ginger, cinnamon, baking soda and salt; gradually add to creamed mixture and mix well. Cover and refrigerate for at least 3 hours.

Shape into 1-in. balls; roll in sugar. Place 3 in. apart on ungreased baking sheets. Flatten to 1/2-in. thickness with a glass dipped in sugar. Bake at 350° for 8-10 minutes or until set. Cool for 2 minutes before removing cookies from pans to wire racks to cool completely.

For the filling, in a small bowl, beat the butter and marshmallow creme until light and fluffy. Gradually beat in confectioners' sugar and extract.

Spread the filling on the bottoms of half of the cookies, about 1 tablespoon on each; top with remaining cookies. **Yield:** about 2 dozen.

Apple Raspberry Crisp

(Pictured below and on page 118)

PREP: 35 min. **BAKE:** 40 min.

Everyone loves the crumble topping and sweet–tart filling in this crisp. It's especially good served with vanilla ice cream.
—*Ginger Price, Elverson, Pennsylvania*

- **10 cups thinly sliced peeled tart apples (about 10 medium)**
- **4 cups fresh raspberries**
- **1/3 cup sugar**
- **3 tablespoons plus 3/4 cup all-purpose flour, divided**
- **1-1/2 cups old-fashioned oats**
- **1 cup packed brown sugar**
- **3/4 cup whole wheat flour**
- **3/4 cup cold butter**

Place the apples and raspberries in a large bowl. Add the sugar and 3 tablespoons all-purpose flour; toss gently to coat. Transfer to a greased 13-in. x 9-in. baking dish.

In a small bowl, combine the oats, brown sugar, whole wheat flour and remaining all-purpose flour. Cut in the

butter until crumbly; sprinkle over top (dish will be full).

Bake, uncovered, at 350° for 40-50 minutes or until the filling is bubbly and the topping is golden brown. Serve warm. **Yield:** 12 servings.

Jam-Topped Mini Cheesecakes

(Pictured above and on page 118)

PREP: 30 min. + chilling

Presto! Our expert Test Kitchen crew transformed cheesecake into finger food in mere minutes. Have fun with this recipe by experimenting with other types of jams and preserves.

- **1 cup graham cracker crumbs**
- **3 tablespoons butter, melted**
- **1 package (8 ounces) cream cheese, softened**
- **1/3 cup sugar**
- **1 teaspoon vanilla extract**
- **1 egg, lightly beaten**
Assorted jams, warmed

In a small bowl, combine graham cracker crumbs and butter. Press gently onto the bottom of 12 paper-lined muffin cups. In another small bowl, beat cream cheese, sugar and vanilla until smooth. Add egg; beat on low until just combined. Spoon over crusts.

Bake at 350° for 15-16 minutes or until the center is set. Cool for 10 minutes before removing from pan to a wire rack to cool completely. Refrigerate for at least 1 hour.

Remove the paper liners; top each cheesecake with 1 teaspoon jam. **Yield:** 1 dozen.

Potluck Pleasers

Looking for a dish to pass? Stand out from the crowd with the sensational recipes in this chapter. Everyone will line up for favorites such as Burrito Lasagna, Chicken Swiss Bundles, Country Bean Bake and Pecan Caramel Bars.

BEST ON THE BUFFET TABLE. Clockwise from top left: Steak Sauce Sloppy Joes (p. 135), Bacon-Swiss Penne (p. 133), Black-and-Blue Pizzas (p. 138) and Sweet Pasta Salad (p. 138).

Pepperoni Pizza Casserole

PREP: 25 min.   **BAKE:** 30 min.

Packed with pizza ingredients, this noodle bake is guaranteed to be popular. If you like, use ground beef instead of turkey.
—Debbie Staley, Mt. Vernon, Illinois

- 1 package (16 ounces) egg noodles
- 2 pounds ground turkey
- 1/3 cup chopped onion
- 1 jar (26 ounces) meatless spaghetti sauce
- 1 can (10 ounces) diced tomatoes and green chilies
- 1 can (8 ounces) mushroom stems and pieces, drained
- 2 cups (8 ounces) shredded part-skim mozzarella cheese
- 2 cups (8 ounces) shredded cheddar cheese
- 1 cup (4 ounces) shredded Parmesan cheese
- 3 ounces sliced turkey pepperoni

In a Dutch oven, cook noodles according to the package directions; drain.

Meanwhile, in a large skillet, cook turkey and onion over medium heat until meat is no longer pink; drain. Stir in spaghetti sauce and tomatoes. Bring to a boil. Reduce heat; simmer, uncovered, for 5 minutes. Stir in noodles.

Transfer to two greased 13-in. x 9-in. baking dishes. Sprinkle each with mushrooms, cheeses and pepperoni.

Bake, uncovered, at 350° for 30-35 minutes or until heated through and cheeses have melted. Let casseroles stand for 5 minutes before serving. **Yield:** 2 casseroles (6 servings each).

Fontina Ham Stromboli

(Pictured below)

PREP: 40 min.   **BAKE:** 30 min.

These stuffed slices seasoned with pesto always come out of the oven golden brown and delicious. The loaves freeze well, too.
—Nancy Piano, Nevada City, California

- 1 large onion, chopped
- 1 tablespoon olive oil
- 1 garlic clove, minced
- 2 loaves (1 pound *each*) frozen bread dough, thawed
- 1/2 cup prepared pesto, *divided*
- 2 teaspoons dried basil
- 1/2 pound sliced deli ham
- 1/2 pound thinly sliced prosciutto *or* additional deli ham
- 1/2 pound sliced fontina cheese
- 1/4 cup grated Parmesan cheese

In a large skillet, saute the onion in oil until tender. Add garlic; cook 1 minute longer. Cool completely.

On two greased baking sheets, roll each loaf of bread dough into a 16-in. x 10-in. rectangle. Spread each with 2 tablespoons pesto; sprinkle with onion mixture and basil. Arrange the ham, prosciutto and fontina cheese over each rectangle to within 1/2 in. of edges.

Roll up jelly-roll style, starting with a long side; pinch seams to seal and tuck ends under.

Brush with the remaining pesto and sprinkle with the Parmesan cheese. Bake at 350° for 30-35 minutes or until golden brown. Cool stromboli for 5 minutes before slicing. **Yield:** 2 loaves (8 servings each).

Easy Molasses Sticky Buns

PREP: 20 min. + rising   **BAKE:** 25 min.

Your family will jump out of bed in the morning when the aroma of these luscious caramel rolls starts wafting through the house. And no one will be disappointed—each bite is heavenly!
—Nancy Foust, Stoneboro, Pennsylvania

- 2 loaves (16 ounces *each*) frozen bread dough, thawed
- 1/3 cup butter, softened
- 1/2 cup sugar
- 1-1/2 teaspoons ground cinnamon

MOLASSES SAUCE:
- 1 cup packed brown sugar
- 1/2 cup butter, cubed
- 1/2 cup water
- 1/4 cup molasses

Roll out each loaf of bread dough into a 10-in. square. Spread with butter to within 1/2 in. of edges. Combine sugar and cinnamon; sprinkle over butter. Roll up jelly-roll style; pinch seams to seal. Cut each loaf into six slices.

For sauce, in a small saucepan, bring the brown sugar, butter, water and molasses to a boil. Pour into a greased 13-in. x 9-in. baking dish. Place rolls, cut side down, in the molasses sauce.

Cover and let rise in a warm place until doubled, about 30 minutes. Bake at 350° for 25-30 minutes or until golden brown. Cool in dish for 5 minutes; invert onto a serving platter. Serve warm. **Yield:** 1 dozen.

Burrito Lasagna

PREP: 35 min. **BAKE:** 30 min. + standing

Years ago, a friend showed me how to make stacked enchiladas. I took the idea even further by creating this zippy lasagna loaded with south-of-the-border ingredients. I serve it with Mexican corn or tortilla chips, and it gets raves from everyone.
—*Deana Briggs, Maud, Texas*

- **2 pounds ground beef**
- **2 cans (10 ounces *each*) enchilada sauce**
- **1 envelope taco seasoning**
- **1 tablespoon ground cumin**
- **1 package (8.8 ounces) ready-to-serve Spanish rice**
- **12 flour tortillas (8 inches), warmed**
- **1 can (15 ounces) refried beans**
- **4 cups (16 ounces) shredded Mexican cheese blend**
- **Optional toppings: salsa, sliced avocado, shredded lettuce, taco sauce *and/or* sour cream**

In a large skillet, cook beef over medium heat until no longer pink; drain. Stir in enchilada sauce, taco seasoning and cumin; heat through.

Heat the Spanish rice according to package directions. Spread each tortilla with about 2 tablespoonfuls refried beans. Spread 1 cup meat mixture into a greased 13-in. x 9-in. baking dish. Layer with 4 tortillas and a third of the Spanish rice, a third of the remaining meat mixture and a third of the cheese. Repeat the layers. Top with the remaining tortillas, Spanish rice and meat mixture (the dish will be full).

Cover and bake at 350° for 20 minutes. Sprinkle with the remaining cheese. Uncover; bake 10-15 minutes longer or until the cheese is melted. Let stand for 10 minutes before serving. Serve with the toppings of your choice. **Yield:** 12 servings.

Bacon-Swiss Penne

(Pictured above right and on page 130)

PREP: 35 min. **BAKE:** 30 min.

I was fortunate to inherit my grandmother's recipe book, which includes this rich, meal-in-one casserole topped with buttery crumbs. I can never get enough of the ooey-gooey cheese, tender chicken, bacon and pasta. It's comfort food at its best!
—*Joseph Sortor, Tampa, Florida*

- **12 ounces uncooked penne pasta**
- **13 bacon strips**
- **1-1/2 pounds boneless skinless chicken breasts, cut into 1-inch cubes**
- **3 tablespoons butter**
- **6 green onions, chopped**
- **3 tablespoons all-purpose flour**
- **4 cups 2% milk**
- **3 cups (12 ounces) shredded cheddar cheese**

- **1-1/2 cups shredded Swiss cheese**
- **1-1/2 cups frozen peas, thawed**
- **3/4 teaspoon pepper**
- **1/2 teaspoon dried thyme**
- **TOPPING:**
- **3/4 cup dry bread crumbs**
- **2 tablespoons butter, melted**

Cook the penne pasta according to package directions.

Meanwhile, in a large skillet, cook bacon in batches over medium heat until crisp. Remove to paper towels; drain, reserving 4 teaspoons drippings. Crumble bacon and set aside.

Saute chicken in butter and drippings until no longer pink. Add onions; cook 1 minute longer. Stir in flour until blended; gradually add milk. Bring to a boil; cook and stir for 2 minutes or until thickened. Stir in the cheeses, peas, pepper, thyme and bacon.

Drain the penne pasta; add to the chicken mixture and toss to coat. Transfer to a greased 13-in. x 9-in. baking dish. In a small bowl, combine bread crumbs and butter; sprinkle over top.

Bake, uncovered, at 350° for 30-35 minutes or until golden brown. **Yield:** 10 servings.

Black Forest Ham Pinwheels

(Pictured above)

PREP: 20 min. + chilling

These appetizers go over big when I bring them to get-togethers. People like the smokiness of the ham and the sweet surprise of the cherries. I appreciate the make-ahead convenience, too.
—*Kate Dampier, Quail Valley, California*

  1 package (8 ounces) cream cheese, softened
  4 teaspoons minced fresh dill
  1 tablespoon lemon juice
  2 teaspoons Dijon mustard
Dash salt and pepper
  1/2 cup dried cherries, chopped
  1/4 cup chopped green onions
  5 flour tortillas (10 inches), room temperature
  1/2 pound sliced deli Black Forest ham
  1/2 pound sliced Swiss cheese

In a small bowl, beat the cream cheese, dill, lemon juice, mustard, salt and pepper until blended. Stir in the dried cherries and onions. Spread over each tortilla; layer with ham and cheese.

   Roll up tightly; wrap rolls in plastic wrap. Refrigerate for at least 2 hours. Cut into 1/2-in. slices. **Yield:** about 3-1/2 dozen.

Root Beer Cupcakes

(Pictured below)

PREP: 15 min. **BAKE:** 20 min. + cooling

Root beer barrel candies and a spiced cakelike batter give these treats old-fashioned appeal. They're always a hit with kids.
—*Dot Kraemer, Cape May Court House, New Jersey*

  1/2 cup butter, softened
  1 cup packed brown sugar
  2 eggs
  2 cups all-purpose flour
  1 teaspoon baking powder
  1/8 teaspoon baking soda
  1/8 teaspoon ground cinnamon
  1/8 teaspoon ground allspice
  1 cup root beer
1-1/2 cups whipped topping
  12 root beer barrel candies, crushed

In a large bowl, cream butter and brown sugar until light and fluffy. Add eggs, one at a time, beating well after each addition. Combine the flour, baking powder, baking soda, cinnamon and allspice; gradually add to creamed mixture alternately with root beer, beating well after each addition.

   Fill paper-lined muffin cups two-thirds full. Bake at 350° for 18-22 minutes or until a toothpick comes out clean. Cool for 10 minutes before removing from pan to a wire rack to cool completely.

   Just before serving, combine whipped topping and crushed candies; frost cupcakes. Refrigerate leftovers. **Yield:** 1 dozen.

Mango Getaway Bars

PREP: 25 min. **BAKE:** 25 min. + cooling

I love the flavor of mangoes, so I came up with these refreshing goodies featuring that sweet fruit. A macadamia–nut crust and a sprinkling of coconut on top add to the tropical taste.
—Patricia Harmon, Baden, Pennsylvania

- 1/2 **cup macadamia nuts**
- 2-1/4 **cups all-purpose flour,** *divided*
- 1/2 **cup confectioners' sugar**
- 1/2 **teaspoon salt**
- 1 **cup cold butter, cubed**
- 1 **medium mango, peeled and chopped**
- 1/2 **cup orange marmalade**
- 1/2 **cup sugar**
- 4 **eggs**
- 1 **teaspoon grated lemon peel**
- 1 **cup flaked coconut**

Place the nuts in a food processor; cover and process until finely chopped. Add 2 cups flour, confectioners' sugar and salt; cover and process until blended. Add the butter; pulse just until mixture is crumbly. Press into an ungreased 13-in. x 9-in. baking pan. Bake at 350° for 15-20 minutes or until lightly browned.

In a clean food processor, combine mango and orange marmalade; cover and process until smooth. Add sugar and remaining flour; process until combined. Add eggs and lemon peel; process just until combined. Pour over crust. Sprinkle with coconut.

Bake for 23-28 minutes or until golden brown around the edges. Cool on a wire rack. Cut into bars. Refrigerate leftovers. **Yield:** 3 dozen.

Pecan Caramel Bars

PREP: 20 min. **BAKE:** 30 min. + cooling

My coworkers often request these for our holiday parties and group lunches. With butterscotch chips, the crunchy bars are a delightfully different way to showcase Georgia pecans.
—Cheryl Guzman, Monroe, Georgia

- 1 **package (12 ounces) vanilla wafers, crushed**
- 2 **tablespoons sugar**
- 3/4 **cup butter, melted**
- 1 **can (14 ounces) sweetened condensed milk**
- 1 **egg**
- 1/2 **teaspoon maple flavoring**
- 1 **cup butterscotch chips**
- 1-1/2 **cups coarsely chopped pecans**

In a small bowl, combine the wafer crumbs, sugar and butter. Press into a greased 13-in. x 9-in. baking pan. Bake at 350° for 8-10 minutes or until lightly browned and set. Cool for 10 minutes on a wire rack.

In a small bowl, beat the sweetened condensed milk, egg and maple flavoring. Stir in the butterscotch chips.

Spread over crust. Sprinkle with pecans. Bake for 18-22 minutes or until golden brown. Cool on a wire rack. Cut into bars. **Yield:** 3 dozen.

Steak Sauce Sloppy Joes

(Pictured above and on page 130)

PREP: 15 min. **COOK:** 30 min.

Everyone enjoys these satisfying sandwiches jazzed up with steak sauce. The recipe makes a big batch and freezes nicely, too.
—Patti Basten, DePere, Wisconsin

- 3 **pounds ground beef**
- 4 **medium onions, chopped**
- 2 **celery ribs, chopped**
- 1 **garlic clove, minced**
- 1 **can (28 ounces) diced tomatoes, undrained**
- 1/4 **cup Worcestershire sauce**
- 1/4 **cup A.1. steak sauce**
- 2 **tablespoons chili powder**
- 2 **tablespoons paprika**
- 1/4 **teaspoon pepper**
- 15 **hamburger buns, split**

In a Dutch oven, cook the beef, onions and celery over medium heat until the meat is no longer pink. Add the garlic; cook 1 minute longer. Drain.

Stir in tomatoes, Worcestershire sauce, steak sauce, chili powder, paprika and pepper. Bring to a boil. Reduce the heat; simmer, uncovered, for 20 minutes or until thickened and heated through. Serve on hamburger buns. **Yield:** 15 servings.

Wow, Whoopie Pies!

SEEMS there's some historical dispute as to whether whoopie pies were invented in Maine or by the Amish of Pennsylvania. What's not in dispute is how quickly these crowd-pleasing goodies were embraced by the rest of the country.

Usually assembled by sandwiching a sweet filling between two soft cookies, these hand-held treats always get smiles. And the pie's the limit when it comes to choosing the flavors of the filling and cookies.

So whoop it up by making a batch for your next potluck, girlfriends' get-together or other event. You'll have as much fun creating them as eating them!

Red Velvet Whoopie Pies

(Pictured below)

PREP: 40 min. **BAKE:** 10 min./batch + cooling

With a drizzle of melted white chips and a sprinkle of pecans, this recipe is a delightful take on classic red velvet cake. Sometimes I substitute canned cream cheese frosting for the filling.
—Judi Dexheimer, Sturgeon Bay, Wisconsin

> 2 ounces semisweet chocolate, chopped
> 3/4 cup butter, softened
> 1 cup sugar
> 2 eggs
> 1/2 cup sour cream
> 1 tablespoon red food coloring
> 1-1/2 teaspoons white vinegar
> 1 teaspoon clear vanilla extract
> 2-1/4 cups all-purpose flour

> 1/4 cup baking cocoa
> 2 teaspoons baking powder
> 1/2 teaspoon salt
> 1/4 teaspoon baking soda

FILLING:
> 1 package (8 ounces) cream cheese, softened
> 1/2 cup butter, softened
> 2-1/2 cups confectioners' sugar
> 2 teaspoons clear vanilla extract

TOPPINGS:
White baking chips, melted
Finely chopped pecans

In a microwave, melt the semisweet chocolate; stir until smooth. Set aside.

In a large bowl, cream butter and sugar until light and fluffy. Beat in the eggs, sour cream, food coloring, vinegar and vanilla. Combine the flour, cocoa, baking powder, salt and baking soda; gradually add to creamed mixture and mix well. Stir in melted chocolate.

Drop by tablespoonfuls 2 in. apart onto parchment paper-lined baking sheets. Bake at 375° for 8-10 minutes or until edges are set. Cool for 2 minutes before removing from pans to wire racks to cool completely.

For the filling, in a large bowl, beat the cream cheese and butter until fluffy. Beat in the confectioners' sugar and vanilla until smooth. Spread filling on the bottoms of half of the cookies, about 1 tablespoon on each. Top with the remaining cookies. Drizzle with melted white baking chips; sprinkle with pecans. Store in the refrigerator. **Yield:** 2 dozen.

Go Bananas Whoopie Pies

PREP: 40 min. **BAKE:** 15 min./batch + cooling

I'm a big fan of peanut butter. When I saw it was an ingredient in these banana-flavored treats, I just had to make them. Using a cookie scoop keeps them nicely rounded and all the same size.
—Jessie Sarrazin, Livingston, Montana

> 1/2 cup butter, softened
> 3/4 cup sugar
> 1/4 cup packed brown sugar
> 1 egg

> 1 teaspoon vanilla extract
> 1/2 cup mashed ripe banana
> 1/2 cup buttermilk
> 2 cups all-purpose flour
> 1/2 teaspoon salt
> 1/2 teaspoon baking powder
> 1/2 teaspoon baking soda

FILLING:
> 1 package (8 ounces) cream cheese, softened
> 1 cup creamy peanut butter
> 3 tablespoons butter, softened
> 1 cup confectioners' sugar
> 1 teaspoon vanilla extract

Additional confectioners' sugar

In a large bowl, cream butter and sugars until light and fluffy. Beat in egg and vanilla. In a small bowl, combine banana and buttermilk. Combine the flour, salt, baking powder and baking soda; gradually add to the creamed mixture alternately with banana mixture.

Drop by tablespoonfuls 2 in. apart onto parchment paper-lined baking sheets. Bake at 350° for 12-15 minutes or until set. Cool for 2 minutes before removing cookies from pans to wire racks to cool completely.

For the filling, in a large bowl, beat the cream cheese, peanut butter and butter until fluffy. Beat in the confectioners' sugar and vanilla until smooth. Spread the filling on the bottoms of half of the cookies, about 1 tablespoon on each; top with the remaining cookies. Dust with additional confectioners' sugar. Store in the refrigerator. **Yield:** 2 dozen.

Chocolate Dream Whoopie Pies

(Pictured above right)

PREP: 40 min. **BAKE:** 15 min./batch + cooling

Chocolate lovers will find these cute, triple–chocolate goodies irresistible. Two yummy cookies, a luscious mousse–like center and miniature semisweet chips...what could be better?
—*Jill Papke, Oconomowoc, Wisconsin*

> 1 package (18-1/4 ounces) chocolate cake mix
> 3 eggs
> 1/2 cup canola oil
> 1 teaspoon vanilla extract

FILLING:
> 2/3 cup sugar
> 2 tablespoons all-purpose flour
> 1/8 teaspoon salt
> 1 cup 2% milk
> 1/2 cup milk chocolate chips
> 2/3 cup shortening
> 1/3 cup butter, softened
> 3/4 teaspoon vanilla extract

GARNISH:
> 1 cup miniature semisweet chocolate chips

In a large bowl, combine the chocolate cake mix, eggs, oil and vanilla; beat on low speed for 30 seconds. Beat on medium for 2 minutes (mixture will be sticky).

Drop by 2 tablespoonfuls 2 in. apart onto greased baking sheets. Bake at 350° for 9-11 minutes or until the edges are set. Cool for 2 minutes before removing to wire racks to cool completely.

For the filling, in a small saucepan, combine the sugar, flour and salt. Gradually add the milk. Bring to a boil; cook and stir for 1-2 minutes or until thickened. Stir in chocolate chips until melted. Transfer to a small bowl; cover and refrigerate until chilled, about 1 hour.

In a large bowl, beat the shortening and butter until fluffy. Beat in chocolate mixture and vanilla.

Spread the chocolate filling on the bottoms of half of the cookies, about 2 tablespoons on each; top with the remaining cookies. Roll the sides in miniature chocolate chips. Store in the refrigerator. **Yield:** about 1 dozen.

SPEEDY SWEETS. Want to treat your family to whoopie pies but have a jam-packed schedule? Save time by picking up soft cookies from your favorite local bakery instead of baking cookies at home. Then simply whip up whatever filling you like and spread it on the cookies.

Sweet Pasta Salad

(*Pictured above and on page 130*)

PREP: 25 min. + chilling

I'm one of 16 children, and I learned a lot about cooking from my mother. This recipe is my version of a much simpler one.
—*June Herke, Watertown, South Dakota*

- 1 package (16 ounces) spiral pasta
- 1 medium cucumber, finely chopped
- 1 jar (8 ounces) whole baby corn, drained and cut into 1/2-inch pieces
- 1 jar (7-1/2 ounces) marinated artichoke hearts, drained
- 1 cup sliced pimiento-stuffed olives
- 1 cup sliced ripe olives
- 1/2 cup finely chopped sweet red pepper
- 1/4 cup finely chopped onion

DRESSING:

- 1 cup canola oil
- 1 cup cider vinegar
- 1 cup sugar
- 1/2 teaspoon pepper
- 2 tablespoons minced fresh parsley

Cook pasta according to package directions. Meanwhile, in a large bowl, combine the cucumber, corn, artichokes, olives, red pepper and onion. Drain pasta and rinse in cold water; stir into vegetable mixture.

In a small bowl, whisk the dressing ingredients. Pour over salad; toss to coat. Cover and refrigerate for at least 2 hours. Serve with a slotted spoon. **Yield:** 16 servings.

Black-and-Blue Pizzas

(*Pictured below and on page 130*)

PREP: 40 min. **BAKE:** 15 min.

Ooey-gooey with cheese and loaded with toppings, these pizzas are delicious and filling. Add a green salad for a complete meal.
—*Michelle Huelskamp, Marion, North Carolina*

- 2 loaves (1 pound *each*) frozen bread dough, thawed
- 8 bacon strips, chopped
- 1 pound boneless skinless chicken breasts, cut into strips
- 5 teaspoons blackened seasoning
- 3 shallots, finely chopped
- 2 garlic cloves, minced
- 1 jar (15 ounces) Alfredo sauce
- 2-1/2 cups sliced fresh shiitake mushrooms
- 1 can (3.8 ounces) sliced ripe olives, drained
- 1/2 cup finely chopped sun-dried tomatoes (not packed in oil)
- 1-1/4 cups (5 ounces) crumbled blue cheese
- 2 tablespoons minced fresh basil or 2 teaspoons dried basil
- 2 tablespoons minced fresh thyme *or* 2 teaspoons dried thyme
- 12 slices provolone cheese
- 3 ounces Parmesan cheese, shaved into strips *or* 3/4 cup grated Parmesan cheese

Roll the bread dough into two 16-in. x 10-in. rectangles; transfer to ungreased baking sheets and build up the edges slightly.

In a large skillet, cook bacon over medium heat until crisp. Remove to paper towels with a slotted spoon; drain, reserving 2 tablespoons drippings. Sprinkle the chicken with blackened seasoning; cook chicken in the drippings until no longer pink. Add shallots and garlic; cook 1 minute longer. Set aside.

Spread sauce over crusts; top with chicken mixture, bacon, mushrooms, olives and tomatoes. Sprinkle with the blue cheese, basil and thyme; top with provolone and Parmesan cheeses.

Bake at 450° for 14-18 minutes or until bubbly and the cheese is melted. **Yield:** 2 pizzas (12 pieces each).

Drizzled Nanaimo Bars

PREP: 40 min. + chilling

Nobody knows for sure who invented Nanaimo bars, but nearly everyone who fixes a panful knows how quickly they disappear! The sweet Canadian treats have a nutty crumb crust, creamy vanilla filling and rich chocolate glaze drizzled on top.
—Alice Maysick, Berrien Center, Michigan

  1 cup butter, cubed
1/2 cup sugar
  2 ounces unsweetened chocolate, chopped
  2 eggs, beaten
  2 teaspoons vanilla extract
  4 cups graham cracker crumbs
  2 cups flaked coconut
  1 cup chopped walnuts
FILLING:
1/2 cup butter, softened
  3 tablespoons 2% milk
  2 tablespoons instant vanilla pudding mix
  2 cups confectioners' sugar
GLAZE:
  8 ounces semisweet chocolate, chopped
  1 tablespoon butter

In large heavy saucepan, combine the butter, sugar and chocolate. Cook and stir over medium-low heat until melted. Whisk a small amount of hot mixture into eggs. Return all to the pan, whisking constantly. Cook and stir over medium-low heat until the mixture reaches 160°. Remove from the heat; stir in vanilla.

In a large bowl, combine the cracker crumbs, coconut and walnuts. Stir in the chocolate mixture until blended. Press into a greased 15-in. x 10-in. x 1-in. pan. Refrigerate for 30 minutes or until set.

For the filling, in a large bowl, beat the butter, milk and pudding mix until blended. Gradually beat in the confectioners' sugar until smooth; spread over crust.

For glaze, in a microwave, melt chocolate and butter; stir until smooth. Drizzle over filling. Refrigerate until set. Cut into bars. **Yield:** 4 dozen.

Chicken Swiss Bundles

(Pictured above)

PREP: 30 min. **BAKE:** 20 min.

These yummy sandwich buns, made with frozen dinner rolls, are a favorite at our house. They're fantastic hot from the oven but also freeze well. I like to serve them with tomato soup.
—Trisha Kruse, Eagle, Idaho

  1 small onion, finely chopped
1/2 cup sliced fresh mushrooms
1-1/2 teaspoons butter
  1 garlic clove, minced
  1 cup cubed cooked chicken breast
1/2 cup chopped roasted sweet red peppers
  1 tablespoon honey mustard
1/4 teaspoon salt
1/4 teaspoon lemon-pepper seasoning
1/4 teaspoon Italian seasoning
  2 cups (8 ounces) shredded Swiss cheese
12 frozen bread dough dinner rolls, thawed
  2 tablespoons butter, melted

In a large skillet, saute onion and mushrooms in butter until tender. Add the garlic; cook 1 minute longer. Add the chicken, peppers, mustard and seasonings; heat through. Remove from the heat; stir in cheese.

Flatten each roll into a 5-in. circle. Place 1/4 cup chicken mixture in the center of six circles. Brush the edges with water; top with the remaining circles. Press edges with a fork to seal.

Place on greased baking sheets; brush with butter. Bake at 350° for 18-22 minutes or until golden brown. Cut bundles in half to serve. **Yield:** 12 servings.

Rhubarb Cheesecake Squares

(Pictured below)

PREP: 20 min. **BAKE:** 35 min. + chilling

Spring is the perfect time to try these rich, tangy cheese squares. They're a decadent way to use your fresh-picked rhubarb.
—*Sharon Schmidt, Mandan, North Dakota*

- 1-1/4 cups all-purpose flour
- 1/2 cup old-fashioned oats
- 1/2 cup packed brown sugar
- 1/2 cup cold butter
- 1 package (8 ounces) cream cheese, softened
- 3/4 cup sugar
- 1/2 teaspoon salt
- 1/2 teaspoon vanilla extract
- 1/4 teaspoon ground cinnamon
- 1/8 teaspoon ground nutmeg
- 1 egg, lightly beaten
- 1-1/2 cups finely chopped fresh *or* frozen rhubarb

In a small bowl, combine flour, oats and brown sugar. Cut in butter until crumbly. Set aside 1 cup crumb mixture; press remaining mixture onto the bottom of a greased 9-in. square baking pan. Set aside.

For filling, in a small bowl, beat the cream cheese and sugar until smooth. Beat in the salt, vanilla, cinnamon and nutmeg. Add the egg; beat on low speed just until combined. Stir in rhubarb. Pour over crust. Sprinkle with reserved crumb mixture.

Bake at 350° for 35-40 minutes or until set. Cool on a wire rack for 1 hour. Refrigerate for at least 2 hours. Cut into squares. **Yield:** 16 squares.

Editor's Note: If using frozen rhubarb, measure rhubarb while still frozen, then thaw completely. Drain in a colander, but do not press liquid out.

Chocolate Mint Treasures

(Pictured above)

PREP: 45 min. **BAKE:** 20 min. + cooling

I adore the combination of chocolate and mint, and these layered triangles take that pairing up a notch by blending dark, milk and white chocolate. Plus, they're pretty enough for parties.
—*Sherry Johnston, Green Cove Springs, Florida*

FIRST LAYER:
- 1/2 cup butter, softened
- 1/2 cup sugar
- 1 egg
- 1/2 teaspoon vanilla extract
- 1 cup all-purpose flour
- 1/4 cup baking cocoa
- 1/8 teaspoon salt

SECOND LAYER:
- 1/2 cup butter, softened
- 1/2 cup sugar
- 1 egg
- 1/2 teaspoon vanilla extract
- 1-1/4 cups all-purpose flour
- 1/8 teaspoon salt
- 1 package (7.05 ounces) After Eight thin mints

DRIZZLE:
- 3 ounces bittersweet chocolate, chopped
- 1 tablespoon butter
- 2 ounces white baking chocolate

In a large bowl, cream butter and sugar until light and fluffy. Beat in egg and vanilla. Combine the flour, cocoa and salt; gradually add to creamed mixture and mix well. Spread into a greased 13-in. x 9-in. baking pan.

For the second layer, in a large bowl, cream the butter and sugar until light and fluffy. Beat in the egg and vanilla. Combine the flour and salt; gradually add to the creamed mixture and mix well. Gently spread over the chocolate layer.

Bake at 350° for 15-18 minutes until golden brown. Remove from the oven; top with mints. Bake 1-2 minutes or until the mints begin to melt; carefully spread mints evenly over the top. Cool completely.

In a microwave, melt bittersweet chocolate and butter; stir until smooth. Drizzle over bars; chill until set. Grate the white chocolate over the top. Chill until set. Cut into triangles. **Yield:** 4 dozen.

Country Bean Bake

PREP: 25 min. **BAKE:** 65 min.

These baked beans of my mother's are the best I've ever tasted. I've brought them to summer and fall picnics, football events, family reunions and other get–togethers, and I always hear rave reviews. An added bonus? Make–ahead convenience!
—Gloria Jarrett, Loveland, Ohio

- 2 pounds bulk pork sausage
- 1 can (16 ounces) Boston baked beans
- 1 can (16 ounces) kidney beans, rinsed and drained
- 1 can (15-1/4 ounces) lima beans, rinsed and drained
- 1 can (16 ounces) butter beans, rinsed and drained
- 1 can (8 ounces) unsweetened crushed pineapple, drained
- 1 medium tart apple, peeled and shredded
- 1 small onion, diced
- 1/2 cup ketchup
- 1/2 cup molasses
- 1 tablespoon lemon juice
- 1 cup (4 ounces) shredded cheddar cheese

In a large skillet, cook sausage over medium heat until no longer pink; drain. In a large bowl, combine the sausage, beans, pineapple, apple, onion, ketchup, molasses and lemon juice.

Transfer to a greased 3-qt. baking dish. Cover and bake at 325° for 60-70 minutes or until thickened and bubbly.

Uncover; sprinkle with cheese. Bake 5 minutes longer or until cheese is melted. **Yield:** 15 servings (2/3 cup each).

Pine Nut Caramel Shortbread

(Pictured at right)

PREP: 30 min. **BAKE:** 20 min. + cooling

I'm a big fan of pine nuts and decided to try substituting them for the pecans in a friend's wonderful caramel bar recipe. The new version turned out great, and now I make them that way often.
—Dara Michalski, Sandy, Utah

- 1 cup plus 2 tablespoons butter, softened
- 3/4 cup packed brown sugar
- 3 cups all-purpose flour
- 1/2 teaspoon salt

FILLING:

- 3/4 cup butter, cubed
- 3/4 cup packed brown sugar
- 1/2 cup honey
- 1/4 cup sugar
- 3 tablespoons heavy whipping cream
- 1/2 teaspoon salt
- 2 cups pine nuts
- 3/4 teaspoon vanilla extract

Coarse salt, optional

In a large bowl, cream butter and sugar until light and fluffy. Combine flour and salt; gradually add to creamed mixture and mix well. Pat onto the bottom of a greased 15-in. x 10-in. x 1-in. baking pan. Prick dough thoroughly with a fork.

Bake at 375° for 15-18 minutes or until golden brown. Cool on a wire rack. Reduce temperature to 325°.

In a large saucepan, combine the butter, brown sugar, honey, sugar, cream and salt. Cook, stirring occasionally, until a candy thermometer reads 234° (soft-ball stage). Remove from the heat; stir in the pine nuts and vanilla. Spread evenly over crust.

Bake for 20-25 minutes or until bubbly. Place pan on a wire rack. Sprinkle the top with coarse salt if desired. Cool completely. Cut into bars. Store in an airtight container. **Yield:** 4 dozen.

Cooking for One or Two

When you want just a few servings, make your meal doubly delightful with recipes such as Asian Mango Chicken, Taco Ramekins, Swiss Potato Gratin and Mini Blueberry Bundt Cakes. Each dish is small in size but big on taste!

PERFECT FOR A PAIR. Clockwise from top left: Bacon Mushroom Chicken (p. 152), Chocolate Malted Bread Pudding (p. 147), Sweet and Sour Pork (p. 144) and Pasta with Chorizo and Spinach (p. 148).

Add the green pepper; cook for 2 minutes. Stir the cornstarch mixture and stir into the pork mixture. Bring to a boil; cook and stir for 2 minutes or until thickened and the green pepper is crisp-tender. Serve over rice if desired. **Yield:** 2 servings.

Spud-Stuffed Peppers

(Pictured below)

PREP: 25 min. **BAKE:** 40 min.

My family and I don't care for rice, so I came up with this tasty stuffed pepper recipe using fresh potatoes from our garden.
—*Joyce Jandera, Hanover, Kansas*

> 2 medium green peppers
> 1/2 pound lean ground beef (90% lean)
> 1 medium potato, peeled and coarsely grated
> 1-1/2 teaspoons chili powder
> 1/4 teaspoon salt
> Dash coarsely ground pepper
> 1/4 cup shredded reduced-fat cheddar cheese

Cut the tops off peppers and remove the seeds. In a large saucepan, cook peppers in boiling water for 4-5 minutes. Drain and rinse in cold water; invert on paper towels.

In a nonstick skillet, cook beef over medium heat until no longer pink; drain. Add the potato; cook and stir for 6-8 minutes or until tender. Stir in the chili powder, salt and pepper. Spoon into peppers.

Place in a 9-in. x 5-in. loaf pan coated with cooking spray. Cover and bake at 350° for 35 minutes. Sprinkle with the cheddar cheese. Bake, uncovered, 5-10 minutes longer or until the peppers are tender and the cheese is melted. **Yield:** 2 servings.

Sweet-and-Sour Pork

(Pictured above and on page 142)

PREP/TOTAL TIME: 30 min.

We like this tangy entree as a quick meal when we've been gone all day. Add more or less minced garlic to suit your taste.
—*Sharon Ryzner, Girard, Ohio*

> 1 tablespoon cornstarch
> 2 tablespoons water
> 3/4 pound boneless lean pork roast, cut into 1-inch cubes
> 1 tablespoon canola oil
> 1 can (8 ounces) pineapple chunks, undrained
> 1/2 cup dark corn syrup
> 1/3 cup white vinegar
> 2 tablespoons ketchup
> 2 tablespoons reduced-sodium soy sauce
> 1 garlic clove, minced
> 1/2 cup chopped green pepper (1-inch pieces)
> Hot cooked rice, optional

In a small bowl, combine the cornstarch and water until smooth; set aside. In a large skillet or wok, cook pork in oil until browned. Add the pineapple, corn syrup, vinegar, ketchup, soy sauce and garlic. Bring to a boil. Reduce heat; simmer, uncovered, for 10 minutes.

Asian Mango Chicken

(Pictured above)

PREP: 25 min. **COOK:** 15 min.

This distinctive chicken dish will brighten any table. The colorful mango and veggies draw you in, and the lively flavors keep you coming back for more. —Jessica Feist, Brookfield, Wisconsin

- 2 boneless skinless chicken breast halves (6 ounces *each*)
- 1 tablespoon sesame *or* canola oil
- 1 tablespoon rice vinegar
- 1 garlic clove, minced
- 1 teaspoon honey
- 1/2 teaspoon green curry paste
- 1 medium mango, peeled and diced
- 1 green onion, finely chopped
- 2 tablespoons diced peeled cucumber
- 2 tablespoons finely chopped sweet red pepper
- 1/8 teaspoon cayenne pepper

Chopped dry roasted peanuts

In a large skillet over medium heat, cook chicken in oil for 4-5 minutes on each side or until a meat thermometer reads 170°. Remove and keep warm. Add rice vinegar, garlic, honey and green curry paste to the pan; cook and stir for 1-2 minutes to allow the flavors to blend. Return chicken to the pan.

Combine the mango, onion, cucumber, red pepper and cayenne. Serve with the chicken. Sprinkle with peanuts.
Yield: 2 servings.

Pear Perfection

PREP: 20 min. **COOK:** 30 min. + chilling

What makes this dessert especially nice is that it can be made in advance and enjoyed any time of year. For example, I use lime sherbet for St. Patrick's Day and pineapple sherbet for Easter. For a yuletide touch, add a sprinkling of pomegranate seeds.
—Pat Neaves, Lees Summit, Missouri

- 1/2 cup pomegranate juice
- 1/4 cup orange juice
- 1-1/2 teaspoons lemon juice
- 1/4 cup sugar
- 1 teaspoon grated lemon peel
- 1 large pear, peeled, halved and cored
- 1 tablespoon semisweet chocolate chips
- 1 tablespoon white baking chips
- 2/3 cup raspberry sherbet
- 2 tablespoons sliced almonds

In a small saucepan, bring juices, sugar and lemon peel to a boil. Reduce heat; carefully add pear halves. Cover and simmer for 8-10 minutes or until tender. Remove pears with a slotted spoon; refrigerate for 1 hour.

Bring the poaching liquid to a boil; cook until liquid is reduced to about 2 tablespoons. Cool.

In a microwave, melt the semisweet chocolate chips and white baking chips in separate bowls; stir until smooth. Drizzle chocolate on a plate. Place pear halves on plate; top with sherbet. Drizzle with the poaching liquid and melted chips. Sprinkle with almonds. Serve immediately. **Yield:** 2 servings.

Let's Get Together Thai Shrimp

(Pictured above)

PREP: 20 min. **COOK:** 15 min.

My husband and I make a point of having at least one "date night" every week, even if that means dinner at home. When we eat in, this is our favorite entree. Although we usually save it for special evenings together, it's easy enough to fix anytime.
—*Marie Saba, San Antonio, Texas*

>   3/4 **pound uncooked medium shrimp, peeled and deveined**
>   1/4 **teaspoon salt**
>   1/4 **teaspoon pepper**
>   2 **tablespoons lime juice,** *divided*
>   1 **shallot, chopped**
>   1 **teaspoon minced fresh gingerroot**
>   1 **garlic clove, minced**
>   1 **tablespoon olive oil**
>   10 **cherry tomatoes, halved**
>   1/2 **cup sliced fresh mushrooms**
>   1/2 **cup reduced-sodium chicken broth**
>   1/2 **cup light coconut milk**
>   1 **teaspoon curry powder**
>   1/2 **teaspoon crushed red pepper flakes**
>   2 **tablespoons chopped salted cashews**
>   2 **tablespoons minced fresh cilantro**

Sprinkle the shrimp with salt, pepper and 1 tablespoon lime juice.

In a large skillet, saute the shallot, ginger and garlic in oil for 1 minute. Add shrimp; cook and stir for 2-3 minutes or until shrimp turn pink. Remove with a slotted spoon and set aside.

Add the cherry tomatoes, mushrooms, chicken broth, coconut milk, curry powder, pepper flakes and remaining lime juice to skillet. Bring to a boil. Reduce heat; simmer, uncovered, for 8-10 minutes or until mushrooms are tender and sauce is slightly reduced, stirring occasionally. Add the shrimp; heat through. Garnish with cashews and cilantro. **Yield:** 2 servings.

Swiss Potato Gratin

(Pictured above right)

PREP: 15 min. **BAKE:** 20 min.

Grated potatoes, minced garlic and creamy Swiss cheese make this side dish a satisfying alternative to the usual mashed or baked potatoes. Plus, the recipe requires just five other ingredients.
—*Connie Bryan, Linwood, Kansas*

>   1-1/2 **cups grated peeled potatoes**
>   1/2 **cup 2% milk**
>   1/4 **cup heavy whipping cream**
>   1/2 **teaspoon salt**
>   1/4 **to 1/2 teaspoon minced garlic**
> **Dash ground nutmeg**

Pepper to taste
   1/4 cup shredded Swiss *or* Gruyere cheese

In a saucepan, combine the potatoes, milk, cream, salt, garlic, nutmeg and pepper. Bring to a boil over medium heat, stirring occasionally.

Pour into a 3-cup baking dish coated with cooking spray. Sprinkle with the cheese. Bake, uncovered, at 425° for 20-25 minutes or until heated through and golden brown. **Yield:** 2 servings.

Meatless Calzones

PREP: 15 min. + rising **BAKE:** 15 min.

Our Test Kitchen pros packed three kinds of cheese and plenty of fresh veggies into these scrumptious baked sandwiches made with frozen dough. Give them a try—you'll never miss the meat!

   2 **frozen Texas-size white dinner rolls**
   1/2 **cup *each* chopped sweet red pepper, fresh mushrooms and broccoli**
   1 **tablespoon chopped green onion**
   1 **garlic clove, minced**
   3 **teaspoons olive oil, *divided***
   1/3 **cup shredded part-skim mozzarella cheese**
   2 **tablespoons grated Parmesan cheese**
   2 **tablespoons crumbled feta cheese**
   1 **tablespoon minced fresh parsley**
   4 **teaspoons Italian salad dressing**

Let the rolls rise until doubled, following the package directions. Meanwhile, in a small skillet, saute the red pepper, mushrooms, broccoli, onion and garlic in 2 teaspoons oil for 2-3 minutes or until crisp-tender. Combine the cheeses and parsley; stir into vegetables.

On a lightly floured surface, roll each dinner roll into a 7-in. circle; brush with salad dressing. Spoon vegetable mixture onto half of each circle; spread to within 1 in. of edges. Fold dough over filling; pinch edges to seal.

Place on an ungreased baking sheet. Brush with the remaining oil. Bake at 350° for 15-20 minutes or until golden brown. **Yield:** 2 servings.

Chocolate Malted Bread Pudding

(Pictured below and on page 142)

PREP: 15 min. + standing **BAKE:** 25 min. + cooling

Some leftover slices of bread, an open can of chocolate syrup and a package of malted milk balls inspired this yummy treat. Adding toasted almonds gives the pudding a pleasing crunch.
                              —Roxanne Chan, Albany, California

   1 **cup cubed day-old bread**
   1/4 **cup coarsely chopped malted milk balls**
   3 **tablespoons semisweet chocolate chips**
   2 **tablespoons sliced almonds, toasted**
   1 **tablespoon chocolate syrup**
   1/2 **cup 2% milk**
   2 **tablespoons cream cheese, softened**
   1 **egg**
   2 **tablespoons malted milk powder**
Whipped cream, optional

Place the bread cubes in two 8-oz. ramekins coated with cooking spray; sprinkle with malted milk balls, chocolate chips and almonds. Drizzle with chocolate syrup.

In a blender, combine the milk, cream cheese, egg and malted milk powder; cover and process until smooth. Pour over bread cube mixture. Let stand for 15 minutes.

Bake at 325° for 25-30 minutes or until the mixture reaches 160°. Cool for 10 minutes before serving. Dollop with whipped cream if desired. **Yield:** 2 servings.

Cook the pasta according to the package directions. Meanwhile, heat oil in a large skillet; crumble chorizo into the pan. Add the onion, mushrooms, artichokes, tomatoes, garlic, oregano, salt and pepper. Cook and stir over medium heat until the chorizo is fully cooked and the vegetables are tender.

Add the spinach; cook and stir for 1-2 minutes or until wilted. Drain pasta; top with chorizo mixture. Sprinkle with cheese. **Yield:** 2 servings.

Shredded Turkey Sandwiches

(*Pictured below*)

PREP/TOTAL TIME: 30 min.

Keep this recipe handy when you have turkey left over from a holiday feast. The saucy sandwiches are a delicious solution.
—*Kathy Nissley, Mount Joy, Pennsylvania*

        1/2 **cup finely chopped onion**
          1 **tablespoon butter**
        1/3 **cup ketchup**
          3 **tablespoons brown sugar**
          4 **teaspoons white vinegar**
      2-1/2 **teaspoons Worcestershire sauce**
          2 **teaspoons prepared mustard**
        1/4 **teaspoon salt**
        1/8 **teaspoon pepper**
          1 **cup shredded cooked turkey**
          2 **kaiser rolls, split**

In a small saucepan, saute the onion in butter. Stir in the ketchup, brown sugar, vinegar, Worcestershire sauce, mustard, salt and pepper. Bring to a boil; reduce heat. Fold in turkey; cover and cook for 5-10 minutes or until heated through. Serve on rolls. **Yield:** 2 servings.

Pasta with Chorizo and Spinach

(*Pictured above and on page 142*)

PREP/TOTAL TIME: 20 min.

This zippy entree looks and tastes special, but it's a cinch to get on the table in 20 minutes. When I get home from work and need a quick dinner, this is one of my favorite choices.
—*Athena Russell, Florence, South Carolina*

      1-1/4 **cups uncooked penne pasta**
          4 **teaspoons olive oil**
        1/3 **pound uncooked chorizo *or* bulk spicy pork sausage**
          1 **small onion, thinly sliced**
          4 **ounces sliced fresh mushrooms**
        1/3 **cup water-packed artichoke hearts, rinsed, drained and quartered**
        1/3 **cup chopped oil-packed sun-dried tomatoes, drained**
          1 **garlic clove, minced**
        1/4 **teaspoon dried oregano**
        1/8 **teaspoon salt**
        1/8 **teaspoon pepper**
          3 **cups chopped fresh spinach**
          2 **tablespoons grated Parmesan cheese**

Herbed Tomatoes

(Pictured above)

PREP/TOTAL TIME: 15 min.

My husband and I grow tomatoes and enjoy this simple salad all summer long. It's great with warm French bread for lunch.
—*Kim Bovino, Milford, Connecticut*

- 2 **medium tomatoes, cut into thin slices**
- 2 **slices sweet onion, separated into rings**
- 4 **teaspoons olive oil**
- 1-1/2 **teaspoons lemon juice**
- 1/4 **teaspoon minced garlic**
- 1 **teaspoon** *each* **minced fresh tarragon, basil and parsley**

Salt and pepper to taste

In a bowl, combine the tomatoes and onion. In another bowl, combine the oil, lemon juice, garlic, herbs, salt and pepper. Pour over the tomatoes and onion; stir gently to coat. **Yield:** 2 servings.

ONION ADVICE. Sweet onions are not suited for long-term storage, so you should use them within several weeks of purchase. When storing sweet onions, keep them cool, dry and separate. Place them in a single layer, wrapped separately in foil or paper towels, in your refrigerator's vegetable bin. If it is not possible to store them in the refrigerator, keep them in the coolest area of your home with good air circulation.

Taco Ramekins

(Pictured below)

PREP: 15 min. **BAKE:** 20 min.

With mild Mexican flavor, these cute little taco cups please young and old alike. They were a hit with my daughter and her friends. Using convenient biscuit/baking mix speeds up the prep.
—*Barbara Willmitch, Youngstown, Ohio*

- 1/4 **pound lean ground beef (90% lean)**
- 1/4 **teaspoon chili powder**
- 1/8 **teaspoon salt**
- 1/8 **teaspoon pepper**
- 3/4 **cup biscuit/baking mix**
- 3 **tablespoons cold water**
- 1 **medium tomato, sliced**
- 1/4 **cup chopped green pepper**
- 2 **tablespoons sour cream**
- 2 **tablespoons mayonnaise**
- 2 **tablespoons shredded cheddar cheese**
- 1 **tablespoon chopped onion**

In a skillet, cook beef over medium heat until no longer pink; drain. Stir in chili powder, salt and pepper. Remove from the heat and set aside.

Combine biscuit mix and water to form a soft dough. Press onto the bottom and up the sides of two 10-oz. ramekins or custard cups coated with cooking spray. Fill with meat mixture; top with tomato and green pepper. Combine the sour cream, mayonnaise, cheese and onion; spread evenly over the tops.

Bake, uncovered, at 375° for 20-25 minutes or until heated through. **Yield:** 2 servings.

Crunchy Peanut Butter Tarts

PREP: 10 min. + chilling

For a fun yet no-fuss treat, try these cute, individual-size tarts. They're guaranteed to satisfy peanut lovers. To lighten them up a bit, use reduced-fat ingredients and a sugar substitute.
—Mary Kelley, Wilmington, North Carolina

 2 ounces cream cheese, softened
 1/4 cup chunky peanut butter
 2 tablespoons sugar
 2 tablespoons sour cream
 1/4 teaspoon vanilla extract
 2 individual graham cracker tart shells
 2 tablespoons whipped topping
Chopped peanuts, optional

In a small bowl, beat the cream cheese, peanut butter and sugar until blended. Stir in sour cream and vanilla. Spoon into graham cracker tart shells. Refrigerate for at least 1 hour.

Top with whipped topping. Sprinkle with peanuts if desired. **Yield:** 2 servings.

Cordon Bleu Bake

(Pictured below)

PREP: 20 min. **BAKE:** 30 min.

This comforting meal-in-one casserole is quick and easy to fix. I can toss in leftover cooked chicken and other extras.
—Helen Musenbrock, O'Fallon, Missouri

 1/2 cup water
 3 tablespoons butter, *divided*
 1 cup stuffing mix
 1 cup frozen mixed vegetables, thawed
 2/3 cup condensed cream of mushroom *or* cream of chicken soup, undiluted, *divided*

 3/4 cup cubed cooked chicken breast
 2 ounces thinly sliced lean deli ham, cut into strips
 1/2 cup shredded Swiss cheese

In a small saucepan, bring water and 1 tablespoon butter to a boil. Stir in stuffing mix. Remove from the heat; cover and let stand for 5 minutes.

Meanwhile, in a shallow 1-qt. baking dish coated with cooking spray, combine the vegetables with 1/3 cup cream soup. Combine the chicken with the remaining cream soup; spoon over the vegetables. Layer with the deli ham and Swiss cheese. Fluff the stuffing with a fork; spoon over cheese. Melt remaining butter; drizzle over stuffing. Bake, uncovered, at 350° for 30-35 minutes or until heated through. **Yield:** 2 servings.

Crunchy Asian Coleslaw

(Pictured above)

PREP: 15 min. + chilling

Here's a flavor-packed twist on traditional creamy coleslaw. The tangy homemade vinaigrette really enhances the fresh veggies.
—Erin Chilcoat, Smithtown, New York

 1 cup shredded Chinese *or* napa cabbage
 1/2 cup sliced water chestnuts, chopped
 1/2 small zucchini, julienned
 2 tablespoons chopped green pepper
4-1/2 teaspoons rice vinegar
 1 teaspoon sugar
 1 teaspoon sesame seeds, toasted
 1 teaspoon reduced-sodium soy sauce
 1/2 teaspoon sesame oil
Dash crushed red pepper flakes

In a small bowl, combine the cabbage, water chestnuts, zucchini and green pepper. In a small bowl, whisk the remaining ingredients. Drizzle over salad; toss to coat. Refrigerate for at least 1 hour. **Yield:** 2 servings.

Cherry-Glazed Lamb Chops

(Pictured above)

PREP/TOTAL TIME: 25 min.

An elegant reduction sauce studded with bits of cherry makes this entree ideal for a quiet dinner with that special someone.
—*Kerry Dingwall, Ponte Vedra, Florida*

- **1 teaspoon dried rosemary, crushed**
- **1/4 teaspoon salt**
- **1/4 teaspoon pepper, *divided***
- **4 lamb loin chops (4 ounces *each*)**
- **1 garlic clove, minced**
- **1/4 cup beef broth**
- **1/4 cup cherry preserves**
- **1/4 cup balsamic vinegar**

Combine the rosemary, salt and 1/8 teaspoon pepper; rub over lamb chops. In a large skillet coated with cooking spray, cook chops over medium heat for 4-6 minutes on each side or until the meat reaches desired doneness (for medium-rare, a meat thermometer should read 145°; medium, 160°; well-done, 170°). Remove and keep warm.

Add the garlic to the pan; cook for 1 minute. Stir in the beef broth, cherry preserves, vinegar and remaining pepper; cook for 2-4 minutes or until thickened. Return chops to the pan; turn to coat. Sprinkle with additional dried rosemary if desired. **Yield:** 2 servings.

Herb Garden Vegetables

(Pictured above)

PREP/TOTAL TIME: 30 min.

I wanted to take advantage of all the vegetables and herbs in our garden, so I came up with this simple but tasty medley.
—*Julie Stella, Champlin, Minnesota*

- **1/4 pound fresh green beans, trimmed**
- **3/4 cup fresh sugar snap peas**
- **1 tablespoon olive oil**
- **3/4 cup julienned zucchini**
- **3/4 cup julienned yellow summer squash**
- **3/4 teaspoon *each* minced fresh rosemary, sage, basil and thyme**
- **1/4 teaspoon crushed red pepper flakes**
- **2 tablespoons crumbled blue cheese**

In a small skillet over medium heat, cook beans and peas in oil for 3 minutes. Add the zucchini, squash, herbs and pepper flakes; cook and stir 3-5 minutes longer or until the vegetables are crisp-tender. Sprinkle with cheese just before serving. **Yield:** 2 servings.

Bacon Mushroom Chicken

(Pictured above and on page 142)

PREP: 25 min. **BAKE:** 20 min.

My brother told me this was the most delicious chicken he'd ever had, and now it's one of my favorites, too. Not only does it have terrific flavor, but it's also a cinch to put together, looks fancy and never fails to get compliments when I serve it to company.
—Kara Cook, Elk Ridge, Utah

    2 bacon strips, halved
    2 boneless skinless chicken breast halves
       (6 ounces *each*)
  1/4 teaspoon seasoned salt
  1/4 cup honey
    2 tablespoons Dijon mustard
    1 tablespoon mayonnaise
    1 tablespoon light corn syrup
  1/2 teaspoon dried minced onion
  1/4 cup sliced fresh mushrooms
  1/3 cup shredded part-skim mozzarella cheese

In a large skillet, cook the bacon over medium heat until crisp. Remove to paper towels; set aside. Flatten chicken to 1/2-in. thickness; sprinkle both sides with seasoned salt. Brown in bacon drippings. Transfer to a 1-qt. baking dish coated with cooking spray.

In a small bowl, combine honey, mustard, mayonnaise, corn syrup and onion; spread 1/4 cup over chicken. Top

with bacon and mushrooms. Sprinkle with cheese. Cover and bake at 350° for 20-25 minutes or until the chicken juices run clear. Serve with the remaining honey mixture. **Yield:** 2 servings.

Dilled Tuna Salad

PREP/TOTAL TIME: 10 min.

When I need something for lunch, I often whip up this creamy tuna salad. It takes only 10 minutes to fix, so I'm on my way in a flash. I love it with kosher dill pickle slices on the side.
—Rebecca Schweizer, Chesapeake, Virginia

  1/4 cup mayonnaise
    1 tablespoon sour cream
    2 to 4 teaspoons minced fresh parsley
    1 to 1-1/2 teaspoons dill weed
  1/8 teaspoon garlic salt
  1/8 teaspoon ground thyme
  1/8 teaspoon pepper
  Dash cayenne pepper
    1 can (6 ounces) light water-packed tuna,
       drained and flaked
    2 tablespoons chopped red onion
    2 cups fresh baby spinach
    5 slices tomato, halved

In a small bowl, whisk the first eight ingredients. Stir in tuna and onion. Serve over spinach. Garnish with tomato slices. **Yield:** 2 servings.

Mini Banana Nut Bread

PREP: 15 min. **BAKE:** 50 min. + cooling

This little banana bread recipe, baked in a mini loaf pan, won several blue ribbons at our county fair and the Nebraska State Fair. I like to use black walnuts because I think they taste best.
—Anna Marie Moore, Aurora, Nebraska

    3 tablespoons shortening
  1/3 cup sugar
    1 egg
  1/4 teaspoon vanilla extract
  2/3 cup all-purpose flour
  1/4 teaspoon baking soda
  1/8 teaspoon salt
  1/2 cup mashed ripe banana (about 1 large)
    3 tablespoons chopped walnuts

In a small bowl, cream the shortening and sugar. Beat in the egg and vanilla. Combine the flour, baking soda and salt; add to creamed mixture alternately with banana. Fold in walnuts.

Transfer to a 5-3/4-in. x 3-in. x 2-in. loaf pan coated with cooking spray. Bake at 325° for 50-55 minutes or until a toothpick inserted near the center comes out clean. Cool for 10 minutes before removing from pan to a wire rack to cool completely. **Yield:** 8 servings.

Crab Fettuccine Alfredo

(Pictured above)

PREP/TOTAL TIME: 25 min.

I just can't resist a plate of this creamy Alfredo. With lots of crab, chicken, broccoli, zucchini and cheese, it's an all-in-one meal.
—*Chris Carattini, Dickinson, North Dakota*

> 4 ounces uncooked fettuccine
> 1/4 cup butter
> 2 teaspoons all-purpose flour
> 3/4 cup 2% milk
> 1/2 cup imitation crabmeat
> 1/2 cup cubed cooked chicken
> 1/2 cup shredded Parmesan cheese
> 1/3 cup chopped fresh broccoli
> 1/3 cup chopped zucchini
> 2 teaspoons minced fresh parsley
> Salt and pepper to taste, optional

Cook the fettuccine according to the package directions. Meanwhile, in a small saucepan, melt butter. Stir in flour until smooth. Gradually whisk in the milk. Bring to a boil; cook and stir for 2 minutes or until thickened. Stir in the remaining ingredients; heat through. Drain fettuccine; top with crab mixture. **Yield:** 2 servings.

EXTRA, EXTRA. Have leftover cooked chicken from last night's dinner? Crab Fettuccine Alfredo (recipe above) is the perfect way to use it up. Feel free to change up this delicious main dish by tossing in different vegetables, too.

Mini Blueberry Bundt Cakes

(Pictured below)

PREP: 20 min. **BAKE:** 25 min. + cooling

Here's a special and yummy dessert for a table of two. The pretty blueberry cakes are drizzled with a sweet lemon icing.
—*Cathy Isaak, Rivers, Manitoba*

> 1/4 cup butter, softened
> 1/2 cup sugar
> 1 egg
> 1/4 cup 2% milk
> 1/2 teaspoon vanilla extract
> 1 cup all-purpose flour
> 1 teaspoon baking powder
> 1/4 teaspoon salt
> 1-1/2 cups fresh *or* frozen blueberries
> **LEMON ICING:**
> 1/2 cup confectioners' sugar
> 1-1/2 teaspoons 2% milk
> 1 teaspoon lemon juice
> **Additional blueberries, optional**

In a small bowl, cream butter and sugar. Beat in the egg, milk and vanilla. Combine the flour, baking powder and salt; stir into creamed mixture. Fold in blueberries.

Pour into three 4-in. fluted tube pans coated with cooking spray. Bake at 350° for 25-30 minutes or until a toothpick inserted near the center comes out clean. Cool for 10 minutes before removing from pans to wire racks to cool completely.

For icing, in a small bowl, combine the confectioners' sugar, milk and lemon juice; drizzle over cakes. Garnish with additional berries if desired. **Yield:** 3 servings.

Editor's Note: If using frozen blueberries, use without thawing to avoid discoloring the batter.

Holiday & Seasonal Celebrations

Special times of the year call for extra-special menus that spread good cheer. Delight everyone with a Fudgy Peppermint Stick Torte for Christmas, Honey-Apple Turkey Breast for Thanksgiving and much more.

FESTIVE FAVORITES. Clockwise from top left: Heavenly Filled Strawberries (p. 157), Hot Buttered Rum (p. 185), Merry Mulled Cider (p. 185), Homemade Irish Cream (p. 185), Best Maple-Cranberry Cheesecake (p. 188) and Cranberry Sauce with Walnuts (p. 178).

Valentine's Day Dinner

WHY GO OUT on February 14 for a pricey dinner at a crowded restaurant? Enjoy the comforts of home and treat your special someone to this elegant menu.

Fresh-tasting Mandarin-Walnut Lettuce Salad is the perfect way to start off your romantic meal. After that appetizing first course, savor an entree of tender Chicken Piccata and a side of Parmesan Rice Pilaf.

Don't forget a decadent dessert! Your sweetie will fall in love with any of the tantalizing delights featured here—Grandma's Red Velvet Cake, Heavenly Filled Strawberries and Soft Valentine Cutouts.

Heavenly Filled Strawberries

(Pictured at left and on page 154)

PREP/TOTAL TIME: 20 min.

These luscious stuffed berries are the perfect bite–size dessert for special occasions. Plus, they're easier to make than they appear.
—Stephen Munro, Beaverbank, Nova Scotia

- 1 pound fresh strawberries
- 2 packages (one 8 ounces, one 3 ounces) cream cheese, softened
- 1/2 cup confectioners' sugar
- 1/4 teaspoon almond extract
- Grated chocolate

Remove stems from strawberries; cut a deep "X" in tip of each strawberry. Gently spread strawberries open.

In a small bowl, beat the cream cheese, confectioners' sugar and extract until light and fluffy. Pipe or spoon about 2 teaspoons into each strawberry; sprinkle with chocolate. Chill until serving. **Yield:** about 3 dozen.

Parmesan Rice Pilaf

PREP/TOTAL TIME: 10 min.

My mom discovered this recipe in a local newspaper years ago, and it's been one of our favorite side dishes ever since. Sometimes I fix more than I need for one meal so I can have leftovers.
—Kellie Mulleavy, Lambertville, Michigan

- 1 small onion, chopped
- 2 tablespoons plus 1-1/2 teaspoons butter
- 1 cup uncooked instant rice
- 1 cup water
- 1 teaspoon beef bouillon granules
- 1/4 teaspoon garlic powder
- 1/4 teaspoon pepper
- 2 tablespoons grated Parmesan cheese
- Fresh marjoram sprig and shaved Parmesan cheese, optional

In a small saucepan, saute onion in butter until tender. Stir in the rice, water, bouillon, garlic powder and pepper; bring to a boil.

Remove from heat; cover and let stand for 5 minutes. Stir in grated Parmesan cheese. Garnish with a sprig of marjoram and shaved Parmesan cheese if desired. **Yield:** 2 servings.

Mandarin-Walnut Lettuce Salad

(Pictured below)

PREP/TOTAL TIME: 15 min.

The sweetened walnuts in this medley add a nice crunch and a taste that complements the mandarin oranges. The dressing is tangy and light, just right for the simple salad ingredients.
—Valerie Gee, Depew, New York

- 4-1/2 teaspoons sugar
- 1-1/2 teaspoons water
- 3 tablespoons chopped walnuts
- 4-1/2 teaspoons olive oil
- 2-1/4 teaspoons tarragon vinegar
- Dash salt
- 2-1/2 cups torn Boston lettuce
- 2/3 cup mandarin oranges

In a small saucepan over medium-low heat, bring sugar and water to a boil, stirring constantly. Add the walnuts; cook and stir for 2-3 minutes or until lightly browned. Spread onto a piece of greased foil; set aside.

In a small bowl, whisk the oil, vinegar and salt. In a salad bowl, combine the lettuce and mandarin oranges. Drizzle with dressing and sprinkle with walnuts; toss to coat. **Yield:** 2 servings.

Chicken Piccata

(Pictured above)

PREP/TOTAL TIME: 25 min.

Chicken makes an elegant entree when it gets draped in a rich wine sauce. I usually serve this with rice or pasta, and it takes longer to cook either of those than it does the main course!
— *Carol Cottrill, Rumford, Maine*

- 2 boneless skinless chicken breast halves (4 ounces *each*)
- 2 tablespoons all-purpose flour
- 1/4 teaspoon salt
- 1/8 teaspoon pepper
- 1 tablespoon canola oil
- 2 tablespoons white wine *or* reduced-sodium chicken broth
- 1 garlic clove, minced
- 1/3 cup reduced-sodium chicken broth
- 1 tablespoon lemon juice
- 1-1/2 teaspoons capers
- 1-1/2 teaspoons butter
- 2 thin lemon slices

Flatten chicken to 1/2-in. thickness. In a shallow bowl, combine the flour, salt and pepper. Add the chicken, one piece at a time, and turn to coat.

In a small skillet, brown chicken in oil for 2-3 minutes on each side or until no longer pink. Remove chicken and keep warm.

Add white wine and garlic to the pan; cook and stir for 30 seconds. Add the broth, lemon juice and capers. Bring to a boil; cook for 1-2 minutes or until slightly thickened. Stir in butter and lemon slices. Return chicken to the pan; heat through. **Yield:** 2 servings.

Grandma's Red Velvet Cake

(Pictured below)

PREP: 30 min.   **BAKE:** 20 min. + cooling

Luscious, layered red velvet cake is one of our family's favorite Christmas traditions, but that showstopping dessert is wonderful for any holiday or special occasion. The version here is different from others I've sampled over the years because it has a mild chocolate taste, and the homemade icing is as light as snow.
— *Kathryn Davison, Charlotte, North Carolina*

- 1/2 cup butter, softened
- 1-1/2 cups sugar
- 2 eggs
- 2 bottles (1 ounce *each*) red food coloring
- 1 tablespoon white vinegar
- 1 teaspoon vanilla extract
- 2-1/4 cups cake flour
- 2 tablespoons baking cocoa
- 1 teaspoon baking soda
- 1 teaspoon salt
- 1 cup buttermilk

FROSTING:
- 1 tablespoon cornstarch
- 1/2 cup water
- 2 cups butter, softened
- 2 teaspoons vanilla extract
- 3-1/2 cups confectioners' sugar

In a large bowl, cream butter and sugar until light and fluffy. Add eggs, one at a time, beating well after each addition. Beat in the food coloring, vinegar and vanilla. Combine the flour, cocoa, baking soda and salt; add to creamed mixture alternately with buttermilk, beating well after each addition.

Pour into two greased and floured 9-in. round baking pans. Bake at 350° for 20-25 minutes or until a toothpick inserted near the center comes out clean. Cool cakes for 10 minutes before removing from pans to wire racks to cool completely.

For frosting, in a small saucepan, combine cornstarch and water until smooth. Cook and stir over medium heat for 2-3 minutes or until thickened and opaque. Cool to room temperature.

In a large bowl, beat the butter and vanilla until light and fluffy. Beat in cornstarch mixture. Gradually add confectioners' sugar; beat until the frosting is light and fluffy. Spread frosting between layers and over top and sides of cake. **Yield:** 14 servings.

COOKIE CREATIONS. Have fun with your Soft Valentine Cutouts (recipe at right) by decorating them to resemble old-fashioned candy hearts. With a ready-to-use tube of decorating icing, pipe words and short phrases such as "Love," "Be Mine" and "For You" onto the cooled cutouts. Use a variety of pretty pastel colors.

Soft Valentine Cutouts

(Pictured above)

PREP: 20 min. + chilling **BAKE:** 10 min.

With this recipe, buttery cutout cookies become lovable treats for February 14. I simply cut the rolled dough with a heart–shaped cookie cutter and sprinkle it with decorative red sugar.
—Helen Giroux, Hampton, New York

- 1/2 **cup butter, softened**
- 1 **cup sugar**
- 1 **egg**
- 1/2 **cup sour cream**
- 1/4 **teaspoon lemon extract**
- 1/4 **teaspoon vanilla extract**
- 2 **cups all-purpose flour**
- 1/2 **teaspoon baking soda**
- 1/8 **teaspoon salt**

Red colored sugar

In a large bowl, cream butter and sugar. Beat in the egg, sour cream and extracts. Combine the flour, baking soda and salt; gradually add to creamed mixture. Cover and refrigerate for 3 hours or until easy to handle.

On a lightly floured surface, roll out dough to 1/4-in. thickness. Cut dough with a floured 2-1/2-in. heart-shaped cookie cutter. Place 1 in. apart on ungreased baking sheets. Sprinkle with colored sugar. Bake at 375° for 8-10 minutes or until lightly browned. Remove to wire racks. **Yield:** about 2 dozen.

Easter Sunday Feast

IS PETER COTTONTAIL on his way down the bunny trail? Spring into action for the Easter holiday with a meal featuring the extra-special fare here.

You'll be up to your ears in compliments when guests see the main course of Supreme Stuffed Crown Roast. Round out your menu with Marinated Cheese-Topped Salad, Marmalade Candied Carrots and Incredible Coconut Cake decorated with a Birds Nest Topper. And serve cute Bird Nests to please the kids!

Incredible Coconut Cake

(Pictured at left)

PREP: 35 min. **BAKE:** 25 min. + chilling

My family and friends absolutely adore this dessert. If you like, decorate it with a Birds Nest Topper (recipe at right).
—Lynne Bassler, Indiana, Pennsylvania

- 5 **eggs, *separated***
- 2 cups sugar
- 1/2 cup butter, softened
- 1/2 cup canola oil
- 1 teaspoon coconut extract
- 1/2 teaspoon vanilla extract
- 1/4 teaspoon almond extract
- 2-1/4 cups cake flour
- 1 teaspoon baking powder
- 1/2 teaspoon baking soda
- 1/4 teaspoon salt
- 1 cup buttermilk
- 2 cups flaked coconut, chopped
- 1/4 teaspoon cream of tartar

FROSTING:
- 2 packages (one 8 ounces, one 3 ounces) cream cheese, softened
- 2/3 cup butter, softened
- 4-1/3 cups confectioners' sugar
- 1-1/4 teaspoons coconut extract
- 2 cups flaked coconut, toasted

Place the egg whites in a large bowl; let stand at room temperature for 30 minutes. In another large bowl, beat the sugar, butter and oil until light and fluffy. Add the egg yolks, one at a time, beating well after each addition. Beat in extracts.

Combine the flour, baking powder, baking soda and salt; add to creamed mixture alternately with buttermilk, beating well after each addition. Stir in coconut.

Add cream of tartar to egg whites; beat until stiff peaks form. Gently fold into batter.

Transfer the batter to three greased and floured 9-in. round baking pans. Bake at 325° for 25-30 minutes or until a toothpick inserted near the center comes out clean. Cool for 10 minutes before removing from pans to wire racks to cool completely.

For frosting, in a small bowl, beat the cream cheese and butter until fluffy. Add confectioners' sugar and extract; beat until smooth.

Place one cake layer on a serving plate; spread with 1/2 cup frosting and sprinkle with 1/3 cup coconut. Repeat. Top with remaining cake layer. Spread remaining frosting over the top and sides of cake; sprinkle with remaining coconut. Refrigerate for 2 hours before cutting. Store in the refrigerator. **Yield:** 16 servings.

Birds Nest Topper

(Pictured at far left)

PREP: 50 min.

Developed by our Test Kitchen pros, this cute creation features edible eggs inside a decorative coconut nest. Use this topper on Incredible Coconut Cake (recipe at left) or any cake you like.

- 2 cups finely shredded unsweetened coconut
- 3 to 4 drops blue food coloring, optional
- 32 large marshmallows
- 1 tablespoon butter
- 3 to 4 cups flaked coconut, toasted

Coconut

In a large resealable plastic bag, combine coconut and food coloring, if desired. Seal the bag and shake to tint coconut; set aside.

In a large microwave-safe bowl, microwave the marshmallows and butter until melted; stir until smooth. Stir in the toasted coconut until combined. With greased hands, shape the mixture into small eggs, about 1-1/2 inches long. Add eggs, a few at a time, to coconut; shake vigorously to coat. Place eggs on a waxed paper-lined sheet; let stand until set.

Shaved Coconut Nest: Pierce the eyes of a fresh coconut with hammer and clean nail. Invert the coconut into a colander set in a bowl to drain the liquid. Using the hammer, crack the coconut in half. With the end of a vegetable peeler, pry the coconut meat from the shell, keeping coconut in large pieces for longer strips. Using the peeler, cut the coconut into very thin strips, cutting along the brown skin for color.

Arrange coconut in single layer on ungreased baking sheets. Let stand at room temperature 1 hour or until dry to the touch. Bake at 350° for 5-10 minutes or until lightly toasted, stirring occasionally. Arrange on cake to form a nest; fill with Coconut Bird Eggs. **Yield:** About 8-12 eggs.

Editor's Note: Look for unsweetened coconut in the baking or health food section of your grocery store.

Bird Nests

(Pictured above)

PREP: 40 min.

I use that perennial Easter favorite—Peeps—for these fun chicks in nests. My kids love to help me create them. White chips, candy eggs and pretzel sticks are the only other ingredients needed.
—*Jessica Boivin, Nekoosa, Wisconsin*

> 2 **packages (10 to 12 ounces *each*) white baking chips**
> 1 **package (10 ounces) pretzel sticks**
> 25 **yellow chicks Peeps candy**
> 1 **package (12 ounces) M&M's eggs *or* other egg-shaped candy**

In a large microwave-safe bowl, melt the white chips; stir until smooth. Set aside 1/2 cup for decorating.

Add pretzel sticks to the remaining chips; stir until coated. Scoop a small amount of mixture onto waxed paper; shape into a nest using two forks. Repeat, forming 25 nests. Dip bottom of Peep into reserved white chips; place in a nest. Add eggs to nests, securing with white chips. Repeat. Let stand until set. **Yield:** 25 servings.

WINGING IT. Get creative with your Bird Nests (recipe above) by experimenting with different ingredients. For example, use chocolate instead of white baking chips. Or, replace the pretzel sticks with chow mein noodles.

Marinated Cheese-Topped Salad

(Pictured below)

PREP: 25 min. + marinating

A tongue-tingling homemade vinaigrette coats this refreshing medley of mixed greens, grape tomatoes, olives and "croutons" of marinated cream cheese. It's delicious! I freeze the cream cheese for about 45 minutes to firm it up so it's easier to cut into cubes.
—*Barbara Estabrook, Rhinelander, Wisconsin*

> 1/2 **cup olive oil**
> 2 **tablespoons minced fresh Italian parsley**
> 2 **tablespoons lemon juice**
> 1 **tablespoon minced fresh oregano**
> 1 **tablespoon red wine vinegar**
> 1 **large garlic clove, minced**
> 1/4 **teaspoon salt**
> 1/8 **teaspoon pepper**
> 1 **package (8 ounces) cream cheese, chilled**
> 4 **cups torn romaine**
> 2 **cups fresh arugula *or* baby spinach**
> 1-1/2 **cups grape tomatoes, halved**
> 2 **shallots, thinly sliced**
> 1/2 **cup medium pitted green olives**

For the dressing, in a small bowl, combine the first eight ingredients. Cut cheese into 1/2-inch cubes; toss with half of the dressing. Cover and refrigerate for 30 minutes.

In a large bowl, combine romaine, arugula, tomatoes, shallots and olives. Drizzle with the remaining dressing; toss to coat. Top with the marinated cheese cubes. Serve immediately. **Yield:** 6 servings.

Supreme Stuffed Crown Roast

(Pictured above)

PREP: 20 min. **BAKE:** 2 hours + standing

I've been making crown roasts for years. This one is beautifully roasted with an apricot glaze and nicely browned stuffing.
—*Isabell Cooper, Cambridge, Nova Scotia*

>   1 pork crown roast (12 ribs and about 8 pounds)
> 1/2 teaspoon seasoned salt
> **STUFFING:**
> 1/4 cup butter, cubed
>   1 cup sliced fresh mushrooms
>   1 medium onion, grated
>   1 celery rib, finely chopped
>   1 cup chopped dried apricots
> 1/2 teaspoon dried savory
> 1/2 teaspoon dried thyme
> 1/4 teaspoon salt
> 1/4 teaspoon pepper
>   3 cups soft bread crumbs
> 1/3 cup apricot preserves

Place roast, rib ends up, in a large shallow roasting pan; sprinkle with seasoned salt. Cover the rib ends with foil. Bake, uncovered, at 350° for 1-1/2 hours.

For the stuffing, in a large skillet, melt butter. Add the mushrooms, onion and celery; saute until tender. Stir in apricots and seasonings. Add bread crumbs; toss to coat.

Carefully spoon stuffing into center of roast. Brush sides of roast with preserves. Bake 45-75 minutes longer or until a meat thermometer reads 160°.

Transfer to a warm serving platter. Remove foil. Let roast stand for 10-15 minutes. Cut between ribs to serve. **Yield:** 12 servings.

Marmalade Candied Carrots

(Pictured above)

PREP/TOTAL TIME: 30 min.

Orange marmalade and brown sugar give these crisp–tender carrots a citrusy–sweet flavor that really dresses them up.
—*Heather Clemmons, Supply, North Carolina*

>   2 pounds fresh baby carrots
> 2/3 cup orange marmalade
>   3 tablespoons packed brown sugar
>   2 tablespoons butter
> 1/2 cup chopped pecans, toasted
>   1 teaspoon rum extract

Place the carrots in a steamer basket; place in a large saucepan over 1 in. of water. Bring to a boil; cover and steam for 12-15 minutes or until crisp-tender.

Meanwhile, in a small saucepan, combine the orange marmalade, brown sugar and butter; cook and stir over medium heat until mixture is thickened and reduced to about 1/2 cup. Stir in pecans and extract.

Place carrots in a large bowl; drizzle with glaze and stir gently to coat. **Yield:** 8 servings.

Mother's Day Brunch

IT MAY be impossible to fully thank Mom for all of the love she's given, lessons she's taught and, of course, meals she's cooked. But you sure can try! Start by pampering her on Mother's Day with a homemade brunch she'll never forget.

You'll do her proud when you dish up any of the delights featured here—Honey Coffee, Classic Long Johns, Elegant Fruit Bliss, Irish Oatmeal Brulee, Italian Brunch Torte, Rosemary-Mustard Sausage Patties and Tropical Suncakes.

Because these sunny specialties are easy to prepare, you'll have plenty of time to spend with Mom. And they taste so good, she's sure to request the recipes!

Rosemary-Mustard Sausage Patties

(Pictured at bottom left in the photo at left)

PREP: 10 min. **BAKE:** 15 min.

I once fixed these delicious, rosemary-seasoned sausage patties for breakfast on Christmas morning, and they're now a favorite throughout the year. I like the fact that the pork mixture can be made a day ahead of time and chilled until it's time to bake.
—Deborah Harris, Colorado Springs, Colorado

- 2 **medium onions, finely chopped**
- 4 **teaspoons olive oil**
- 2 **teaspoons minced fresh rosemary** *or*
  3/4 teaspoon dried rosemary, crushed
- 4 **teaspoons stone-ground mustard**
- 1/2 **teaspoon pepper**
- 2 **pounds bulk pork sausage**

In a large skillet, saute the onions in oil until tender. Add the rosemary; cook 1 minute longer. Transfer to a large bowl; stir in the mustard and pepper. Crumble sausage over mixture; mix well. Shape mixture by 1/4 cupfuls into thin patties.

Place patties in ungreased 15-in. x 10-in. x 1-in. baking pans. Bake at 375° for 12-15 minutes or until the meat is no longer pink. Drain if necessary on paper towels. **Yield:** 16 sausage patties.

Elegant Fruit Bliss

(Pictured at top in the photo at left)

PREP/TOTAL TIME: 20 min.

This colorful, refreshing salad is nice enough to serve as a light dessert. A mild dressing made with peach nectar and honey adds a hint of sweetness to the pretty assortment of fresh fruit.
—Peggy West, Georgetown, Delaware

- 1 **medium cantaloupe, peeled, seeded and cubed**
- 2 **large navel oranges, peeled and sectioned**
- 2 **cups cubed fresh pineapple**
- 2 **medium kiwifruit, peeled and sliced**
- 1 **cup green grapes**
- 1 **cup red grapes**
- 3/4 **cup peach** *or* **apricot nectar**
- 1/4 **cup honey**
- 2 **tablespoons lemon juice**
- 2 **tablespoons balsamic vinegar**

In a large bowl, combine the first six ingredients. In a small bowl, whisk the peach nectar, honey, lemon juice and vinegar; drizzle over fruit and toss to coat. Chill until serving. **Yield:** 13 servings (3/4 cup each).

Tropical Suncakes

(Pictured at bottom right in the photo at left)

PREP: 25 min. **COOK:** 5 min./batch

My daughter-in-law, who is a fantastic cook, introduced me to these tender, citrusy pancakes. With ricotta cheese and a simple strawberry-orange sauce, they're a wonderful change of pace.
—Ginger Sullivan, Cutler Bay, Florida

- 1/2 **cup all-purpose flour**
- 4 **teaspoons sugar**
- 1/2 **teaspoon baking powder**
- 1/4 **teaspoon salt**
- 4 **eggs,** *separated*
- 1-1/3 **cups ricotta cheese**
- 1/2 **cup milk**
- 1 **tablespoon grated orange peel**
- **STRAWBERRY ORANGE SAUCE:**
- 2 **cups frozen unsweetened strawberries**
- 1/4 **cup orange juice**
- 2 **tablespoons sugar**
- 2 **teaspoons grated orange peel**

In a large bowl, combine the flour, sugar, baking powder and salt. Combine the egg yolks, ricotta cheese, milk and orange peel; stir into the dry ingredients just until moistened. Beat the egg whites until stiff peaks form; fold into the batter.

Pour batter by 1/4 cupfuls onto a greased hot griddle; turn when bubbles form on top. Cook until second side is golden brown.

Meanwhile, in a small saucepan, combine the sauce ingredients. Bring to a boil. Reduce the heat; simmer, uncovered, for 5-10 minutes or until syrupy. Serve with suncakes. **Yield:** 16 suncakes (1-1/4 cups sauce).

Place between two paper towels and blot to remove excess liquid. In a large bowl, whisk six eggs, Parmesan cheese, Italian seasoning and pepper.

Layer the prepared crust with half of the ham, salami, provolone cheese, red peppers, spinach mixture and egg mixture. Repeat layers.

Separate remaining crescent dough; press triangles together to form a top crust. Place over casserole. Whisk remaining egg; brush over dough.

Bake, uncovered, at 350° for 1 to 1-1/4 hours or until a thermometer reads 160°. Cover loosely with foil if the top browns too quickly. Carefully run a knife around the edge of the pan to loosen; remove the sides of pan. Let stand for 20 minutes before slicing. **Yield:** 12 servings.

Honey Coffee

(Pictured below)

PREP/TOTAL TIME: 10 min.

For a quick pick-me-up in the morning or anytime, sip a cup of this pleasantly sweet java from our Test Kitchen pros. It was inspired by the taste of a traditional Spanish latte.

- 2 cups hot strong brewed coffee (French *or* other dark roast)
- 1/2 cup milk
- 1/4 cup honey
- 1/8 teaspoon ground cinnamon
- Dash ground nutmeg
- 1/4 teaspoon vanilla extract

In a small saucepan, combine the coffee, milk, honey, cinnamon and nutmeg. Cook and stir until heated through. (Do not boil.) Remove from the heat; stir in the vanilla. Pour into cups or mugs; serve immediately. **Yield:** 4 servings.

Italian Brunch Torte

(Pictured above)

PREP: 50 min. **BAKE:** 1 hour + standing

This impressive layered breakfast bake filled with deli meat and cheese is one of our most-requested dishes, and it can be served warm or cold. We like it with a salad of greens and tomatoes.
—*Danny Diamond, Farmington Hills, Michigan*

- 2 tubes (8 ounces *each)* refrigerated crescent rolls, *divided*
- 1 package (6 ounces) fresh baby spinach
- 1 cup sliced fresh mushrooms
- 1 teaspoon olive oil
- 7 eggs
- 1 cup grated Parmesan cheese
- 2 teaspoons Italian seasoning
- 1/8 teaspoon pepper
- 1/2 pound thinly sliced deli ham
- 1/2 pound thinly sliced hard salami
- 1/2 pound sliced provolone cheese
- 2 jars (12 ounces *each)* roasted sweet red peppers, drained, sliced and patted dry

Place a greased 9-in. springform pan on a double thickness of heavy-duty foil (about 18 in. square). Securely wrap foil around pan. Separate one tube crescent dough into eight triangles; press onto the bottom of prepared pan. Bake at 350° for 10-15 minutes or until set.

Meanwhile, in a large skillet over medium heat, cook spinach and mushrooms in oil until the spinach is wilted.

Classic Long Johns

PREP: 30 min. + rising **COOK:** 5 min./batch + cooling

I remember my mother making wonderful doughnuts like these. You can frost them with the maple or chocolate glaze, then top them with chopped nuts, jimmies, toasted coconut or sprinkles.
—Ann Sorgent, Fond du Lac, Wisconsin

- 2 packages (1/4 ounce *each*) active dry yeast
- 1/2 cup warm water (110° to 115°)
- 1/2 cup half-and-half cream
- 1/4 cup sugar
- 1/4 cup shortening
- 1 egg
- 1 teaspoon salt
- 1/2 teaspoon ground nutmeg
- 3 to 3-1/2 cups all-purpose flour
Oil for deep-fat frying
MAPLE FROSTING:
- 1/4 cup packed brown sugar
- 2 tablespoons butter
- 1 tablespoon half-and-half cream
- 1/8 teaspoon maple flavoring
- 1 cup confectioners' sugar
CHOCOLATE FROSTING:
- 2 ounces semisweet chocolate, chopped
- 2 tablespoons butter
- 1 cup confectioners' sugar
- 2 tablespoons boiling water
- 1 teaspoon vanilla extract

In a large bowl, dissolve the yeast in warm water. Add cream, sugar, shortening, egg, salt, nutmeg and 3 cups flour. Beat until smooth. Stir in enough remaining flour to form a soft dough (dough will be sticky).

Turn dough onto a floured surface; knead until smooth and elastic, about 6-8 minutes. Place in a greased bowl, turning once to grease the top. Cover and let rise in a warm place until doubled, about 1 hour.

Punch dough down; divide in half. Turn onto a lightly floured surface; roll each half into a 12-in. x 6-in. rectangle. Cut into 3-in. x 2-in. rectangles. Place on greased baking sheets. Cover and let rise in a warm place until doubled, about 30 minutes.

In an electric skillet or deep fryer, heat oil to 375°. Fry long johns, a few at a time, until golden brown on both sides. Drain on paper towels.

For the maple frosting, combine the brown sugar and butter in a small saucepan. Bring to a boil; cook and stir for 2 minutes or until sugar is dissolved. Remove from the heat; stir in the cream and maple flavoring. Add the confectioners' sugar; beat for 1 minute or until smooth. Frost cooled long johns.

For the chocolate frosting, in a microwave, melt the chocolate and butter. Stir until smooth. Stir in remaining ingredients. Spread over the cooled long johns; let stand until set. **Yield:** 2 dozen.

Irish Oatmeal Brulee

(Pictured above)

PREP: 15 min. + simmering **BROIL:** 5 min.

With mild maple flavor and a crispy broiled topping, my oatmeal is a comforting yet special morning treat. I sometimes replace the raisins with dried cherries and add star anise for extra spice.
—Rose Ann Wilson, Germantown, Wisconsin

- 8 cups 2% milk
- 2 cups steel-cut oats
- 1 cinnamon stick (3 inches)
- 1 orange peel strip (1 to 3 inches)
Dash salt
- 3/4 cup dried cranberries
- 1/2 cup golden raisins
- 1/2 cup maple syrup
Buttermilk, optional
- 1/2 cup packed brown sugar

In a large heavy saucepan, bring the milk to a boil over medium heat. Add the oats, cinnamon, orange peel and salt. Reduce heat; simmer for 30 minutes or until thick and creamy, stirring occasionally.

Remove from the heat; discard cinnamon and orange peel. Stir in the cranberries, golden raisins, maple syrup and a small amount of buttermilk if desired. Cover and let stand for 2 minutes.

Transfer to eight ungreased 6-oz. ramekins. Place on a baking sheet. Sprinkle with brown sugar. Broil 8 in. from the heat for 4-7 minutes or until the sugar is caramelized. Serve immediately. **Yield:** 8 servings.

Editor's Note: Steel-cut oats are also known as Scotch oats or Irish oatmeal.

Sweet Treats for July Fourth

FROM the tiniest towns to the biggest cities, the Fourth of July calls for special festivities—spectacular fireworks, marching bands and cookouts galore. So why serve just any old dessert?

Bring some patriotic pizzazz to your holiday menu with sparkling miniature sweets such as Razzy Jazzy Berry Tarts arranged to resemble a flag. Keep things classic with a fruit-packed Bluebarb Pie, or present a real showstopper like Red Velvet Crepe Cakes or Red, White and Blue Cheesecake.

Hosting kids? Thrill them with tot-friendly treats—Firecracker Cupcakes and Strawberry Patch Frost.

Red, White and Blue Cheesecake

(Pictured at left)

PREP: 40 min. **BAKE:** 1-1/4 hours + chilling

I made this rich dessert for the Fourth of July, and it was a hit. With red and blue berries on top, it looks and tastes good.
—*Connie LaFond, Troy, New York*

- 1-1/2 **cups all-purpose flour**
- 1/3 **cup sugar**
- 1 **teaspoon grated lemon peel**
- 3/4 **cup cold butter**
- 2 **egg yolks**
- 1/2 **teaspoon vanilla extract**

FILLING:
- 5 **packages (8 ounces *each*) cream cheese, softened**
- 1 **cup sugar**
- 1/4 **cup half-and-half cream**
- 3 **tablespoons all-purpose flour**
- 1/2 **teaspoon grated lemon peel**
- 1/4 **teaspoon salt**
- 1/4 **teaspoon vanilla extract**
- 2 **eggs, lightly beaten**
- 1 **egg yolk**
- 1 **cup crushed strawberries**
- 1 **cup crushed blueberries**

Fresh mixed berries and currants, optional

In a large bowl, combine the flour, sugar and lemon peel. Cut in butter until crumbly. Whisk egg yolks and vanilla; add to flour mixture, tossing with a fork until the dough forms a ball.

Press onto the bottom and 3 in. up the sides of a greased 9-in. springform pan. Place the pan on a baking sheet. Bake at 400° for 12-15 minutes or until golden brown. Cool on a wire rack.

For filling, in a large bowl, beat cream cheese and sugar until smooth. Beat in the cream, flour, lemon peel, salt and vanilla. Add the eggs and yolk; beat on low speed just until combined.

Divide the batter in half. Fold the crushed strawberries and crushed blueberries into half of the batter. Pour into the crust. Top with the remaining batter. Return pan to baking sheet.

Bake at 400° for 10 minutes. Reduce heat to 300°; bake 60-70 minutes longer or until center is almost set. Cool on a wire rack for 10 minutes. Carefully run a knife around the edge of pan to loosen; cool 1 hour longer. Refrigerate overnight. Remove sides of pan.

Garnish with mixed berries and currants, if desired. **Yield:** 16 servings.

Strawberry Patch Frost

PREP/TOTAL TIME: 5 min.

Fresh strawberries become a luscious chilled treat in this pretty and simple beverage from our Test Kitchen staff. What a great way to cool down on a hot summer's day!

- 2 **tablespoons strawberry jam**
- 1 **teaspoon water**
- 3 **scoops strawberry ice cream**
- 1/2 **cup sliced fresh strawberries**
- 1/4 **cup heavy whipping cream *or* half-and-half cream**
- 1 **cup chilled strawberry *or* raspberry sparkling water**

Whipped cream
Colored sprinkles

In a tall glass, combine strawberry jam and water. Add ice cream, strawberries and cream. Top with sparkling water. Garnish with whipped cream and sprinkles. Serve immediately. **Yield:** 1 serving.

CHEESECAKE CHECKLIST. Keep these helpful tips in mind when making cheesecakes:

- Before preheating the oven, arrange the oven racks so that the cheesecake will bake in the center of the oven.
- For best results, use regular cream cheese unless the recipe specifically calls for a reduced-fat or fat-free product.
- To avoid lumps in the cheescake batter, always soften the cream cheese at room temperature for about 30 minutes before mixing.

Firecracker Cupcakes

(Pictured below)

PREP/TOTAL TIME: 30 min.

Thrill the kids—and kids at heart—at patriotic parties with these fuss-free goodies. If you like, tint the whipped topping red and blue to make the cute cupcakes even more colorful.

—Erin Glass, White Hall, Maryland

> 5 red pull-and-peel licorice
> 6 drops red food coloring
> 1 cup flaked coconut, *divided*
> 4 drops blue food coloring
> 1 carton (12 ounces) frozen whipped topping, thawed
> 24 cupcakes
> Assorted red and blue sprinkles, optional

Cut each licorice twist into five pieces; pull apart one end of each to make firecracker fuses. Set aside.

In a resealable plastic bag, combine 1/4 teaspoon water and red food coloring; add 1/2 cup coconut. Seal the bag and shake to tint the coconut. In another bag, combine 1/4 teaspoon water and blue food coloring; add the remaining coconut. Seal bag and shake to tint.

Spread whipped topping over cupcakes; decorate with coconut or sprinkles as desired. Insert firecracker fuses into tops. Refrigerate until serving. **Yield:** 2 dozen.

Red Velvet Crepe Cakes

(Pictured above)

PREP: 1-1/4 hours **COOK:** 25 min.

This special cake is sure to impress. I've found that the first crepe never works—it's the number one rule of crepe-making—so keep trying. You'll be glad you did! I sometimes scrape a vanilla bean into the frosting mixture instead of using vanilla extract.

—Crystal Heaton, Alton, Utah

> 1 package (18-1/4 ounces) red velvet cake mix
> 2-3/4 cups whole milk
> 1 cup all-purpose flour
> 3 eggs
> 3 egg yolks
> 1/4 cup butter, melted
> 3 teaspoons vanilla extract
> **FROSTING:**
> 5 packages (3 ounces *each*) cream cheese, softened
> 1-1/4 cups butter, softened
> 1/2 teaspoon salt
> 12 cups confectioners' sugar
> 5 teaspoons vanilla extract
> Fresh blueberries, optional

In a large bowl, combine the red velvet cake mix, milk, flour, eggs, egg yolks, butter and vanilla; beat on low speed for 30 seconds. Beat on medium for 2 minutes.

Heat a lightly greased 8-in. nonstick skillet over medium heat; pour 1/4 cup batter into center of skillet. Lift and tilt the pan to coat bottom evenly. Cook until top

appears dry; turn and cook 15-20 seconds longer. Remove to a wire rack. Repeat with remaining batter, greasing skillet as needed. When cool, stack crepes with waxed paper or paper towels in between.

For the frosting, in a large bowl, beat the cream cheese, butter and salt until fluffy. Add confectioners' sugar and vanilla; beat until smooth.

To assemble two crepe cakes, place one crepe on each of two cake plates. Spread each with one rounded tablespoon frosting to within 1/2 in. of edges. Repeat layers until all crepes are used. Spread the remaining frosting over tops and sides of crepe cakes. Garnish with berries if desired. **Yield:** 2 crepe cakes (8 servings each).

Bluebarb Pie

PREP: 50 min. + chilling **BAKE:** 40 min. + cooling

If you're a fan of classic strawberry–rhubarb pie, you'll want to taste this scrumptious twist. Plenty of blueberries provide a sweet counterpoint to the tartness, with mouthwatering results.
—*Steve Gyuro, Franklin, Wisconsin*

> 2 **cups all-purpose flour**
> 1 **teaspoon salt**
> 2/3 **cup shortening**
> 6 **to 8 tablespoons ice water**

FILLING:

> 1-1/2 **cups sugar**
> 3 **tablespoons quick-cooking tapioca**
> 1/4 **teaspoon salt**
> 4 **cups sliced fresh *or* frozen rhubarb, thawed**
> 2 **cups fresh *or* frozen blueberries, thawed**
> 1 **tablespoon butter**
> 1 **teaspoon 2% milk**

Coarse sugar *or* additional granulated sugar, optional

In a small bowl, combine the flour and salt; cut in the shortening until crumbly. Gradually add water, tossing with a fork until the dough forms a ball. Divide dough in half so that one portion is slightly larger than the other; wrap each in plastic wrap. Refrigerate for 4 hours or until easy to handle.

On a lightly floured surface, roll out larger portion of dough to fit a 9-in. deep-dish pie plate. Transfer pastry to pie plate. Trim pastry even with edge.

For filling, in a large bowl, combine the sugar, tapioca and salt. Add rhubarb and blueberries; toss to coat. Let stand for 15 minutes. Transfer to crust. Dot with butter.

Roll out remaining pastry to fit top of pie. Place over filling. Trim, seal and flute edges. Cut slits in pastry. Brush with milk; sprinkle with coarse sugar if desired.

Bake at 400° for 40-45 minutes or until crust is golden brown and filling is bubbly. Cover edges with foil during the last 15 minutes to prevent overbrowning if necessary. Cool on a wire rack. **Yield:** 8 servings.

Editor's Note: If using frozen rhubarb, measure the rhubarb while still frozen, then thaw completely. Drain in a colander, but do not press liquid out.

Razzy Jazzy Berry Tarts

(Pictured below)

PREP: 1 hour **BAKE:** 20 min.

I serve these fun treats every year at my family's Independence Day celebration. The festive flag display shown in the photo uses 48 of the tarts, so you'll need to make a batch and a half.
—*Nicole Chatron, Tulsa, Oklahoma*

> 1 **cup butter, softened**
> 2 **packages (3 ounces *each*) cream cheese, softened**
> 2 **cups all-purpose flour**
> 1/2 **teaspoon salt**
> 1-1/2 **cups fresh blueberries**
> 2/3 **cup blueberry preserves**
> 1-1/2 **cups fresh raspberries**
> 2/3 **cup seedless raspberry jam**

In a large bowl, beat the butter and cream cheese until smooth. Combine the flour and salt; gradually add to creamed mixture.

Drop dough by scant tablespoonfuls into 36 greased miniature muffin cups. With well-floured hands, press dough onto the bottoms and up the sides of cups; flute edges if desired.

Bake the tarts at 325° for 20-25 minutes or until golden brown. Cool for 5 minutes before removing from pans to wire racks to cool completely.

On a lightly floured surface, roll the remaining dough to 1/8-in. thickness. Cut stars with a floured 1-1/2-in. star-shaped cookie cutter; cut 1/4-in. stripes with a small knife. Place stars and stripes on ungreased baking sheets. Bake at 325° for 4-6 minutes or until lightly browned.

In a small bowl, combine blueberries and blueberry preserves; spoon into half of the tarts. In another bowl, combine raspberries and raspberry jam; spoon into the remaining tarts. Top with cutouts. **Yield:** 3 dozen.

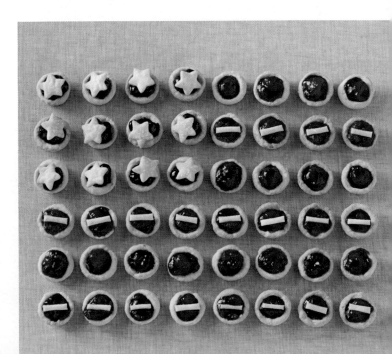

Fresh-Baked for Fall

AS THE LEAVES tumble down and the weather turns brisk, nothing tastes better than a warm-you-up baked treat fresh from the oven. Here, you'll find a special selection of autumn-inspired delights you and your family are sure to love.

Crave the fall flavor of pumpkin? We've featured an array of tempting goodies, from a flaky batch of biscuits and two tender loaves of bread to a rich and creamy cheesecake pie.

Enjoy this cool, colorful season even more by indulging in fruity Apple Crisp Muffins and irresistible Double Chocolate Orange Brownies. Yum!

Apple Crisp Muffins

(Pictured at left)

PREP: 30 min. **BAKE:** 20 min.

Cream cheese filling makes these dessert-like muffins moist and tender, and the oats and nuts in the topping add crunch.
—Connie Boll, Chilton, Wisconsin

- 2 cups all-purpose flour
- 1/3 cup packed brown sugar
- 2 teaspoons baking powder
- 1/2 teaspoon salt
- 1/2 teaspoon ground cinnamon
- 1 egg, beaten
- 1 cup 2% milk
- 1/2 cup canola oil
- 2 cups finely chopped peeled apples

FILLING:

- 1 package (8 ounces) cream cheese, softened
- 2 tablespoons maple syrup
- 4 teaspoons grated orange peel
- 1/4 teaspoon ground nutmeg

TOPPING:

- 1/4 cup all-purpose flour
- 1/4 cup old-fashioned oats
- 1/4 cup packed brown sugar
- 1/4 teaspoon ground cinnamon
- 3 tablespoons cold butter
- 1/4 cup chopped pecans

In a large bowl, combine flour, sugar, baking powder, salt and cinnamon. In another bowl, combine the egg, milk and oil. Stir into the dry ingredients just until moistened. Fold in the apples. Fill greased or paper-lined muffin cups three-fourths full.

In a small bowl, beat filling ingredients until smooth. Drop by tablespoonfuls into centers of muffins.

For topping, in a small bowl, combine the flour, oats, brown sugar and cinnamon. Cut in butter until crumbly. Stir in pecans. Sprinkle over filling. Bake at 400° for 16-20 minutes or until a toothpick inserted in muffin comes out clean. Cool for 5 minutes before removing from pan to wire rack. **Yield:** 1 dozen.

Double Chocolate Orange Brownies

(Pictured below)

PREP: 15 min. **BAKE:** 30 min. + cooling

My husband and I love the flavor combination of chocolate and orange, so he suggested I try creating a treat featuring both. My citrusy, sugar-dusted brownies were the yummy result.
—Elinor Townsend, North Grafton, Massachusetts

- 3/4 cup butter, cubed
- 4 ounces unsweetened chocolate, chopped
- 3 eggs
- 2 cups sugar
- 1 teaspoon orange extract
- 1 cup all-purpose flour
- 1 cup (6 ounces) semisweet chocolate chips

Confectioners' sugar

In a microwave, melt the butter and chocolate; stir until smooth. Cool slightly. In a large bowl, beat the eggs and sugar. Stir in the chocolate mixture. Beat in the extract. Gradually add flour to chocolate mixture.

Pour into a greased 13-in. x 9-in. baking dish. Sprinkle with the chocolate chips. Bake at 350° for 30-35 minutes or until a toothpick inserted near the center comes out clean (do not overbake).

Cool completely on a wire rack. Cut into squares. Just before serving, sprinkle brownies with confectioners' sugar. **Yield:** 2 dozen.

Pumpkin Cheesecake Pie

(Pictured below)

PREP: 30 min. **BAKE:** 45 min. + chilling

If you're looking for a classic fall dessert, try this rich and creamy cheesecake pie. For an elegant presentation, use a paper doily when sprinkling on the cinnamon to create a pretty pattern.
—*Sharon Crockett, La Palma, California*

- 1-1/2 cups crushed gingersnap cookies
- 1 tablespoon sugar
- 1/4 cup butter, melted

FILLING:
- 2 packages (8 ounces *each*) cream cheese, softened
- 3/4 cup sugar
- 2 eggs, lightly beaten
- 1 can (15 ounces) solid-pack pumpkin
- 1 teaspoon ground cinnamon
- 1/4 teaspoon ground ginger
- 1/4 teaspoon ground nutmeg
- 1/8 teaspoon salt

TOPPING:
- 1 cup (8 ounces) sour cream
- 1/4 cup sugar
- 1 teaspoon vanilla extract

Ground cinnamon, optional

In a small bowl, combine gingersnap crumbs and sugar. Stir in butter. Press onto the bottom and up the sides of a greased 9-in. deep-dish pie plate. Bake at 350° for 8-10 minutes or until lightly browned.

In a large bowl, beat the cream cheese and sugar until smooth. Add eggs; beat on low speed just until combined. Stir in the pumpkin, cinnamon, ginger, nutmeg and salt.

Pour into the crust. Bake for 35-40 minutes or until the center is almost set.

In a small bowl, combine the sour cream, sugar and vanilla. Spread over the pie. Bake 8-12 minutes longer or until set. Cool on a wire rack. Cover and refrigerate for at least 4 hours. Sprinkle with cinnamon if desired. **Yield:** 8-10 servings.

Pumpkin Patch Biscuits

PREP: 20 min. **BAKE:** 20 min.

To meet the demand, I usually prepare a double batch of these tender, fluffy biscuits. My dad loves their pumpkin flavor and always requests them for Father's Day and his birthday.
—*Liza Taylor, Seattle, Washington*

- 1-3/4 cups all-purpose flour
- 1/4 cup packed brown sugar
- 2-1/2 teaspoons baking powder
- 1/2 teaspoon salt
- 1/4 teaspoon baking soda
- 1/2 cup plus 1-1/2 teaspoons cold butter, *divided*
- 3/4 cup canned pumpkin
- 1/3 cup buttermilk

In a large bowl, combine the flour, brown sugar, baking powder, salt and baking soda. Cut in 1/2 cup butter until the mixture resembles coarse crumbs. Combine pumpkin and buttermilk; stir into the crumb mixture just until moistened.

Turn dough onto a lightly floured surface; knead 8-10 times. Pat or roll out to 1-in. thickness; cut with a floured 2-1/2-in. biscuit cutter. Place 1 in. apart on a greased baking sheet.

Bake at 425° for 18-22 minutes or until golden brown. Melt the remaining butter; brush over the biscuits. Serve warm. **Yield:** 6 biscuits.

Swirled Pumpkin Yeast Bread

(Pictured at top right)

PREP: 45 min. + rising **BAKE:** 55 min. + cooling

I call this my "hostess gift" bread, but it's fantastic any time at all. Swirls of cinnamon–sugar make each slice irresistible.
—*Shirley Runkle, St. Paris, Ohio*

- 4-1/2 to 5 cups all-purpose flour
- 3 cups whole wheat flour
- 2 cups quick-cooking oats
- 2/3 cup packed brown sugar
- 2-1/2 teaspoons pumpkin pie spice
- 1-1/2 teaspoons salt
- 1 teaspoon sugar
- 2 packages (1/4 ounce *each*) active dry yeast
- 1-1/2 cups warm water (120° to 130°)
- 1 cup canned pumpkin
- 1/3 cup unsweetened applesauce
- 1/3 cup canola oil
- 2 eggs, lightly beaten

1/2 **cup raisins**
FILLING:
  1/4 **cup butter, softened**
  1/2 **cup packed brown sugar**
    1 **teaspoon ground cinnamon**

In a large bowl, combine 2 cups all-purpose flour, whole wheat flour, oats, brown sugar, pie spice, salt, sugar and yeast. Beat in the warm water, pumpkin, applesauce and oil just until moistened. Add the eggs; beat until smooth. Stir in enough remaining all-purpose flour to form a firm dough. Add raisins.

Turn onto a lightly floured surface; knead until smooth and elastic, about 6-8 minutes. Place in a greased bowl, turning once to grease top. Cover and let rise in a warm place until doubled, about 1 hour.

Punch dough down. Turn onto a lightly floured surface; divide in half. Roll each portion of dough into an 18-in. x 9-in. rectangle; brush with butter to within 1/2 in. of edges. Combine the brown sugar and cinnamon; sprinkle over dough. Roll up jelly-roll style, starting with a short side; pinch seam to seal.

Place seam side down in two greased 9-in. x 5-in. loaf pans. Cover and let rise until doubled, about 30 minutes.

Bake at 350° for 55-65 minutes or until golden brown. Cool for 10 minutes before removing from pans to wire racks. **Yield:** 2 loaves (16 slices each).

Rustic Pumpkin Bread

(Pictured at right)

PREP: 25 min. **BAKE:** 1 hour + cooling

This recipe came from a coworker who brought it to an office party. The nutty loaf is so good, I now bake it every year for the holidays. The recipe includes three yummy variations at the end.
—*Sandy Sandaval, Sandy Valley, Nevada*

    3 **cups sugar**
    1 **can (15 ounces) solid-pack pumpkin**
    1 **cup canola oil**
    4 **eggs**
  2/3 **cup water**
3-1/2 **cups all-purpose flour**
    2 **teaspoons baking soda**
    1 **teaspoon salt**
    1 **teaspoon ground cinnamon**
    1 **teaspoon ground nutmeg**
  1/2 **teaspoon ground cloves**
  1/2 **cup chopped pecans**
TOPPING:
  1/3 **cup all-purpose flour**
  1/4 **cup packed brown sugar**
  1/2 **teaspoon ground cinnamon**
    2 **tablespoons cold butter**
  1/4 **cup chopped pecans**

In a large bowl, beat the sugar, pumpkin, oil, eggs and water until blended. In a large bowl, combine the flour, baking soda, salt, cinnamon, nutmeg and cloves; gradually beat into the pumpkin mixture until blended. Stir in pecans.

Pour into two greased 9-in. x 5-in. loaf pans. For the topping, in a small bowl, combine the flour, brown sugar and cinnamon; cut in the butter until mixture resembles coarse crumbs. Stir in pecans. Sprinkle over batter.

Bake at 350° for 60-65 minutes or until a toothpick inserted near the center comes out clean. Cool loaves for 10 minutes before removing from the pans to wire racks. **Yield:** 2 loaves (16 slices each).

Cranberry Pumpkin Bread: Fold in 1-1/2 cups fresh or thawed frozen cranberries with the pecans.

Pistachio Pumpkin Bread: Substitute pistachios for pecans in the batter and topping.

Pumpkin Chip Bread: Fold in 1 cup miniature semisweet chocolate chips with the pecans.

Thanksgiving Gathering

DINING TABLES are always at their most bountiful on Turkey Day. Looking for extra-special fare for your menu? Feast your eyes on the selection here!

A main course of Honey-Apple Turkey Breast will be the centerpiece of your holiday meal. For standout side dishes, consider Shoepeg Corn Supreme, Hazelnut and Pear Salad, Roasted Garlic Mashed Potatoes and Cranberry Sauce with Walnuts.

Have plenty of vanilla ice cream or whipped cream on hand to top off fresh-baked slices of golden, fruity Cranberry-Pecan Pear Pie. With such a luscious dessert, everyone will be sure to save room!

Honey-Apple Turkey Breast

(Pictured at left)

PREP: 10 min. **BAKE:** 2 hours + standing

I saw this recipe in a diabetics' cookbook, and even people who are not on a special diet love it. The sweetness of the honey comes through when I use the leftovers in casseroles and soups, too.
—*Rita Reinke, Wauwatosa, Wisconsin*

- 3/4 cup thawed apple juice concentrate
- 1/3 cup honey
- 1 tablespoon ground mustard
- 1 bone-in turkey breast (6 to 7 pounds)

In a small saucepan, combine apple juice concentrate, honey and mustard. Cook over low heat for 2-3 minutes or just until blended, stirring occasionally.

Remove the skin from the turkey if desired; place on a rack in a foil-lined shallow roasting pan. Pour honey mixture over turkey.

Bake, uncovered, at 325° for 2 to 2-1/2 hours or until a meat thermometer reads 180°, basting with pan juices every 30 minutes. (Cover loosely with foil if the turkey browns too quickly.) Cover and let stand for 15 minutes before carving. **Yield:** 12-14 servings.

Cranberry-Pecan Pear Pie

(Pictured at right)

PREP: 30 min. **BAKE:** 55 min. + cooling

This is one of my favorite desserts to make in the fall. The spiced filling pairs perfectly with the buttery, flaky crust. I always make two of these luscious pies because one just isn't enough!
—*Frances Benthin, Scio, Oregon*

- 2 cups all-purpose flour
- 1/2 teaspoon salt
- 3/4 cup cold butter
- 6 tablespoons cold water

FILLING:
- 4 cups sliced peeled fresh pears (about 5 medium)
- 1/2 cup chopped dried cranberries
- 1/2 cup chopped pecans
- 1/2 cup honey
- 1/4 cup butter, melted
- 3 tablespoons cornstarch
- 2 tablespoons grated lemon peel
- 1 teaspoon ground cinnamon
- 1 tablespoon milk
- 1-1/2 teaspoons sugar

In a bowl, combine the flour and salt. Cut in butter until crumbly. Gradually add water, tossing with a fork until dough forms a ball. Roll out half of the pastry to fit a 9-in. pie plate; transfer pastry to pie plate.

In a bowl, combine pears, dried cranberries, pecans, honey, butter, cornstarch, lemon peel and cinnamon; pour into crust. Roll out remaining pastry; make a lattice crust. Trim, seal and flute edges. Brush with milk; sprinkle with sugar.

Bake at 400° for 15 minutes. Reduce heat to 350°; bake 40-50 minutes longer or until crust is golden brown and filling is bubbly. Cool on a wire rack. **Yield:** 8 servings.

Shoepeg Corn Supreme

(Pictured above)

PREP: 10 min.   **BAKE:** 25 min.

I dress up canned corn with green pepper, cream of celery soup and cheddar cheese for a deluxe, holiday-worthy side dish. The butter-flavored cracker coating is the crowning touch.
—Linda Roberson, Collierville, Tennessee

- 1 small green pepper, chopped
- 1 small onion, chopped
- 1 celery rib, chopped
- 2 tablespoons olive oil
- 3 cans (7 ounces *each*) white *or* shoepeg corn, drained
- 1 can (10-3/4 ounces) condensed cream of celery soup, undiluted
- 1 cup (8 ounces) sour cream
- 1/2 cup shredded sharp cheddar cheese
- 1/4 teaspoon pepper
- 1-1/2 cups crushed butter-flavored crackers
- 3 tablespoons butter, melted

In a large skillet, saute the green pepper, onion and celery in oil until tender. Remove from the heat; stir in the corn, cream of celery soup, sour cream, cheddar cheese and pepper. Transfer mixture to a greased 11-in. x 7-in. baking dish.

Combine cracker crumbs and butter; sprinkle over the top. Bake, uncovered, at 350° for 25-30 minutes or until bubbly. **Yield:** 8 servings.

Roasted Garlic Mashed Potatoes

PREP: 20 min.   **BAKE:** 30 min. + cooling

Yukon Golds give this variation of mashed potatoes a buttery color and hearty texture. I've taken the garlicky spuds to many potlucks, and I never have any leftovers to take home.
—Marilyn Geary-Symons, Portland, Oregon

- 1 whole garlic bulb
- 1 teaspoon olive oil
- 2-1/2 pounds Yukon Gold potatoes, peeled and quartered
- 2 cups chicken broth, *divided*
- 1/4 cup butter, softened
- 1/4 teaspoon pepper
- 1/8 teaspoon salt

Remove papery outer skin from garlic bulb (do not peel or separate cloves). Cut top off bulb; brush with oil. Wrap in heavy-duty foil. Bake at 425° for 30-35 minutes or until softened. Cool for 10-15 minutes.

Meanwhile, place the potatoes in a large saucepan and cover with water. Bring to a boil. Reduce heat; cover and cook for 15-20 minutes or until tender.

Place 1 cup broth in a blender. Squeeze softened garlic into blender; cover and process until blended. Drain the potatoes; place in a large bowl. Add butter, pepper, salt, garlic mixture and remaining broth; beat until smooth. **Yield:** 8 servings.

Cranberry Sauce with Walnuts

(Pictured below and on page 154)

PREP: 5 min.   **COOK:** 35 min.

Apricot preserves, a splash of lemon juice and toasted walnuts make this tangy cranberry sauce delightfully different.
—Dee Buckley, Salado, Texas

2 cups sugar
1 cup water
1 package (12 ounces) fresh *or* frozen cranberries
1/2 cup apricot preserves
1/4 cup lemon juice
1/2 cup chopped walnuts, toasted

In a large saucepan over medium heat, bring the sugar and water to a boil. Simmer, uncovered, for 10 minutes. Stir in the cranberries. Cook until the cranberries pop, about 15 minutes.

Remove from the heat. Stir in apricot preserves and lemon juice. Transfer to a bowl. Serve warm, at room temperature or chilled. Stir in the walnuts just before serving. **Yield:** 3-1/2 cups.

Hazelnut and Pear Salad

(Pictured above)

PREP/TOTAL TIME: 25 min.

My husband, daughter and I raise hazelnuts, and this crunchy salad is a favorite. I sprinkle the finished dish with those nuts and blend them with the dressing. Our home state of Oregon grows pears and cherries, too, so I included them in my recipe.
—Karen Kirsch, Saint Paul, Oregon

1/3 cup plus 1/2 cup chopped hazelnuts, toasted, *divided*
2 tablespoons plus 1/2 cup chopped red onion, *divided*
2 tablespoons water
4-1/2 teaspoons balsamic vinegar
4-1/2 teaspoons sugar
1/2 teaspoon salt
1 garlic clove, halved
1/8 teaspoon paprika
1/4 cup olive oil
1 package (5 ounces) spring mix salad greens
1 medium pear, thinly sliced
1/2 cup crumbled Gorgonzola cheese
1/4 cup dried cherries

For the dressing, place 1/3 cup hazelnuts, 2 tablespoons onion, water, vinegar, sugar, salt, garlic and paprika in a food processor; cover and process until blended. While processing, gradually add oil in a steady stream.

In a bowl, combine salad greens and remaining onion; add 1/2 cup dressing and toss to coat. Divide among six salad plates.

Top each salad with pear, Gorgonzola cheese, cherries and remaining hazelnuts; drizzle with the remaining dressing. Serve immediately. **Yield:** 6 servings.

A Dickens of a Christmas

FOR MANY, Charles Dickens' *A Christmas Carol* is a beloved part of the holidays. Published in December 1843, the book was an instant success and continues to inspire yuletide celebrations today.

As the tale of Ebenezer Scrooge, Bob Cratchit and Tiny Tim proves, there's magic in this season. So why not bring a little of it to your dining room table for your family? Enjoy traditional delights such as Christmas Goose with Orange Glaze, Old-Fashioned Fruit Compote, Tiny Tim's Plum Pudding, Walnut Mincemeat Pie and Wassail Bowl Punch.

With the Dickens-era menu featured here, you can dine like the Cratchit family of Victorian England—with all of our modern-day comforts, of course!

Christmas Goose With Orange Glaze

(Pictured at left)

PREP: 15 min. **BAKE:** 2-3/4 hours + standing

Steeped in tradition and rich with flavor, a golden-brown goose is an impressive centerpiece for your feast. The delicious aroma and tangy glaze make this bird one even Scrooge would love.
—*Terri Draper, Columbus, Montana*

- 1 **domestic goose (10 to 12 pounds)**
- 1 **teaspoon salt**
- 1/2 **teaspoon rubbed sage**
- 1/4 **teaspoon pepper**
- 6 **small navel oranges,** *divided*
- 1/3 **cup light corn syrup**
- 2 **tablespoons sugar**

Sprinkle the goose with salt, sage and pepper; prick skin well with a fork. Cut three oranges into quarters; place in the goose cavity. Tuck wings under goose; tie drumsticks together. Place breast side up on a rack in a roasting pan.

Bake, uncovered, at 350° for 2-3/4 to 3-1/4 hours or until a meat thermometer reads 180°. (Cover loosely with foil if goose browns too quickly). If necessary, drain fat from pan as it accumulates.

Cut the peel from the remaining oranges into long thin strips; cut oranges into sections, discarding membranes. Set aside.

Place goose on a serving platter; cover and let stand for 15 minutes. Meanwhile, in a small skillet over medium heat, cook and stir the corn syrup and sugar until the sugar is dissolved. Stir in the orange sections and orange peel; heat through.

Brush the glaze over goose. Spoon orange sections and peel around goose. **Yield:** 10 servings.

Old-Fashioned Fruit Compote

(Pictured below)

PREP: 15 min. **COOK:** 1 hour

A perfect partner for your Christmas goose or other main course, this warm but refreshing medley can simmer while you prepare the rest of your menu. Or, save time on the holiday by fixing this compote a day ahead, then reheat it before serving.
—*Shirley Glaab, Hattiesburg, Mississippi*

- 1 **can (20 ounces) pineapple chunks, undrained**
- 1 **package (18 ounces) pitted dried plums**
- 1 **can (15-1/4 ounces) sliced peaches, undrained**
- 1 **can (11 ounces) mandarin oranges, undrained**
- 1 **jar (10 ounces) maraschino cherries, drained**
- 1 **package (6 ounces) dried apricots**
- 2 **packages (3-1/2 ounces each) dried blueberries**
- 1/2 **cup golden raisins**
- 4 **lemon peel strips**
- 1 **cinnamon stick (3 inches)**

In a Dutch oven, combine all ingredients. Bring to a boil. Reduce the heat; cover and simmer for 50-60 minutes or until fruit is tender. Serve warm or at room temperature. **Yield:** 8 cups.

Wassail Bowl Punch

(Pictured above)

PREP: 10 min. **COOK:** 1 hour

On frosty days, my guests love relaxing with mugs of this punch. The blend of spice, fruit and citrus is wonderful. Prepare this beverage before heading out for winter activities, let it heat up in the slow cooker, then sip away the chill when you return.
—*Margaret Harms, Jenkins, Kentucky*

- 4 **cups hot brewed tea**
- 4 **cups cranberry juice**
- 4 **cups unsweetened apple juice**
- 2 **cups orange juice**
- 1 **cup sugar**
- 3/4 **cup lemon juice**
- 3 **cinnamon sticks (3 inches)**
- 12 **whole cloves**

In a 5-qt. slow cooker, combine the first six ingredients. Place cinnamon sticks and cloves on a double thickness of cheesecloth; bring up corners of cloth and tie with string to form a bag. Add to slow cooker.

   Cover and cook on high for 1 hour or until the punch begins to boil. Discard the spice bag. Serve warm. **Yield:** 3-1/2 quarts.

Tiny Tim's Plum Pudding

(Pictured at right)

PREP: 30 min. **COOK:** 2 hours

In the classic novel "A Christmas Carol," everyone claps for plum pudding. Our family made this warm dessert a holiday tradition of our own, and it really is something to applaud.
—*Ruthanne Karel, Hudsonville, Michigan*

- 1/2 **cup butter, softened**
- 3/4 **cup packed brown sugar**
- 3 **eggs**
- 3/4 **cup dry bread crumbs**
- 1/2 **cup all-purpose flour**
- 1 **teaspoon ground cinnamon**
- 1/2 **teaspoon baking soda**
- 1/2 **teaspoon ground nutmeg**
- 1/4 **teaspoon salt**
- 1/4 **teaspoon ground cloves**
- 2 **cans (15 ounces *each*) plums, drained, pitted and chopped**
- 1-3/4 **cups chopped dates**
- 1 **cup golden raisins**
- 1 **cup shredded carrots**
- 1/2 **cup dried currants**
- 1 **tablespoon grated orange peel**

HARD SAUCE:
- 1/2 **cup butter, softened**
- 3 **cups confectioners' sugar**
- 1/4 **cup dark rum *or* orange juice**

In a large bowl, cream the butter and brown sugar until light and fluffy. Beat in eggs. Combine the bread crumbs, flour, cinnamon, baking soda, nutmeg, salt and cloves; gradually beat into the creamed mixture. Fold in the plums, dates, raisins, carrots, currants and orange peel.

   Pour into a well-greased 8-cup pudding mold, metal gelatin mold or ovenproof bowl; cover tightly. Place on a rack in a stockpot; add 3 in. of hot water to pot. Bring to a gentle boil; cover and steam for 2 to 2-1/2 hours or until a toothpick inserted near the center comes out clean, adding water as needed. Let stand for 5 minutes before unmolding.

   In a small bowl, beat the butter, confectioners' sugar and rum until smooth. Unmold pudding onto a serving plate; cut into wedges. Serve warm with sauce. **Yield:** 12 servings (1-1/2 cups hard sauce).

Walnut Mincemeat Pie

(Pictured above)

PREP: 15 min. **BAKE:** 40 min. + cooling

Here's a delightful twist on old-fashioned mincemeat pie. This version is sweeter, creamier, easier to make and oh, so yummy!
—*Mary Reagan, Warsaw, New York*

Pastry for single-crust pie (9 inches)
- 1 cup sugar
- 2 tablespoons all-purpose flour
- 1/8 teaspoon salt
- 3 eggs, lightly beaten
- 1/4 cup butter, melted
- 1 cup prepared mincemeat
- 1/2 cup chopped walnuts

Line a 9-in. pie plate with pastry; flute edges. Line pastry shell with a double thickness of heavy-duty foil. Bake at 450° for 5 minutes. Remove foil; bake 5 minutes longer. Cool on a wire rack. Reduce heat to 350°.

In a large bowl, combine the sugar, flour and salt. Stir in the eggs, butter, mincemeat and walnuts until blended. Pour into crust.

Bake for 40-45 minutes or until a knife inserted near the center comes out clean. Cover the edges with foil during the last 15 minutes to prevent overbrowning if necessary. Cool on a wire rack. **Yield:** 6-8 servings.

Zesty Winter Vegetables

PREP: 30 min. **COOK:** 10 min.

With a rich and delicious horseradish sauce, this quintessential English side dish will add zip to your Christmas dinner.
—*Lisa Leaper-Shuck, Worthington, Ohio*

- 1-1/4 pounds pearl onions
- 1-1/2 pounds fresh brussels sprouts
- 2 teaspoons all-purpose flour
- 1/8 teaspoon ground allspice
- 3/4 cup heavy whipping cream
- 3 tablespoons prepared horseradish
- 3 tablespoons butter
- 1-1/4 teaspoons minced fresh thyme *or*
  1/2 teaspoon dried thyme

In a large saucepan, bring 6 cups water to a boil. Add the onions; boil for 3 minutes. Drain and rinse in cold water; peel.

Meanwhile, cut the brussels sprouts in half. In a large skillet, bring 1/2 in. of water to a boil. Add sprouts; cover and cook for 5-8 minutes or until crisp-tender. Drain. In a small bowl, combine the flour, allspice, heavy whipping cream and horseradish.

In the same skillet, melt butter over medium heat. Add the vegetables, cream mixture and thyme. Cook and stir until the cream mixture is thickened and the vegetables are tender. **Yield:** 9 servings.

Merry Drinks and Desserts

WHAT Christmas gathering is complete without a selection of special beverages and sweet treats? Here, you'll find the best of both so you can make your get-togethers as cheery as can be.

Offer guests toasty-warm mugs of Merry Mulled Cider, Hot Malted Chocolate, Homemade Irish Cream or Hot Buttered Rum. These wintry drinks will quench everyone's thirst in a festive way.

After dinner, make eyes light up with a tempting dessert such as Festive Napoleons with Thyme Cream, Peppermint Cream Pound Cake, Holiday Ambrosia Cake, Fudgy Peppermint Stick Torte, Pecan Kringle Sticks or Best Maple-Cranberry Cheesecake.

Hot Buttered Rum

(Pictured at left in the photo at left and on page 154)

PREP/TOTAL TIME: 15 min.

I received this recipe from a friend more than 30 years ago, and I think of her every winter when I prepare a batch. You can store the mix in the freezer, then stir up a hot beverage anytime.
—*Joyce Moynihan, Lakeville, Minnesota*

- 1 **cup butter, softened**
- 1/2 **cup confectioners' sugar**
- 1/2 **cup packed brown sugar**
- 2 **cups vanilla ice cream, softened**
- 1 **teaspoon ground cinnamon**
- 1 **teaspoon ground nutmeg**

EACH SERVING:
- 1/2 **cup boiling water**
- 1 **to 3 tablespoons rum**

In a large bowl, cream the butter and sugars until light and fluffy. Beat in the ice cream, cinnamon and nutmeg. Cover and store in the freezer.

For each serving, place 1/2 cup butter mixture in a mug; add the boiling water and stir to dissolve. Stir in the rum. **Yield:** 7 servings (3-1/2 cups mix).

Homemade Irish Cream

(Pictured at bottom in the photo at left and on page 154)

PREP/TOTAL TIME: 10 min.

Add some yummy flavor to your cup of joe with a splash of this sweet cream. It's an alcohol-free version of the Irish classic.
—*Marcia Severson, Hallock, Minnesota*

- 1 **can (12 ounces) evaporated milk**
- 1 **cup heavy whipping cream**
- 1/2 **cup 2% milk**
- 1/4 **cup sugar**

- 2 **tablespoons chocolate syrup**
- 1 **tablespoon instant coffee granules**
- 2 **teaspoons vanilla extract**
- 1/4 **teaspoon almond extract**

EACH SERVING:
- 1/2 **cup brewed coffee**

In a blender, combine the first eight ingredients; cover and process until smooth. Store in refrigerator. For each serving, place coffee in a mug. Stir in 1/3 cup Irish cream. Heat mixture in a microwave if desired. **Yield:** 3-1/3 cups.

Editor's Note: Irish whiskey may be added to this recipe if desired.

Merry Mulled Cider

(Pictured at top in the photo at far left and on page 154)

PREP/TOTAL TIME: 25 min.

When our children were younger, I always made warm cider for Christmas Eve. This herbal version featuring fresh rosemary was a favorite. The kids are now grown and gone, but my husband and I still enjoy a mug or two during the holiday season.
—*Sue Gronholz, Beaver Dam, Wisconsin*

- 7 **cups apple cider *or* juice**
- 1 **cup cranberry juice**
- 2 **tablespoons brown sugar**
- 1 **cinnamon stick (3 inches)**
- 1 **fresh rosemary sprig**
- 2/3 **cup orange juice**

In a Dutch oven, bring the apple cider, cranberry juice, brown sugar, cinnamon and rosemary to a boil. Reduce heat; cover and simmer for 10-15 minutes or until flavors are blended.

Discard cinnamon and rosemary; stir in orange juice. Serve warm. **Yield:** 8 servings (2 quarts).

TURNING UP THE HEAT. A warm beverage such as Merry Mulled Cider (recipe above) is the perfect thirst-quencher for a Christmastime gathering or other winter party. Want to serve your hot beverage in a serving bowl? Avoid shattering the bowl by making sure it's heat-resistant and by warming it with warm water before pouring in the hot beverage.

If you don't have a heat-resistant bowl, serve your beverage in a chafing dish, fondue pot, slow cooker or an attractive pan on the stovetop.

In a small bowl, beat the heavy whipping cream until it begins to thicken. Add 1/4 cup confectioners' sugar and extract; beat until soft peaks form. In another bowl, beat cream cheese and remaining confectioners' sugar until smooth. Fold in the whipped cream, then 3/4 cup crushed peppermint candies.

Place the bottom cake layer on a serving plate; top with one-fourth of the filling. Repeat the layers three times. Refrigerate for at least 1 hour.

Just before serving, sprinkle remaining candies over the top. **Yield:** 16 servings.

Peppermint Cream Pound Cake

(Pictured below)

PREP: 35 min. **BAKE:** 1 hour + cooling

When I wanted a new version of a tried-and-true pound cake, I created this because I really like festively colored peppermint candies and the flavor of peppermint for Christmas.
—*Carolyn Webster, Winston-Salem, North Carolina*

   1 **cup unsalted butter, softened**
1/2 **cup butter-flavored shortening**
   2 **cups sugar**
   6 **eggs**
   1 **teaspoon vanilla extract**
1/2 **teaspoon peppermint extract**
   3 **cups all-purpose flour**
   1 **teaspoon baking powder**
   1 **cup heavy whipping cream**
1/2 **cup finely crushed peppermint candies**
GLAZE:
1-1/2 **cups confectioners' sugar**
   1 **teaspoon unsalted butter, melted**
1/4 **teaspoon vanilla extract**
1/8 **teaspoon salt**
   4 **to 5 tablespoons heavy whipping cream**
Additional crushed peppermint candies

Fudgy Peppermint Stick Torte

(Pictured above)

PREP: 25 min. **BAKE:** 20 min. + chilling

I came up with this torte based on a chocolate cake a friend made for me several years ago. I love the fact that it contains brown sugar instead of granulated sugar. Big slices are wonderful for a special meal because they look absolutely spectacular.
—*Mary Shivers, Ada, Oklahoma*

1-1/2 **cups butter, softened**
3-1/4 **cups packed brown sugar**
   4 **eggs**
   2 **teaspoons vanilla extract**
   4 **cups all-purpose flour**
1-1/4 **cups baking cocoa**
   2 **teaspoons baking powder**
   1 **teaspoon salt**
   1 **teaspoon baking soda**
2-1/2 **cups cold water**
FILLING:
1-1/2 **cups heavy whipping cream**
1/2 **cup confectioners' sugar,** *divided*
1/4 **teaspoon peppermint extract**
   1 **package (8 ounces) cream cheese, softened**
   1 **cup crushed peppermint candies,** *divided*

In a large bowl, cream the butter and brown sugar until light and fluffy. Add the eggs, one at a time, beating well after each addition. Beat in vanilla. Combine the flour, cocoa, baking powder, salt and baking soda; add to the creamed mixture alternately with the cold water, beating well after each addition.

Transfer batter to four greased and floured 9-in. round baking pans. Bake at 350° for 18-22 minutes or until a toothpick inserted near the center comes out clean. Cool cakes for 10 minutes before removing from the pans to wire racks to cool completely.

In a large bowl, cream the butter, shortening and sugar until light and fluffy. Add eggs, one at a time, beating well after each addition. Beat in extracts. Combine flour and baking powder; add to creamed mixture alternately with whipping cream. Fold in peppermint candies.

Transfer to a well-greased and floured 10-in. fluted tube pan. Bake at 325° for 1 to 1-1/4 hours or until a toothpick inserted near the center comes out clean. Cool cake for 10 minutes before removing from pan to a wire rack to cool completely.

In a small bowl, combine confectioners' sugar, butter, vanilla and salt. Stir in enough heavy whipping cream to achieve a drizzling consistency. Drizzle over cake. Sprinkle with additional peppermint candies. Refrigerate leftovers. **Yield:** 12 servings.

Pecan Kringle Sticks

PREP: 40 min. + chilling **BAKE:** 20 min./batch

We're fans of this kringle's flakiness and the fact that it's not too sweet. It just melts in your mouth! Delight holiday guests by serving pieces on your cookie platter alongside the other treats.
—Connie Vjestica, Brookfield, Illinois

- 2 cups all-purpose flour
- 1 cup cold butter
- 1 cup sour cream

FILLING:
- 1 egg white
- 1 teaspoon vanilla extract
- 1/2 cup sugar
- 1 cup chopped pecans
- 1-1/4 cups confectioners' sugar
- 2 tablespoons 2% milk

Place flour in a large bowl; cut in butter until crumbly. Stir in the sour cream. Wrap in plastic wrap. Refrigerate for 1 to 1-1/2 hours or until easy to handle.

In a small bowl, beat egg white and vanilla on medium speed until soft peaks form. Gradually beat in sugar on high until stiff peaks form. Fold in pecans.

Divide the dough into four portions. Roll one portion into a 12-in. x 6-in. rectangle; place on an ungreased baking sheet. Spread a fourth of the egg white mixture lengthwise down the center. Fold in sides of pastry to meet in the center. Repeat.

Bake at 375° for 18-22 minutes or until lightly browned. Combine confectioners' sugar and milk; drizzle over warm pastries. **Yield:** 4 kringles (6 servings each).

Holiday Ambrosia Cake

(Pictured above right)

PREP: 40 min. **BAKE:** 50 min. + cooling

Adding pineapple, coconut and pineapple juice to an old recipe for fruitcake made it extra moist and gave it tropical flair.
—Dotty Stodulski, North Port, Florida

- 1/2 cup butter, softened
- 1 cup sugar
- 4 eggs
- 1 teaspoon coconut extract
- 2-1/2 cups all-purpose flour
- 1 teaspoon baking powder
- 1/2 teaspoon salt
- 1/2 cup unsweetened pineapple juice
- 2-1/4 cups flaked coconut
- 1-1/2 cups chopped candied pineapple
- 1 cup chopped macadamia nuts
- 1 cup golden raisins
- 1/2 cup chopped dried mangoes
- 1/2 cup chopped green candied cherries
- 1/2 cup chopped red candied cherries

COCONUT GLAZE:
- 1 cup confectioners' sugar
- 2 tablespoons coconut milk *or* milk
- 1/4 teaspoon coconut extract
- 1/4 teaspoon vanilla extract

In a large bowl, cream butter and sugar until light and fluffy. Add eggs, one at a time, beating well after each addition. Beat in the extract. Combine the flour, baking powder and salt; add to the creamed mixture alternately with pineapple juice, beating well after each addition. Fold in the coconut, pineapple, macadamia nuts, raisins, mangoes and candied cherries.

Transfer to a greased and floured 10-in. fluted tube pan. Bake at 350° for 50-60 minutes or until a toothpick inserted near the center comes out clean. Cool cake for 10 minutes before removing from the pan to a wire rack to cool completely.

In a small bowl, combine the confectioners' sugar, coconut milk and extracts. Drizzle the glaze over cake. **Yield:** 12 servings.

Best Maple-Cranberry Cheesecake

(Pictured above and on page 154)

PREP: 30 min. **BAKE:** 1-1/4 hours + chilling

This lovely cheesecake may look intimidating, but it's not hard to prepare. If you fix just one holiday dessert, this should be it!
—Tonya Burkhard, Davis, Illinois

- 2 cups graham cracker crumbs
- 1/3 cup butter, melted
- 3 tablespoons sugar
- 1/2 teaspoon ground cinnamon

FILLING:
- 1-1/2 cups maple syrup
- 3 packages (8 ounces *each*) cream cheese, softened
- 1/2 cup packed brown sugar
- 2/3 cup sour cream
- 3 tablespoons all-purpose flour
- 2 teaspoons vanilla extract
- 1/4 teaspoon salt
- 4 eggs, lightly beaten

COMPOTE:
- 2 cups fresh *or* frozen cranberries, thawed
- 2/3 cup dried cranberries
- 1 cup maple syrup
- 1/2 cup packed brown sugar

Place a greased 9-in. springform pan on a double thickness of heavy-duty foil (about 18 in. square). Securely wrap the foil around pan.

Combine the graham cracker crumbs, butter, sugar and cinnamon; press onto the bottom and 1-1/2 in. up the sides of prepared pan. Place pan on a baking sheet. Bake at 375° for 8-10 minutes or until set. Cool on a wire rack. Reduce heat to 325°.

Meanwhile, place the maple syrup in a small saucepan. Bring to a boil; cook until syrup is reduced to about 1 cup. Cool to room temperature; set aside.

In a large bowl, beat cream cheese and brown sugar until smooth. Beat in the sour cream, flour, vanilla, salt and cooled syrup. Add eggs; beat on low speed just until combined. Pour into the crust. Place springform pan in a large baking pan; add 1 in. of hot water to larger pan.

Bake at 325° for 1-1/4 to 1-1/2 hours or until the center is just set and top appears dull. Remove springform pan from water bath. Cool on a wire rack for 10 minutes. Carefully run a knife around edge of pan to loosen; cool 1 hour longer. Refrigerate overnight. Remove sides of pan.

In a large saucepan, combine the cranberries, maple syrup and brown sugar. Cook over medium heat until the cranberries pop, about 10 minutes. Serve warm with cheesecake. **Yield:** 16 servings (2 cups compote).

Hot Malted Chocolate

(Pictured below)

PREP/TOTAL TIME: 20 min.

What's better on a cold day than a mug of rich hot chocolate? Malted milk powder makes this version even yummier.
—Christy Meinecke, Mansfield, Texas

- 4 cups 2% milk
- 1 cup heavy whipping cream
- 1/2 cup sugar
- 1 cup milk chocolate chips
- 1/3 cup malted milk powder
- 2 teaspoons vanilla extract

In a large saucepan, heat milk over medium heat until bubbles form around sides of pan.

Meanwhile, in a small bowl, beat the heavy whipping cream until it begins to thicken. Add sugar; beat until soft peaks form.

Whisk chocolate chips and milk powder into milk until the chocolate is melted. Remove from the heat; whisk in vanilla. Pour into mugs. Spoon whipped cream over the top. **Yield:** 5 servings.

Festive Napoleons With Thyme Cream

(Pictured above)

PREP: 50 min. **BAKE:** 10 min./batch + cooling

I like to experiment with seasonings, and thyme adds a surprising twist that works well with the honey and fruit in these desserts. They take a bit of extra time to assemble, but they're worth it!
—Bridget Klusman, Otsego, Michigan

- **5 egg whites**
- **1 cup turbinado (washed raw) sugar**
- **1-1/4 teaspoons vanilla extract**
- **1/4 teaspoon salt**
- **1-1/4 cups all-purpose flour**
- **2/3 cup butter, softened**
- **2 tablespoons plus 1-1/2 teaspoons walnut or canola oil**
- **1-2/3 cups chopped walnuts, toasted**

CRANBERRY FILLING:
- **4 tangerines**
- **1 package (12 ounces) fresh or frozen cranberries**
- **1/2 cup turbinado (washed raw) sugar**

THYME CREAM:
- **1 carton (8 ounces) Mascarpone cheese**
- **1 cup (8 ounces) plain yogurt**
- **1/3 cup honey**
- **1/2 teaspoon minced fresh thyme**

Additional chopped toasted walnuts

In a small bowl, beat the egg whites, sugar, vanilla and salt until foamy. Gradually beat in flour. Beat in butter and oil. Fold in toasted walnuts.

With a pencil, draw five 3-in. circles on a sheet of parchment paper. Place the paper, pencil mark down, on a baking sheet. Spread a heaping tablespoonful of batter over each circle. Bake at 400° for 8-10 minutes or until the edges begin to brown. Remove to wire racks to cool completely. Repeat with the remaining batter, making 30 cookies.

Using a vegetable peeler, remove the peel from one tangerine. Peel and seed the remaining tangerines and place in a food processor. Add the cranberries, sugar and tangerine peel. Cover and process until chopped. Transfer to a large saucepan. Cook over medium heat until thickened, about 10 minutes. Cool.

For the thyme cream, beat Mascarpone cheese, yogurt, honey and thyme until thickened. Place one cookie on a small plate. Spread with 1 tablespoon cranberry filling and 1 tablespoon thyme cream. Repeat the layers twice. Repeat with the remaining cookies, cranberry filling and thyme cream. Sprinkle with additional toasted walnuts. **Yield:** 10 servings.

'Mom's Best'

What's better than Mom's home cooking? In this chapter, four cooks fondly recall the recipes for their favorite made-by-mom dishes, from a lively array of classic Cuban specialties to delightful baked goods for Christmas.

FAMILY-PLEASING FARE. Clockwise from top left: Cuban Black Beans (p. 198), Nena's Papas Rellenas (p. 198), Berry Delightful Spinach Salad (p. 203) and Grandma's Oatmeal Raisin Cookies (p. 193).

CREAM-FILLED
CHOCOLATE- SUPREME MUFFINS

BLUE-RIBBON RYE BREAD

GRANDMA'S OATMEAL RAISIN
COOKIES

Jumbo Zucchini Chip Muffins

Signed, Sealed and Delivered

This mom is known for her thoughtful (and yummy) gifts from the kitchen—especially during the Christmas season.

By Libby Spicker, North Ogden, Utah

FOR AS LONG AS I can remember, my mom, Susanne Spicker (pictured at left), of North Ogden, Utah, has planned a gift to give to friends and neighbors at Christmas. Most often, it's homemade from her own kitchen.

She loves sharing her delicious rye bread, spiced tea mix, holiday cookies and more. Over the years, she has given goodies to as many as 140 people.

Her gifts are beautifully wrapped in colored cellophane or decorative freezer bags, holiday boxes or tins. My mom does calligraphy (and has taught classes), so she likes to write a poem or saying to accompany each present. One year, she gave pint jars of homemade salsa and a bag of chips with a tag that read, "You're 'nacho' ordinary neighbor!"

My brothers, sisters and I used to help Mom with the gifts and always did the delivering. We're all grown up now—my two sisters and older brother are married; my younger brother and I live at home—but we continue to keep the traditions we had as children, from our holiday gift-baking days to our Christmas Eve feast.

Mom's recipe collection is huge, but I've shared some of her yummiest baked treats here—Grandma's Oatmeal Raisin Cookies, Jumbo Zucchini Chip Muffins, Cream-Filled Chocolate-Supreme Muffins and Blue-Ribbon Rye Bread.

Whether it's a holiday or a weeknight, Mom has made a point of serving well-balanced meals with lean meats and fresh fruits and vegetables. She also stresses the importance of cleanliness and order when preparing foods. "If you get it out, put it away," she says.

My mom taught piano lessons in our home until we were all in school. Then, she started substitute teaching, which she still does. She also creates beautiful flower arrangements for a local dentist's office.

As a result of her teaching skills (and patience), all of us kids are quite accomplished cooks—even my brothers. My parents have five grandchildren, and I'm sure they'll grow up to be good cooks, too.

Thanks to Mom, I've found that cooking and baking are wonderful ways to express myself. Keeping close as a family has been an added bonus. We joke that a family that bakes together, stays together. I know that in our family, this is certainly true!

Grandma's Oatmeal Raisin Cookies

PREP: 25 min. **BAKE:** 10 min./batch

- 2 cups raisins, chopped
- 2 cups boiling water
- 3/4 cup butter-flavored shortening
- 1 cup sugar
- 3 eggs
- 2-1/2 cups all-purpose flour
- 2 cups old-fashioned oats
- 1-1/4 teaspoons baking soda
- 1/2 teaspoon salt
- 2 cups chopped walnuts

Place raisins in a small bowl. Cover with boiling water; let stand for 5 minutes. Drain and set aside.

In a large bowl, cream shortening and sugar until light and fluffy. Beat in eggs. Combine the flour, oats, baking soda and salt; gradually add to creamed mixture and mix well. Stir in walnuts and raisins.

Drop by rounded tablespoonfuls 2 in. apart onto greased baking sheets. Flatten with a glass. Bake at 325° for 8-10 minutes or until bottoms are browned. Remove to wire racks. **Yield:** 4 dozen.

Jumbo Zucchini Chip Muffins

PREP: 30 min. BAKE: 30 min. + cooling

- 3 cups all-purpose flour
- 1-1/2 cups sugar
- 3 teaspoons ground cinnamon
- 2 teaspoons baking powder
- 1 teaspoon salt
- 1/2 teaspoon baking soda
- 3 eggs, beaten
- 2/3 cup canola oil
- 3 teaspoons vanilla extract
- 2 cups shredded zucchini
- 1 package (11-1/2 ounces) milk chocolate chips
- 1 cup chopped walnuts

MASCARPONE FROSTING:
- 1/2 cup butter, softened
- 1 package (3 ounces) cream cheese, softened
- 1/3 cup Mascarpone cheese
- 1/4 cup confectioners' sugar
- 1/2 teaspoon vanilla extract
- 1/4 cup finely chopped walnuts, optional

In a large bowl, combine the first six ingredients. In another bowl, combine the eggs, oil and vanilla. Stir into dry ingredients just until moistened. Fold in the zucchini, chips and walnuts.

Fill paper-lined jumbo muffin cups three-fourths full. Bake at 350° for 30-35 minutes or until a toothpick

Blue-Ribbon Rye Bread

PREP: 40 min. + rising BAKE: 20 min. + cooling

- 1 package (1/4 ounce) active dry yeast
- 1 tablespoon sugar
- 2-1/4 cups warm water (110° to 115°)
- 1/4 cup packed brown sugar
- 1/4 cup shortening
- 1/4 cup molasses
- 1 tablespoon caraway seeds
- 1 teaspoon salt
- 1 cup rye flour
- 3-1/2 to 4 cups all-purpose flour

In a large bowl, dissolve yeast and sugar in warm water. Stir in the brown sugar, shortening, molasses, caraway seeds and salt. Add rye flour and 1-3/4 cups all-purpose flour; beat until smooth. Stir in enough remaining all-purpose flour to form a soft dough.

Turn dough onto a floured surface; knead until smooth and elastic, about 6-8 minutes. Place in a greased bowl, turning once to grease the top. Cover and let rise in a warm place until doubled, about 1 hour.

Punch dough down; shape into three loaves. Place on greased baking sheets. Cover and let rise until doubled, about 1 hour.

Bake at 350° for 20-25 minutes or until golden brown. Remove from pans to wire racks to cool. **Yield:** 3 loaves (12 slices each).

inserted near the center comes out clean. Cool muffins for 5 minutes before removing from pans to wire racks to cool completely.

In a large bowl, beat the butter and cheeses until fluffy. Add confectioners' sugar and vanilla; beat until smooth. Pipe a dollop of frosting onto each muffin. Sprinkle with walnuts if desired. **Yield:** 1 dozen.

Cream-Filled Chocolate-Supreme Muffins

PREP: 30 min. **BAKE:** 25 min. + cooling

- 3 cups all-purpose flour
- 2 cups sugar
- 1/2 cup baking cocoa
- 2 teaspoons baking soda
- 1 teaspoon salt
- 2 cups cold water
- 3/4 cup canola oil
- 1 egg
- 2 tablespoons white vinegar
- 2 teaspoons vanilla extract

FILLING:
- 4 ounces cream cheese, softened
- 1/4 cup sugar
- 1/8 teaspoon salt
- 2 tablespoons beaten egg
- 1/2 teaspoon vanilla extract
- 3/4 cup milk chocolate chips

Confectioners' sugar, optional

In a large bowl, combine the flour, sugar, cocoa, baking soda and salt. In another bowl, combine the water, oil, egg, vinegar and vanilla. Stir into dry ingredients just until moistened.

For filling, beat the cream cheese, sugar and salt until smooth. Beat in egg and vanilla. Fold in chips.

Fill 12 paper-lined jumbo muffin cups half full with batter. Drop heaping tablespoonfuls of the cream cheese mixture into center of each; cover with remaining batter.

Bake at 350° for 25-30 minutes or until a toothpick inserted in muffin comes out clean. Cool the muffins for 5 minutes before removing from the pans to wire racks to cool completely. Sprinkle with confectioners' sugar if desired. **Yield:** 1 dozen.

Nena's Papas Rellenas

CUBAN BLACK BEANS

ARROZ CON LECHE
(RICE PUDDING)

NO-FUSS AVOCADO ONION SALAD

Cooking to a Cuban Beat

A Havana-born mom isn't afraid to mix things up in the kitchen, but the classic dishes of Cuba remain closest to her heart.

By Marina Castle, North Hollywood, California

MY MOTHER, Nena Linares (pictured at left), wanted to be a journalist and write about the world and its many cuisines. But love got in the way; she got married and became a homemaker instead.

She may not have had the chance to write about food, but my mom has had plenty of opportunities to prepare it. When my brother, Rick, and I were growing up, she made breakfast, lunch and dinner, plus snacks 24/7. There was always something ready in the fridge or on the stove for us to eat. And everything was from scratch.

The food she put on the table was a mouthwatering blend of cultures. Mom, who lives in Los Angeles, was born in Cuba; her parents were transplants from Spain. Early on, she learned the basics of French and Spanish cooking from her grandmother. Her mother-in-law showed her how to fix authentic Cuban food, and our Sicilian stepdad, Fred, taught her the Italian classics.

We couldn't get enough of her fluffy steamed white rice, which she prepared every day. I loved it topped with a velvety ocean of her Cuban Black Beans. Mom made the best black beans I've ever tasted, and I've had many variations.

But the dish I like most of all is still Nena's Papas Rellenas. A friend described them best: "They're like shepherd's pie rolled into a ball." You'll find Mom's recipes for both of those dishes here, along with No-Fuss Avocado Onion Salad and Arroz Con Leche (Rice Pudding) to round out the meal.

When Mom and Fred were entertaining, she would feed my brother and me early, and we'd go to our rooms to read or watch TV. Now and then, she'd pop in with some goodies just for us.

Rick and I couldn't resist taking a peek at the grown-up party. I loved watching mom dance in her beautiful dresses and heels. In fact, she always dressed up. She once told me that a young woman needed to be at her best, whether she was at home or out with friends.

Both my mother and stepdad shared their cooking skills with me, and I've now passed them on to my own children. I frequently make her steamed rice, her wonderful black beans and papas rellenas. Every time we enjoy them, I feel reconnected with Mom's heritage—in the most delicious way possible!

Arroz Con Leche (Rice Pudding)

PREP: 5 min. COOK: 30 min.

- 1-1/2 cups water
- 1/2 cup uncooked long grain rice
- 1 cinnamon stick (3 inches)
- 1 cup sweetened condensed milk
- 3 tablespoons raisins

In a small saucepan, combine water, rice and cinnamon stick. Bring to a boil. Reduce heat; simmer, uncovered, for 15-20 minutes or until water is absorbed.

Stir in the sweetened condensed milk and raisins. Bring to a boil. Reduce the heat; simmer, uncovered, for 10-15 minutes or until thick and creamy, stirring frequently. Discard the cinnamon stick. Serve pudding warm or cold. **Yield:** 4 servings.

Nena's Papas Rellenas

PREP: 45 min. **COOK:** 5 min./batch

2-1/2 **pounds potatoes (about 8 medium), peeled and cut into wedges**
1 **pound lean ground beef (90% lean)**
1 **small green pepper, finely chopped**
1 **small onion, finely chopped**
1/2 **cup tomato sauce**
1/2 **cup sliced green olives with pimientos**
1/2 **cup raisins**
1-1/4 **teaspoons salt,** *divided*
1-1/4 **teaspoons pepper,** *divided*
1/2 **teaspoon paprika**
1 **teaspoon garlic powder**
2 **eggs, lightly beaten**
1 **cup seasoned bread crumbs**
Oil for deep-fat frying

Place potatoes in a large saucepan and cover with water. Bring to a boil. Reduce heat; cover and cook for 15-20 minutes or until tender.

Meanwhile, in a large skillet, cook ground beef, green pepper and onion over medium heat until the meat is no longer pink; drain. Stir in the tomato sauce, green olives, raisins, 1/4 teaspoon salt, 1/4 teaspoon pepper and paprika; heat through.

Drain the potatoes; mash with the garlic powder and remaining salt and pepper. Shape 2 tablespoons potatoes into a patty; place a heaping tablespoonful of filling in the center. Shape the potatoes around filling, forming a ball. Repeat.

Place the eggs and seasoned bread crumbs in separate shallow bowls. Dip the potato balls in the eggs, then roll in the bread crumbs. In an electric skillet or deep fryer, heat oil to 375°. Fry the potato balls, a few at a time, for 1-2 minutes or until golden brown. Drain on paper towels. **Yield:** 2-1/2 dozen.

Editor's Note: Instead of frying the papas rellenas, you may place them on baking sheets and bake at 450° for 20 minutes or until heated through.

No-Fuss Avocado Onion Salad

PREP/TOTAL TIME: 20 min.

3 **medium ripe avocados, peeled and thinly sliced**
1 **large sweet onion, halved and thinly sliced**
1/3 **cup olive oil**
1/4 **cup stone-ground mustard**
2 **tablespoons lemon juice**
1 **tablespoon honey**

Arrange avocados and onion on a large platter. In a small bowl, whisk the remaining ingredients; drizzle over the vegetables. **Yield:** 12 servings.

Cuban Black Beans

PREP: 20 min. + soaking **COOK:** 1-3/4 hours

2 **cups dried black beans, rinsed**
1 **bay leaf**
3 **medium green peppers, chopped**
2 **medium onions, chopped**
1/2 **cup olive oil**
6 **garlic cloves, minced**
1 **can (15 ounces) tomato puree**
1/2 **cup sherry** *or* **chicken broth**
2 **tablespoons sugar**
3/4 **teaspoon salt**

Soak the beans according to package directions. Drain and rinse beans, discarding liquid. Place beans in a large saucepan; add 6 cups water and bay leaf. Bring to a boil. Reduce the heat; cover and simmer for 1-1/2 to 2 hours or until tender.

Meanwhile, in a large skillet, saute the green peppers and onions in the oil until tender. Add the garlic; cook 1 minute longer.

Stir in the tomato puree, sherry, sugar and salt. Bring to a boil. Reduce heat; simmer, uncovered, for 8-10 minutes or until thickened. Drain the beans; discard bay leaf. Stir beans into tomato mixture. **Yield:** 9 servings.

ARTICHOKE MUSHROOM LASAGNA

BERRY DELIGHTFUL SPINACH SALAD

LUSCIOUS LIME SLUSH

Lemon Dream Cheesecake

Making Dishes, Doing Dishes

A mother's home cooking brings her family around the dinner table (and the sink) for plenty of love, laughter and special times together.

By Julie Herzfeldt, Manitowoc, Wisconsin

COOKING came easily to my mom, Bonnie Jost (pictured at left), who learned the basics from her mother and grandmother. When she became a wife and mom herself, cooking became part of life—and she really took a shine to it.

Mom and Dad raised my brother, sister and me on the farm my grandma grew up on, near Manitowoc, Wisconsin. So Mom had everything at her fingertips, from the beef cattle, chickens and pigs we raised to the fresh garden produce. I can't remember ever having a meal from a box; everything was cooked from scratch. When vegetables weren't in season, Mom relied on the bounty she and Dad canned each year.

My dad grew up with meat-and-potato meals, so that's what Mom usually fixed for dinner—and they were wonderful. But as much meat as we had access to, Mom loved her vegetables more. It shows in the scrumptious recipes of hers that I've shared here—Luscious Lime Slush, Artichoke Mushroom Lasagna, Berry Delightful Spinach Salad and a special treat, Lemon Dream Cheesecake.

Our family always ate supper together, even with Mom working nights. Both of my parents went back to school when my brother, sister and I were older. Dad is an electrician, and Mom's a nurse.

They still have the farm, so we kids and our families are the lucky recipients of meat and canned produce. They often have us all over for supper. Mom calls us kids her treasures, our spouses her stars and her seven grandchildren her angels. While Mom loves to cook, her real love is those grandkids!

With all the cooking and canning my parents do, we're always telling them to get a dishwasher. But Mom says the best thing about making meals is doing the dishes, because that's when we have time to talk—and there's always a lot of laughter.

Luscious Lime Slush

PREP: 20 min. + freezing

- 9 cups water
- 4 individual green tea bags
- 2 cans (12 ounces *each*) frozen limeade concentrate, thawed
- 2 cups sugar
- 2 cups lemon rum *or* rum
- 7 cups lemon-lime soda, chilled

In a Dutch oven, bring the water to a boil. Remove from the heat; add tea bags. Cover and steep for 3-5 minutes. Discard tea bags.

Stir in the limeade concentrate, sugar and lemon rum. Transfer to a 4-qt. freezer container; cool. Cover and freeze for 6 hours or overnight.

To use frozen limeade mixture: Combine the limeade mixture and lemon-lime soda in a 4-qt. pitcher. Or for one serving, combine 1/2 cup limeade mixture and 1/4 cup lemon-lime soda in a glass. Serve slush immediately. **Yield:** 28 servings (3/4 cup each).

Artichoke Mushroom Lasagna

PREP: 30 min. BAKE: 1 hour + standing

- 1 pound sliced baby portobello mushrooms
- 2 tablespoons butter
- 3 garlic cloves, minced
- 2 cans (14 ounces *each*) water-packed artichoke hearts, rinsed, drained and chopped
- 1 cup chardonnay *or* other white wine
- 1/4 teaspoon salt
- 1/4 teaspoon pepper

SAUCE:
- 1/4 cup butter, cubed
- 1/4 cup all-purpose flour
- 3-1/2 cups 2% milk
- 2-1/2 cups shredded Parmesan cheese
- 1 cup chardonnay *or* other white wine

ASSEMBLY:
- 9 no-cook lasagna noodles
- 4 cups (16 ounces) shredded part-skim mozzarella cheese, *divided*

In a large skillet, saute the mushrooms in the butter until tender. Add the garlic; cook 1 minute longer. Add the artichokes, wine, salt and pepper; cook over medium heat until liquid is evaporated.

For the sauce, in a large saucepan over medium heat, melt butter. Stir in the flour until smooth; gradually add milk. Bring to a boil; cook and stir for 1 minute or until thickened. Stir in Parmesan cheese and wine.

Spread 1 cup sauce into a greased 13-in. x 9-in. baking dish. Layer with three noodles, 1-2/3 cups sauce, 1 cup mozzarella and 1-1/3 cups artichoke mixture. Repeat the layers twice.

Cover and bake at 350° for 45 minutes. Sprinkle with remaining mozzarella cheese. Bake, uncovered, 15-20 minutes longer or until the cheese is melted. Let stand for 15 minutes before cutting. **Yield:** 12 servings.

Lemon Dream Cheesecake

PREP: 30 min. BAKE: 55 min. + chilling

- 2 cups graham cracker crumbs
- 6 tablespoons butter, melted
- 1/4 cup sugar

FILLING:
- 4 packages (8 ounces *each*) cream cheese, softened
- 1 cup sugar
- 1/2 cup heavy whipping cream
- 1/4 cup lemon juice
- 2 tablespoons all-purpose flour
- 1 tablespoon grated lemon peel
- 2-1/2 teaspoons vanilla extract
- 1 teaspoon lemon extract
- 10 drops yellow food coloring, optional
- 5 eggs, lightly beaten

In a small bowl, combine the cracker crumbs, butter and sugar. Press onto the bottom and 2 in. up the sides of a greased 10-in. springform pan. Place pan on a baking sheet. Bake at 325° for 10 minutes. Cool on a wire rack.

In a large bowl, beat cream cheese and sugar until smooth. Beat in cream, juice, flour, peel, extracts and food coloring if desired. Add eggs; beat on low speed just until combined. Pour into crust. Return pan to baking sheet.

Bake for 55-65 minutes or until center is almost set. Cool on a wire rack for 10 minutes. Carefully run a knife around edge of pan to loosen; cool 1 hour longer. Refrigerate overnight. Remove sides of pan. **Yield:** 16 servings.

Berry Delightful Spinach Salad

PREP: 35 min.

- 1/2 cup sugar
- 1 cup chopped pecans
- 1 package (6 ounces) fresh baby spinach
- 2 cups sliced fresh strawberries
- 1 cup fresh blueberries

DRESSING:
- 1/4 cup balsamic vinegar
- 2/3 cup fresh strawberries
- 1 teaspoon sugar

- 3/4 teaspoon onion powder
- 1/2 teaspoon salt
- 1/4 teaspoon pepper
- 2/3 cup olive oil

In a small heavy skillet over medium-low heat, cook the sugar until it begins to melt. Gently drag the melted sugar to the center of pan so sugar melts evenly. Cook, without stirring, until sugar is dark reddish brown, about 15 minutes.

Remove from the heat; stir in pecans. Pour onto a foil-lined baking sheet; cool completely. Break pecans apart if necessary.

In a salad bowl, combine the spinach, strawberries and blueberries. Place the first six dressing ingredients in a blender; cover and process until pureed. While processing, gradually add the olive oil to the mixture in a steady stream.

Just before serving, drizzle salad with dressing; toss to coat. Top with sugared pecans. **Yield:** 8 servings.

ZUCCHINI SALSA VERDE

ROASTED TOMATO SALSA

SWEET & SPICY PINEAPPLE SALSA

Sweet & Spicy Pineapple Salsa

It Takes Two to Salsa

A daughter and her birth mother reunited—and formed an instant bond over their love of cooking and Mexican food.

By Anne Tegtmeier, Portland, Oregon

IT'S DIFFICULT to put into words what it's like to meet your birth mother for the very first time.

I met mine, Donna Kelly (shown at left in the photo at left), when I was 27, and we connected powerfully, quickly and permanently—in part because of our love of cooking.

We were living about as far away from one another as you can get in this country: I in Connecticut, Donna in Oregon. So we got to know each other through hand-written letters, long phone calls and regular emails.

When we finally met in San Diego, we embraced immediately. Although it was a while before I met Donna's husband, Jim, and their four children—Katy, Amy, Matt and Jake—once we took that step, we all grew close.

It was during that first meeting that Donna and I discovered we share a love of food. She was raised in Tucson, Arizona, a few miles from the Mexican border. So, unlike a lot of kids who grew up on peanut butter sandwiches, Donna lunched on bean burritos.

Mexican and Southwestern food happens to be both her specialty and my favorite cuisine, so I envy her expertise. Donna's salsas, which I've shared here, are the best. Everyone raves over her tongue-tingling blends—Sweet & Spicy Pineapple Salsa, Roasted Tomato Salsa and Zucchini Salsa Verde.

Donna's been known to leave pint jars of her creations on the porches or car seats of those she loves. This has earned her the nickname Salsa Fairy. (See the box on page 206 for some of Donna's best tips.)

Donna loves to cook for her friends and family—and always from scratch. Whenever I visit, we spend most of our time planning meals, grocery shopping, cooking and eating. We'll use any excuse to go wild!

In fact, we enjoy cooking together so much that we wrote a cookbook, *101 Things to Do With Tofu.* I won second place on the Food Network's Ultimate Recipe Showdown with one of the recipes, my Ultimate Veggie Chili. We also collaborated on a blog to tell our story through food, one post at a time.

Donna does all this while holding down a demanding job as a prosecuting attorney in Provo, Utah. I live in Portland, Oregon now and feel so fortunate to be even closer to Donna and her family. Life holds so many more special times for us—and a lot more cooking!

Sweet & Spicy Pineapple Salsa

PREP/TOTAL TIME: 30 min.

- 1/2 fresh pineapple, peeled, cored and cut into 1/2-inch slices
- 2 jalapeno peppers
- 1 medium mango, peeled and finely chopped
- 1/4 cup finely chopped onion
- 2 green onions, finely chopped
- 3 tablespoons minced fresh cilantro
- 3 tablespoons lime juice
- 2 tablespoons olive oil
- 2 tablespoons honey
- 1/8 teaspoon salt
- 1/8 teaspoon pepper
- 1/8 teaspoon hot pepper sauce

Moisten a paper towel with cooking oil; using long-handled tongs, lightly coat the grill rack. Grill the pineapple, covered, over medium heat for 3 to 5 minutes on each side or until golden brown. Grill jalapenos until tender, turning occasionally.

Let pineapple and jalapenos cool slightly; finely chop and transfer to a large bowl. Add remaining ingredients. Chill at least 2 hours. Before serving, allow salsa to come to room temperature. **Yield:** 2 cups.

Editor's Note: We recommend wearing disposable gloves when cutting hot peppers. Avoid touching your face.

In a food processor, process the uncooked and roasted tomatoes in batches until chunky. Transfer all tomatoes to a large bowl.

Place the cilantro, lime juice, garlic, lime peel and remaining oil in the food processor. Cover and process until blended; add to tomatoes.

Stir in pepper, jalapeno peppers, green onions, cumin, paprika, chipotle pepper, salt and hot sauce. Let stand 1 hour to allow flavors to blend. Serve with tortilla chips. **Yield:** 8 cups.

Editor's Note: We recommend wearing disposable gloves when cutting hot peppers. Avoid touching your face.

Zucchini Salsa Verde

PREP: 25 min. GRILL: 20 min.

- 1 large sweet onion, cut into wedges
- 2 poblano peppers, cut into 1-inch pieces
- 2 medium zucchini, cut into 1-inch pieces
- 4 tomatillos, husks removed and quartered
- 3 jalapeno peppers, halved and seeded
- 2 tablespoons canola oil
- 2 tablespoons lime juice
- 1 tablespoon Louisiana-style hot sauce
- 1-1/2 teaspoons grated lime peel
- 1/4 teaspoon salt
- 2 teaspoons honey, optional

In a large bowl, combine the first six ingredients. Transfer to a grill wok or basket.

Grill vegetables, covered, over medium heat for 18-22 minutes or until slightly charred and tender, stirring occasionally.

Cool slightly. Finely chop and transfer to a small bowl. Stir in the lime juice, hot sauce, lime peel, salt and honey, if desired. **Yield:** 3 cups.

Editor's Note: We recommend wearing disposable gloves when cutting hot peppers. Avoid touching your face.

Roasted Tomato Salsa

PREP/TOTAL TIME: 25 min.

- 12 large tomatoes, halved and seeded, *divided*
- 2 tablespoons olive oil, *divided*
- 1 bunch fresh cilantro, trimmed
- 1/4 cup lime juice
- 4 garlic cloves, peeled
- 2 teaspoons grated lime peel
- 1 large sweet yellow pepper, finely chopped
- 6 jalapeno peppers, minced
- 12 green onions, thinly sliced
- 1 tablespoon ground cumin
- 1 tablespoon smoked paprika
- 1 tablespoon ground chipotle pepper
- 2 teaspoons salt
- 1/4 teaspoon Louisiana-style hot sauce

Tortilla chips

Arrange six tomatoes cut side down on a 15-in. x 10-in. x 1-in. baking pan; drizzle with 1 tablespoon oil. Broil 4 in. from the heat until the skin blisters, about 4 minutes. Cool slightly; drain well.

SALSA SUCCESS. Donna Kelly, nicknamed the Salsa Fairy, shares these suggestions for making and serving salsa:

- To add a charred flavor to any salsa, place your tomatoes, onions and chilies on the grill for a few minutes over very high heat.
- To can a salsa, simply add one tablespoon of apple cider vinegar to a pint of salsa before canning. Once you open the jar of salsa, add a little bit of sugar or honey to counterbalance the acidity.
- For an instant yummy dip, mix one part salsa and one part cottage cheese.

Field Editor Favorites

Taste of Home magazine is edited by cooks across North America. In this chapter, you'll meet five of them and see what they love to serve their families and friends. Then, enjoy making and serving these specialties yourself!

COOK'S CHOICE. Clockwise from top left: Inside-Out Veggie Dip (p. 212), Grilled Cheese & Tomato Flatbreads (p. 228), Espresso Cream Cake (p. 220) and 1-2-3 Grilled Salmon (p. 220).

PARTY PITAS

BRIE-APPLE PASTRY BITES

INSIDE-OUT VEGGIE DIP

Smoky Pecan Puffs

A Family Affair

This mother and daughter-in-law team up in the kitchen
not only at Christmastime, but year-round.

*By Awynne Thurstenson, Siloam Springs, Arkansas,
& Judie Thurstenson, Colcord, Oklahoma*

FIELD EDITORS Awynne Thurstenson (pictured at left in the photo at left) and Judie Thurstenson may live in different states, but they are only a few miles apart... and they often collaborate in the kitchen.

"Awynne and I have cooked together many times," says Judie of her mother-in-law. "She helped me prepare the food for my daughter's graduation party and her wedding. Usually, when we walk into each other's kitchen, the first words are, 'OK, what do you need me to do?'"

A stay-at-home mom, Judie and her husband, Jeff, who runs their screen printing and embroidery shop, have three children and a grandson. Awynne, a church administrator whose husband, Joe, is a retired human resources manager, enjoys spending time with their children, 15 grandchildren and great grandson.

"Every week, I fix a big Sunday lunch for family and friends—up to 40 people," says Awynne. "If Judie beats me home from church, she picks up whatever needs doing. She's right at home in my kitchen.

"When Christmas dinner is at my house, Judie helps me plan the menu. She is one of five daughters-in-law, and they all pitch in."

The two phone each other frequently when one is planning a meal, shower or other event to get ideas or second opinions. "We always know that if one of us needs a helping hand with anything, the other one is just a phone call away," says Judie.

They share a lot of recipes, too, like the scrumptious appetizers featured here. They're ideal for get-togethers during the Christmas season.

A tray of Smoky Pecan Puffs always impresses party guests. For an extra-festive look, cut the pastry with a small star-shaped cutter.

Greek vinaigrette and Greek olives give Party Pitas Mediterranean flair. The dainty mini sandwiches are easy to make with store-bought deli turkey.

Brie-Apple Pastry Bites offer a tangy burst of flavor. And the festive color of Inside-Out Veggie Dip makes it perfect for the holidays.

Rely on these recipes at Christmastime, and—like Awynne and Judie—you'll spread plenty of cheer!

Brie-Apple Pastry Bites

PREP: 30 min. **BAKE:** 15 min.

- 1 package (17.3 ounces) frozen puff pastry, thawed
- 1 round (8 ounces) Brie cheese, cut into 1/2-inch cubes
- 1 medium apple, chopped
- 2/3 cup sliced almonds
- 1/2 cup chopped walnuts
- 1/4 cup dried cranberries

Ground nutmeg

Unfold puff pastry; cut each sheet into 24 squares. Gently press squares onto the bottoms of 48 greased miniature muffin cups.

Combine cheese, apple, nuts and cranberries; spoon into cups. Bake at 375° for 12-15 minutes or until cheese is melted. Sprinkle with nutmeg. **Yield:** 4 dozen.

Unfold the puff pastry; cut into 1-in. squares. Place on parchment paper-lined baking sheets. Whisk the egg and water; brush over squares. Sprinkle with poppy seeds. Bake at 400° for 8-10 minutes or until golden brown.

In a small bowl, combine the cream cheese, sherry and Liquid Smoke if desired; stir in pecans and onion.

Split each pastry square horizontally; spread with 3/4 teaspoon cream cheese mixture. Replace tops. **Yield:** 81 appetizers.

Inside-Out Veggie Dip

PREP: 35 min. + chilling

- 2 large cucumbers
- 16 cherry tomatoes
- 1 package (8 ounces) cream cheese, softened
- 1/4 cup finely chopped sweet red pepper
- 2 tablespoons finely chopped celery
- 2 tablespoons finely chopped green onion
- 1 tablespoon finely chopped carrot
- 1 teaspoon garlic powder
- 1/2 teaspoon salt
- 1/2 teaspoon onion powder

Peel strips from cucumbers to create decorative edges if desired; cut into 1/2-in. slices. Finely chop two slices; set aside. With a small spoon, scoop some of the seeds from the remaining slices.

Cut a thin slice from the bottoms of tomatoes to allow them to rest flat. Cut a thin slice from tops of tomatoes; scoop out pulp, leaving a 1/4-in. shell. Invert onto paper towels to drain.

In a large bowl, combine the cream cheese, red pepper, celery, onion, carrot, seasonings and chopped cucumber.

Fill tomatoes and cucumber slices with cream cheese mixture, about 1 teaspoon in each. Refrigerate for at least 1 hour. **Yield:** 3-1/2 dozen.

Party Pitas

PREP/TOTAL TIME: 25 min.

- 4 whole wheat pita pocket halves
- 1/3 cup Greek vinaigrette
- 1/2 pound thinly sliced deli turkey
- 1 jar (7-1/2 ounces) roasted sweet red peppers, drained and patted dry
- 2 cups fresh baby spinach
- 24 pitted Greek olives
- 24 frilled toothpicks

Brush insides of pita pockets with vinaigrette; fill with turkey, peppers and spinach. Cut each pita pocket into six wedges.

Thread olives onto toothpicks; use to secure wedges. **Yield:** 2 dozen.

Smoky Pecan Puffs

PREP: 30 min. BAKE: 10 min.

- 1 sheet frozen puff pastry, thawed
- 1 egg
- 1 tablespoon water
- 1 tablespoon poppy seeds
- 1 package (8 ounces) cream cheese, softened
- 2 tablespoons sherry
- 1/2 teaspoon Liquid Smoke, optional
- 1/4 cup finely chopped pecans
- 1 tablespoon finely chopped onion

SOUTHWEST BEEF BRISKET

HONEY-OF-A-MEAL CHICKEN

25-MINUTE TURKEY CHILI

Presto Mexican Peppers

Cooking Therapy

A journey of healing in both body and spirit passed squarely through this resourceful Field Editor's kitchen.

By Traci Wynne, Denver, Pennsylvania

WHEN I was growing up, my family spent most Sundays at my grandparents' house, having supper around their big dining room table.

Grandma was an amazing cook, and the aromas that came out of her kitchen were so mouthwatering that it was hard to wait for dinner.

Those memories made such an impact on me that I wanted to prepare delicious foods, too. My mother, who's also a wonderful cook, tried to teach me, but she doesn't use recipes. So I ended up buying a gazillion cookbooks to figure out how to make the foods I enjoy. Eventually, I began experimenting and coming up with my own recipes.

Then an accident left me permanently disabled. I will always walk with a cane or crutches, depending on how I'm doing. After years of physical therapy and other treatments, I found that returning to the kitchen was one of the most beneficial remedies for both my body and spirit.

Because I can't bend down to put food in the oven or lift heavy pots and dishes, I had to rely on the assistance of my wonderful parents, who have always been there for me. Recently, I married my husband, Michael, an operating room nurse in the U.S. Army Medical Corps, who's a huge help as well.

I also turned to kitchen appliances that make cooking easier, such as my pressure cooker. I got interested in pressure cooking because it's how my mom prepared her wonderful beef stew. The meat would be so tender that it just fell apart.

Pressure cookers not only tenderize, they cook really fast—and the steam seals in nutrients. I was afraid of pressure cookers when I was younger, but they've come a long way in safety and are now much easier to use. Plus, I can fill one on the counter instead of having to get help to use the oven.

Some of my favorite pressure-cooker dishes are Honey-of-a-Meal Chicken, Southwest Beef Brisket, Presto Mexican Peppers and 25-Minute Turkey Chili. I've shared those recipes here.

For me, cooking is much more than therapy—it is my passion. I feel at peace when I'm able to do it. And making someone smile with something I've prepared and served is the cherry on top.

Honey-of-a-Meal Chicken

PREP/TOTAL TIME: 30 min.

- 4 **bone-in chicken breast halves, skin removed (8 ounces *each*)**
- 2 **tablespoons olive oil**
- 1 **medium onion, finely chopped**
- 1 **cup chicken broth**
- 2 **tablespoons spicy brown mustard**
- 1/2 **teaspoon pepper**
- 2 **tablespoons honey**

In a pressure cooker, brown the chicken breasts in oil in batches. Set the chicken aside. Saute the onion in the drippings until tender. Stir in chicken broth, mustard and pepper. Return chicken to the pan. Close cover securely according to manufacturer's directions.

Bring pressure cooker to full pressure over high heat. Reduce heat to medium-high and cook for 8 minutes. (Pressure regulator should maintain a slow steady rocking motion or release of steam; adjust the heat if needed.) Immediately cool according to manufacturer's directions until pressure is completely reduced. Remove chicken and keep warm.

Stir honey into the sauce. Bring to a boil. Reduce heat; simmer, uncovered, for 8-10 minutes or until thickened. Serve with chicken. **Yield:** 4 servings.

Southwest Beef Brisket

PREP: 25 min. + marinating **COOK:** 55 min.

- 1 fresh beef brisket (3 pounds)
- 1 small onion, finely chopped
- 1 serrano pepper, seeded and minced
- 4 teaspoons brown sugar
- 1 tablespoon chili powder
- 1 tablespoon cider vinegar
- 2 garlic cloves, minced
- 1/2 teaspoon salt
- 1/2 teaspoon ground cumin
- 4 teaspoons canola oil
- 2-1/2 cups water
- 2 cans (10 ounces *each*) diced tomatoes and green chilies
- 1 medium onion, sliced

Cut the beef brisket in half. In a large resealable plastic bag, combine the chopped onion, serrano pepper, brown sugar, chili powder, cider vinegar, garlic, salt and cumin. Add the brisket; seal the bag and turn to coat. Refrigerate overnight.

In a pressure cooker, brown brisket in oil on all sides. Add the water, tomatoes and sliced onion. Close cover securely according to manufacturer's directions.

Bring cooker to full pressure over high heat. Reduce heat to medium-high and cook for 55 minutes. (Pressure regulator should maintain a slow steady rocking motion or release of steam; adjust heat if needed.) Remove from the heat; allow pressure to drop on its own. Remove beef to a platter; serve with tomato mixture. **Yield:** 8 servings.

Editor's Note: This is a fresh beef brisket, not corned beef. We recommend wearing disposable gloves when cutting hot peppers. Avoid touching your face.

Presto Mexican Peppers

PREP/TOTAL TIME: 30 min.

- 4 medium green, sweet red, orange *and/or* yellow peppers
- 1 egg, beaten
- 1 cup salsa
- 1-1/2 cups crushed tortilla chips
- 1 medium onion, chopped
- 1/2 cup minced fresh cilantro
- 1 red chili pepper, seeded and finely chopped
- 3 garlic cloves, minced
- 2 teaspoons ground cumin
- 1 pound lean ground beef (90% lean)
- 1/2 cup shredded Mexican cheese blend

Sour cream and additional salsa, optional

Cut tops off of the peppers and remove seeds. In a large bowl, combine the egg, salsa, chips, onion, cilantro, chili pepper, garlic and cumin. Crumble beef over mixture and mix well; spoon into peppers.

Pour 1-1/2 cups water into pressure cooker. Place the peppers on steamer tray in pressure cooker; top with a piece of foil. Close the cover securely according to the manufacturer's directions.

Bring cooker to full pressure over high heat. Reduce heat to medium-high and cook for 10 minutes. (Pressure regulator should maintain a slow steady rocking motion or release of steam; adjust heat if needed.) Remove from the heat; immediately cool according to manufacturer's directions until pressure is completely reduced.

Sprinkle peppers with cheese. Serve with sour cream and additional salsa if desired. **Yield:** 4 servings.

Editor's Note: We recommend wearing disposable gloves when cutting hot peppers. Avoid touching your face.

25-Minute Turkey Chili

PREP/TOTAL TIME: 25 min.

- **1-1/4 pounds ground turkey**
- **1 can (16 ounces) kidney beans, rinsed and drained**
- **1 can (15 ounces) black beans, rinsed and drained**
- **1 can (14-1/2 ounces) Mexican stewed tomatoes, undrained**
- **1 can (8 ounces) tomato sauce**
- **1 small sweet red pepper, finely chopped**
- **1 small onion, chopped**
- **1/2 cup beef broth**
- **1 jalapeno pepper, seeded and minced**
- **2 tablespoons chili powder**
- **1/2 teaspoon salt**
- **1/4 teaspoon pepper**

Crumble turkey into a pressure cooker. Add remaining ingredients; stir to combine.

Close the cover securely according to manufacturer's directions. Bring the pressure cooker to full pressure over high heat. Reduce the heat to medium-high and cook for 5 minutes. (Pressure regulator should maintain a slow steady rocking motion or release of steam; adjust the heat if needed.)

Immediately cool according to the manufacturer's directions until pressure is completely reduced. Stir chili. **Yield:** 8 servings (2 quarts).

Editor's Note: We recommend wearing disposable gloves when cutting hot peppers. Avoid touching your face.

RED HOT. Jalapenos and other chili peppers contain a skin irritant called capsaicin. When handling them, it's a good idea not only to wear gloves and avoid touching your face, but also to wash your hands and cutting surface thoroughly with hot, soapy water when finished.

MEDITERRANEAN CHIPS & DIP

BLUE CHEESE SLAW

ESPRESSO CREAM CAKE

1-2-3 Grilled Salmon

Toast Master

Once this Arizona Field Editor learned the fundamentals of cooking (starting with toast), everything else was gravy.

By Nicole Clayton, Prescott, Arizona

YOU COULD SAY I had my first taste of cooking when I was 10 years old. Well, it wasn't exactly cooking—on weekends, I made toast at a local restaurant while my mom waited tables.

I guess I did OK with the toast; by the time I was in high school, I was promoted to the position of cook on the busiest shift at the restaurant—weekend breakfast and lunch.

Because Mom was also working a second job, I started helping out with the cooking at home, too. I thought, *How hard can it be?* I can make a pretty mean piece of toast!

I tried to imitate my mom, who was a great cook, but she never used recipes. So I learned by trial and error. I'd make a simple macaroni and cheese, for example, and I'd change it up by throwing in some chicken and vegetables.

That's how I cook to this day—by putting my own spin on things. I'll try a recipe as it's written the first time, then play around with the seasonings or substitute one ingredient for another.

My family and I are trying to eat healthier, so the other day I made burgers with ground chicken instead of beef, adding mayonnaise, garlic and fresh rosemary. Everyone loved the results!

My husband, Robert, also enjoys cooking. Before we had children, he'd get home from work—he's the branch manager of a bank—and get dinner started. Now that I'm home during the day with our young sons, Andrew and Garrett, preparing dinner usually falls to me.

Luckily, my family doesn't mind being guinea pigs for my kitchen experiments. I like to tinker with dishes my husband normally doesn't care for, then add a tasty twist so he'll eat them.

I did exactly that with 1-2-3 Grilled Salmon and Mediterranean Chips & Dip. I've shared those recipes here, as well as yummy Blue Cheese Slaw and Espresso Cream Cake.

Andrew usually eats what Robert and I eat and isn't picky at all. Still, the household rule is to try something at least once; then, if you don't like it, you can have something else. So far, we haven't had to use the second part of that rule!

Mediterranean Chips & Dip

PREP/TOTAL TIME: 30 min.

- 1 can (15-1/2 ounces) white kidney *or* cannellini beans, rinsed and drained
- 1/3 cup olive oil
- 2 garlic cloves, peeled
- 2 tablespoons lemon juice
- 1/4 cup packed fresh parsley sprigs
- 1/4 teaspoon salt
- 1/4 teaspoon coarsely ground pepper

CHIPS:

- 4 whole pita breads
- 2 tablespoons olive oil
- 3/4 teaspoon dried oregano
- 1/8 teaspoon salt
- 1/8 teaspoon coarsely ground pepper

Place the first seven ingredients in a food processor; cover and process until smooth.

For pita chips, cut each pita bread into eight wedges; place on ungreased baking sheets. Brush with oil and sprinkle with seasonings. Bake at 400° for 4-6 minutes or until golden brown. Serve with dip. **Yield:** 8 servings.

In a large bowl, dissolve espresso powder in water; cool. Stir in cheese.

In a small bowl, beat cream until it begins to thicken. Gradually add confectioners' sugar; beat until soft peaks form. Stir 1/2 cup cream into the cheese mixture; fold in remaining cream.

Serve the mascarpone cream with angel food cake. Drizzle each serving with coffee liqueur and dust with cocoa. **Yield:** 8 servings.

1-2-3 Grilled Salmon

PREP: 10 min. + marinating GRILL: 5 min.

- 1/3 **cup olive oil**
- 3 **tablespoons reduced-sodium soy sauce**
- 2 **tablespoons Dijon mustard**
- 1/2 **teaspoon dried minced garlic**
- 6 **salmon fillets (5 ounces *each*)**

In a small bowl, combine oil, soy sauce, Dijon mustard and garlic. Pour half of marinade into a large resealable plastic bag. Add the salmon fillets; seal bag and turn to coat. Refrigerate for 30 minutes. Refrigerate remaining marinade.

Drain fish and discard marinade. Moisten a paper towel with cooking oil; using long-handled tongs, lightly coat the grill rack. Grill salmon, covered, over high heat for 5-10 minutes or until the fish flakes easily with a fork. Drizzle with reserved marinade. **Yield:** 6 servings.

Blue Cheese Slaw

PREP: 40 min. + chilling

- 4 **cups shredded green cabbage**
- 4 **cups shredded red cabbage**
- 4 **large carrots, shredded**

DRESSING:
- 1 **cup mayonnaise**
- 2 **tablespoons Dijon mustard**
- 1 **tablespoon stone-ground mustard**
- 1 **tablespoon cider vinegar**
- 1/2 **teaspoon celery salt**
- 1/4 **teaspoon salt**
- 1/4 **teaspoon coarsely ground pepper**
- 1-1/2 **cups (6 ounces) crumbled blue cheese**
- 1/4 **cup minced fresh parsley**

In a large bowl, combine cabbages and carrots. In a small bowl, combine the mayonnaise, mustards, vinegar, celery salt, salt and pepper. Pour over cabbage mixture; toss to coat. Stir in cheese and parsley. Refrigerate for at least 2 hours. **Yield:** 10 servings.

Espresso Cream Cake

PREP/TOTAL TIME: 25 min.

- 2 **tablespoons instant espresso powder**
- 2 **tablespoons hot water**
- 1 **carton (8 ounces) Mascarpone cheese**
- 1 **cup heavy whipping cream**
- 1/3 **cup confectioners' sugar**
- 1 **prepared angel food cake (8 to 10 ounces)**
- 1/2 **cup coffee liqueur**
- 2 **teaspoons baking cocoa**

LEMON BREAKFAST PARFAITS

COOL BEANS SALAD

Saucy Thai Beef Noodles

A Moving Experience

A Wisconsin Field Editor's vast treasury of recipes reflects
the varied places she has lived and cooked.

By Janelle Lee, Appleton, Wisconsin

I'M NOT that different from a lot of busy moms—I'm active in the PTA, help out at my kids' school and enjoy fixing wholesome, delicious meals for my family.

Perhaps I've moved a little more than some people; we lived in Louisiana, Idaho and Oregon before moving to Wisconsin. In every place, though, I've picked up different tastes and new cooking styles, and I've made many friends. I've also collected, tried and shared countless recipes. But if you're like me, you can never have too many recipes!

Three of my favorites reflect my wide range of cooking influences. Saucy Thai Beef Noodles is always a popular entree in our house. I like the make-ahead convenience of Cool Beans Salad, and Lemon Breakfast Parfaits give us a great kick-start in the morning.

An Iowa native, I didn't know anything about cooking Cajun when I moved to Louisiana, where I met my husband, Denny. After we got married, we'd get together with friends about once a month to play a card game called pokeno. During those games, I sampled new dishes featuring crawfish, shrimp and other Cajun delights, many of them spicy.

It took a while to adjust to the spiciness, but now I make a mean gumbo. It's got more of a kick than anything I once thought I could tolerate.

The move to Idaho didn't result in sacks of potato recipes, but I was part of a cooking club—though we usually went out to eat and talk about recipes! Our time in Oregon was a feast of salmon and tuna; it was also where I first sampled sushi.

We've lived in Wisconsin now for six years, and of course, I quickly learned how to prepare bratwurst in onions, sweet peppers and beer. I've accumulated a lot of cheese recipes, too.

Although I learned the most in Louisiana, I have collected more recipes in Wisconsin because, for the past four years, I've been part of a cooking club that's helped expand my culinary skills. Five friends and I get together each month to prepare themed entrees that we take home to our families for dinner that night.

So far, I've filled an entire notebook with recipes and started a second one. So, while we're settled here in Wisconsin, my travels in cooking continue.

Cool Beans Salad

PREP/TOTAL TIME: 20 min.

- 3 cups cooked basmati rice
- 1 can (16 ounces) kidney beans, rinsed and drained
- 1 can (15 ounces) black beans, rinsed and drained
- 1-1/2 cups frozen corn, thawed
- 4 green onions, sliced
- 1 small sweet red pepper, chopped
- 1/4 cup minced fresh cilantro

DRESSING:

- 1/2 cup olive oil
- 1/4 cup red wine vinegar
- 1 tablespoon sugar
- 1 garlic clove, minced
- 1 teaspoon salt
- 1 teaspoon ground cumin
- 1 teaspoon chili powder
- 1/4 teaspoon pepper

In a large bowl, combine the first seven ingredients. In a small bowl, whisk dressing ingredients; pour over salad and toss to coat. Chill until serving. **Yield:** 6 servings.

Saucy Thai Beef Noodles

PREP/TOTAL TIME: 30 min.

- 1/2 cup 2% milk
- 1/2 cup creamy peanut butter
- 1/4 cup soy sauce
-   2 tablespoons brown sugar
-   2 tablespoons sherry
-   2 garlic cloves, minced
- 1/4 teaspoon crushed red pepper flakes
-   3 drops hot pepper sauce
- 12 ounces uncooked spaghetti
-   1 beef top sirloin steak (1 pound), thinly sliced
- 1-1/2 teaspoons canola oil, *divided*
- 1/2 cup thinly sliced fresh carrot
- 1/2 cup julienned sweet red pepper
-   1 cup fresh snow peas
-   2 green onions, sliced
- 1/4 cup chopped salted peanuts
-   2 tablespoons minced fresh cilantro

In a small saucepan, bring the first eight ingredients just to a boil, stirring constantly. Remove from the heat; set aside.

Cook the spaghetti according to package directions.

In a large skillet or wok, stir-fry beef in 1/2 teaspoon oil until no longer pink. Remove and keep warm.

Stir-fry the carrot and red pepper in the remaining oil for 3-4 minutes. Add snow peas and onions; stir-fry 2-3 minutes longer or until vegetables are crisp-tender. Return beef to skillet.

Drain the noodles; add to the pan. Add the peanut sauce and toss to coat. Sprinkle with the peanuts and cilantro. **Yield:** 6 servings.

Lemon Breakfast Parfaits

PREP: 25 min. + cooling

- 3/4 cup fat-free milk
- **Dash salt**
- 1/3 cup uncooked couscous
- 1/2 cup reduced-fat sour cream
- 1/2 cup lemon yogurt
-   1 tablespoon honey
- 1/4 teaspoon grated lemon peel
-   1 cup sliced peeled kiwifruit
-   1 cup fresh blueberries
-   1 cup fresh raspberries
- **Chopped crystallized ginger and minced fresh mint**

In a small saucepan, bring milk and salt to a boil. Stir in couscous. Remove from the heat; cover and let stand for 5-10 minutes or until milk is absorbed. Fluff with a fork; cool.

In a small bowl, combine sour cream, yogurt, honey and lemon peel. Stir in couscous.

Combine the kiwi, blueberries and raspberries; spoon 1/4 cup of fruit mixture into each of six parfait glasses. Layer with the couscous mixture and remaining fruit mixture. Garnish with the crystallized ginger and fresh mint. **Yield:** 6 servings.

PARFAIT POSSIBILITIES. Easy Lemon Breakfast Parfaits (recipe above) are an energy-boosting and wholesome way to start off the day. Want more options for morning parfaits? Try any of these memorable combinations:

• Layer some pineapple chunks, fresh or frozen raspberries, vanilla yogurt, ripe banana slices and dates or raisins, then top it all off with a sprinkling of sliced almonds.

• Mix sweetened applesauce with a little ground nutmeg and spoon it into glasses with vanilla yogurt and prepared granola with raisins.

• For a refreshing taste of the tropics, combine pineapple yogurt with nutmeg and add prepared granola, mandarin oranges, fresh raspberries and unsweetened pineapple tidbits.

Garden Vegetable Pasta Salad

GRILLED CHEESE
& TOMATO FLATBREADS

SMOKY GARLIC
AND SPICE CHICKEN

Grill Power

A Pennsylvania Field Editor combines two of her passions—
food and the outdoors—every time she fires up the grill.

By Tina Repak Mirilovich, Johnstown, Pennsylvania

I DON'T KNOW exactly when, but my enthusiasm for food and cooking started early on. My mom, who was a fantastic cook and baker, said I would stop watching *Sesame Street* so I could pull up a stool and help her in the kitchen.

I remember her guiding me as I tore lettuce for salads, coated pork chops with breading and stirred up batches of holiday cookies. Over the years, my fascination with food—making it and eating it—has never waned.

I even got into the food business, producing packaged polenta and pizza crust mixes. But the real joy comes from cooking for my family and friends, or giving them a gift of food to show my appreciation or gratitude.

They'd probably all agree that grilling is my specialty, and there isn't much I haven't prepared on a grill. I have three grills—two charcoal kettle grills and one gas one. They're nothing fancy, but they serve their purpose, which is grilling everything from chunks of provolone cheese (which I serve with crusty bread—yum!) and romaine lettuce to clams, whole smoked turkeys and grilled pizzas.

I've shared a few favorite recipes here, including Grilled Cheese & Tomato Flatbreads. A wonderful appetizer or entree, it combines grilled pizza and a cheesy flatbread recipe I discovered years ago.

A soy sauce-based marinade makes Smoky Garlic and Spice Chicken an entree that's moist, crisp and delicious. And Garden Vegetable Pasta Salad is a versatile side dish that gets Mediterranean flair from olives and feta cheese.

One of the great things about grilling, in addition to the fabulous flavors, is that I can do it outdoors. I can't get enough of summer, so I spend every possible minute outside cooking, vegetable gardening and enjoying meals on the patio with my husband, Anthony.

He's a foodie, too, so our vacations usually center around unique restaurants and dining experiences, whether we're staying at a resort here in Pennsylvania or escaping our cold winters by fleeing to Florida. We go to Disney World every year, but more for the restaurants than the park itself.

In fact, it's not unusual for us to schedule the itinerary of our trip around the reservations we have at special restaurants. Talk about loving food!

Smoky Garlic and Spice Chicken

PREP: 20 min. + marinating **GRILL:** 1 hr. + standing

- 1/3 cup reduced-sodium soy sauce
- 3 tablespoons lime juice
- 6 garlic cloves, minced
- 1 tablespoon olive oil
- 1 tablespoon ground cumin
- 1 teaspoon paprika
- 1/2 teaspoon dried oregano
- 1/2 teaspoon pepper
- 1 broiler/fryer chicken (3 to 4 pounds), split in half lengthwise

In a large resealable plastic bag, combine the first eight ingredients. Add the chicken; seal bag and turn to coat. Refrigerate for 8 hours or overnight.

Drain and discard marinade. Moisten a paper towel with cooking oil; using long-handled tongs, lightly coat the grill rack. Prepare grill for indirect heat, using a drip pan.

Place the chicken cut side down over the drip pan and grill, covered, over indirect medium heat for 1 to 1-1/4 hours or until a meat thermometer reads 180°, turning occasionally. Let stand for 10 minutes before carving.
Yield: 4 servings.

Garden Vegetable Pasta Salad

PREP: 40 min. GRILL: 10 min.

- **1 pound fusilli *or* pasta of your choice**
- **2 medium eggplant**
- **2 medium zucchini**
- **2 medium yellow summer squash**
- **1 large red onion, cut into 1/2-inch slices**
- **1 medium sweet red pepper, cut in half and seeds removed**
- **1/4 cup olive oil**
- **1/2 teaspoon salt**
- **1/4 teaspoon pepper**
- **3 plum tomatoes, chopped**
- **1-1/2 cups (6 ounces) crumbled feta cheese**
- **2 cans (2-1/4 ounces *each*) sliced ripe olives, drained**
- **2 tablespoons minced fresh parsley**

PARMESAN VINAIGRETTE:

- **3/4 cup olive oil**
- **1/3 cup grated Parmesan cheese**
- **1/3 cup white wine vinegar**
- **3 tablespoons lemon juice**
- **1 teaspoon sugar**
- **1 garlic clove, minced**
- **1 teaspoon salt**
- **1/2 teaspoon dried oregano**
- **1/2 teaspoon pepper**

Cook the fusilli pasta according to package directions; drain pasta and rinse in cold water. Place in a large bowl and set aside.

Meanwhile, cut eggplant, zucchini and summer squash lengthwise into 3/4-in.-thick slices. Brush the eggplant, zucchini, summer squash, red onion and red pepper with oil; sprinkle with salt and pepper. Grill vegetables, covered, over medium heat for 4-6 minutes on each side or until crisp-tender. When cool enough to handle, cut into cubes.

Add the plum tomatoes, feta cheese, ripe olives, parsley and grilled vegetables to pasta. In a small bowl, whisk the vinaigrette ingredients. Pour vinaigrette over the salad; toss to coat. Cover and refrigerate until serving. **Yield:** 26 servings (3/4 cup each).

Grilled Cheese & Tomato Flatbreads

PREP: 30 min. GRILL: 5 min.

- **1 package (8 ounces) cream cheese, softened**
- **2/3 cup grated Parmesan cheese, *divided***
- **2 tablespoons minced fresh parsley, *divided***
- **1 tablespoon minced chives**
- **2 garlic cloves, minced**
- **1/2 teaspoon minced fresh thyme**
- **1/4 teaspoon salt**
- **1/4 teaspoon pepper**
- **1 tube (13.8 ounces) refrigerated pizza crust**
- **2 tablespoons olive oil**
- **3 medium tomatoes, thinly sliced**

In a small bowl, beat the cream cheese, 1/3 cup Parmesan cheese, 1 tablespoon parsley, chives, garlic, thyme, salt and pepper until blended.

Unroll the pizza crust dough and cut in half. On a lightly floured surface, roll out each portion of pizza crust dough into a 12-in. x 6-in. rectangle; brush each side with oil. Grill, covered, over medium heat for 1-2 minutes or until the bottoms are lightly browned. Remove from the grill.

Spread the grilled sides of crust with cheese mixture. Sprinkle with the remaining Parmesan cheese; top with the tomatoes. Return to the grill. Cover and cook for 2-3 minutes or until the crust is lightly browned and the cheese is melted, rotating halfway through cooking to ensure an evenly browned crust. Sprinkle with the remaining parsley. **Yield:** 2 flatbreads (12 servings each).

ABOUT EGGPLANTS. Garden Vegetable Pasta Salad (recipe at left) gets extra flavor and color from eggplants. Choose eggplants that have a smooth skin; avoid those with soft or brown spots. Refrigerate them for up to 5 days in a plastic bag. Young and tender eggplants do not need to be peeled before using; larger ones may be bitter and will taste better when peeled.

Quick Fixes

You'll always have time for a hearty, home-cooked meal, no matter how full your schedule becomes. Simply turn to the no-fuss specialties found here. They each come together in 30 minutes or less yet offer all the flavor you crave!

FAST FAVORITES. Clockwise from top left: Presto Pasta (p. 237), Loaded Flank Steak (p. 241), Raspberry & Rosemary Sundaes (p. 238) and Relish the Radish Salad (p. 249).

Garlic Parmesan Orzo

(Pictured below)

PREP/TOTAL TIME: 15 min.

My buttery pasta dish was inspired by something similar I tasted a while ago. It calls for orzo, which cooks quickly and is a nice change from ordinary pasta shapes. Best of all, it makes a superb side dish anytime—no matter how hectic things get! The garlic and Parmesan cheese really stand out.

—Stephanie Moon, Boise, Idaho

> 2 cups uncooked orzo pasta
> 3 teaspoons minced garlic
> 1/2 cup butter, cubed
> 1/2 cup grated Parmesan cheese
> 1/4 cup 2% milk
> 2 tablespoons minced fresh parsley
> 1 teaspoon salt
> 1/4 teaspoon pepper

Cook orzo according to package directions; drain. In a large skillet, saute garlic in butter until tender. Add the orzo, Parmesan cheese, milk, parsley, salt and pepper. Cook and stir until heated through. **Yield:** 8 servings.

Grilled Salmon Packets

(Pictured below left)

PREP/TOTAL TIME: 25 min.

Cleanup's a snap with this convenient entree prepared and cooked in a foil wrapper. That's always a welcomed time–saving treat during the week. —Tim Weber, Bettendorf, Iowa

> 4 salmon steaks (6 ounces *each*)
> 1 teaspoon lemon-pepper seasoning
> 1 cup shredded carrots
> 1/2 cup julienned sweet yellow pepper
> 1/2 cup julienned green pepper
> 4 teaspoons lemon juice
> 1 teaspoon dried parsley flakes
> 1/2 teaspoon salt
> 1/4 teaspoon pepper

Sprinkle salmon with lemon-pepper. Place each salmon steak on a double thickness of heavy-duty foil (about 12 in. square). Top with carrots and peppers. Sprinkle with remaining ingredients.

Fold foil around fish and seal tightly. Grill, covered, over medium heat for 15-20 minutes or until fish flakes easily with a fork. **Yield:** 4 servings.

Lemon & Garlic New Potatoes

PREP/TOTAL TIME: 25 min.

This is a simplified version of a recipe my Costa Rican host sister used to make when I was in the Peace Corps. It has become a favorite side dish at my house.

—Katie Bartle, Parkville, Missouri

> 1 pound small red potatoes
> 2 tablespoons olive oil
> 2 garlic cloves, minced
> 1/4 cup shredded Parmesan cheese
> 2 tablespoons lemon juice
> 1/4 teaspoon salt
> 1/4 teaspoon pepper

Place potatoes in a large saucepan and cover with water. Bring to a boil. Cover and cook for 10-15 minutes or until tender; drain.

In the same pan, cook potatoes in oil over medium-high heat for 4-6 minutes or until browned. Add garlic; cook 1 minute longer. Remove from the heat, stir in the cheese, lemon juice, salt and pepper. **Yield:** 4 servings.

PARMESAN POINTER. When a recipe calls for shredded Parmesan cheese, simply use the cheese that is found in small bags or containers in the dairy section of your grocery store.

Classic Cashew Beef

(Pictured above)

PREP/TOTAL TIME: 30 min.

My family loves stir–fries, and I love them even more because they are healthy and easy to prepare. I've been making this recipe for many years. —Sherri Melotik, Oak Creek, Wisconsin

- 4 teaspoons cornstarch
- 4 teaspoons soy sauce
- 1 teaspoon sesame oil
- 1 teaspoon oyster sauce
- 1/4 teaspoon ground ginger

Dash cayenne pepper

- 1/2 cup cold water
- 1 pound beef top sirloin steak, cut into 1/2-in pieces
- 2 tablespoons canola oil, *divided*
- 8 green onions, cut into 1-in. lengths
- 2/3 cup lightly salted cashews
- 2 garlic cloves, minced

Hot cooked rice

In a small bowl, combine the first seven ingredients until smooth; set aside.

In a large skillet or wok, stir-fry beef in 1 tablespoon oil until no longer pink. Remove and keep warm. Stir-fry onions, cashews and garlic in remaining oil for 1 minute.

Stir cornstarch mixture and add to the pan. Bring to a boil; cook and stir for 2 minutes or until thickened. Add beef; heat through. Serve with rice. **Yield:** 4 servings.

Sesame Green Beans

(Pictured above)

PREP/TOTAL TIME: 30 min.

Vibrant and flavorful, these beans will be a welcome accompaniment to any menu. With delightful Asian–inspired flair, they're wonderful with light dishes such as marinated and grilled salmon. —Noelle Myers, Grand Forks, North Dakota

- 1 pound fresh green beans, trimmed
- 1 medium sweet red pepper, julienned
- 1 tablespoon sesame seeds
- 1 tablespoon rice vinegar
- 1 tablespoon sesame oil
- 1 tablespoon reduced-sodium soy sauce
- 1/4 teaspoon salt
- 1/4 teaspoon pepper

Place beans and red pepper in a 15-in. x 10-in. x 1-in. baking pan coated with cooking spray. Combine the remaining ingredients. Drizzle mixture over vegetables; stir to coat.

Bake, uncovered, at 425° for 20-25 minutes or until beans are tender, stirring once. **Yield:** 6 servings.

Ham It Up Primavera

(Pictured at left)

PREP/TOTAL TIME: 30 min.

I adapted this recipe from a cookbook my husband and I received when we got married. We simply love all the veggies, especially the fresh asparagus. Simply drop the ham for a colorful side dish or meatless entree. —Angelia Holland, Plano, Texas

- 1 package (16 ounces) spaghetti
- 1 pound fresh asparagus, trimmed and cut into 1-inch pieces
- 2 medium carrots, cut into 1/4-inch slices
- 1/2 cup butter, cubed
- 1/2 pound sliced fresh mushrooms
- 2 medium zucchini, halved and cut into 1/4-inch slices
- 2 cups cubed fully cooked ham
- 1 package (10 ounces) frozen peas, thawed
- 8 green onions, chopped
- 3 teaspoons dried basil
- 1-1/2 teaspoons salt
- 1/4 teaspoon white pepper
- 1/4 teaspoon ground nutmeg
- 1-1/2 cups heavy whipping cream
- 1 cup grated Parmesan cheese, *divided*

Cook spaghetti according to package directions. Meanwhile, in a large skillet, saute asparagus and carrots in butter for 3 minutes. Add mushrooms and zucchini; saute until crisp-tender.

Stir in the ham, peas, onions, basil, salt, pepper and nutmeg. Add the cream. Bring to a boil; cook and stir for 2 minutes.

Drain spaghetti; place in a large bowl. Add vegetable mixture and 1/2 cup cheese; toss to combine. Serve with remaining cheese. **Yield:** 12 servings.

Southwest Turkey Soup

PREP/TOTAL TIME: 30 min.

Ground turkey and a handful of other ingredients are all that's required for this satisfying soup that is nicely spiced with salsa, green chilies and chili powder. I think that it's simply perfect on busy weeknights, particularly when chilly winter months set in. —Genise Krause, Sturgeon Bay, Wisconsin

- 1 pound ground turkey
- 1 tablespoon olive oil
- 2 cans (16 ounces *each*) kidney beans, rinsed and drained
- 2 cans (14-1/2 ounces *each*) chicken broth
- 2 cups frozen corn
- 1 cup salsa
- 1 can (4 ounces) chopped green chilies
- 1 to 2 tablespoons chili powder

Sour cream and minced fresh cilantro

Sweet Onion Bread Skillet

(Pictured above)

PREP: 25 min. **BAKE:** 10 min.

Because there are just a few ingredients in this recipe, you'll get the best results if you use the finest-quality ingredients, such as fresh Vidalia onions and aged Parmesan cheese. —Lisa Speer, Palm Beach, Florida

- 1 large sweet onion, thinly sliced
- 2 tablespoons butter
- 2 tablespoons olive oil, *divided*
- 1 can (13.8 ounces) refrigerated pizza crust
- 1/4 cup grated Parmesan cheese

In a large skillet, saute onion in butter and 1 tablespoon oil until softened. Reduce heat to medium-low; cook, stirring occasionally, for 15 to 20 minutes or until golden brown. Set aside.

Brush bottom and sides of a 10-in. ovenproof skillet with remaining oil. Unroll dough into skillet; flatten dough and build up edge slightly. Top with onion mixture and cheese. Bake at 450° for 10-12 minutes or until golden brown. Cut into wedges. **Yield:** 4 servings.

In a Dutch oven, cook turkey in oil over medium heat until meat is no longer pink; drain.

Add the beans, broth, corn, salsa, chilies and chili powder. Bring to a boil. Reduce heat; cover and simmer for 10-15 minutes to allow flavors to blend. Serve with sour cream and cilantro. **Yield:** 6 servings (2-1/2 quarts).

Presto Beef Stew

(Pictured below)

PREP/TOTAL TIME: 30 min.

This quick, flavorful dinner for two couldn't be faster. Just combine sauteed mushrooms with shredded beef, then serve with golden-brown biscuits. Sometimes I even add a few sliced green onions to the stew. —*Karla Johnson, East Helena, Montana*

- **2 individually frozen biscuits**
- **2 tablespoons butter**
- **2 cups sliced fresh mushrooms**
- **1 package (17 ounces) refrigerated beef roast au jus**
- **1/4 teaspoon pepper**
- **2 tablespoons cornstarch**
- **1 cup cold water**

Bake biscuits according to package directions.

Meanwhile, in a large saucepan over medium heat, melt butter. Add mushrooms; cook and stir until tender. Shred beef with two forks; add to the pan. Add pepper. Combine cornstarch and water until smooth; stir into stew. Bring to a boil; cook and stir for 1-2 minutes or until mixture is thickened.

Divide stew between two bowls; top each with a biscuit. **Yield:** 2 servings.

Sausage Hash

(Pictured above)

PREP/TOTAL TIME: 30 min.

I created this easy and quick recipe one night by trying to work with what I had in the refrigerator. I often serve this hearty hash for brunch. Regular or spicy sausage can be used, and red potatoes make it more colorful.

—*Kari Caven, Post Falls, Idaho*

- **1/2 pound bulk pork sausage**
- **2-1/2 cups cubed cooked potatoes**
- **1 cup thinly sliced sweet onion**
- **1 cup sliced fresh mushrooms**
- **2 tablespoons butter**
- **1/4 teaspoon salt**
- **1/4 teaspoon pepper**

In a large heavy skillet over medium heat, cook the sausage until no longer pink; drain and set aside.

In the same skillet, cook the potatoes, onion and mushrooms in butter until potatoes are lightly browned. Stir in the sausage, salt and pepper; heat through. **Yield:** 2 servings.

Teriyaki Mahi Mahi

(Pictured above)

PREP/TOTAL TIME: 20 min.

This glazed fish is good with rice, vegetables or salad. Blotting the fillets before cooking allows a nice brown crust to form. Cod or halibut can be used, too.

—Michelle Ibarrientos, Torrance, California

  4 **mahi mahi fillets (6 ounces *each*)**
1/4 **teaspoon garlic powder**
1/4 **teaspoon pepper**
  1 **tablespoon canola oil**
  1 **teaspoon minced fresh gingerroot**
1/4 **cup reduced-sodium teriyaki sauce**

Sprinkle mahi mahi with garlic powder and pepper. In a large skillet, cook mahi mahi in oil over medium-high heat for 4-5 minutes on each side or until fish flakes easily with a fork. Remove and keep warm.

In the same skillet, saute ginger for 30 seconds. Stir in the teriyaki sauce; heat through. Serve over mahi mahi. **Yield:** 4 servings.

Hummus & Veggie Wrap Up

PREP/TOTAL TIME: 15 min.

I had a sandwich similar to this once when I stopped at a diner while on a long and arduous walk. I enjoyed it so much that I modified it to my own taste and now have it for lunch on a regular basis. Everyone at work wants to know how to make it.

—Michael Steffens, Indianapolis, Indiana

  2 **tablespoons hummus**
  1 **whole wheat tortilla (8 inches)**
1/4 **cup torn mixed salad greens**
  2 **tablespoons finely chopped sweet onion**
  2 **tablespoons thinly sliced cucumber**
  2 **tablespoons alfalfa sprouts**
  2 **tablespoons shredded carrot**
  1 **tablespoon balsamic vinaigrette**

Spread the hummus over the wheat tortilla. Layer with mixed salad greens, chopped onion, sliced cucumber, alfalfa sprouts and shredded carrot.

Drizzle with balsamic vinaigrette. Roll up tightly and serve. **Yield:** 1 serving.

Terrific Turkey Club

PREP/TOTAL TIME: 10 min.

Stone-ground mustard and tangy cranberry sauce combine to liven up a traditional turkey sandwich. I've added celery for a refreshing crunch. —*Janet Sanders, Pine Mountain, Georgia*

- 1 teaspoon stone-ground mustard
- 1 rye *or* wheat sandwich roll, split
- 2 ounces Gouda cheese, sliced
- 1 teaspoon jellied cranberry sauce
- 2 slices deli turkey
- 1 tablespoon thinly sliced celery

Spread the mustard on roll bottom. Layer with cheese, cranberry sauce, turkey and celery. Replace the roll top. **Yield:** 1 serving.

Presto Pasta

(*Pictured below and on page 230*)

PREP/TOTAL TIME: 20 min.

When the temperature and humidity rise, this easy, breezy pasta is just the ticket to help you play it cool.
—*Debbie Verdini, Yardley, Pennsylvania*

- 8 ounces linguine
- 4 cups fresh baby spinach
- 1-1/2 cups julienned roasted sweet red peppers
- 4 garlic cloves, minced
- 3 tablespoons olive oil
- 1 can (6 ounces) pitted ripe olives, drained
- 1/4 teaspoon salt
- 1/8 teaspoon pepper

Cook linguine according to package directions. Meanwhile, in a large skillet over medium heat, cook the spinach, peppers and garlic in oil until spinach is wilted.

Drain the linguine; toss with the spinach mixture, olives, salt and pepper. Serve pasta warm or at room temperature. **Yield:** 9 servings.

Stovetop Orzo Medley

(*Pictured above*)

PREP/TOTAL TIME: 30 min.

A burst of butter and a colorful array of vegetables make this pretty pasta good enough for company. Use a blend of exotic mushrooms to make it extra special.
—*Marie Rizzio, Interlochen, Michigan*

- 1-1/4 cups uncooked orzo pasta
- 2 shallots, finely chopped
- 1 tablespoon olive oil
- 3/4 pound fresh snow peas
- 1/2 pound assorted fresh mushrooms (such as portobello, button *and/or* shiitake), thinly sliced
- 1/4 cup pine nuts
- 2 tablespoons butter
- 1 teaspoon salt
- 1/2 teaspoon coarsely ground pepper
- 1/4 cup finely chopped sweet red pepper

Cook orzo according to package directions.

Meanwhile, in a large skillet, saute shallots in oil for 2 minutes. Add peas and mushrooms; cook 3 minutes longer. Add pine nuts; cook and stir until the vegetables are tender.

Drain the orzo; stir in the shallot mixture, butter, salt and pepper until blended. Sprinkle with the red pepper. **Yield:** 8 servings.

Dessert In a Dash

IF YOU have a family of sweet-tooths but not hours to spend making desserts, look here! You'll be serving up special treats in a snap thanks to these luscious but lickety-split recipes.

Surprise everyone on a hectic weeknight with an after-dinner delight such as Raspberry & Rosemary Sundaes, Rocky Road Pudding Cups, Tipsy Roasted Peaches or Cherry Pie Chimis. You'll finish your meal in a short but sweet way—each fast favorite is ready to eat in less than 30 minutes.

They're so yummy, you'll want to make them even on days when you aren't crunched for time.

Raspberry & Rosemary Sundaes

(Pictured below and on page 230)

PREP/TOTAL TIME: 15 min.

When my rosemary bush overtook my herb garden one summer, I created these surprising sundaes for grown-ups. The rosemary goes beautifully with the fresh raspberries and peach ice cream. However, you can substitute any flavor of ice cream you'd like.
—Lisa Renshaw, Kansas City, Missouri

  2 cups fresh *or* frozen raspberries
1/3 cup sugar
  1 tablespoon balsamic vinegar
  1 teaspoon minced fresh rosemary
  1 tablespoon butter
  3 cups peach ice cream

In a large skillet over medium heat, cook the raspberries, sugar, vinegar and rosemary in butter until heated through. Drizzle sauce over ice cream; serve immediately. **Yield:** 6 servings.

Rocky Road Pudding Cups

(Pictured above)

PREP/TOTAL TIME: 25 min.

Dressed up with nuts and marshmallows, this fudgy homemade pudding will delight kids of all ages. For a lunch box treat, assemble the pudding cups directly in small plastic containers with tight-fitting lids.   —Carole Fraser, Toronto, Ontario

  1/2 cup sugar
  1/3 cup baking cocoa
  3 tablespoons cornstarch
2-1/2 cups 2% milk
  2 eggs, beaten
1-1/4 cups semisweet chocolate chips, *divided*
  1/2 cup chopped pecans, toasted
  1/2 cup miniature marshmallows

In a large heavy saucepan, combine the sugar, cocoa and cornstarch. Stir in milk until smooth. Cook and stir over medium-high heat until thickened and bubbly. Reduce heat to low; cook and stir 2 minutes longer.

Remove from the heat. Stir a small amount of hot mixture into eggs; return all to the pan, stirring constantly. Bring to a gentle boil; cook and stir 2 minutes longer. Remove from the heat; stir in 1 cup chips until melted.

Spoon into dessert dishes, 1/2 cup in each; sprinkle with pecans, marshmallows and remaining chips. Serve immediately. **Yield:** 6 servings.

Tipsy Roasted Peaches

(Pictured below)

PREP/TOTAL TIME: 20 min.

Roasting frozen peaches in a simple brandy sauce turns them into a decadent topping for toasted pound cake. Whipped cream and crunchy almonds are fast finishing touches.
—*Susan Martin, Oshkosh, Wisconsin*

- 1/3 **cup brandy**
- 1/3 **cup honey**
- 3 **tablespoons butter**
- 2 **cups frozen unsweetened sliced peaches**
- 4 **slices pound cake, toasted**
- 1/2 **cup heavy whipping cream, whipped**
- 3 **tablespoons sliced almonds, toasted**

In a small saucepan, combine the brandy, honey and butter; heat through. Keep warm.

Combine peaches and 3 tablespoons brandy mixture; transfer to a greased 15-in. x 10-in. x 1-in. baking pan. Bake at 400° for 10-15 minutes or until tender.

To assemble, place toasted pound cake on four dessert plates. Top with peaches and remaining brandy mixture. Garnish servings with the whipped cream and almonds. **Yield:** 4 servings.

Cherry Pie Chimis

(Pictured above)

PREP/TOTAL TIME: 25 min.

In New Mexico, we love to make these yummy fried pies for dessert. Because they call for flour tortillas and convenient canned pie filling, they're a snap to put together when time is short. —*Terry Dominguez, Silver City, New Mexico*

- 2 **cans (21 ounces *each*) cherry pie filling**
- 6 **flour tortillas (10 inches)**
- **Oil for deep-fat frying**
- **Confectioners' sugar**

Spoon pie filling down the center of each tortilla; fold sides and ends over filling and roll up. Seal with toothpicks.

In an electric skillet or deep fryer, heat oil to 375°. Fry chimichangas, a few at a time, for 2 minutes on each side or until golden brown on both sides. Drain on paper towels. Dust with confectioners' sugar. Serve immediately. **Yield:** 6 servings.

FAST FIX. For dessert in a hurry, slice a prepared angel food cake into thirds horizontally. Place bottom layer on a platter. Spread 1/2 quart of softened ice cream over cake; top with middle cake layer. Spread another 1/2 quart of ice cream over cake; add top cake layer. Wrap cake, and freeze at least 2 hours before serving. Serve with dollops of whipped cream.

Buttery-Onion Corn on the Cob

(Pictured above)

PREP/TOTAL TIME: 20 min.

My mother has relied on this recipe for years. Every time I make it for company, they rave and can't believe how easy it is!
—*Lisa Denson, Decatur, Alabama*

- 1/2 **cup butter, melted**
- 1 **envelope onion soup mix**
- 4 **medium ears sweet corn, husks removed**

In a small bowl, combine butter and soup mix; rub over corn. Place each ear of corn on a 12-in. x 10-in. piece of heavy-duty foil. Fold foil over corn and seal tightly.

Bake at 450° for 15-20 minutes or until corn is tender, turning packet once. **Yield:** 4 servings.

Apple-Green Bean Saute

PREP/ TOTAL TIME: 25 min.

Green beans get a sweet treatment from a bit of apple and a taste of honey. Even kids who don't want to eat their vegetables will give in to this side dish! —*Kimberly Ronio, Audubon, Pennsylvania*

- 1 **pound fresh green beans, trimmed**
- 1 **large apple, peeled and chopped**
- 1 **tablespoon canola oil**
- 1/2 **cup chopped walnuts**
- 1/2 **cup honey**
- 1 **tablespoon sesame seeds, toasted**

In a large skillet, saute beans and apple in oil for 3 minutes. Add walnuts; cook and stir until vegetables are crisp-tender. Stir in honey and sesame seeds; heat through. **Yield:** 5 servings.

Bok Choy Toss

PREP/TOTAL TIME: 20 min.

Chop some fresh veggies, add a gingery bottled dressing and savor this unique salad that's big on flavor and crunch. Toss in cubes of last night's leftover chicken, slices of cooked beef or even a few cooked and peeled shrimp, and you have a refreshing entree that feeds a crowd. It's perfect when you need a potluck contribution but don't have a lot of time. How cool is that?
—*Andrew McDowell, Lake Villa, Illinois*

- 1 **head bok choy, thinly sliced**
- 3 **medium tomatoes, seeded and chopped**
- 1 **yellow summer squash, quartered and sliced**
- 1/4 **cup orange ginger vinaigrette**
- 2 **tablespoons sesame seeds, toasted**

In a large bowl, combine the bok choy, tomatoes and squash. Drizzle with dressing and toss to coat. Sprinkle with sesame seeds. Serve immediately. **Yield:** 10 servings.

Tom & Ava Sandwiches

PREP/TOTAL TIME: 15 min.

An appealing blend of textures and flavors makes every bite of this meatless option a winner. And if your kids are among the many trying out vegetarianism, you might just be glad to have this trick up your sleeve. Slices of garden–fresh cucumbers would add a delightful touch!
—*Lisa Bennett, Riley, Oregon*

- 8 **slices whole wheat bread**
- 1/2 **cup cream cheese, softened**
- 1 **medium ripe avocado, peeled and thinly sliced**
- 1 **large tomato, thinly sliced**
- 8 **slices red onion**
- 1 **cup alfalfa sprouts**

Spread four slices bread with cream cheese. Layer with avocado, tomato, onion and sprouts. Top with remaining bread. **Yield:** 4 servings.

Loaded Flank Steak

(Pictured above right and on page 230)

PREP/TOTAL TIME: 30 min.

For a delicious steak dinner, try this recipe. The simple stuffing makes it elegant enough to serve to guests, yet it's quick enough for a busy weeknight entree. No one ever suspects that the decadent meal comes together in just half an hour. It's sure to become a new favorite in your home.
—*Tammy Thomas, Mustang, Oklahoma*

- 1/2 **cup butter, softened**
- 6 **bacon strips, cooked and crumbled**
- 3 **green onions, chopped**
- 2 **tablespoons ranch salad dressing mix**
- 1/2 **teaspoon pepper**
- 1 **beef flank steak (1-1/2 to 2 pounds)**

In a small bowl, combine the first five ingredients. Cut a deep slit in steak, forming a pocket. Stuff butter mixture into slit.

Grill the flank steak, covered, over medium heat, or broil 4-6 in. from the heat, for 6-7 minutes on each side or until meat reaches desired doneness (for medium-rare, a meat thermometer should read 145°; medium, 160°; well-done, 170°).

To serve, thinly slice across the grain. **Yield:** 6 servings.

HOT TOPIC. It's easy to tell whether your grill is hot, medium-hot, medium, etc. Hold your hand 4 inches over the coals. Count the number of seconds you can hold your hand in place before the heat forces you to pull away. If you can hold your hand above the fire for no more than 2 seconds, the heat level is "hot" (about 500°). If you can only hold your hand above the coals for 3 seconds, the heat level is "medium-hot" (about 400°). If you can hold your hand above the heat source for no more than 4 seconds, the heat level is "medium" (about 350°). If you can hold your hand in place for about 5 seconds, the heat level is "low" (about 300°).

Bistro Beef Sandwich

PREP/TOTAL TIME: 15 min.

Red pepper lends a nice crunch to this satisfying roast beef sandwich. If you like garlic, you'll love the zing added by the garlic–herb spread.   —David Locke, Woburn, Massachusetts

- 2 slices rye bread
- 1 tablespoon garlic-herb cheese spread
- 3 slices deli roast beef
- 2 slices tomato
- 1 romaine leaf
- 1/4 cup julienned sweet red pepper
- 2 teaspoons French salad dressing

Spread one bread slice with cheese spread. Layer with beef, tomato, lettuce and red pepper. Spread remaining bread with salad dressing; place on top. **Yield:** 1 serving.

Corn Muffin Ham & Cheese

(Pictured below)

PREP/TOTAL TIME: 20 min.

You can put leftover corn bread muffins to good use and put a new twist on a ham and cheese sandwich in the process. Dill in the mayonnaise adds a lively spark.
—Jennifer Warner, Huntertown, Indiana

- 6 corn muffins
- 1/4 cup mayonnaise
- 2 tablespoons bacon bits
- 1/8 teaspoon dill weed
- 1/8 teaspoon dried parsley flakes
- 12 slices deli ham
- 6 slices cheddar cheese
- 1/4 cup thinly sliced cucumber

Cut each muffin in half horizontally. In a small bowl, combine the mayonnaise, bacon bits, dill and parsley. Spread over muffin bottoms. Layer with ham, cheese and cucumber. Replace muffin tops. **Yield:** 6 servings.

Very Veggie Frittata

(Pictured above)

PREP/TOTAL TIME: 25 min.

We enjoy this colorful frittata often. Wedges are not only great for breakfast or brunch, but also for a tasty meatless dinner. The sour cream gives the eggs great flavor and texture.
—Teri Condon, Burley, Idaho

- 5 eggs
- 1/4 cup sour cream
- 1/4 teaspoon salt
- 1/8 teaspoon pepper
- 1 cup (4 ounces) shredded cheddar cheese, *divided*
- 2 green onions, chopped
- 1 cup chopped fresh mushrooms
- 1/2 cup *each* chopped sweet red, yellow and green pepper
- 1/4 cup chopped onion
- 1 tablespoon butter

Hot pepper sauce, optional

In a large bowl, whisk the eggs, sour cream, salt and pepper. Stir in 3/4 cup cheese and the green onions; set aside. In a 9-in. ovenproof skillet, saute the mushrooms, sweet peppers and onion in butter until tender. Reduce heat; top with egg mixture. Cover and cook for 4-6 minutes or until nearly set.

Uncover skillet; sprinkle with remaining cheese. Broil 3-4 in. from the heat for 2-3 minutes or until eggs are completely set. Let stand for 5 minutes. Cut into wedges. Serve with pepper sauce, if desired. **Yield:** 4 servings.

Pour into two greased 9-in. pie plates. Bake at 350°
for 15 minutes or until a knife inserted near the center
comes out clean.

Meanwhile, in a small saucepan, melt the butter. Stir in
the cornstarch, salt and pepper until smooth. Gradually
add milk.

Bring to a boil; cook and stir for 2 minutes or until
thickened. Reduce heat; stir in cheese until melted.

To serve, cut each omelet into six wedges. Stack two
wedges on each serving plate with cheese sauce drizzled
between and on top. **Yield:** 6 servings.

Chutney Chicken Croissants

(Pictured below)

PREP/TOTAL TIME: 10 min.

*The complex flavors of the chutney perfectly complement the
cream cheese in this wonderfully unique sandwich. It's a great
way to use up any leftover chicken you might have on hand.
Croissants always make sandwiches seem special, and I truly
think this one is pretty enough for an occasion such as a bridal or
baby shower.* —Jane Ingraham, San Marcos, California

   3 tablespoons reduced-fat cream cheese
   3 tablespoons mango chutney
   2 croissants, split
   2 lettuce leaves
   2 slices red onion
   1 cup shredded cooked chicken breast

Spread cream cheese and chutney over croissant
bottoms. Layer with lettuce, onion and chicken. Replace
tops. **Yield:** 2 servings.

Omelet Wedges With Cheese Sauce

(Pictured above)

PREP/TOTAL TIME: 30 min.

*Our kids wake up early when these fluffy, layered omelets are
on the menu. A savory cheese sauce tastefully tops each piece,
making them seem extra special...without much extra effort!
The quick dish would even be ideal for special-occasion
breakfasts or holiday brunches.*
      —Amy Transue, Catasauqua, Pennsylvania

   6 eggs, *separated*
   1/2 teaspoon salt
   1/4 cup cornstarch
Dash pepper
   1/3 cup water
SAUCE:
   1 tablespoon butter
   1 tablespoon cornstarch
   1/4 teaspoon salt
Dash pepper
   1 cup milk
   2 cups (8 ounces) shredded cheddar cheese

In a small bowl, beat egg whites and salt until stiff peaks
form. In a large bowl, beat the cornstarch, egg yolks and
pepper until lemon-colored. Add water; mix well. Fold in
the egg whites.

In a large saucepan, cook the tortellini according to package directions.

Meanwhile, in a small saucepan, cook garlic in butter for 1 minute. Stir in flour until blended; gradually add milk. Bring to a boil; cook and stir for 2 minutes or until mixture is thickened.

Add marinara sauce, cream cheese, onions, salt and pepper; cook and stir until cream cheese is melted and sauce is heated through. Drain tortellini; serve with sauce. **Yield:** 6 servings.

Easy Sausage & Ravioli

(Pictured below)

PREP/TOTAL TIME: 25 min.

This saucy combo of frozen ravioli and Italian sausage is sure to please the whole family. It's great served with garlic bread and a simple salad. —*Misty Williams, Grain Valley, Missouri*

> 3 **Italian sausage links (4 ounces *each*)**
> 1 **package (25 ounces) frozen cheese ravioli**
> 2 **cups spaghetti sauce**
> 3/4 **cup cubed process cheese (Velveeta)**
> 1/4 **teaspoon garlic powder**
> 1/4 **teaspoon pepper**

Place sausage in a large skillet and cover with water; bring to a boil. Reduce heat; cover and simmer for 10-12 minutes or until no longer pink. Drain. Cut sausage into bite-size pieces.

Meanwhile, cook the ravioli according to package directions. In a small saucepan, heat the spaghetti sauce, cheese, garlic powder and pepper until cheese is melted. Drain ravioli; stir in sauce and sausage. **Yield:** 4 servings.

Rich & Creamy Tortellini

(Pictured above)

PREP: 15 min. **COOK:** 20 min.

This simple recipe mimics one of my favorite menu items at a local Italian restaurant. Now we can enjoy this delicious dish without going out. —*Molly Seidel, Edgewood, New Mexico*

> 1 **package (9 ounces) refrigerated cheese tortellini *or* ravioli**
> 2 **garlic cloves, minced**
> 4 **teaspoons butter**
> 4-1/2 **teaspoons all-purpose flour**
> 1 **cup 2% milk**
> 1 **jar (15 ounces) marinara sauce**
> 4 **ounces cream cheese, cubed**
> 2 **green onions, thinly sliced**
> 1/8 **teaspoon salt**
> 1/8 **teaspoon pepper**

SIMPLE SOLUTION. To remove skin from garlic cloves, lay a clove on a clean, flat rubber jar opener. Fold one side of the opener over and roll garlic on a flat surface with your palm.

Blue Cheese-Stuffed Steaks

(Pictured below)

PREP/TOTAL TIME: 30 min.

For a fast, fancy dinner, try my tender beef with a mild blue cheese stuffing. Grape tomatoes sauteed in garlic make a colorful and flavorful accompaniment.

—*Teddy Devico, Warren, New Jersey*

- 10 **garlic cloves, peeled**
- 2 **tablespoons canola oil**
- 4 **cups grape tomatoes**
- 4 **boneless beef top loin steaks (8 ounces *each*)**
- 1/2 **cup crumbled blue cheese**
- 1/2 **teaspoon salt**
- 1/4 **teaspoon pepper**

In a large skillet, saute garlic in oil until tender. Cover and cook over low heat for 5-7 minutes or until golden and softened. Add tomatoes; cook and stir until tomatoes just begin to burst. Remove from the skillet; set aside and keep warm.

Cut a pocket in the thickest part of each steak; fill with blue cheese. Sprinkle with salt and pepper.

In the same skillet, cook steaks over medium heat for 4-5 minutes on each side or until meat reaches desired doneness (for medium-rare, a meat thermometer should read 145°; medium, 160°; well-done, 170°). Serve with tomato mixture. **Yield:** 4 servings.

Editor's Note: Top loin steak may be labeled as strip steak, Kansas City steak, New York strip steak, ambassador steak or boneless club steak in your region.

BLT Salad

(Pictured above)

PREP: 25 min. + chilling

This basic pasta salad is great for gatherings and a favorite of everyone I know! I like to keep the ingredients in separate containers in the fridge. Just toss it all together for one or more servings whenever needed.

—*Mary Sigfusson, Mankato, Minnesota*

- 2 **cups uncooked spiral pasta**
- 1 **package (1 pound) sliced bacon, chopped**
- 1 **large tomato, seeded and chopped**
- 1/2 **cup ranch salad dressing**
- 3 **cups torn romaine**

Cook the pasta according to package directions. Meanwhile, in a large skillet, cook bacon over medium heat until crisp. Remove to paper towels with a slotted spoon to drain.

Drain pasta and rinse in cold water; place in a large bowl. Add the bacon, tomato and dressing. Toss to coat. Refrigerate until serving.

Just before serving, add the torn romaine and toss to coat. **Yield:** 6 servings.

Chicken and Asian Slaw

(Pictured above)

PREP/TOTAL TIME: 20 min.

Sesame ginger salad dressing adds refreshing flavor to this pairing of broiled chicken and an exotic homemade coleslaw.
—*Melissa Jelinek, Menomonee Falls, Wisconsin*

- **2 cups cubed fresh pineapple**
- **2 cups sliced bok choy**
- **2 cups shredded red cabbage**
- **1/3 cup plus 1/4 cup sesame ginger salad dressing, *divided***
- **4 boneless skinless chicken breast halves (4 ounces *each*)**

In a large bowl, combine the pineapple, bok choy, cabbage and 1/3 cup dressing; toss to coat. Chill.

Brush chicken with remaining dressing; transfer to a 15-in. x 10-in. x 1-in baking pan. Broil 4 in. from the heat for 4-5 minutes on each side or until a meat thermometer reads 170°.

Divide slaw among four bowls. Slice chicken; arrange over slaw. Serve immediately. **Yield:** 4 servings.

Dee's Grilled Tuna With Greens

(Pictured at far right)

PREP/TOTAL TIME: 30 min.

Slices of tender tuna top this colorful combo of fresh spinach, grape tomatoes, corn and edamame (green soy beans).
—*De'Lawrence Reed, Durham, North Carolina*

- **1 pound tuna steaks**
- **2 teaspoons olive oil**
- **1/4 teaspoon salt**
- **1/4 teaspoon pepper**
- **6 cups fresh baby spinach**
- **1 cup grape tomatoes**
- **3/4 cup frozen shelled edamame, thawed**
- **1/2 cup frozen corn, thawed**

CITRUS VINAIGRETTE:
- **2 tablespoons olive oil**
- **1 tablespoon minced fresh basil**
- **1 tablespoon white wine vinegar**
- **1 tablespoon honey**
- **1 tablespoon lime juice**
- **1 tablespoon lemon juice**
- **1 tablespoon orange juice**
- **1/8 teaspoon salt**
- **1/8 teaspoon pepper**

Moisten a paper towel with cooking oil; using long-handled tongs, lightly coat the grill rack. Brush tuna with olive oil; sprinkle with salt and pepper. Grill, covered, over high heat or broil 3-4 in. from the heat for 2-3 minutes on each side for rare; cook longer if desired. Let stand for 5 minutes.

In a large bowl, combine the spinach, tomatoes, edamame and corn. In a small bowl, whisk the vinaigrette ingredients; drizzle over salad and toss to coat. Divide salad among four plates; slice tuna and arrange over salads. Serve immediately. **Yield:** 4 servings.

Sesame Wonton Chips

(Pictured at right)

PREP/TOTAL TIME: 25 min.

These crispy crackers are a nice change from chips. They make a great side to salad or soup, but they also are a flavorful snack.
—*Kristin Arnett, Elkhorn, Wisconsin*

- **12 wonton wrappers**
- **1 tablespoon sesame oil**
- **1 tablespoon reduced-sodium soy sauce**
- **1/2 teaspoon sugar**
- **1/4 teaspoon garlic salt**

Black sesame seeds *and/or* sesame seeds

Cut wrappers diagonally in half; place on a greased baking sheet. In a bowl, combine the next four ingredients; brush over strips. Sprinkle with seeds. Bake at 400° for 3-5 minutes or until crisp. **Yield:** 2 dozen.

SWIFT SNACKS. Use wonton wrappers to make quick appetizers. Spritz both sides of wrappers with refrigerated butter-flavored spray. Press into mini muffin cups and bake at 350° for 4 to 5 minutes or until lightly browned. Add a filling from the deli, and bake 5 minutes longer.

Olive 'n' Fig Chicken

(Pictured above)

PREP/TOTAL TIME: 25 min.

Olive fans will enjoy the elegance of this easy entree. I love green olives and figs, so I put them together with chicken for a salty–sweet combination that's perfect for a special meal.
—*Carol Hull, Hermiston, Oregon*

> 4 **boneless skinless chicken breast halves
>   (5 ounces** *each*)
> 1/4 **teaspoon garlic salt**
> 1/4 **teaspoon lemon-pepper seasoning**
> 2 **tablespoons olive oil**
> 1 **jar (6.35 ounces) green olive tapenade**
> 2 **tablespoons fig preserves**
> **Sliced pimiento-stuffed olives, optional**

Flatten chicken to 1/2-inch thickness; sprinkle with the garlic salt and lemon-pepper. In a large skillet, cook chicken in oil over medium heat for 4-5 minutes on each side or until a meat thermometer reads 170°. Remove and keep warm.

In the same skillet, cook tapenade and fig preserves over medium heat until heated through, stirring to loosen browned bits from pan. Return chicken to the pan; cook on low heat for 2-3 minutes or until chicken is heated through. Garnish with the sliced olives if desired. **Yield:** 4 servings.

Peppered Pork Pitas

(Pictured below)

PREP/TOTAL TIME: 20 min.

The combination of tender pork and sweet red peppers in these sandwiches will appeal to the whole family. Sometimes, I add caramelized onions. They're especially good with garlic mayo. Have fun experimenting with your own variations.
—*Katherine White, Clemmons, North Carolina*

- 1 pound boneless pork loin chops, cut into thin strips
- 1 tablespoon olive oil
- 2 teaspoons coarsely ground pepper
- 2 garlic cloves, minced
- 1 jar (12 ounces) roasted sweet red peppers, drained and julienned
- 4 whole pita breads, warmed

In a small bowl, combine the pork, oil, pepper and garlic; toss to coat. In a large skillet, saute pork mixture until no longer pink. Add red peppers; heat through. Serve with pita breads. **Yield:** 4 servings.

Relish the Radish Salad

(Pictured above)

PREP/TOTAL TIME: 15 min.

I love the fresh taste and pretty color of this bold-flavored medley. Serve it on the side or as a relish atop a veggie burger.
—*Kim Drewiske, De Pere, Wisconsin*

- 10 radishes, thinly sliced
- 8 green onions, thinly sliced
- 3 tablespoons minced fresh parsley
- 3 tablespoons lime juice
- 2 tablespoons olive oil
- 2 teaspoons honey
- 1/2 teaspoon salt
- 1/2 teaspoon ground cumin
- 1/4 teaspoon pepper
- 1/8 teaspoon cayenne pepper

In a bowl, combine the first three ingredients. In another bowl, whisk the remaining ingredients. Pour over radish mixture and toss to coat. **Yield:** 4 servings.

FRESHNESS IS IN THE BAG. You only need a few tablespoons of minced fresh parsley for the radish salad. You can keep the rest of the bunch in the refrigerator for several weeks. Wash the entire bunch in warm water, shake off all excess moisture, wrap it in a paper towel and seal it in a plastic bag. If you need longer storage time, remove the paper towel and place the sealed bag in the freezer. Then simply break off and crumble the amount of parsley you need for soups, stews and other cooked dishes.

Cooking Lighter

Whether you're on a special diet or simply watching what you eat, you can rely on Beef Barley Stew, Deluxe Grilled Cheese and the other delicious recipes here. Each one includes Nutrition Facts, and most include Diabetic Exchanges.

GUILT-FREE FARE. Clockwise from top left: Shrimp & Tortellini in Tomato Cream (p. 270), Grilled Stuffed Pork Tenderloin (p. 258), Portobello Beef Stew with Cranberry Pilaf (p. 269) and Apricot-Glazed Turkey Breast (p. 264).

Barbecue Beef Sandwiches

(Pictured above)

PREP/TOTAL TIME: 30 min.

A quick, tangy sauce gives these family-pleasing sandwiches lots of zip. I've had this recipe for years, and we never get tired of it.
—*Sharon Zagar, Gardner, Illinois*

  1-1/2 **pounds lean ground beef (90% lean)**
      2 **celery ribs, sliced**
      1 **large onion, chopped**
      1 **can (8 ounces) tomato sauce**
   1/4 **cup ketchup**
      2 **tablespoons brown sugar**
      2 **tablespoons barbecue sauce**
      1 **tablespoon prepared mustard**
      1 **tablespoon Worcestershire sauce**
      6 **hamburger buns, split**

In a large nonstick skillet, cook the beef, celery and onion over medium heat until meat is no longer pink; drain.

Stir in tomato sauce, ketchup, brown sugar, barbecue sauce, mustard and Worcestershire sauce. Bring to a boil. Reduce heat; simmer, uncovered, for 10-15 minutes to allow the flavors to blend. Spoon 3/4 cup onto each

hamburger bun. **Yield:** 6 servings.

Nutrition Facts: 1 sandwich equals 348 calories, 11 g fat (4 g saturated fat), 56 mg cholesterol, 719 mg sodium, 35 g carbohydrate, 2 g fiber, 27 g protein. **Diabetic Exchanges:** 3 lean meat, 2 starch.

Asian Turkey Lettuce Wraps

(Pictured below)

PREP/TOTAL TIME: 20 min.

Frozen chopped vegetables make these lettuce wraps a snap. Add some Asian chile sauce if you'd like to spice them up a bit.
—*Susan Riley, Allen, Texas*

  1-1/4 **pounds extra-lean ground turkey**
      1 **package (16 ounces) frozen stir-fry vegetable blend, thawed**
   1/3 **cup reduced-sodium teriyaki sauce**
   1/4 **cup hoisin sauce**
      3 **tablespoons reduced-fat creamy peanut butter**
      2 **tablespoons minced fresh gingerroot**
      1 **tablespoon rice vinegar**
      1 **tablespoon sesame oil**
      3 **garlic cloves, minced**
      4 **green onions, chopped**
   10 **Boston lettuce leaves**
Additional hoisin sauce, optional

In a large nonstick skillet coated with cooking spray, cook and stir turkey over medium heat until no longer pink.

Coarsely chop the stir-fry vegetables; add to the pan. Stir in the teriyaki sauce, hoisin sauce, peanut butter, ginger, vinegar and oil. Stir-fry over medium-high heat for 5 minutes. Add garlic; cook 1 minute longer.

Remove from the heat; stir in the onions. Place a scant 1/2 cup turkey mixture on each lettuce leaf; fold the lettuce over filling. Serve with additional hoisin sauce if desired. **Yield:** 5 servings.

Nutrition Facts: 2 lettuce wraps (calculated without additional hoisin sauce) equals 275 calories, 8 g fat (1 g saturated fat), 45 mg cholesterol, 686 mg sodium, 19 g carbohydrate, 4 g fiber, 34 g protein. **Diabetic Exchanges:** 3 very meat, 1-1/2 fat, 1 starch, 1 vegetable.

Veggie Tuna Burgers

PREP/TOTAL TIME: 30 min.

You don't have to be a so-called health nut to enjoy the taste of these moist and nutritious burgers. They take just 30 minutes to fix and always get my children to eat their veggies.
—*Laura Davis, Ruston, Louisiana*

- 1/4 **cup finely chopped onion**
- 1 **garlic clove, minced**
- 1 **cup** *each* **shredded zucchini, yellow summer squash and carrots**
- 1 **egg, lightly beaten**
- 2 **cups soft whole wheat bread crumbs**
- 1 **can (6 ounces) light water-packed tuna, drained and flaked**
- 1/4 **teaspoon salt**
- 1/4 **teaspoon pepper**
- 1 **teaspoon butter**
- 6 **hamburger buns, split**
- 6 **slices reduced-fat cheddar cheese**
- 6 **lettuce leaves**
- 6 **slices tomato**

In a large nonstick skillet coated with cooking spray, saute the onion and garlic for 1 minute. Add the zucchini, yellow squash and carrots; saute until tender. Drain and cool to room temperature.

In a large bowl, combine the egg, bread crumbs, tuna, salt and pepper. Add vegetable mixture. Shape into six 3-1/2-in. patties.

Coat the same skillet again with cooking spray; cook the patties in butter for 3-5 minutes on each side or until lightly browned. Serve on buns with cheese, lettuce and tomato. **Yield:** 6 servings.

Nutrition Facts: 1 burger equals 275 calories, 8 g fat (4 g saturated fat), 58 mg cholesterol, 643 mg sodium, 32 g carbohydrate, 3 g fiber, 20 g protein. **Diabetic Exchanges:** 2 starch, 2 lean meat, 1 vegetable.

ZIPPY ZUCCHINI. Zucchini is thin-skinned and easily damaged, so handle it carefully. Wash it just before using it. If you need to grate zucchini for Veggie Tuna Burgers (recipe above) or another recipe, leave the stem on to give you a grip.

Chicken Tacos with Pineapple Pico de Gallo

(Pictured above)

PREP/TOTAL TIME: 30 min.

These zesty chicken tacos are not only lower in fat and calories, but also guaranteed to satisfy your cravings for Mexican food. Pineapple and mango bring a burst of refreshing flavor.
—*Jenny Flake, Newport Beach, California*

- 1 **cup chopped fresh pineapple**
- 1/2 **cup chopped peeled mango**
- 2 **tablespoons minced fresh cilantro**
- 1 **tablespoon finely chopped red onion**
- 1 **tablespoon lime juice**
- 3/4 **teaspoon salt,** *divided*
- 2 **cups cubed cooked chicken breast**
- 1/2 **teaspoon ground cumin**
- 1/4 **teaspoon salt-free garlic seasoning blend**
- 8 **corn tortillas (6 inches), warmed**

For pico de gallo, in a small bowl, combine the pineapple, mango, cilantro, onion, lime juice and 1/4 teaspoon salt. Set aside.

In a large nonstick skillet coated with cooking spray, cook and stir the chicken, cumin, seasoning blend and remaining salt until heated through. Spoon 1/4 cup onto each tortilla. Fold in sides. Serve with pico de gallo. **Yield:** 4 servings.

Nutrition Facts: 2 chicken tacos with 1/3 cup pico de gallo equals 257 calories, 4 g fat (1 g saturated fat), 54 mg cholesterol, 572 mg sodium, 33 g carbohydrate, 4 g fiber, 24 g protein. **Diabetic Exchanges:** 3 lean meat, 1-1/2 starch, 1/2 fruit.

Blackened Chicken and Beans

(Pictured below)

PREP/TOTAL TIME: 15 min.

My husband loves any spicy dish, but this is a low-fat one we can both enjoy. While the chicken is cooking, I fix individual salads of lettuce and veggies. Just like that, dinner's done!
—Christine Zongker, Spring Hill, Kansas

  2 **teaspoons chili powder**
1/4 **teaspoon salt**
1/4 **teaspoon pepper**
  4 **boneless skinless chicken breast halves (4 ounces *each*)**
  1 **tablespoon canola oil**
  1 **can (15 ounces) black beans, rinsed and drained**
  1 **cup frozen corn, thawed**
  1 **cup chunky salsa**

Combine the chili powder, salt and pepper; rub over both sides of the chicken. In a large nonstick skillet, cook the chicken in oil over medium heat for 4-5 minutes on each side or until a meat thermometer reads 170°. Remove chicken and keep warm.

Add the black beans, corn and salsa to skillet; bring to a boil. Reduce heat; cover and simmer for 2-3 minutes or until heated through. Transfer to a serving dish; serve with chicken. **Yield:** 4 servings.

Nutrition Facts: 1 chicken breast half with 3/4 cup bean mixture equals 297 calories, 7 g fat (1 g saturated fat), 63 mg cholesterol, 697 mg sodium, 30 g carbohydrate, 10 g fiber, 33 g protein. **Diabetic Exchanges:** 3 lean meat, 2 starch, 1 fat.

Blue Cheese-Topped Steaks

(Pictured above)

PREP/TOTAL TIME: 30 min.

These juicy tenderloin steaks, lightly crusted with blue cheese and bread crumbs, are special enough for a holiday feast. Drizzled with the rich wine sauce, the beef melts in your mouth.
—Tiffany Vancil, San Diego, California

    2 **tablespoons crumbled blue cheese**
4-1/2 **teaspoons dry bread crumbs**
4-1/2 **teaspoons minced fresh parsley**
4-1/2 **teaspoons minced chives**
Dash pepper
    4 **beef tenderloin steaks (4 ounces *each*)**
1-1/2 **teaspoons butter**
    1 **tablespoon all-purpose flour**
  1/2 **cup reduced-sodium beef broth**
    1 **tablespoon Madeira wine**
  1/8 **teaspoon browning sauce, optional**

In a small bowl, combine the blue cheese, bread crumbs, parsley, chives and pepper. Press mixture onto one side of each steak.

In a large nonstick skillet coated with cooking spray, cook the steaks over medium-high heat for 2 minutes on each side. Transfer to a 15-in. x 10-in. x 1-in. baking pan coated with cooking spray.

Bake at 350° for 6-8 minutes or until the meat reaches desired doneness (for medium-rare, a meat thermometer should read 145°; medium, 160°; well-done, 170°).

Meanwhile, in a small saucepan, melt the butter. Whisk in flour until smooth. Gradually whisk in beef broth and wine. Bring to a boil; cook and stir for 2 minutes or until thickened. Stir in browning sauce if desired. Serve with steaks. **Yield:** 4 servings.

Nutrition Facts: 1 steak equals 228 calories, 11 g fat (5 g saturated fat), 78 mg cholesterol, 197 mg sodium, 4 g carbohydrate, trace fiber, 26 g protein. **Diabetic Exchanges:** 3 lean meat, 1/2 fat.

Gingered Beef Stir-Fry

(Pictured below)

PREP/TOTAL TIME: 20 min.

Stir-fry is always a popular supper in our house, especially on busy nights. My oldest son really likes this beef recipe that has pleasant ginger flavor, sweet red peppers and snap peas.
—Debbie Williams, Ashland, Ohio

  1-1/2 **teaspoons sugar**
     1 **teaspoon cornstarch**
   1/4 **cup cold water**
     3 **tablespoons reduced-sodium soy sauce**
     2 **teaspoons sesame oil,** *divided*
     1 **beef flank steak (1 pound), cut into thin strips**
     1 **jar (8 ounces) whole baby corn, drained**
   1/4 **cup julienned sweet red pepper**
     2 **teaspoons minced fresh gingerroot**
     2 **teaspoons minced garlic**
   1/4 **pound fresh sugar snap peas**
     3 **cups hot cooked rice**

In a small bowl, combine the sugar and cornstarch. Stir in the water, soy sauce and 1 teaspoon oil until smooth; set aside. In a large nonstick skillet or wok, stir-fry beef in remaining oil for 4-5 minutes or until no longer pink.

Add the whole baby corn, sweet red pepper, ginger and garlic; stir-fry for 2-3 minutes or until the vegetables are crisp-tender. Add the sugar snap peas; stir-fry 30 seconds longer.

Stir the soy sauce mixture and add to the pan. Bring to a boil; cook and stir for 2 minutes or until thickened. Serve with rice. **Yield:** 4 servings.

Nutrition Facts: 1 cup beef mixture with 3/4 cup rice equals 377 calories, 12 g fat (4 g saturated fat), 48 mg cholesterol, 618 mg sodium, 41 g carbohydrate, 2 g fiber, 25 g protein. **Diabetic Exchanges:** 3 lean meat, 2 starch, 1 vegetable, 1/2 fat.

Herb-Rubbed Pork Chops

(Pictured above)

PREP/TOTAL TIME: 25 min.

When company's coming and time's short, I often turn to these delicious pork chops. Jazzed up with herbs, they're on the lighter side but don't taste that way. Everyone raves about them.
—Sharon Denton, Mt. Airy, Maryland

     1 **teaspoon dried parsley flakes**
     1 **teaspoon dried marjoram**
     1 **teaspoon rubbed sage**
   1/8 **teaspoon garlic powder**
   1/8 **teaspoon salt**
   1/8 **teaspoon pepper**
     2 **bone-in pork loin chops (3/4 inch thick and 6 ounces** *each***)**
  1-1/2 **teaspoons olive oil,** *divided*
   1/4 **cup reduced-sodium chicken broth**
     2 **tablespoons sherry** *or* **additional reduced-sodium chicken broth**

In a small bowl, combine the parsley, marjoram, sage, garlic powder, salt and pepper. Brush both sides of pork chops with 1 teaspoon oil; rub with herb mixture.

In a large nonstick skillet coated with cooking spray, cook the pork chops in remaining oil over medium heat for 3-4 minutes on each side or until lightly browned. Remove and keep warm. Add chicken broth and sherry or additional broth to skillet, stirring to loosen browned bits. Bring to a boil.

Return the pork chops to the pan. Reduce heat; cover and simmer for 4-5 minutes or until a meat thermometer reads 160°. Serve the pork chops with the pan juices. **Yield:** 2 servings.

Nutrition Facts: 1 chop with 3 tablespoons pan juices equals 221 calories, 11 g fat (3 g saturated fat), 74 mg cholesterol, 282 mg sodium, 1 g carbohydrate, trace fiber, 26 g protein. **Diabetic Exchanges:** 3 lean meat, 1 fat.

1/2 cup finely chopped onion
1/4 cup beer *or* nonalcoholic beer
  1 tablespoon Worcestershire sauce
  2 garlic cloves, minced
  1 teaspoon salt
1/4 teaspoon pepper
1-1/2 pounds lean ground beef
  6 rye rolls *or* whole wheat hamburger buns, split
  6 lettuce leaves
 12 tomato slices

In a large bowl, combine the first six ingredients. Crumble the ground beef over the mixture and mix well. Shape into six patties.

Moisten a paper towel with cooking oil; using long-handled tongs, lightly coat the grill rack. Cover and grill over medium-high heat or broil 4 in. from the grill for 4-5 minutes on each side or until a meat thermometer reads 160° and juices run clear.

Serve burgers on rolls with lettuce and tomato slices. **Yield:** 6 servings.

Nutrition Facts: 1 burger equals 307 calories, 12 g fat (4 g saturated fat), 70 mg cholesterol, 686 mg sodium, 25 g carbohydrate, 4 g fiber, 25 g protein. **Diabetic Exchanges:** 3 lean meat, 2 starch.

Chipotle-Sparked Mustard Salmon

(Pictured above)

PREP/TOTAL TIME: 25 min.

These baked salmon fillets get amazing flavor from horseradish, dill, mustard, lemon-pepper seasoning and chipotle.
—*Helen Conwell, Portland, Oregon*

  6 salmon fillets (4 ounces *each*)
1/4 cup reduced-fat mayonnaise
1/4 cup prepared horseradish
1/4 cup stone-ground mustard
1/4 teaspoon lemon-pepper seasoning
  1 teaspoon minced chipotle pepper in adobo sauce
  1 teaspoon snipped fresh dill

Place salmon in a foil-lined 15-in. x 10-in. x 1-in. baking pan. Combine the mayonnaise, horseradish, mustard, lemon-pepper and chipotle pepper; spread over fillets.

Bake at 350° for 15-20 minutes or until fish flakes easily with a fork. Sprinkle with dill. **Yield:** 6 servings.

Nutrition Facts: 1 fillet equals 260 calories, 16 g fat (3 g saturated fat), 70 mg cholesterol, 407 mg sodium, 4 g carbohydrate, 1 g fiber, 23 g protein. **Diabetic Exchanges:** 3 lean meat, 1/2 fat.

Hearty Backyard Burgers

PREP/TOTAL TIME: 25 min.

While these delicious, lean burgers are cooking, I toast rye rolls or whole wheat buns on the grill for a few minutes.
—*Paula LeFevre, Garden, Michigan*

Cajun Shrimp and Rice

(Pictured below)

PREP/TOTAL TIME: 10 min.

I have a friend with Celiac's disease, and I like to serve this when she comes over for lunch. The zippy dish of shrimp, peas and rice suits her dietary needs and pleases everyone who tries it.
—*Ruth Miller, Boyertown, Pennsylvania*

1 **package (8.8 ounces) ready-to-serve long grain rice**
1 **pound uncooked medium shrimp, peeled and deveined**
2 **teaspoons Cajun seasoning**
1 **tablespoon olive oil**
1 **tablespoon butter**
1-1/2 **teaspoons minced garlic**
1 **package (6 ounces) frozen snow peas, thawed**

Cook rice according to package directions. Meanwhile, in a large skillet, saute the shrimp and Cajun seasoning in oil and butter until the shrimp turn pink. Add garlic; cook 1 minute longer. Add the peas and rice. Cook 2-3 minutes or until heated through. **Yield:** 4 servings.

Nutrition Facts: 1 cup equals 269 calories, 8 g fat (3 g saturated fat), 176 mg cholesterol, 550 mg sodium, 23 g carbohydrate, 1 g fiber, 21 g protein. **Diabetic Exchanges:** 3 lean meat, 1-1/2 starch, 1/2 fat.

Sweet Onion 'n' Sausage Spaghetti

(Pictured above)

PREP/TOTAL TIME: 30 min.

Sweet onion seasons the turkey sausage in this yummy dish. I toss in cheese, cream, basil and tomatoes for a meal in minutes.
—*Mary Relyea, Canastota, New York*

6 **ounces uncooked whole wheat spaghetti**
3/4 **pound Italian turkey sausage links, casings removed**

2 **teaspoons olive oil**
1 **sweet onion, thinly sliced**
1 **pint cherry tomatoes, halved**
1/2 **cup loosely packed fresh basil leaves, thinly sliced**
1/2 **cup half-and-half cream**
Shaved Parmesan cheese, optional

Cook the spaghetti according to the package directions. Meanwhile, in a large nonstick skillet over medium heat, cook the sausage in oil for 5 minutes. Add the onion; cook 8-10 minutes longer or until meat is no longer pink and onion is tender.

Stir in tomatoes and basil; heat through. Add cream; bring to a boil. Drain the spaghetti; toss with sausage mixture. Garnish with cheese if desired. **Yield:** 5 servings.

Nutrition Facts: 1-1/4 cups (calculated without Parmesan cheese) equals 305 calories, 11 g fat (4 g saturated fat), 48 mg cholesterol, 442 mg sodium, 33 g carbohydrate, 6 g fiber, 18 g protein. **Diabetic Exchanges:** 2 lean meat, 1-1/2 starch, 1 vegetable, 1 fat.

STICKY SOLUTION. To prevent spaghetti from sticking together during cooking, use a large kettle or Dutch oven and 3 quarts of water for every 8 ounces of pasta you'll be cooking. Add 1 tablespoon olive or vegetable oil to the water, then let the water come to a full rolling boil before adding the pasta. Stir it several times during cooking to separate the strands.

Grilled Stuffed Pork Tenderloin

(Pictured below and on page 250)

PREP: 20 min. + marinating **GRILL:** 25 min.

Here's a real treat from the grill that's easier to prepare than it looks. We pair the stuffed tenderloin with a mixed salad.
—*Bobbie Carr, Lake Oswego, Oregon*

- 2 pork tenderloins (3/4 pound *each*)
- 3/4 cup dry red wine *or* reduced-sodium beef broth
- 1/3 cup packed brown sugar
- 1/4 cup ketchup
- 2 tablespoons reduced-sodium soy sauce
- 2 garlic cloves, minced
- 1 teaspoon curry powder
- 1/2 teaspoon minced fresh gingerroot
- 1/4 teaspoon pepper
- 1-1/4 cups water
- 2 tablespoons butter
- 1 package (6 ounces) stuffing mix

Cut a lengthwise slit down the center of each tenderloin to within 1/2 in. of bottom. In a large resealable plastic bag, combine the wine or broth, brown sugar, ketchup, soy sauce, garlic, curry, ginger and pepper; add pork. Seal bag and turn to coat; refrigerate for 2-3 hours.

In a small saucepan, bring water and butter to a boil. Stir in stuffing mix. Remove from the heat; cover and let stand for 5 minutes. Cool.

Drain and discard marinade. Open tenderloins so they lie flat; spread stuffing down the center of each. Close tenderloins; tie at 1-1/2-in. intervals with kitchen string.

Moisten a paper towel with cooking oil; using long-handled tongs, lightly coat the grill rack. Prepare grill for indirect heat using a drip pan. Place pork over drip pan; grill pork, covered, over indirect medium-hot heat for 25-40 minutes or until a meat thermometer reads 160°. Let stand 5 minutes before slicing. **Yield:** 6 servings.

Nutrition Facts: 1 serving equals 296 calories, 9 g fat (4 g saturated fat), 73 mg cholesterol, 678 mg sodium, 24 g carbohydrate, 1 g fiber, 27 g protein. **Diabetic Exchanges:** 3 lean meat, 1-1/2 starch, 1 fat.

Broiled Scallops

(Pictured above)

PREP/TOTAL TIME: 25 min.

As empty nesters, my husband and I often enjoy these scallops. The two mini baking dishes create the perfect portions.
—*Susan Coryell, Huddleston, Virginia*

- 2 green onions, sliced
- 1 garlic clove, minced
- 2 teaspoons olive oil
- 12 ounces sea scallops
- 2 teaspoons minced fresh parsley
- 1 teaspoon finely chopped fresh basil
- 1/4 cup vermouth *or* chicken broth
- 1/8 teaspoon salt
- 1/8 teaspoon white pepper
- 1/3 cup soft bread crumbs
- 2 teaspoons butter

In a nonstick skillet, saute onions and garlic in oil until tender. Add the scallops, parsley and basil; cook and stir over medium heat until the scallops are firm and opaque. Add vermouth or broth, salt and pepper; cook, uncovered, over medium-low heat for 1 minute.

Divide the mixture evenly between two ovenproof 1-1/2-cup dishes. Sprinkle with the bread crumbs; dot with butter. Broil 4-6 in. from the heat until crumbs are golden. **Yield:** 2 servings.

Nutrition Facts: 1 serving equals 296 calories, 10 g fat (3 g saturated fat), 66 mg cholesterol, 506 mg sodium, 13 g carbohydrate, 1 g fiber, 30 g protein. **Diabetic Exchanges:** 4 lean meat, 2 fat, 1 starch.

Peach-Glazed Beef Fillets

(Pictured below)

PREP/TOTAL TIME: 30 min.

When I'm in the kitchen, I love combining fruits and chilies to come up with new glazes. This recipe uses peach preserves and ancho chili powder, which lends a nice smokey flavor. I like to serve the juicy fillets over rice, potatoes or cheesy grits.
—*Anna Ginsberg, Austin, Texas*

- 2 **beef tenderloin steaks (5 ounces** *each***)**
- 1/4 **teaspoon salt**
- 1/8 **teaspoon pepper**
- 1 **teaspoon canola oil**
- 1/4 **cup peach preserves**
- 2 **tablespoons chicken broth**
- 1 **tablespoon balsamic vinegar**
- 2 **teaspoons minced fresh cilantro**
- 3/4 **teaspoon ground ancho chili pepper**
- 1 **garlic clove, minced**

Sprinkle the beef with salt and pepper. In a large skillet, cook steaks in oil over medium heat for 5-8 minutes on each side or until the meat reaches desired doneness (for medium-rare, a meat thermometer should read 145°; medium, 160°; well-done, 170°).

In a small bowl, combine remaining ingredients; pour over steaks. Cook for 1-2 minutes or until glaze is heated through. **Yield:** 2 servings.

Nutrition Facts: 1 fillet with 3-1/2 teaspoons glaze equals 350 calories, 12 g fat (4 g saturated fat), 89 mg cholesterol, 422 mg sodium, 28 g carbohydrate, trace fiber, 30 g protein. **Diabetic Exchanges:** 4 lean meat, 2 fruit, 1/2 fat.

Saucy Portobello Pitas

(Pictured above)

PREP: 25 min. **COOK:** 10 min.

Hearty portobello mushrooms replace the ground lamb in this healthier version of a gyro. The meat-free sandwiches have the refreshing, cucumber-mint yogurt sauce of the Greek classic.
—*Lisa Hundley, Aberdeen, North Carolina*

CUCUMBER SAUCE:
- 1 **cup (8 ounces) reduced-fat plain yogurt**
- 1/2 **cup chopped peeled cucumber**
- 1/4 **to 1/3 cup minced fresh mint**
- 1 **tablespoon grated lemon peel**
- 1 **tablespoon lemon juice**
- 1 **teaspoon garlic powder**

PITAS:
- 4 **large portobello mushrooms, stems removed**
- 1/2 **teaspoon pepper**
- 1/4 **teaspoon onion powder**
- 1/4 **teaspoon garlic powder**
- 1/4 **teaspoon Greek seasoning**
- 2 **tablespoons canola oil**
- 8 **pita pocket halves, warmed**
- 8 **thin slices red onion, separated into rings**
- 8 **slices tomato**

In a small bowl, combine cucumber sauce ingredients. Cover and refrigerate until serving.

Sprinkle the mushrooms with pepper, onion powder, garlic powder and Greek seasoning. In a large skillet, cook mushrooms in oil for 3-5 minutes on each side or until tender.

Cut pita breads in half; line each with a slice of onion and tomato. Cut mushrooms in half; place in pitas. Serve with cucumber sauce. **Yield:** 4 servings.

Nutrition Facts: 2 filled pita halves with 1/3 cup sauce equals 303 calories, 9 g fat (1 g saturated fat), 3 mg cholesterol, 411 mg sodium, 45 g carbohydrate, 4 g fiber, 11 g protein. **Diabetic Exchanges:** 3 starch, 1 fat.

Vegetable Scrambled Eggs

(Pictured above)

PREP/TOTAL TIME: 10 min.

These scrambled eggs are packed with green pepper, green onions and tomato for an instantly healthy start to the day.
—*Marilyn Ipson, Rogers, Arkansas*

- 1 cup egg substitute
- 1/2 cup chopped green pepper
- 1/4 cup sliced green onions
- 1/4 cup fat-free milk
- 1/4 teaspoon salt
- 1/8 teaspoon pepper
- 1 small tomato, chopped and seeded

In a small bowl, combine egg substitute, green pepper, onions, milk, salt and pepper. Pour into a nonstick skillet coated with cooking spray. Cook and stir over medium heat until the eggs are nearly set. Add the tomato; cook and stir until completely set. **Yield:** 2 servings.
   Nutrition Facts: 1 serving equals 90 calories, trace fat (trace saturated fat), 1 mg cholesterol, 563 mg sodium, 8 g carbohydrate, 2 g fiber, 14 g protein. **Diabetic Exchanges:** 2 lean meat, 1 vegetable.

So Easy Gazpacho

PREP: 10 min. + chilling

My daughter got this recipe from a college friend and gave it to me. Now I often serve the yummy chilled soup as an appetizer when entertaining, and it ends up being the talk of the party.
—*Lorna Sirtoli, Cortland, New York*

- 2 cups tomato juice
- 4 medium tomatoes, peeled and finely chopped
- 1/2 cup chopped seeded peeled cucumber
- 1/3 cup finely chopped onion

- 1/4 cup olive oil
- 1/4 cup cider vinegar
- 1 teaspoon sugar
- 1 garlic clove, minced
- 1/4 teaspoon salt
- 1/4 teaspoon pepper

In a large bowl, combine all ingredients. Cover and refrigerate soup for at least 4 hours or until chilled. **Yield:** 5 servings.
   Nutrition Facts: 1 cup equals 146 calories, 11 g fat (2 g saturated fat), 0 cholesterol, 387 mg sodium, 11 g carbohydrate, 2 g fiber, 2 g protein.

Mimi's Lentil Medley

(Pictured below)

PREP: 40 min.

I created this salad with what I had on hand. My husband gave it high praise when he said, "Let's have this again soon!"
—*Mary Ann Hazen, Rochester Hills, Michigan*

- 1 cup dried lentils, rinsed
- 2 cups water
- 2 cups sliced fresh mushrooms
- 1 medium cucumber, cubed
- 1 medium zucchini, cubed
- 1 small red onion, chopped
- 1/2 cup chopped sun-dried tomatoes (not packed in oil)
- 1/2 cup rice vinegar
- 1/4 cup minced fresh mint
- 3 tablespoons olive oil
- 2 teaspoons honey
- 1 teaspoon dried basil
- 1 teaspoon dried oregano
- 4 cups fresh baby spinach, chopped
- 1 cup (4 ounces) crumbled feta cheese
- 4 bacon strips, cooked and crumbled

In a small saucepan, bring the lentils and water to a boil. Reduce heat; cover and simmer for 20-25 minutes or until tender. Drain and rinse in cold water.

Transfer lentils to a large bowl. Add the mushrooms, cucumber, zucchini, onion and tomatoes. Whisk the rice vinegar, mint, oil, honey, basil and oregano. Drizzle over the lentil mixture; toss to coat. Add the spinach, feta cheese and bacon; toss to combine. Serve immediately. **Yield:** 8 servings.

Nutrition Facts: 1-1/4 cups equals 226 calories, 9 g fat (3 g saturated fat), 11 mg cholesterol, 299 mg sodium, 25 g carbohydrate, 10 g fiber, 12 g protein. **Diabetic Exchanges:** 2 fat, 1 starch, 1 vegetable.

Turkey Cutlets With Cool Pepper Sauce

PREP/TOTAL TIME: 25 min.

Crisp breading surrounds tender turkey cutlets in this refreshing main course. Topped with a sauce of sour cream, mayonnaise, lemon and jalapeno pepper, it has just the right kick.
—Jeannie Klugh, Lancaster, Pennsylvania

- 3 tablespoons reduced-fat sour cream
- 2 tablespoons reduced-fat mayonnaise
- 2 tablespoons minced seeded jalapeno pepper
- 2 teaspoons lemon juice
- 1/4 teaspoon grated lemon peel
- 1/8 teaspoon plus 1/4 teaspoon pepper, *divided*
- 1/2 cup seasoned bread crumbs
- 2 tablespoons grated Parmesan cheese
- 1 tablespoon minced fresh parsley
- 1 garlic clove, minced
- 1 package (17.6 ounces) turkey breast cutlets
- 1 tablespoon olive oil
Lemon wedges and sliced jalapeno peppers, optional

For the sauce, in a small bowl, combine the sour cream, mayonnaise, jalapeno pepper, lemon juice, lemon peel and 1/8 teaspoon pepper; set aside.

In a large resealable plastic bag, combine the seasoned bread crumbs, Parmesan cheese, parsley, garlic and remaining pepper. Add the turkey, a few pieces at a time, and shake to coat.

In a large nonstick skillet, cook turkey in oil in batches over medium heat for 1-2 minutes on each side or until no longer pink. Serve with the sauce. Garnish with lemon wedges and jalapeno peppers if desired. **Yield:** 4 servings (1/2 cup sauce).

Editor's Note: We recommend wearing disposable gloves when cutting hot peppers. Avoid touching your face.

Nutrition Facts: 4 ounces cooked turkey with 2 tablespoons sauce equals 242 calories, 9 g fat (2 g saturated fat), 78 mg cholesterol, 296 mg sodium, 9 g carbohydrate, 1 g fiber, 31 g protein. **Diabetic Exchanges:** 4 very lean meat, 1-1/2 fat, 1/2 starch.

Northwest Salmon Salad

(Pictured above)

PREP: 45 min.

I put my favorite Northwest ingredients—hazelnuts, fresh salmon and blueberries—in this dish. The fish and dressing are great in sandwiches, too. —Elda Clevenger, Dexter, Oregon

- 1 salmon fillet (1 pound)
- 1/2 teaspoon salt
- 1/2 teaspoon plus 1/8 teaspoon coarsely ground pepper, *divided*
- 2 tablespoons lemon juice, *divided*
- 4 fresh dill sprigs
- 1 cup chopped peeled cucumber
- 1/2 cup reduced-fat sour cream
- 1/4 cup finely chopped sweet red pepper
- 1/4 cup snipped fresh dill
- 3 tablespoons capers, drained
- 8 cups torn Bibb lettuce
- 1 medium peach, peeled and sliced
- 1/4 cup chopped hazelnuts
- 1/4 cup fresh blueberries
- 4 thin slices red onion, separated into rings

Place salmon on a greased baking sheet; sprinkle with salt and 1/2 teaspoon pepper. Drizzle with 1 tablespoon lemon juice; top with dill sprigs.

Bake, uncovered, at 425° for 15-18 minutes or until fish flakes easily with a fork. Flake salmon into large pieces.

In a small bowl, combine the cucumber, sour cream, red pepper, snipped dill, capers and remaining pepper and lemon juice.

Divide the lettuce among four plates. Top with peach, hazelnuts, blueberries, onion and salmon. Serve with the dressing. **Yield:** 4 servings.

Nutrition Facts: 1 serving equals 305 calories, 18 g fat (4 g saturated fat), 67 mg cholesterol, 571 mg sodium, 13 g carbohydrate, 3 g fiber, 25 g protein. **Diabetic Exchanges:** 3 lean meat, 2 fat, 1 starch.

Pork Chops with Blue Cheese Sauce

(Pictured below)

PREP/TOTAL TIME: 30 min.

Even if you aren't a huge fan of blue cheese, you're sure to enjoy the mild flavor of the sauce paired with these pork chops.
—Kathy Specht, Clinton, Montana

  4 bone-in pork loin chops (7 ounces *each*)
  1 teaspoon coarsely ground pepper
SAUCE:
  1 green onion, finely chopped
  1 garlic clove, minced
  1 teaspoon butter
  1 tablespoon all-purpose flour
  2/3 cup fat-free milk
  3 tablespoons crumbled blue cheese
  1 tablespoon white wine *or* reduced-sodium chicken broth

Sprinkle pork chops on both sides with pepper. Broil 3-4 in. from the heat for 4-6 minutes on each side or until a meat thermometer reads 160°.

Meanwhile, in a small saucepan, saute the green onion and garlic in butter until tender. Sprinkle with the flour; stir until blended. Gradually add the milk. Bring to a boil; cook and stir for 2 minutes or until thickened. Add the blue cheese and wine; heat through. Serve the sauce with chops. **Yield:** 4 servings.

Nutrition Facts: 1 pork chop with 3 tablespoons sauce equals 263 calories, 11 g fat (5 g saturated fat), 94 mg cholesterol, 176 mg sodium, 5 g carbohydrate, trace fiber, 33 g protein. **Diabetic Exchanges:** 5 lean meat.

Oven-Fried Fish Nuggets

PREP/TOTAL TIME: 25 min.

My husband and I love fried fish but are trying to cut back on the fat in our diets. After sampling the baked nuggets I created, he said they taste just as good—and that's saying a lot!
—LaDonna Reed, Ponca City, Oklahoma

  1/3 cup seasoned bread crumbs
  1/3 cup crushed cornflakes
  3 tablespoons grated Parmesan cheese
  1/2 teaspoon salt
  1/4 teaspoon pepper
1-1/2 pounds cod fillets, cut into 1-inch cubes
Butter-flavored cooking spray

In a shallow bowl, combine the seasoned bread crumbs, cornflakes, Parmesan cheese, salt and pepper. Coat the fish with butter-flavored spray, then roll in the bread crumb mixture.

Place on a baking sheet coated with cooking spray. Bake at 375° for 15-20 minutes or until fish flakes easily with a fork. **Yield:** 4 servings.

Nutrition Facts: 1 serving equals 171 calories, 2 g fat (1 g saturated fat), 66 mg cholesterol, 415 mg sodium, 7 g carbohydrate, trace fiber, 29 g protein. **Diabetic Exchanges:** 5 lean meat, 1/2 starch.

Spinach and Mushroom Smothered Chicken

PREP/TOTAL TIME: 30 min.

(Pictured above right)

With a mushroom and spinach topping tucked under a blanket of melted provolone cheese, these chicken breasts stay nice and moist. It's an extra–special entree for guests and also makes a great weeknight choice because it's done in 30 minutes.
—Katrina Wagner, Grain Valley, Missouri

  3 cups fresh baby spinach
1-3/4 cups sliced fresh mushrooms
  3 green onions, sliced
  2 tablespoons chopped pecans
1-1/2 teaspoons olive oil
  4 boneless skinless chicken breast halves (4 ounces *each*)
  1/2 teaspoon rotisserie chicken seasoning
  2 slices reduced-fat provolone cheese, halved

In a large skillet, saute the spinach, mushrooms, onions and pecans in oil until mushrooms are tender. Set aside and keep warm.

Sprinkle the chicken with seasoning. Moisten a paper towel with cooking oil; using long-handled tongs, lightly coat the grill rack.

Grill chicken, covered, over medium heat or broil 4 in. from the heat for 4-5 minutes on each side or until a meat thermometer reads 170°.

Top with provolone cheese. Cover and grill 2-3 minutes longer or until the cheese is melted. To serve, top each chicken breast half with the reserved spinach mixture. **Yield:** 4 servings.

Nutrition Facts: 1 chicken breast half equals 203 calories, 9 g fat (2 g saturated fat), 68 mg cholesterol, 210 mg sodium, 3 g carbohydrate, 2 g fiber, 27 g protein. **Diabetic Exchanges:** 3 lean meat, 1 vegetable, 1 fat.

Spicy Sweet-Sour Pork

PREP/TOTAL TIME: 30 min.

I mix tender pork with pineapple and peppers in this tangy main dish. Not too sweet or sour, it gets zip from red pepper flakes.
—Shannon Talmage, Alexandria, Indiana

- 1 can (8 ounces) pineapple chunks
- 1 tablespoon cornstarch
- 2 tablespoons reduced-sodium soy sauce
- 1 teaspoon brown sugar
- 1/8 to 1/4 teaspoon crushed red pepper flakes
- 1/2 pound pork tenderloin, cut into 2-inch strips
- 2 teaspoons canola oil
- 1/2 cup green pepper strips
- 1/2 cup sweet red pepper strips

Hot cooked rice, optional

Drain the pineapple, reserving the pineapple juice in a 1-cup measuring cup; set the pineapple aside. Add enough water to pineapple juice to measure 1/2 cup. In a small bowl, combine the cornstarch, soy sauce, brown sugar, red pepper flakes and reserved juice mixture until smooth. Set aside.

In a nonstick skillet or wok, stir-fry pork in hot oil until meat is no longer pink. Remove and keep warm. In the same skillet, stir-fry peppers for 3-4 minutes or until just crisp-tender.

Return the meat to skillet; add the reserved pineapple. Stir the pineapple juice mixture; add to skillet. Bring to a boil; cook and stir for 2 minutes or until thickened. Serve

with rice if desired. **Yield:** 2 servings.

Nutrition Facts: 1 cup pork mixture (calculated without rice) equals 277 calories, 9 g fat (2 g saturated fat), 63 mg cholesterol, 661 mg sodium, 24 g carbohydrate, 2 g fiber, 24 g protein. **Diabetic Exchanges:** 3 lean meat, 1 fruit, 1 fat, 1/2 starch.

Soft Fish Tacos

(Pictured below)

PREP/TOTAL TIME: 25 min.

These soft tacos feature the combination of tilapia and coleslaw. It may seem unusual, but after one bite, everyone's hooked!
—Carrie Billups, Florence, Oregon

- 4 cups coleslaw mix
- 1/2 cup fat-free tartar sauce
- 1/2 teaspoon salt
- 1/2 teaspoon ground cumin
- 1/4 teaspoon pepper
- 1-1/2 pounds tilapia fillets
- 2 tablespoons olive oil
- 1 tablespoon lemon juice
- 10 corn tortillas (6 inches), warmed

Shredded cheddar cheese, chopped tomato and sliced avocado, optional

In a large bowl, toss the coleslaw mix, tartar sauce, salt, cumin and pepper; set aside. In a large nonstick skillet coated with cooking spray, cook tilapia in oil and lemon juice over medium heat for 4-5 minutes on each side or until fish flakes easily with a fork.

Place the tilapia on tortillas; top with coleslaw mixture. Serve with cheese, tomato and avocado if desired. **Yield:** 5 servings.

Nutrition Facts: 2 tacos (calculated without optional toppings) equals 310 calories, 8 g fat (2 g saturated fat), 66 mg cholesterol, 542 mg sodium, 31 g carbohydrate, 4 g fiber, 29 g protein. **Diabetic Exchanges:** 4 very lean meat, 2 starch, 1 fat.

Roasted Butternut Linguine

PREP: 10 min. **BAKE:** 45 min.

Squash is one of our favorite vegetables, and this is my husband's favorite main dish during fall. He looks forward to it all year.
—Kim Caputo, Cannon Falls, Minnesota

- 4 cups cubed peeled butternut squash
- 1 medium red onion, chopped
- 3 tablespoons olive oil
- 1/4 teaspoon crushed red pepper flakes
- 1/2 pound uncooked linguine
- 2 cups shredded Swiss chard
- 1 tablespoon minced fresh sage
- 1/2 teaspoon salt
- 1/4 teaspoon pepper

Place the butternut squash and onion in a 15-in. x 10-in. x 1-in. baking pan coated with cooking spray. Combine the oil and red pepper flakes; drizzle over the vegetables and toss to coat.

Bake, uncovered, at 350° for 45-50 minutes or until tender, stirring occasionally.

Meanwhile, cook the pasta according to the package directions; drain and place in a large bowl. Add squash mixture, Swiss chard, sage, salt and pepper; toss to combine. **Yield:** 4 servings.

Nutrition Facts: 1-1/2 cups equals 384 calories, 12 g fat (2 g saturated fat), 0 cholesterol, 344 mg sodium, 64 g carbohydrate, 6 g fiber, 10 g protein.

Apricot-Glazed Turkey Breast

(Pictured above and on page 250)

PREP: 10 min. **BAKE:** 1-1/2 hours + standing

Basted with a fuss-free glaze, this wonderfully moist and tender turkey bakes to a lovely golden brown. Make it the centerpiece of your holiday table—you and your guests will be glad you did!
—Greg Fontenot, The Woodlands, Texas

- 1/2 cup apricot preserves
- 1/4 cup balsamic vinegar
- 1/4 teaspoon pepper
- Dash salt
- 1 bone-in turkey breast (5 pounds)

Combine the preserves, vinegar, pepper and salt. Place turkey breast on a rack in a large shallow roasting pan.

Bake, uncovered, at 325° for 1-1/2 to 2 hours or until a meat thermometer reads 170°, basting every 30 minutes with apricot mixture. (Cover loosely with foil if the turkey browns too quickly.) Cover and let stand for 15 minutes before slicing. **Yield:** 15 servings.

Nutrition Facts: 3 ounces cooked turkey equals 156 calories, 1 g fat (trace saturated fat), 78 mg cholesterol, 64 mg sodium, 8 g carbohydrate, trace fiber, 28 g protein.
Diabetic Exchanges: 4 lean meat, 1/2 starch.

Dijon-Crusted Chicken Breasts

(Pictured above right)

PREP/TOTAL TIME: 25 min.

If you're craving fried chicken, rely on this recipe. With its crisp and flavorful coating, you won't miss the higher-fat version.
—Jacqueline Correa, Landing, New Jersey

- 1/3 cup dry bread crumbs
- 1 tablespoon grated Parmesan cheese
- 1 teaspoon Italian seasoning
- 1/2 teaspoon dried thyme
- 1/4 teaspoon salt
- 1/4 teaspoon pepper
- 4 boneless skinless chicken breast halves (4 ounces *each*)
- 2 tablespoons Dijon mustard
- 1 teaspoon olive oil
- 1 teaspoon reduced-fat margarine

Place the first six ingredients in a shallow bowl. Brush the chicken breast halves with Dijon mustard; roll in the crumb mixture.

In a large nonstick skillet, cook chicken breast halves in oil and margarine over medium heat for 5-6 minutes on

each side or until a meat thermometer reads 170°. **Yield:** 4 servings.

Editor's Note: This recipe was tested with Parkay Light stick margarine.

Nutrition Facts: 1 chicken breast half equals 169 calories, 5 g fat (1 g saturated fat), 63 mg cholesterol, 380 mg sodium, 6 g carbohydrate, trace fiber, 24 g protein. **Diabetic Exchanges:** 3 lean meat, 1/2 starch, 1/2 fat.

Grilled Veggie Tortillas

PREP/TOTAL TIME: 25 min.

Wondering what to do with an overabundant garden harvest? Put it to delicious use in this pizza-like entree loaded with herbs and veggies. As soon as I tried it, I knew it was a keeper.
—*Sharon Delaney-Chronis, South Milwaukee, Wisconsin*

- 1 **medium zucchini, cut lengthwise into 1/2-inch slices**
- 1 **yellow summer squash, cut lengthwise into 1/2-inch slices**
- 1 **small sweet red pepper, cut in half**
- 2 **tablespoons olive oil,** *divided*
- 1/2 **teaspoon salt**
- 1 **large tomato, chopped**
- 1/4 **cup reduced-fat mayonnaise**
- 2 **tablespoons prepared pesto**
- 1 **tablespoon minced fresh basil**
- 1 **tablespoon minced fresh oregano**
- 4 **whole wheat tortillas (8 inches)**
- 1 **cup (4 ounces) shredded part-skim mozzarella cheese**

Brush the zucchini, summer squash and red pepper with 1 tablespoon oil. Sprinkle with salt. Grill the vegetables over medium heat for 4-5 minutes on each side or until tender. Cut into 1/2-in. cubes and place in a small bowl; stir in tomato.

Combine the mayonnaise, pesto, basil and oregano; set aside. Brush both sides of the tortillas with remaining

oil. Grill, uncovered, over medium heat for 2-3 minutes or until puffed.

Remove from the grill. Spread grilled sides with sauce; top with vegetable mixture. Sprinkle with cheese. Grill, covered, for 2-3 minutes or until cheese is melted. **Yield:** 4 servings.

Nutrition Facts: 1 tortilla equals 390 calories, 23 g fat (6 g saturated fat), 24 mg cholesterol, 785 mg sodium, 31 g carbohydrate, 4 g fiber, 14 g protein. **Diabetic Exchanges:** 3 fat, 1-1/2 starch, 1 medium-fat meat, 1 vegetable.

Southwestern Goulash

(Pictured below)

PREP/TOTAL TIME: 30 min.

I had some leftover fresh cilantro in the refrigerator and didn't want it to go to waste. So I tossed it into this zippy goulash full of lean ground beef and macaroni. Everyone loved it!
—*Vikki Rebholz, West Chester, Ohio*

- 1 **cup uncooked elbow macaroni**
- 1 **pound lean ground beef (90% lean)**
- 1 **medium onion, chopped**
- 1 **can (28 ounces) diced tomatoes, undrained**
- 2/3 **cup frozen corn**
- 1 **can (8 ounces) tomato sauce**
- 1 **can (4 ounces) chopped green chilies**
- 1/2 **teaspoon ground cumin**
- 1/2 **teaspoon pepper**
- 1/4 **teaspoon salt**
- 1/4 **cup minced fresh cilantro**

Cook the macaroni according to the package directions. Meanwhile, in a Dutch oven over medium heat, cook beef and onion until meat is no longer pink; drain. Stir in the tomatoes, corn, tomato sauce, chilies, cumin, pepper and salt. Bring to a boil. Reduce heat; simmer, uncovered, for 3-4 minutes or until heated through.

Drain macaroni; add to meat mixture. Stir in cilantro and heat through. **Yield:** 6 servings.

Nutrition Facts: 1-1/3 cups equals 224 calories, 6 g fat (2 g saturated fat), 37 mg cholesterol, 567 mg sodium, 24 g carbohydrate, 4 g fiber, 19 g protein. **Diabetic Exchanges:** 2 lean meat, 2 vegetable, 1 starch.

Anytime Frittata

(Pictured below)

PREP/TOTAL TIME: 30 min.

We enjoy frittatas often at our house because they're a great way to use up leftover vegetables, cheese and meat. Enjoy this tomato and feta variation with fruit and biscuits for a light dinner.
—*Lynne Van Wagenen, Salt Lake City, Utah*

- 1-1/4 **cups egg substitute**
- 2 **eggs**
- 1/2 **teaspoon dried oregano**
- 1/8 **teaspoon pepper**
- 1 **small onion, chopped**
- 1 **garlic clove, minced**
- 1 **teaspoon butter**
- 3 **plum tomatoes, chopped**
- 1/2 **cup crumbled feta cheese**
- 2 **tablespoons capers, drained**

In a small bowl, whisk the egg substitute, eggs, oregano and pepper; set aside. In a 10-in. oven-proof skillet, saute onion and garlic in butter for 2 minutes. Stir in tomatoes; heat through.

Pour the reserved egg mixture into skillet. Reduce heat; cover and cook for 4-6 minutes or until nearly set.

Sprinkle with cheese and capers. Broil 3-4 in. from the heat for 2-3 minutes or until eggs are completely set. Let stand for 5 minutes. Cut into wedges. **Yield:** 4 servings.

Nutrition Facts: 1 wedge equals 138 calories, 6 g fat (3 g saturated fat), 116 mg cholesterol, 465 mg sodium, 6 g carbohydrate, 2 g fiber, 14 g protein. **Diabetic Exchanges:** 2 lean meat, 1 vegetable, 1/2 fat.

Viva Panzanella

(Pictured above)

PREP: 40 min.

Add some white beans to a traditional Italian salad of tomatoes and bread, and you have a wonderful meatless entree. With a tongue–tingling dressing, it leaves you feeling satisfied.
—*Patricia Levenson, Santa Ana, California*

- 3/4 **pound sourdough bread, cubed (about 8 cups)**
- 2 **tablespoons olive oil**
- 2-1/2 **pounds tomatoes (about 8 medium), chopped**
- 1 **can (15 ounces) white kidney *or* cannellini beans, rinsed and drained**
- 1 **can (14 ounces) water-packed artichoke hearts, rinsed, drained and quartered**
- 1 **cup thinly sliced roasted sweet red peppers**
- 1/2 **cup fresh basil leaves, thinly sliced**
- 1/3 **cup thinly sliced red onion**
- 1/4 **cup Greek olives, quartered**
- 3 **tablespoons capers, drained**

DRESSING:
- 1/4 **cup balsamic vinegar**
- 3 **tablespoons minced fresh parsley**
- 3 **tablespoons olive oil**
- 3 **tablespoons lemon juice**
- 2 **tablespoons white wine vinegar**
- 3 **teaspoons minced fresh thyme *or* 1 teaspoon dried thyme**
- 1-1/2 **teaspoons minced fresh marjoram *or* 1/2 teaspoon dried marjoram**
- 1-1/2 **teaspoons minced fresh oregano *or* 1/2 teaspoon dried oregano**
- 1 **garlic clove, minced**

In a large bowl, toss the sourdough bread with oil and transfer to a baking sheet. Bake at 450° for 8-10 minutes or until golden brown. Cool to room temperature.

In a large bowl, combine tomatoes, beans, artichokes, red peppers, basil, red onion, Greek olives, capers and sourdough bread.

In a small bowl, whisk the dressing ingredients. Drizzle over the salad and toss to coat. Serve immediately. **Yield:** 6 servings.

Nutrition Facts: 2-2/3 cups equals 424 calories, 15 g fat (2 g saturated fat), 0 cholesterol, 1,047 mg sodium, 59 g carbohydrate, 7 g fiber, 13 g protein.

Tasty Italian Chicken

PREP/TOTAL TIME: 30 min.

My friend prepared this main dish and brought it to my husband and me after our first child was born. I trimmed down the recipe a bit to reduce the fat and carbohydrates. The lighter version is just as good, and it gets on the table in 30 minutes flat.
—Beth Ann Stein, Richmond, Indiana

- 1/2 **cup chopped onion**
- 1-1/8 **teaspoons paprika,** *divided*
- 3 **teaspoons olive oil,** *divided*
- 1-1/4 **cups water**
- 1/4 **cup tomato paste**
- 1 **bay leaf**
- 1/2 **teaspoon reduced-sodium chicken bouillon granules**
- 1/2 **teaspoon Italian seasoning**
- 1/4 **cup all-purpose flour**
- 1-1/2 **teaspoons grated Parmesan cheese**
- 1/2 **teaspoon salt**
- 1/4 **teaspoon garlic powder**
- 1/4 **teaspoon dried oregano**
- 1-1/2 **pounds chicken tenderloins**

In a small saucepan, saute the onion and 1/8 teaspoon paprika in 1 teaspoon oil until tender. Stir in the water, tomato paste, bay leaf, bouillon and Italian seasoning. Bring to a boil. Reduce the heat; simmer, uncovered, for 10 minutes.

Meanwhile, in a large resealable plastic bag, combine the flour, Parmesan cheese, salt, garlic powder, oregano and remaining paprika. Add the chicken; seal the bag and shake to coat.

In a large nonstick skillet coated with cooking spray, cook half of the chicken in 1 teaspoon oil for 2-3 minutes on each side or until chicken is no longer pink. Remove and keep warm; repeat with the remaining chicken and oil. Discard the bay leaf. Serve the sauce with chicken.
Yield: 6 servings.

Nutrition Facts: 4 ounces cooked chicken with 3 tablespoons sauce equals 163 calories, 3 g fat (trace saturated fat), 67 mg cholesterol, 287 mg sodium, 8 g carbohydrate, 1 g fiber, 27 g protein. **Diabetic Exchanges:** 3 very lean meat, 1/2 starch, 1/2 fat.

Tex-Mex Pork Chops

(*Pictured below*)

PREP/TOTAL TIME: 20 min.

I entered my Southwestern pork chops in a recipe contest and was thrilled when they won. Plenty of salsa, cumin and green chilies give them the zip they need to be called Tex–Mex.
—Jo Ann Dalrymple, Claremore, Oklahoma

Butter-flavored cooking spray
- 1 **small onion, chopped**
- 6 **boneless pork loin chops (5 ounces** *each***)**
- 1 **cup salsa**
- 1 **can (4 ounces) chopped green chilies**
- 1/2 **teaspoon ground cumin**
- 1/4 **teaspoon pepper**

In a large skillet coated with butter-flavored cooking spray, saute the onion until tender. Add pork chops; cook over medium heat for 5-6 minutes on each side or until a meat thermometer reads 160°.

Combine the salsa, chilies, cumin and pepper; pour over pork. Bring to a boil. Reduce heat; cover and simmer until heated through. **Yield:** 6 servings.

Nutrition Facts: 1 pork chop equals 223 calories, 8 g fat (3 g saturated fat), 68 mg cholesterol, 433 mg sodium, 9 g carbohydrate, 5 g fiber, 32 g protein. **Diabetic Exchanges:** 4 lean meat, 1 vegetable.

Cran-Orange Pork Tenderloin

(Pictured above)

PREP/TOTAL TIME: 30 min.

Cranberries and oranges are natural choices for flavoring pork in fall. Warm up your family on a cool autumn day with this comforting main course from our Test Kitchen.

- 1/4 teaspoon garlic salt
- 1/4 teaspoon pepper
- 1/8 teaspoon ground mustard
- 1/8 teaspoon ground cinnamon
- 1 pork tenderloin (1 pound)

CRAN-ORANGE SAUCE:
- 1/2 cup dried cranberries
- 1/4 cup plus 1 tablespoon orange juice, *divided*
- 1/8 teaspoon ground ginger

Dash ground cloves
- 1 can (11 ounces) mandarin oranges
- 1 tablespoon cornstarch

In a small bowl, combine the first four ingredients; rub over the pork. Place on a rack in a shallow roasting pan. Bake, uncovered, at 425° for 25-28 minutes or until a meat thermometer reads 160°.

Meanwhile, in a small saucepan, combine cranberries, 1/4 cup orange juice, ginger and cloves. Drain mandarin oranges, reserving the juice; set oranges aside. Add the reserved juice to the cranberry mixture. Bring to a boil. Reduce heat; cover and simmer for 5 minutes. Combine the cornstarch and remaining orange juice until smooth; stir into the saucepan. Bring to a boil; cook and stir for 1 minute or until thickened. Fold in oranges. Serve with sliced pork. **Yield:** 4 servings.

Nutrition Facts: 1 serving equals 242 calories, 4 g fat (1 g saturated fat), 63 mg cholesterol, 163 mg sodium, 29 g carbohydrate, 1 g fiber, 23 g protein.

Greek Isle Pizza

(Pictured below)

PREP/TOTAL TIME: 30 min.

I wanted to create a pizza based on the delicious salads I enjoyed while visiting the Greek island of Corfu more than 20 years ago. The pie I came up with is so good and easy to make, too.
—*Amanda Cooke, Los Angeles, California*

- 1 prebaked 12-inch thin pizza crust
- 1/2 cup chopped oil-packed sun-dried tomatoes plus 1 tablespoon of the oil, *divided*
- 1 small red onion, thinly sliced
- 1 teaspoon olive oil
- 2 garlic cloves, minced
- 1 teaspoon dried rosemary, crushed
- 1/4 teaspoon pepper

Grated lemon peel, optional
- 2 cups fresh baby spinach, chopped
- 1-1/4 cups crumbled feta cheese
- 1/4 cup Greek olives, pitted and chopped
- 4 slices part-skim mozzarella cheese

Place crust on an ungreased 12-in. pizza pan; brush with oil from the sun-dried tomatoes. Set aside.

In a small skillet, saute the onion in oil until tender. Add garlic; cook 1 minute longer. Remove from the heat; stir in the rosemary, pepper and lemon peel if desired. Spread over crust. Top with spinach and tomatoes.

Sprinkle with feta cheese and Greek olives; top with mozzarella cheese. Bake at 425° for 10-12 minutes or until

crust is golden brown and cheese is melted. Let stand for 10 minutes before cutting. **Yield:** 6 slices.

Nutrition Facts: 1 slice equals 328 calories, 16 g fat (6 g saturated fat), 23 mg cholesterol, 725 mg sodium, 30 g carbohydrate, 3 g fiber, 15 g protein. **Diabetic Exchanges:** 2 starch, 1 high-fat meat, 1 fat.

Asparagus Ham Dinner

PREP/TOTAL TIME: 25 min.

I've been preparing this light meal for my family for a long time, and we never get tired of it. With asparagus, tomato, pasta and chunks of ham, it's a tempting blend of tastes and textures.
—*Rhonda Zavodny, David City, Nebraska*

    2 cups uncooked spiral pasta
  3/4 pound fresh asparagus, cut into 1-inch pieces
    1 medium sweet yellow pepper, julienned
    1 tablespoon olive oil
    3 cups diced fresh tomatoes (about 6 medium)
    6 ounces boneless fully cooked ham, cubed
  1/4 cup minced fresh parsley
  1/2 teaspoon salt
  1/2 teaspoon dried oregano
  1/2 teaspoon dried basil
  1/8 to 1/4 teaspoon cayenne pepper
  1/4 cup shredded Parmesan cheese

Cook the pasta according to the package directions. Meanwhile, in a large nonstick skillet, saute asparagus and yellow pepper in oil until tender. Add tomatoes and ham; heat through.

Drain the pasta; add to the vegetable mixture. Stir in seasonings. Sprinkle with cheese. **Yield:** 6 servings.

Nutrition Facts: 1-1/3 cups equals 198 calories, 5 g fat (1 g saturated fat), 17 mg cholesterol, 559 mg sodium, 27 g carbohydrate, 3 g fiber, 12 g protein. **Diabetic Exchanges:** 1 starch, 1 lean meat, 1 vegetable, 1/2 fat.

Portobello Beef Stew With Cranberry Pilaf

(Pictured above right and on page 250)

PREP: 25 min. **COOK:** 2-3/4 hours

Love beef stew? Take it in a different direction with this special recipe. It features portobello mushrooms and is served with a berry-filled rice pilaf. I round out the menu with a green salad.
—*Rebecca Ames, Wylie, Texas*

  1/4 cup all-purpose flour
    2 garlic cloves, minced
  1/2 teaspoon salt
  1/2 teaspoon coarsely ground pepper
    1 pound beef stew meat
    1 tablespoon canola oil
    1 pound sliced baby portobello mushrooms
    1 cup white wine

    1 cup reduced-sodium beef broth
    1 teaspoon dried thyme
    1 teaspoon dried rosemary, crushed
    2 tablespoons cornstarch
    2 tablespoons water
PILAF:
  1/3 cup chopped onion
  1/3 cup chopped celery
    1 tablespoon butter
    1 cup uncooked long grain rice
  1/3 cup dried cranberries
    2 cups reduced-sodium beef broth

In a large resealable plastic bag, combine the flour, garlic, salt and pepper. Add the beef, a few pieces at a time, and shake to coat.

In a Dutch oven, brown beef in oil in batches. Remove and set aside. Add portobello mushrooms to the pan; saute until tender. Return beef to the pan. Add the wine, broth, thyme and rosemary, stirring to loosen browned bits from pan. Bring to a boil.

Reduce heat; cover and simmer for 2-1/2 to 3 hours or until beef is tender. Combine cornstarch and water until smooth; gradually stir into stew. Bring to a boil; cook and stir for 2 minutes or until slightly thickened.

Meanwhile, in a large saucepan, saute onion and celery in butter until tender. Add rice and cranberries; cook and stir for 3-4 minutes or until rice is lightly browned. Add the broth. Bring to a boil. Reduce heat; cover and simmer for 15-20 minutes or until rice is tender. Fluff with a fork. Serve with stew. **Yield:** 6 servings.

Nutrition Facts: 3/4 cup stew with 1/2 cup rice equals 330 calories, 10 g fat (3 g saturated fat), 55 mg cholesterol, 324 mg sodium, 39 g carbohydrate, 2 g fiber, 20 g protein. **Diabetic Exchanges:** 2-1/2 starch, 2 lean meat, 1 fat.

Tomato Walnut Tilapia

(Pictured below)

PREP/TOTAL TIME: 20 min.

Sliced tomato, bread crumbs and crunchy walnuts really dress up the tilapia fillets in this delightful, summery main dish. I often serve it with cooked julienned carrots and green beans.
—*Phyl Broich-Wessling, Garner, Iowa*

  4 **tilapia fillets (4 ounces** *each*)
1/4 **teaspoon salt**
1/4 **teaspoon pepper**
  1 **tablespoon butter**
  1 **medium tomato, thinly sliced**
TOPPING:
1/2 **cup soft bread crumbs**
1/4 **cup chopped walnuts**
  2 **tablespoons lemon juice**
1-1/2 **teaspoons butter, melted**

Sprinkle fillets with salt and pepper. In a large ovenproof skillet coated with cooking spray, cook fillets in butter over medium-high heat for 2-3 minutes on each side or until lightly browned.

    Place the tomato slices over fish. Combine the topping ingredients; spoon over tomato. Broil 3-4 in. from the heat for 2-3 minutes or until topping is lightly browned and fish flakes easily with a fork. **Yield:** 4 servings.

    Nutrition Facts: 1 fillet equals 205 calories, 10 g fat (3 g saturated fat), 67 mg cholesterol, 265 mg sodium, 7 g carbohydrate, 1 g fiber, 24 g protein. **Diabetic Exchanges:** 3 lean meat, 2 fat, 1/2 starch.

Shrimp & Tortellini in Tomato Cream

(Pictured above)

PREP: 20 min. **COOK:** 30 min.

This shrimp and pasta combination featuring a cheesy, creamy sauce is one of my husband's all-time favorites. It's on the lighter side, but he has no idea because it tastes so good.
—*Mary Kay LaBrie, Clermont, Florida*

  1 **package (9 ounces) refrigerated cheese tortellini**
  1 **pound uncooked medium shrimp, peeled and deveined**
  1 **tablespoon olive oil,** *divided*
  2 **teaspoons grated lemon peel**
1/4 **teaspoon pepper,** *divided*
Dash crushed red pepper flakes
  2 **shallots, chopped**
  2 **garlic cloves, minced**
  2 **cans (14-1/2 ounces** *each***) no-salt-added diced tomatoes, undrained**
  1 **bottle (8 ounces) clam juice**
1/2 **cup white wine**
  2 **tablespoons balsamic vinegar**
  4 **fresh thyme sprigs**
1/4 **cup grated Parmesan and Romano cheese blend**
1/4 **cup half-and-half cream**
10 **fresh basil leaves, thinly sliced**
  2 **tablespoons minced chives**
Shredded Parmesan cheese and minced fresh parsley, optional

Cook tortellini according to package directions. Meanwhile, in a large nonstick skillet, cook shrimp in 2 teaspoons oil until shrimp turn pink. Stir in lemon peel, 1/8 teaspoon pepper and pepper flakes. Remove and keep warm.

In the same skillet, cook shallots in remaining oil over low heat for 10-15 minutes or until golden brown, stirring occasionally. Add garlic; cook 1 minute longer.

Add tomatoes, clam juice, white wine, vinegar, thyme and remaining pepper. Bring to a boil; cook until liquid is reduced by half, about 10 minutes. Remove from the heat; discard the thyme sprigs. Stir in the cheese, cream, basil, chives and shrimp.

Drain tortellini; stir into shrimp mixture. Sprinkle with shredded cheese and parsley if desired. **Yield:** 4 servings.

Nutrition Facts: 1-1/2 cups (calculated without shredded cheese) equals 449 calories, 14 g fat (6 g saturated fat), 182 mg cholesterol, 723 mg sodium, 46 g carbohydrate, 5 g fiber, 33 g protein. **Diabetic Exchanges:** 4 lean meat, 2 starch, 2 vegetable, 1 fat.

California Chicken Wraps

(Pictured below)

PREP/TOTAL TIME: 15 min.

In recipes like this one, I prefer to use hummus instead of mayo. With feta cheese, these chicken wraps have amazing flavor.
—Donna Munch, El Paso, Texas

- 1/3 **cup prepared hummus**
- 4 **whole wheat tortillas (8 inches)**
- 2 **cups cubed cooked chicken breast**
- 1/4 **cup chopped roasted sweet red peppers**
- 1/4 **cup crumbled feta cheese**
- 1/4 **cup thinly sliced fresh basil leaves**

Spread hummus on tortillas; top with chicken, peppers, cheese and basil. Roll up. **Yield:** 4 servings.

Nutrition Facts: 1 wrap equals 300 calories, 8 g fat (2 g saturated fat), 58 mg cholesterol, 408 mg sodium, 26 g carbohydrate, 3 g fiber, 27 g protein. **Diabetic Exchanges:** 3 lean meat, 2 starch.

Tomato-Basil Pita Pizzas

(Pictured above)

PREP/TOTAL TIME: 20 min.

You'll need just five basic ingredients and 20 minutes to assemble these yummy pizzas. Enjoy them as appetizers or entrees.
—Barbra Annino, Galena, Illinois

- 2 **pita breads (6 inches)**
- 2 **plum tomatoes, thinly sliced**
- 8 **fresh basil leaves, thinly sliced**
- 1/4 **cup shredded Asiago cheese**
- 2 **teaspoons olive oil**

Place the pita breads on an ungreased baking sheet. Layer with tomatoes, basil and cheese; drizzle with oil. Bake at 350° for 12-14 minutes or until cheese is melted. **Yield:** 2 servings.

Nutrition Facts: 1 pizza equals 269 calories, 9 g fat (3 g saturated fat), 12 mg cholesterol, 362 mg sodium, 37 g carbohydrate, 2 g fiber, 10 g protein. **Diabetic Exchanges:** 2 starch, 1 lean meat, 1 vegetable, 1 fat.

BEAUTIFUL BASIL. To easily slice the basil leaves for the recipes on this page, stack the leaves neatly in the same direction, then roll the stack lengthwise into a tight cigar shape. Slice across the rolled leaves to form thin strips.

Craving Comfort Food

WATCHING your diet? It doesn't have to mean that comfort foods—those rich, ooey-gooey, home-style favorites everyone loves—are off-limits.

Indulge in a steaming bowl of Beef Barley Stew... dig into tender Country Chicken with Gravy...pair Deluxe Grilled Cheese with your favorite soup...or enjoy a plate of creamy Ranch Ham 'n' Cheese Pasta. You can do so guilt-free with the knowledge that each dish is lower in fat and calories.

Why not serve one of these satisfying, sure-to-please main dishes for dinner tonight? Your family will never guess they're on the lighter side.

Ranch Ham 'n' Cheese Pasta

PREP/TOTAL TIME: 25 min.

Our Test Kitchen pros took a pasta recipe from Kathy Heller, Colorado Springs, Colorado, and lightened it up—deliciously!

- 1 **package (16 ounces) penne pasta**
- 1 **tablespoon butter**
- 1 **tablespoon all-purpose flour**
- 1 **cup fat-free milk**
- 2 **teaspoons dried parsley flakes**
- 1 **teaspoon garlic salt**
- 1 **teaspoon salt-free lemon-pepper seasoning**
- 1/2 **teaspoon garlic powder**
- 1/2 **teaspoon dried minced onion**
- 1/2 **teaspoon dill weed**
- 1/4 **teaspoon onion powder**
- 1/8 **teaspoon pepper**
- 1 **cup (8 ounces) reduced-fat sour cream**
- 2 **cups cubed fully cooked lean ham**
- 1-1/2 **cups (6 ounces) shredded reduced-fat Mexican cheese blend**
- 1/4 **cup shredded Parmesan cheese**

Cook pasta according to package directions; drain. In a Dutch oven, melt the butter; whisk in the flour until smooth. Gradually add the milk and seasonings. Bring to a boil; cook and stir for 2 minutes or until thickened.

Reduce the heat; fold in sour cream until blended. Add ham and pasta; cook and stir until heated through. Remove from heat; stir in cheese blend until melted. Sprinkle with Parmesan cheese. **Yield:** 10 servings.

Nutrition Facts: 1 cup equals 306 calories, 9 g fat (5 g saturated fat), 27 mg cholesterol, 612 mg sodium, 38 g carbohydrate, 2 g fiber, 20 g protein. **Diabetic Exchanges:** 2-1/2 starch, 2 lean meat.

HOME-STYLE SIDE. Want to treat your family to a whole plateful of comfort food? Savor every drop of gravy in Country Chicken with Gravy (recipe at right) with a side of mashed potatoes.

Country Chicken with Gravy

(Pictured above)

PREP/TOTAL TIME: 30 min.

This classic chicken with a creamy gravy looks and tastes so good, it's hard to believe that it's lower in fat and calories.
—*Ruth Helmuth, Abbeville, South Carolina*

- 3/4 **cup crushed cornflakes**
- 1/2 **teaspoon poultry seasoning**
- 1/2 **teaspoon paprika**
- 1/4 **teaspoon salt**
- 1/4 **teaspoon dried thyme**
- 1/4 **teaspoon pepper**
- 2 **tablespoons fat-free evaporated milk**
- 4 **boneless skinless chicken breast halves (4 ounces *each*)**
- 2 **teaspoons canola oil**

GRAVY:
- 1 **tablespoon butter**
- 1 **tablespoon all-purpose flour**
- 1/4 **teaspoon pepper**
- 1/8 **teaspoon salt**
- 1/2 **cup fat-free evaporated milk**
- 1/4 **cup condensed chicken broth, undiluted**
- 1 **teaspoon sherry *or* additional condensed chicken broth**
- 2 **tablespoons minced chives**

In a shallow bowl, combine the first six ingredients. Place milk in another shallow bowl. Dip chicken in milk, then roll in cornflake mixture.

In a large nonstick skillet coated with cooking spray, cook the chicken breast halves in oil over medium heat for 6-8 minutes on each side or until a meat thermometer reads 170°.

Meanwhile, in a small saucepan, melt butter. Stir in the flour, pepper and salt until smooth. Gradually stir in the milk, broth and sherry. Bring to a boil; cook and stir for 1-2 minutes or until thickened. Stir in chives. Serve with chicken. **Yield:** 4 servings.

Nutrition Facts: 1 chicken breast half with 2 tablespoons gravy equals 274 calories, 8 g fat (3 g saturated fat), 72 mg cholesterol, 569 mg sodium, 20 g carbohydrate, trace fiber, 28 g protein. **Diabetic Exchanges:** 3 lean meat, 1 starch, 1/2 fat.

Deluxe Grilled Cheese

(Pictured below)

PREP/TOTAL TIME: 15 min.

Love grilled cheese but think it doesn't fit your diet? With a few simple tricks, our Test Kitchen experts show how you can actually boost the fantastic flavor of that sandwich while slashing the fat, calories and cholesterol to less than half.

- 1 small onion, halved and thinly sliced
- 4 slices French bread (1/2 inch thick)
- Butter-flavored cooking spray
- 1 ounce herbed fresh goat cheese
- 1/2 small tart apple, thinly sliced
- 1/2 cup shredded reduced-fat cheddar cheese

In a small skillet coated with cooking spray, saute onion until tender; set aside.

Place the bread slices on a baking sheet; spritz with butter-flavored cooking spray. Broil 4 in. from the heat for 2-3 minutes or until golden brown.

Spread the goat cheese over the untoasted sides of two bread slices. Top with the apple slices and reserved onion; sprinkle with cheddar cheese. Broil 2-3 minutes longer or until the cheese is melted. Top with the

remaining bread slices. **Yield:** 2 servings.

Nutrition Facts: 1 sandwich equals 225 calories, 12 g fat (6 g saturated fat), 30 mg cholesterol, 400 mg sodium, 18 g carbohydrate, 2 g fiber, 12 g protein. **Diabetic Exchanges:** 2 medium-fat meat, 1 starch.

Beef Barley Stew

(Pictured above)

PREP/TOTAL TIME: 30 min.

On a cool autumn or winter day, nothing satisfies like a big bowl of hot and hearty stew. Packed with lean ground beef and barley, this one has a comforting, chili-like appeal everyone enjoys. Just add a fresh-baked batch of your favorite rolls or biscuits.
—Lisa Kolenich, Regina, Saskatchewan

- 1/2 pound lean ground beef (90% lean)
- 1/2 cup sliced celery
- 1/3 cup chopped onion
- 1-3/4 cups water
- 2 teaspoons reduced-sodium beef bouillon granules
- 1-1/2 teaspoons chili powder
- 1/4 teaspoon pepper
- 1/2 cup quick-cooking barley
- 1 can (14-1/2 ounces) diced tomatoes, undrained

In a large saucepan, cook the beef, celery and onion over medium heat until meat is no longer pink and vegetables are tender; drain.

Stir in water, beef bouillon, chili powder and pepper. Bring to a boil. Stir in the barley. Reduce heat; cover and simmer for 10-12 minutes or until barley is tender. Stir in tomatoes; heat through. **Yield:** 4 cups.

Nutrition Facts: 1-1/3 cups equals 269 calories, 7 g fat (3 g saturated fat), 37 mg cholesterol, 456 mg sodium, 33 g carbohydrate, 9 g fiber, 20 g protein. **Diabetic Exchanges:** 2 lean meat, 1-1/2 starch, 1 vegetable.

Jiffy Ground Pork Skillet

(Pictured below)

PREP/TOTAL TIME: 30 min.

Some people call it the dinner hour, but many of us call it rush hour! To slow down the pace, try this super-fast but delicious ground pork skillet. It's finished and ready for the table in only 30 minutes, so it's perfect for hectic weeknights.
—Brigitte Schaller, Flemington, Missouri

> 1-1/2 cups uncooked penne pasta
> 1 pound ground pork
> 1/2 cup chopped onion
> 1 can (14-1/2 ounces) stewed tomatoes
> 1 can (8 ounces) tomato sauce
> 1 teaspoon Italian seasoning
> 1 medium zucchini, cut into 1/4-inch slices

Cook the pasta according to the package directions. Meanwhile, in a large skillet, cook pork and onion over medium heat until meat is no longer pink; drain. Add the tomatoes, tomato sauce and Italian seasoning. Bring to a boil. Reduce heat; cover and cook for 5 minutes to allow flavors to blend.

Drain pasta; add to skillet. Stir in zucchini. Cover and cook for 3-5 minutes or until the zucchini is crisp-tender. **Yield:** 6 servings.

Nutrition Facts: 1-1/4 cups equals 263 calories, 12 g fat (4 g saturated fat), 50 mg cholesterol, 339 mg sodium, 22 g carbohydrate, 2 g fiber, 18 g protein. **Diabetic Exchanges:** 2 lean meat, 2 vegetable, 1 starch, 1/2 fat.

Kielbasa Apple Kabobs

(Pictured above)

PREP/TOTAL TIME: 25 min.

I rely on smoked turkey sausage to make these kabobs different from most. The meaty chunks are skewered with tart apples and colorful peppers, then basted with a mildly sweet glaze.
—Edna Hoffman, Hebron, Indiana

> 1/4 cup sugar
> 1 tablespoon cornstarch
> 3/4 cup cranberry juice
> 2 tablespoons cider vinegar
> 2 teaspoons soy sauce
> 1 pound smoked turkey kielbasa, cut into 1-1/2-inch pieces
> 2 medium tart apples, cut into wedges
> 1 medium sweet red pepper, cut into 1-inch pieces
> 1 medium green pepper, cut into 1-inch pieces

In a large saucepan, combine sugar and cornstarch. Stir in cranberry juice, vinegar and soy sauce. Bring to a boil; cook and stir for 1-2 minutes or until thickened.

On eight metal or soaked wooden skewers, alternately thread sausage, apples and peppers. Grill, uncovered, over indirect heat for 8 minutes or until heated through, turning and brushing with the glaze occasionally. **Yield:** 8 servings.

Nutrition Facts: 1 kabob equals 136 calories, 3 g fat (1 g saturated fat), 35 mg cholesterol, 636 mg sodium, 17 g carbohydrate, 1 g fiber, 10 g protein. **Diabetic Exchanges:** 1 starch, 1 lean meat.

Southwestern Beef Strips

PREP/TOTAL TIME: 20 min.

Flavor-packed seasonings give this filling entree from our Test Kitchen pros some zip. Serve the stir-fried beef and veggies over fettuccine for a family-pleasing, all-in-one supper.

- 1-1/2 **pounds beef top sirloin steak, cut into thin strips**
- 1 **medium onion, sliced**
- 1 **medium sweet red pepper, cut into thin strips**
- 2 **tablespoons taco seasoning**
- 1/4 **teaspoon salt**
- 1/4 **teaspoon pepper**
- 2 **tablespoons canola oil**
- 1 **can (15 ounces) black beans, rinsed and drained**
- 1-1/2 **cups frozen corn, thawed**
- 1/2 **cup picante sauce**
- 2 **teaspoons dried cilantro flakes**

Hot cooked fettuccine, optional

In a large skillet, stir-fry the beef, onion, red pepper, taco seasoning, salt and pepper in oil until meat is no longer pink. Stir in the black beans, corn, picante sauce and cilantro; heat through. Serve with fettuccine if desired. **Yield:** 6 servings.

Nutrition Facts: 1-1/3 cups beef mixture (calculated without fettuccine) equals 291 calories, 11 g fat (3 g saturated fat), 63 mg cholesterol, 777 mg sodium, 22 g carbohydrate, 5 g fiber, 27 g protein.

Tomato-Melon Chicken Salad

(Pictured above right)

PREP/TOTAL TIME: 15 min.

Nothing says summer like picking watermelon, tomatoes and raspberries, then tossing them together in a salad. The addition of grilled chicken makes it a satisfying yet refreshing meal.
—Betsy Hite, Wilton, California

- 4 **medium tomatoes, cut into wedges**
- 2 **cups cubed seedless watermelon**
- 1 **cup fresh raspberries**
- 1/4 **cup minced fresh basil**
- 1/4 **cup olive oil**
- 2 **tablespoons balsamic vinegar**
- 1/4 **teaspoon salt**
- 1/4 **teaspoon pepper**
- 9 **cups torn mixed salad greens**
- 4 **grilled chicken breasts (4 ounces *each*), sliced**

In a large bowl, combine the tomatoes, watermelon and raspberries. In a small bowl, whisk the basil, oil, balsamic vinegar, salt and pepper. Drizzle over tomato mixture; toss to coat. Divide the salad greens among 6 serving plates; top with the tomato mixture and grilled chicken. **Yield:** 6 servings.

Nutrition Facts: 1-1/2 cups equals 368 calories, 16 g fat (3 g saturated fat), 113 mg cholesterol, 230 mg sodium, 14 g carbohydrate, 5 g fiber, 44 g protein.

Spicy Chicken Tenders

PREP/TOTAL TIME: 15 min.

These spiced-up chicken bites boast the traditional East Indian flavors of cinnamon, ginger and curry. Pair this simple main course with rice and vegetables, and you'll have a terrific dinner.
—Carol Dodds, Aurora, Ontario

- 1 **tablespoon water**
- 1/4 **teaspoon salt**
- 1/4 **teaspoon crushed red pepper flakes**
- 1/4 **teaspoon curry powder**
- 1/8 **teaspoon *each* ground turmeric, ginger and cinnamon**
- 1/8 **teaspoon paprika**
- 1/2 **pound chicken tenderloins**

In a small bowl, combine the water and seasonings; brush over both sides of the chicken tenders. Place in a large resealable plastic bag; seal bag and refrigerate for 15 minutes.

Place the chicken tenders on a broiler pan coated with cooking spray. Broil 3-4 in. from the heat for 3 minutes on each side or until the chicken is no longer pink. **Yield:** 2 servings.

Nutrition Facts: 3 ounces cooked chicken equals 108 calories, 1 g fat (trace saturated fat), 67 mg cholesterol, 343 mg sodium, 1 g carbohydrate, trace fiber, 26 g protein. **Diabetic Exchange:** 3 very lean meat.

Entrees on a Budget

Eating well doesn't have to mean spending beyond your budget. Just consider the money-saving main dishes here! From Margherita Pita Pizzas to Chicken Tamales, each family-pleasing entree costs less than $2 per serving.

WALLET-FRIENDLY FARE. Clockwise from top left: Chicken Tamales (p. 283), Spanish Beef Hash (p. 279), French Canadian Tourtieres (p. 278) and Dutch Meatballs (Bitterballen) (p. 282).

French Canadian Tourtieres

(Pictured above and on page 276)

PREP: 45 min. **BAKE:** 40 min.

Each fall, my big sister and I prepare about 20 of these meat pies to use at Christmas, give as gifts and freeze for drop–in guests.
—Pat Menee, Carberry, Manitoba

- 4 celery ribs
- 4 medium carrots
- 2 large onions
- 2 garlic cloves, peeled
- 4 pounds ground pork
- 2 pounds ground veal
- 2 pounds bulk pork sausage
- 1 can (14-1/2 ounces) chicken broth
- 1/2 cup minced fresh parsley
- 1 tablespoon salt
- 1 teaspoon pepper
- 1 teaspoon dried basil
- 1 teaspoon dried rosemary, crushed
- 1 teaspoon cayenne pepper
- 1 teaspoon ground mace
- 1 teaspoon ground cloves
- 1 cup dry bread crumbs

Pastry for four double-crust pies (9 inches)

Coarsely chop the celery, carrots and onions; place in a food processor with garlic. Cover and process until finely chopped; set aside.

In a stockpot or two Dutch ovens, cook the vegetables, pork, veal and sausage until the meat is no longer pink; drain. Stir in the chicken broth, parsley and seasonings. Reduce heat; cover and cook on low for 20 minutes. Stir in the bread crumbs.

Line four 9-in. pie plates with the bottom crusts; trim

pastry even with edges. Fill each with about 4 cups filling. Roll out remaining pastry to fit tops of pies; place over filling. Trim, seal and flute edges. Cut slits in pastry. Cover and freeze some of the pies for up to 3 months if desired.

Cover the edges of the remaining pies loosely with foil. Bake at 400° for 25 minutes. Reduce heat to 350°; remove foil and bake 15-20 minutes longer or until the crusts are golden brown.

To bake frozen pies: Unwrap pies; cover edges loosely with foil. Bake at 400° for 25 minutes. Reduce heat to 350°; remove foil and bake 50-60 minutes longer or until crusts are golden brown. **Yield:** 4 pies (8 servings each).

Cola Hot Wings

(Pictured below)

PREP: 15 min. **GRILL:** 20 min.

These delectable wings are good any time of year. My husband likes them so much, he'll stand out in the snow to grill them!
—Lisa Linville, Randolph, Nebraska

- 3 pounds chicken wings
- 1 cup Louisiana-style hot sauce
- 1 can (12 ounces) cola
- 1 tablespoon soy sauce
- 1/4 teaspoon cayenne pepper
- 1/4 teaspoon pepper

Blue cheese salad dressing

Cut the chicken wings into three sections; discard wing tip sections. In a small bowl, combine the hot sauce, cola, soy sauce, cayenne and pepper.

Prepare grill for indirect heat, using a drip pan. Moisten a paper towel with cooking oil; using long-handled tongs, lightly coat grill rack. Grill wings, covered, over indirect medium heat for 10 minutes. Turn; grill 10-20 minutes longer or until juices run clear, basting occasionally with sauce. Serve with dressing. **Yield:** about 2-1/2 dozen.

Editor's Note: Uncooked chicken wing sections (wingettes) may be substituted for whole chicken wings.

Italian Spiral Meat Loaf

(*Pictured above*)

PREP: 40 min.   **BAKE:** 1-1/4 hours

Take classic comfort food to new heights with this yummy recipe. Sausage, pizza sauce and mozzarella give it an Italian accent.
—*Megan Krumm, Schererville, Indiana*

    2 eggs, beaten
    1 cup pizza sauce, *divided*
    1 cup seasoned bread crumbs
    1 medium onion, chopped
    1 medium green pepper, chopped
    1 teaspoon dried oregano
    1 garlic clove, minced
  1/2 teaspoon salt
  1/4 teaspoon pepper
    2 pounds lean ground beef (90% lean)
    1 pound bulk Italian sausage
  1/2 pound sliced deli ham
    2 cups (8 ounces) shredded part-skim mozzarella cheese, *divided*
    1 jar (6 ounces) sliced mushrooms, drained

In a large bowl, combine the eggs, 3/4 cup pizza sauce, bread crumbs, onion, green pepper, oregano, garlic, salt and pepper. Crumble beef and sausage over mixture and mix well.

On a piece of parchment paper, pat beef mixture into a 12-in. x 10-in. rectangle. Layer the ham, 1-1/2 cups cheese and mushrooms over beef mixture to within 1 in. of edges. Roll up jelly-roll style, starting with a short side and peeling parchment paper away as you roll. Seal seam and ends. Place seam side down in a greased 13-in. x 9-in. baking dish; brush with remaining pizza sauce.

Bake, uncovered, at 375° for 1 hour. Sprinkle with the remaining cheese. Bake 15-20 minutes longer or until no

pink remains and a meat thermometer reads 160°. Using two large spatulas, carefully transfer the meat loaf to a serving platter. **Yield:** 12 servings.

Spanish Beef Hash

(*Pictured below and on page 276*)

PREP: 40 min.   **COOK:** 30 min.

When I was in middle school, I made this for my entire class. The hearty main dish smells great as it cooks and tastes even better.
—*Thomas Reynolds, Tampa, Florida*

    1 pound ground beef
    2 cups chopped sweet yellow, red *and/or* green peppers
    1 small onion, chopped
    3 garlic cloves, minced
    2 small potatoes, peeled and cut into 3/4-inch cubes
    2 medium tomatoes, chopped
    1 can (8 ounces) tomato sauce
  2/3 cup chopped pitted green olives
  1/2 cup sliced fresh mushrooms
  1/2 cup dry red wine *or* beef broth
    1 tablespoon Louisiana-style hot sauce
    1 tablespoon Worcestershire sauce
1-1/2 teaspoons reduced-sodium soy sauce
    1 teaspoon pepper
  1/2 teaspoon salt
  1/2 teaspoon dried oregano
  1/4 teaspoon Cajun seasoning
Hot cooked rice

In a Dutch oven, cook beef, peppers, onion and garlic over medium heat until meat is no longer pink; drain. Add the potatoes, tomatoes, tomato sauce, green olives, mushrooms, red wine and seasonings.

Bring to a boil. Reduce heat; simmer, uncovered, for 30-35 minutes or until potatoes are tender. Serve with rice. **Yield:** 6 servings.

Cut a lengthwise slit down the center of the roast to within 1/2 in. of the bottom. Open the roast so it lies flat. Starting at the center, split each half of roast horizontally to within 1/2 in. of edge. Open halves so roast lies flat. Cover with plastic wrap. Flatten to 1/2-in. thickness. Remove plastic.

Brush roast with apple butter; spoon sausage mixture over the top. Roll up jelly-roll style, starting with a long side. Tie with kitchen string at 2-in. intervals. Place on a rack in a shallow baking pan.

Bake, uncovered, at 350° for 1 to 1-1/2 hours or until a meat thermometer reads 160°. Let stand for 10-15 minutes before slicing. In a small saucepan, heat the sauce ingredients until smooth. Serve with roast. **Yield:** 12 servings (1-1/4 cups sauce).

Editor's Note: This recipe was tested with commercially prepared apple butter.

Margherita Pita Pizzas

(Pictured below)

PREP/TOTAL TIME: 20 min.

This refreshing pizza on a pita–bread crust is my favorite way to use the plum tomatoes from our garden. My husband does all of the planting, and I do the harvesting and cooking.
—Rosemarie Weleski, Natrona Hts., Pennsylvania

  4 **pita breads (6 inches)**
  2 **teaspoons olive oil**
  2 **garlic cloves, minced**
  2 **cups (8 ounces) shredded part-skim mozzarella cheese**
  3 **plum tomatoes, thinly sliced**
1/4 **teaspoon garlic powder**
  1 **teaspoon Italian seasoning**
Thinly sliced fresh basil, optional

Stuffed Pork Loin With Currant Sauce

(Pictured above)

PREP: 30 min. **BAKE:** 1 hour + standing

With a mouthwatering sausage stuffing, this is a great entree to serve any time of year, especially on holidays. The pretty sauce is the perfect accompaniment. I add a garnish of fresh parsley.
—Gloria Bradley, Naperville, Illinois

3/4 **cup chopped walnuts, toasted**
3/4 **pound bulk pork sausage**
  1 **medium apple, peeled and finely chopped**
  1 **garlic clove, minced**
  1 **egg, beaten**
  1 **tablespoon minced fresh parsley**
1/4 **teaspoon salt**
1/4 **teaspoon pepper**
  1 **boneless whole pork loin roast (3 to 4 pounds)**
1/3 **cup apple butter**
SAUCE:
  1 **cup red currant jelly**
  2 **tablespoons honey**
  1 **tablespoon dried currants**
  2 **teaspoons cider vinegar**
1/4 **teaspoon hot pepper sauce**

Place the walnuts in a food processor; cover and process until ground. Set aside.

In a large skillet, cook the sausage, apple and garlic over medium heat until meat is no longer pink. Drain; cool slightly. Stir in the ground walnuts, egg, parsley, salt and pepper.

Place pita breads on an ungreased baking sheet; brush with oil. Top with the garlic, 1 cup mozzarella cheese, tomatoes, garlic powder and remaining cheese; sprinkle with Italian seasoning.

Bake at 425° for 10-12 minutes or until cheese is melted. Top with basil if desired. **Yield:** 4 servings.

Grandma Edna's Cajun Pork

PREP: 35 min. **COOK:** 6 hours

My grandma, Edna Mills, used to prepare this every year as part of our Christmas dinner. She's now gone, but our family still carries on the delicious tradition of her Cajun pork.
—Tonya Cline, Greenville, Ohio

- 1 small onion
- 1 celery rib
- 1 small green pepper
- 3 tablespoons butter
- 3 garlic cloves, minced
- 2 teaspoons dried thyme
- 1 teaspoon paprika
- 1/2 teaspoon each salt, white pepper and pepper
- 1/2 teaspoon ground mustard
- 1/2 teaspoon hot pepper sauce
- 1 boneless whole pork loin roast (4 pounds)
- 2 tablespoons cornstarch
- 2 tablespoons cold water

Finely chop the vegetables. In a large skillet, saute the vegetables in the butter until tender. Add the garlic; cook 1 minute longer. Stir in seasonings and pepper sauce.

Cut the roast in half. Cut several slits in roast to within 1/2 in. of bottom. Place in a 4-qt. slow cooker. Spoon the onion mixture between slits and over top of meat. Cover and cook on low for 6-8 hours or until pork is tender.

Transfer the roast to a serving platter; keep warm. Pour cooking juices into a small saucepan. Combine cornstarch and water until smooth; stir into pan. Bring to a boil; cook and stir for 2 minutes or until thickened. Serve with roast. **Yield:** 12 servings (2-1/4 cups sauce).

FLAT-OUT EASY. Planning to prepare delicious Crispy Buffalo Chicken Roll-Ups (recipe above right)? To flatten the chicken breasts, use this simple technique:
1. Hold a sharp knife parallel to a cutting board and along one long side of the chicken breast; cut the breast almost in half, leaving it attached at one side.
2. Open the breast so it lies flat; cover it with plastic wrap. Using the flat side of a meat mallet, lightly pound the breast to 1/4-inch thickness.
3. Remove the plastic wrap from the chicken and continue according to the recipe.

Crispy Buffalo Chicken Roll-Ups

(Pictured above)

PREP: 15 min. **BAKE:** 30 min.

With their crunchy cornflake crust and blue cheese filling, these winning chicken rolls are so easy to make but look like I fussed. My family and friends love it when these are on the menu.
—Lisa Keys, Middlebury, Connecticut

- 4 boneless skinless chicken breast halves (6 ounces *each*)
- 3/4 teaspoon salt
- 1/2 teaspoon pepper
- 1/4 cup crumbled blue cheese
- 1/4 cup hot pepper sauce
- 2 tablespoons mayonnaise
- 1 cup crushed cornflakes

Flatten chicken breasts to 1/4-in. thickness. Season with salt and pepper; sprinkle with blue cheese. Roll up each from a short side and secure with toothpicks.

In a shallow bowl, combine the hot pepper sauce and mayonnaise. Place cornflakes in a separate shallow bowl. Dip the chicken in pepper sauce mixture, then coat with cornflakes. Place seam side down in a greased 11-in. x 7-in. baking dish.

Bake, uncovered, at 400° for 30-35 minutes or until the chicken is no longer pink. Discard the toothpicks. **Yield:** 4 servings.

Raspberry Turkey Tenderloins

(Pictured above)

PREP: 20 min. **GRILL:** 15 min.

Quick to prepare and even quicker to grill, this entree is always a winner at our house. We love the raspberry and mustard flavors. If you prefer, substitute chicken breasts for the turkey.
—*JoAnn Handley, Mount Dora, Florida*

- 1/2 cup seedless raspberry jam
- 1/3 cup cider vinegar
- 1/4 cup Dijon mustard
- 1 teaspoon grated orange peel
- 1/2 teaspoon minced fresh thyme *or* 1/8 teaspoon dried thyme
- 4 turkey breast tenderloins (6 ounces *each*)
- 1/8 teaspoon salt

In a small saucepan, combine the first five ingredients. Cook and stir for 2-3 minutes or until heated through. Set aside 1/4 cup for serving.

Sprinkle the turkey with salt. Moisten a paper towel with cooking oil; using long-handled tongs, lightly coat the grill rack. Grill turkey, covered, over medium heat or broil 4 in. from the heat for 13-18 minutes or until a meat thermometer reads 170°, turning occasionally. Baste with remaining sauce during last 5 minutes of cooking.

Let stand for 5 minutes before slicing. Serve with the reserved sauce. **Yield:** 6 servings.

Family-Favorite Pasta Sauce

PREP: 30 min. **COOK:** 1-3/4 hours

This hearty, Italian-style meat sauce has a wonderful sweetness. It's the recipe I use for spaghetti, lasagna and gnocchi.
—*Jody Bober, St. Clairsville, Ohio*

- 1 pound bulk Italian sausage
- 1 large sweet onion, chopped
- 3 garlic cloves, minced
- 1 tablespoon olive oil
- 1 can (28 ounces) diced tomatoes, undrained
- 1 can (6 ounces) Italian tomato paste
- 1/2 cup water
- 2 tablespoons minced fresh parsley
- 1 tablespoon brown sugar
- 1 tablespoon balsamic vinegar
- 2 teaspoons dried basil
- 1 teaspoon salt
- 1/2 teaspoon Italian seasoning
- 1/4 teaspoon coarsely ground pepper

Hot cooked pasta of your choice

In a large saucepan, cook the sausage, onion and garlic in oil over medium heat until meat is no longer pink; drain.

Stir in the tomatoes, tomato paste, water, parsley, brown sugar, vinegar and seasonings. Bring to a boil. Reduce heat; simmer, uncovered, for 1-1/2 hours or until flavors are blended. Serve with pasta. **Yield:** 8 servings.

Dutch Meatballs (Bitterballen)

(Pictured below and on page 276)

PREP: 30 min. + chilling **COOK:** 5 min./batch

For a Christmas party one year, I fixed a dish representing each guest's heritage. Talk about a hit! These moist Dutch Meatballs boast a crispy coating. —*Tracey Rosato, Markham, Ontario*

- 3 tablespoons butter
- 3 tablespoons all-purpose flour

1/2 cup beef broth
1 beef top sirloin steak (3/4 pound), cut into 1/2-inch cubes
1/4 cup minced fresh parsley
1/4 teaspoon salt
1/4 teaspoon ground nutmeg
1/8 teaspoon pepper
1-1/3 cups dry bread crumbs
2 eggs
1 teaspoon milk
1 teaspoon canola oil
Oil for deep-fat frying
Stone-ground mustard, optional

In a large saucepan, melt butter over medium heat. Stir in flour until smooth. Gradually add broth; bring to a boil. Cook and stir for 1 minute or until thickened. Carefully add meat and parsley; cook and stir for 2-5 minutes or until meat is no longer pink. Stir in the salt, nutmeg and pepper. Transfer to a bowl; refrigerate for 3-4 hours or until chilled.

Place bread crumbs in a small shallow bowl. In another bowl, whisk the eggs, milk and oil. Drop meat mixture by tablespoonfuls into bread crumbs; shape into balls. Dip meatballs in egg mixture, then coat again with crumbs. In an electric skillet or deep fryer, heat oil to 375°.

Fry meatballs, a few at a time, for 2-4 minutes or until golden brown on all sides. Drain on paper towels. Serve hot with mustard if desired. **Yield:** 2-1/2 dozen.

Chicken Tamales

(Pictured above right and on page 276)

PREP: 2-1/2 hours + soaking **COOK:** 45 min.

I love making my own tamales. This recipe may look complicated and time-consuming, but it's easier than it seems—and definitely worth the effort. My family requests these yummy bundles often.
—*Cindy Pruitt, Grove, Oklahoma*

20 dried corn husks
1 broiler/fryer chicken (3 to 4 pounds), cut up
3 quarts water
1 medium onion, quartered
2 teaspoons salt
1 garlic clove, crushed
DOUGH:
1 cup shortening
3 cups masa harina
CHICKEN CHILI FILLING:
6 tablespoons canola oil
6 tablespoons all-purpose flour
3/4 cup chili powder
1/2 teaspoon salt
1/4 teaspoon garlic powder
1/4 teaspoon pepper
2 cans (2-1/4 ounces *each*) sliced ripe olives, drained

Place corn husks in a large bowl; cover with cold water and soak for at least 2 hours.

Meanwhile, in a Dutch oven, combine the chicken, water, onion, salt and garlic. Bring to a boil. Reduce heat; cover and simmer for 45-60 minutes or until the meat is tender. Remove chicken from broth; set aside until cool enough to handle. Strain broth; skim fat. Finely chop or shred chicken.

For dough, in a large bowl, beat the shortening until light and fluffy, about 1 minute. Add small amounts of the masa harina alternately with 2 cups reserved broth, beating until well blended.

Drop a small amount of dough into a cup of cold water; dough should float to the top. If dough does not float, continue beating until dough is light enough to float.

In a Dutch oven, heat oil over medium heat; stir in flour until blended. Cook and stir for 7-9 minutes or until lightly browned. Stir in the spices, chicken and 4 cups reserved broth. Bring to a boil. Reduce heat; simmer, uncovered, for 45 minutes or until filling is thickened, stirring occasionally.

Drain corn husks and pat dry. Place a corn husk on a work surface with the small end pointing away from you. Place 3 tablespoons dough over the half of husk closest to you, patting dough to within 1 in. of edges. Top with 2 tablespoons chicken mixture and 2 teaspoons olives. Lifting one long side, fold husk over filling so that edges meet, enclosing filling in husk. Fold ends of husk over tamale; tie with string. Repeat.

In a large steamer basket, position tamales upright. Place basket in a Dutch oven over 1 in. of water. Bring to a boil; cover and steam for 45-50 minutes or until dough peels away from husk, adding hot water to pan as needed. Remove husks before eating. **Yield:** 10 servings.

Editor's Note: Look for dried corn husks and masa harina in the ethnic aisle.

Southwest Chicken Stromboli

(Pictured above)

PREP: 30 min. + rising **BAKE:** 25 min.

I prefer Italian food, but my brother's favorite fare is Mexican. So I combined them and created this stromboli. He loved it! The made-from-scratch dough comes together in a bread machine.
—*Carly Curtin, Ellicott City, Maryland*

- 3/4 cup water (70° to 80°)
- 1 tablespoon canola oil
- 1 tablespoon nonfat dry milk powder
- 1 tablespoon sugar
- 1 teaspoon salt
- 2-1/4 cups bread flour
- 1/4 cup yellow cornmeal
- 1 teaspoon active dry yeast

FILLING:
- 1 small onion, finely chopped
- 1 small sweet yellow pepper, finely chopped
- 1 tablespoon canola oil
- 1-1/2 cups shredded cooked chicken breast
- 3/4 cup salsa
- 2/3 cup shredded Mexican cheese blend
- 1/2 cup refried beans
- 3/4 teaspoon ground cumin
- 1/4 teaspoon garlic powder
- 1/4 teaspoon chili powder
- 1/4 teaspoon dried oregano

EGG WASH:
- 1 egg white, beaten
- 1 tablespoon water
  Sour cream, optional

In bread machine pan, place the first eight ingredients in the order suggested by manufacturer. Select dough setting (check the dough after 5 minutes of mixing; add 1 to 2 tablespoons of water or flour if needed).

Meanwhile, for filling, in a large skillet, saute onion and pepper in oil until crisp-tender. Stir in the chicken, salsa, cheese, beans and seasonings; heat through. Remove from the heat; set aside.

When cycle is completed, turn the dough onto a lightly floured surface. Roll dough to a 14-in. x 12-in. rectangle. Spread the filling over half of dough to within 1/2 in. of edges. Fold dough over filling; pinch seams to seal and tuck ends under. Combine egg white and water; brush over dough. Cut slits in top.

Place on an ungreased baking sheet. Bake at 350° for 25-30 minutes or until golden brown. Let stromboli stand for 5 minutes before cutting. Serve with sour cream if desired. **Yield:** 6 servings.

Nutty Chicken Stir-Fry

PREP: 20 min. **COOK:** 15 min.

My daughter often treats our family to this zippy stir-fry full of chicken and veggies. The peanuts and chunky peanut butter give it a nice crunch. Leftovers are great…if there are any!
—*Shirley Conrad, High Amana, Iowa*

- 1 pound boneless skinless chicken breasts, chopped
- 1 tablespoon canola oil
- 1 package (16 ounces) frozen stir-fry vegetable blend
- 6 garlic cloves, minced
- 2 tablespoons brown sugar
- 4 teaspoons cornstarch
- 3/4 teaspoon ground ginger
- 1/2 cup chicken broth
- 1/3 cup reduced-sodium soy sauce
- 1/4 cup chunky peanut butter
- 5 to 6 drops hot pepper sauce
- 3 cups shredded cabbage
- 3/4 cup salted peanuts, chopped
  Hot cooked rice

In a large skillet or wok, stir-fry chicken in oil for 2 minutes. Add the vegetables; cook 4 minutes longer. Add garlic; stir-fry until chicken is no longer pink and vegetables are crisp-tender.

In a small bowl, combine the brown sugar, cornstarch and ginger; stir in the broth, soy sauce, peanut butter and pepper sauce until blended. Pour over chicken mixture.

Bring to a boil; cook and stir for 2 minutes or until thickened. Add the cabbage; cook 2 minutes longer or until crisp-tender. Sprinkle with peanuts. Serve with rice. **Yield:** 5 servings.

Meaty Sun-Dried Tomato Sauce

PREP: 35 min. **COOK:** 8 hours

Marinated artichokes, green pepper and sun-dried tomatoes are wonderful additions to this hearty, slow-cooked pasta sauce.
—*Aysha Schurman, Ammon, Idaho*

- 1 pound bulk Italian sausage
- 1/2 pound ground beef
- 1 medium red onion, chopped
- 1 medium green pepper, chopped
- 2 celery ribs, chopped
- 3 garlic cloves, minced
- 3 cans (14-1/2 ounces *each*) diced tomatoes
- 1 can (6 ounces) Italian tomato paste
- 1 jar (7-1/2 ounces) marinated quartered artichoke hearts, drained and chopped
- 1 cup sun-dried tomatoes (not packed in oil), chopped
- 3 tablespoons minced fresh parsley
- 1-1/2 teaspoons minced fresh rosemary or 1/2 teaspoon dried rosemary, crushed
- 1 bay leaf
- 1 teaspoon pepper
- 1/2 teaspoon salt

In a large skillet, cook sausage, beef, onion, green pepper, celery and garlic over medium heat until the meat is no longer pink; drain. Transfer to a 4-qt. slow cooker.

Stir in the remaining ingredients. Cover and cook on low for 8-10 hours. Discard bay leaf. **Yield:** 12 servings.

Easy Breezy Turkey Loaf

PREP: 10 min. **BAKE:** 1 hour 5 min.

Think you can't make meat loaf that tastes like Mom's? Try this super-simple variation that calls for ground turkey, seasoned bread crumbs and just a handful of other ingredients.
—*Jo Ann Shappard, Vincennes, Indiana*

- 1 cup seasoned bread crumbs
- 1 cup garden-style spaghetti sauce, *divided*
- 1 medium onion, chopped
- 1 egg
- 1 teaspoon salt
- 1 teaspoon pepper
- 1-1/2 pounds ground turkey

In a large bowl, combine bread crumbs, 1/2 cup spaghetti sauce, onion, egg, salt and pepper. Crumble turkey over the mixture and mix well. Pat into an ungreased 9-in. x 5-in. loaf pan.

Bake, uncovered, at 350° for 1 hour. Spread remaining spaghetti sauce over the loaf. Bake 5-10 minutes longer or until a meat thermometer reads 165° and juices run clear. **Yield:** 6 servings.

French Onion Pizza au Gratin

(Pictured below)

PREP: 30 min. **BAKE:** 10 min.

I adore French onion soup…and am also a big fan of pizza after a busy workday. This unique, delicious pie lets me enjoy both.
—*Bonnie Long, Lakewood, Ohio*

- 1 large onion, sliced
- 2 tablespoons brown sugar
- 2 tablespoons olive oil, *divided*
- 3 tablespoons balsamic vinegar
- 3 garlic cloves, minced
- 1 tablespoon bourbon, optional
- 1 cup sliced fresh mushrooms
- 1/4 pound thickly sliced deli roast beef, coarsely chopped
- 1 prebaked 12-inch pizza crust
- 3/4 cup French onion dip
- 3/4 cup shredded part-skim mozzarella cheese
- 1 medium sweet red pepper, chopped
- 3/4 cup shredded Gruyere or Swiss cheese
- 1 teaspoon minced fresh rosemary

In a large skillet, saute the onion with the brown sugar in 1 tablespoon oil until softened. Reduce the heat to medium-low; cook, stirring occasionally, for 30 minutes or until deep golden brown. Stir in the vinegar and garlic. Remove from the heat; add bourbon if desired. Continue cooking until liquid is nearly evaporated.

In another skillet, saute mushrooms in remaining oil until tender; add roast beef and heat through.

Place the pizza crust on a pizza pan; spread with the French onion dip. Sprinkle with the mozzarella cheese, onion mixture, red pepper, mushroom mixture and Gruyere cheese.

Bake at 425° for 10-15 minutes or until cheese is melted. Sprinkle with rosemary. **Yield:** 8 slices.

Slow Cooked Carnitas

(Pictured below)

PREP: 20 min. **COOK:** 6 hours

This hearty entree is delicious and easy to prepare in your slow cooker. Sometimes, instead of using tortillas, I put the shredded pork mixture on top of lettuce for a Southwestern salad.
—Lisa Glogow, Aliso VIejo, California

   1 **boneless pork shoulder butt roast (3 to 4 pounds)**
   3 **garlic cloves, thinly sliced**
   2 **teaspoons olive oil**
1/2 **teaspoon salt**
1/2 **teaspoon pepper**
   1 **bunch green onions, chopped**
1-1/2 **cups minced fresh cilantro**
   1 **cup salsa**
1/2 **cup chicken broth**
1/2 **cup tequila** *or* **additional chicken broth**
   2 **cans (4 ounces *each*) chopped green chilies**
 12 **flour tortillas (8 inches), warmed**
Fresh cilantro leaves, sliced red onion and chopped tomatoes, optional

Cut the roast in half; place in a 5-qt. slow cooker. Sprinkle with garlic, oil, salt and pepper. Add the onions, cilantro, salsa, broth, tequila and chilies. Cover and cook on low for 6-8 hours or until meat is tender.

Remove meat; cool slightly. Shred with two forks and return to the slow cooker; heat through. Spoon about 2/3 cup meat mixture onto each tortilla; serve with the toppings of your choice. **Yield:** 12 servings.

Pastitsio

(Pictured above)

PREP: 35 min. **BAKE:** 30 min. + standing

My guests always gobble up this authentic Greek beef and pasta casserole. And they savor every drop of the creamy white sauce!
—Amanda Briggs, Greenfield, Wisconsin

   1 **package (7 ounces) uncooked elbow macaroni**
   1 **pound ground beef** *or* **lamb**
   1 **medium onion, chopped**
   1 **garlic clove, minced**
   1 **can (8 ounces) tomato sauce**
   1 **teaspoon salt,** *divided*
1/4 **teaspoon dried oregano**
1/8 **teaspoon pepper**
1/4 **teaspoon ground cinnamon, optional**
1/2 **cup grated Parmesan cheese,** *divided*
   3 **tablespoons butter**
   3 **tablespoons all-purpose flour**
1-1/2 **cups 2% milk**
   1 **egg, beaten**

Cook the macaroni according to the package directions. Meanwhile, in a large skillet, cook the beef, onion and garlic over medium heat until meat is no longer pink; drain. Stir in the tomato sauce, 1/2 teaspoon salt, oregano, pepper and cinnamon if desired; heat through.

Drain macaroni; place half of macaroni in a greased 9-in. square baking pan. Sprinkle with 1/4 cup cheese. Layer with meat mixture and remaining macaroni. Set aside.

In a small saucepan, melt the butter; stir in flour and remaining salt until smooth. Gradually add milk. Bring to a boil; cook and stir for 2 minutes or until thickened.

Remove from the heat. Stir a small amount of the hot mixture into egg; return all to pan, stirring constantly.

Bring to a gentle boil; cook and stir for 2 minutes. Remove from the heat; stir in the remaining cheese. Pour sauce over macaroni.

Bake, uncovered, at 350° for 30-35 minutes or until golden brown. Let stand for 10 minutes before serving. **Yield:** 4 servings.

Spiral Stromboli

(Pictured below)

PREP: 15 min. **BAKE:** 20 min.

I got this recipe from my mom, and everyone who tries it loves it. Serve the stromboli for lunch or as a quick, casual dinner.
—*Beth Bruhn, Willmar, Minnesota*

- 1 **tube (11 ounces) refrigerated crusty French loaf**
- 3/4 **cup shredded part-skim mozzarella cheese**
- 3/4 **cup shredded cheddar cheese**
- 1/4 **pound thinly sliced hard salami**
- 1/4 **pound thinly sliced deli ham**
- 1 **jar (2 ounces) diced pimientos, drained**
- 1 **tablespoon butter, melted**
- 3 **tablespoons shredded Parmesan cheese**

Unroll the dough on a lightly floured surface. Pat into a 14-in. x 12-in. rectangle; sprinkle mozzarella and cheddar cheeses to within 1/2 in. of edges. Layer with salami, ham and pimientos.

Roll up tightly jelly-roll style, starting from a short side; pinch the seam to seal. Place seam side down on an ungreased baking sheet. Brush with butter; sprinkle with Parmesan cheese.

Bake at 375° for 20-25 minutes or until golden brown. Cool on a wire rack for 5 minutes. Cut with a serrated knife. Serve warm. Refrigerate leftovers. **Yield:** 6 servings.

Hawaiian Chicken

(Pictured above)

PREP: 20 min. **BAKE:** 20 min.

Who says you can't have a taste of the tropics on a weeknight? This tangy chicken is done in a flash, and my husband and sons rave about it.
—*Kara Cook, Elk Ridge, Utah*

- 1/2 **cup all-purpose flour**
- 1 **teaspoon salt**
- 1/4 **teaspoon pepper**
- 6 **boneless skinless chicken breast halves (6 ounces *each*)**
- 3 **tablespoons canola oil**
- 1 **cup sugar**
- 2 **tablespoons cornstarch**
- 1 **teaspoon chicken bouillon granules**
- 1/4 **teaspoon ground ginger**
- 1 **can (20 ounces) unsweetened sliced pineapple**
- 1/2 **cup cider vinegar**
- 1 **tablespoon soy sauce**
- 1 **medium green pepper, cut into rings**

Hot cooked rice

In a large resealable plastic bag, combine the flour, salt and pepper. Add chicken, one piece at a time, and shake to coat. In a skillet, brown the chicken in oil. Transfer to a greased 13-in. x 9-in. baking dish.

In a small saucepan, combine the sugar, cornstarch, chicken bouillon and ginger. Drain the pineapple into a 2-cup measuring cup; set pineapple aside. Add enough cold water to juice to measure 1-1/4 cups. Stir in the cider vinegar and soy sauce. Gradually whisk into sugar mixture. Bring to a boil; cook and stir for 2 minutes or until thickened.

Pour sauce over chicken; top with green pepper and reserved pineapple. Bake, uncovered, at 350° for 20-30 minutes or until a meat thermometer reads 170°. Serve with rice. **Yield:** 6 servings.

Tasteful Get-Togethers

Hosting a party is fun and fuss-free when you rely on the themed menus in this chapter. From a spicy Mexican fiesta to terrific tailgating and a fondue feast, these spectacular bashes will thrill guests with delicious, festive fare.

FUN-FILLED FOOD. Clockwise from top left: Sweet-Tart Rhubarb Crepes (p. 296), Topsy-Turvy Sangria (p. 295), Caramel Apple Fondue (p. 301) and Fruity Halibut Steaks (p. 292).

Flavors of the Far East

ASIAN FOOD offers a wide range of exotic flavors, from spicy wasabi, ginger and red chili paste to subtler cilantro and lime. Why not invite friends over to take a trip —with their taste buds—to the Far East?

The special spread here showcases tongue-tingling hors d'oeuvres you can easily assemble in your own kitchen. Everyone is sure to love finger foods such as Phyllo Shrimp with Dipping Sauce, Steamed Pork and Shrimp Dumplings, Asian Meatballs, Thai Pork Salad Wraps and Creamy Wasabi Spread.

So immerse your guests in a different culture—and serve them appetizers from the other side of the world!

Thai Pork Salad Wraps

(Pictured at right)

PREP: 20 min. **COOK:** 15 min.

You can substitute ground beef or chicken in the filling of these tasty lettuce wraps. I season them with lime and cilantro.
—*Diane Hixon, Niceville, Florida*

- 3/4 **pound ground pork**
- 2 **tablespoons dry bread crumbs**
- 1/2 **cup minced fresh cilantro**
- 1/2 **cup minced fresh mint**
- 2 **green onions, chopped**
- 1/4 **cup lime juice**
- 4 **teaspoons fish *or* soy sauce**
- 1/8 **teaspoon cayenne pepper**
- 8 **Bibb lettuce leaves**
- 1-1/2 **cups finely shredded cabbage**

In a small skillet over medium heat, cook pork until no longer pink; drain. Stir in bread crumbs. Stir in the cilantro, mint, onions, lime juice, fish sauce and cayenne.

Top each lettuce leaf with 3 tablespoons each of pork mixture and cabbage. Roll up. **Yield:** 8 servings.

Steamed Pork and Shrimp Dumplings

(Pictured above right)

PREP: 40 min. **COOK:** 10 min./batch

These delicious dumplings are the perfect finger food. Pick them up by the stem, dunk them in dipping sauce and enjoy!
—*Steve Niederloh, Champlin, Minnesota*

- 1 **pound boneless pork loin chops, cut up**
- 1/2 **pound uncooked medium shrimp, peeled and deveined**
- 10 **whole water chestnuts**
- 2 **tablespoons cornstarch**
- 1 **green onion, chopped**
- 2 **tablespoons rice vinegar**
- 1 **teaspoon minced fresh gingerroot**
- 1 **tablespoon sesame oil**

- 1 **tablespoon sherry *or* chicken broth**
- 1 **tablespoon reduced-sodium soy sauce**
- 1 **package (12 ounces) wonton wrappers**
- 12 **romaine leaves**

DIPPING SAUCE:
- 1/4 **cup reduced-sodium soy sauce**
- 1-1/2 **teaspoons finely chopped green onion**
- 1/2 **teaspoon sesame oil**

Place the first 10 ingredients in a food processor; cover and process until finely chopped.

Place 2 teaspoons pork mixture in the center of a wonton wrapper. (Keep remaining wrappers covered with a damp paper towel until ready to use.) Moisten the edges with water. Bring corners of wonton wrapper over filling and twist to form a bundle; pinch edges to seal. Repeat.

Line a steamer basket with three lettuce leaves. Arrange a fourth of the dumplings 1 in. apart over lettuce; place in a large saucepan over 1 in. of water. Bring to a boil; cover and steam for 10-12 minutes or until a meat thermometer reads 160°. Discard lettuce. Repeat.

Combine sauce ingredients; serve with hot dumplings. **Yield:** 52 dumplings.

Asian Meatballs

PREP: 30 min. **BAKE:** 15 min.

My mother creates her own recipes for wonderful Asian-inspired menus. Inspired by her mouthwatering specialties, I came up with these pork sausage meatballs to complement her meals.
—Amanda Kotlan, Spokane, Washington

- 2 green onions, finely chopped
- 1 teaspoon butter
- 1 egg, beaten
- 3 tablespoons soy sauce
- 1/2 cup dry bread crumbs
- 1/4 cup finely chopped water chestnuts
- 3 garlic cloves, minced
- 1 tablespoon minced fresh gingerroot
- 1 pound bulk pork sausage
- 1 tablespoon sesame seeds, toasted

SAUCE:
- 1/3 cup mayonnaise
- 1 tablespoon rice vinegar
- 1-1/2 teaspoons prepared wasabi

In a small skillet, saute the onions in butter until tender. Transfer to a large bowl. Add the egg, soy sauce, bread crumbs, water chestnuts, garlic and ginger. Crumble the sausage over mixture and mix well.

Shape into 1-in. balls. Place on an ungreased broiler pan. Bake at 350° for 15-20 minutes or until no longer pink; drain. Sprinkle with sesame seeds.

Combine mayonnaise, rice vinegar and wasabi; serve with meatballs. **Yield:** 2 dozen (1/3 cup sauce).

Phyllo Shrimp With Dipping Sauces

PREP/TOTAL TIME: 30 min.

I fixed this appetizer when I had leftover phyllo dough in the freezer. The shrimp is great for a party because it looks elegant but is easy to put together. I serve it with two different sauces so guests can decide what mood they're in—sweet or spicy!
—Sonali Ruder, New York, New York

- 12 uncooked large shrimp
- 1/8 teaspoon salt
- 1/8 teaspoon pepper
- 6 sheets phyllo dough (14 inches x 9 inches)
- 2 tablespoons butter, melted
- 3 tablespoons canola oil

SWEET CILANTRO LIME SAUCE:
- 2 tablespoons lime juice
- 2 tablespoons honey
- 2 tablespoons minced fresh cilantro
- 1 tablespoon reduced-sodium soy sauce
- 1 teaspoon sesame oil
- 1 garlic clove, minced

Dash crushed red pepper flakes

SPICY MAYONNAISE:
- 2 tablespoons mayonnaise
- 2 teaspoons Thai red chili paste

Peel and devein the shrimp, leaving tails on. Sprinkle with salt and pepper. Stack six sheets of phyllo dough on a work surface; brush the top sheet with butter. Cut into 12 strips from long side.

Place one shrimp on each strip; roll up. In a large skillet over medium heat, cook shrimp in oil for 2-3 minutes on each side or until shrimp turn pink.

In a small bowl, whisk cilantro lime sauce ingredients. In another bowl, combine mayonnaise and chili paste. Serve sauces with shrimp. **Yield:** 1 dozen.

Creamy Wasabi Spread

(Pictured below)

PREP/TOTAL TIME: 10 min.

Sesame seeds make an attractive coating for this simple cracker spread. Look for rice crackers in the ethnic food aisle—you can use any flavor, but I think the wasabi ones are best.
—Tammie Balon, Boyce, Virginia

- 1 package (8 ounces) cream cheese
- 1/4 cup prepared wasabi
- 2 tablespoons sesame seeds, toasted
- 2 tablespoons soy sauce

Rice crackers

Place the cream cheese on a cutting board; split into two layers. Spread wasabi over bottom half; replace top layer.

Press both sides into sesame seeds. Place on a shallow serving plate; pour soy sauce around cheese. Serve with crackers. **Yield:** 8 servings.

Backyard Barbecue Bash

WHEN the weather's fine, take the party outdoors for some fresh-air fun—and, of course, scrumptious food! You'll have the picnic table covered when you fire up the special cookout menu here.

To spark appetites, create mouthwatering aromas by putting zippy Jalapeno Popper Burgers, Marvelous Mediterranean Vegetables, Fruity Halibut Steaks and Stacey's Famous BBQ Chicken on the grill. When guests dig in, they'll see that the taste of these main dishes doesn't disappoint.

With a spread this sensational, your backyard barbecue bash is sure to be a blazing success!

Jalapeno Popper Burgers

PREP: 30 min. **GRILL:** 15 min.

What do you get when you combine a jalapeno popper and a hamburger? This fantastic recipe! It takes the classic ingredients of the pepper appetizer and encases them in a juicy beef patty.
—*Jo Davison, Naples, Florida*

 3 jalapeno peppers, halved lengthwise and seeded
 1 teaspoon olive oil
 6 bacon strips, cooked and crumbled
 1 package (3 ounces) cream cheese, softened
 2 garlic cloves, minced
 1 teaspoon salt
 1 teaspoon lemon-pepper seasoning
 1/2 teaspoon pepper
 1/4 teaspoon paprika
 2 pounds ground beef
 4 slices pepper Jack cheese
 4 hamburger buns, split
 4 lettuce leaves
 1 large tomato, sliced
 3/4 cup guacamole

Brush the jalapeno peppers with oil. Grill, covered, over medium heat for 3-5 minutes or until tender, turning occasionally. When cool enough to handle, finely chop. In a small bowl, combine the bacon, cream cheese and jalapeno until blended.

In a large bowl, combine the garlic, salt, lemon-pepper seasoning, pepper and paprika. Crumble the ground beef over the mixture and mix well. Shape into eight thin patties. Spoon the bacon mixture onto the center of four patties; top with remaining patties and press edges firmly to seal.

Grill burgers, covered, over medium heat or broil 4 in. from heat for 6-7 minutes on each side or until a meat thermometer reads 160° and juices run clear. Top with pepper Jack cheese. Cover and cook 1-2 minutes longer or until pepper Jack cheese is melted.

Grill buns, cut side down, over medium heat for 30-60 seconds or until toasted. Serve the burgers on buns with lettuce, tomato and guacamole. **Yield:** 4 servings.

Fruity Halibut Steaks

(Pictured above and on page 288)

PREP/TOTAL TIME: 30 min.

My friends and family rave about this colorful, delicious halibut every time I serve it. I like to prepare and refrigerate the salsa about 4 hours in advance so the flavors have time to blend.
—*Patricia Nieh, Portola Vally, California*

 1 cup chopped fresh pineapple
 1 cup chopped peeled mango
 2/3 cup chopped sweet red pepper
 1 medium tomato, seeded and chopped
 1/3 cup chopped seeded peeled cucumber
 1/4 cup minced fresh cilantro
 2 tablespoons chopped seeded jalapeno pepper
 2 tablespoons lime juice
 6 halibut steaks (8 ounces *each*)
 2 tablespoons olive oil
 1/2 teaspoon salt
 1/2 teaspoon pepper

In a small bowl, combine the first eight ingredients; chill until serving.

Brush the halibut steaks with the oil; sprinkle with salt and pepper. Moisten a paper towel with cooking oil; using long-handled tongs, lightly coat the grill rack. Grill halibut, covered, over high heat or broil 3-4 in. from the heat for 3-5 minutes on each side or until the fish flakes easily with a fork. Serve with salsa. **Yield:** 6 servings.

Editor's Note: We recommend wearing disposable gloves when cutting hot peppers. Avoid touching your face.

Stacey's Famous BBQ Chicken

PREP: 45 min. **GRILL:** 40 min.

I smother this chicken with a finger-lickin', lip-smacking sauce everyone loves. I make big batches and give jars of it as gifts.
—*Stacey Nerness, Spencer, Iowa*

- 2-1/2 cups ketchup
- 1/2 cup packed brown sugar
- 1/2 cup honey
- 1/4 cup Liquid Smoke
- 1/4 cup molasses
- 1 serrano pepper, finely chopped
- 2 tablespoons prepared mustard
- 1 tablespoon white wine vinegar
- 1 tablespoon Worcestershire sauce
- 2 teaspoons onion powder
- 2 teaspoons garlic powder
- 1/4 teaspoon cayenne pepper
- 4 chicken leg quarters
- 1/2 teaspoon salt
- 1/2 teaspoon pepper

In a large saucepan, combine the first 12 ingredients. Bring to a boil. Reduce the heat; simmer, uncovered, for 30 minutes to allow flavors to blend. Set aside 1/2 cup sauce for basting; cover and refrigerate remaining sauce.

Sprinkle chicken with salt and pepper. Moisten a paper towel with cooking oil; using long-handled tongs, lightly coat the grill rack. Prepare grill for indirect heat, using a drip pan. Place chicken skin side down over drip pan and grill, covered, over indirect medium heat for 20 minutes. Turn; grill 20-30 minutes longer or until juices run clear, basting occasionally with reserved sauce. **Yield:** 4 servings plus 3 cups leftover sauce.

Marvelous Mediterranean Vegetables

(Pictured at right)

PREP: 25 min. + marinating **GRILL:** 10 min.

With lots of cookouts to plan in summer, I created this side that goes with everything. Fix it earlier in the day and let it marinate, then toss it on the grill. —*Cathy Godberson, Oakville, Ontario*

- 3 large portobello mushrooms
- 1 *each* medium sweet red, orange and yellow peppers
- 1 medium zucchini
- 10 fresh asparagus spears, cut into 2-inch lengths
- 1 small onion, sliced and separated into rings
- 3/4 cup grape tomatoes
- 1/2 cup fresh sugar snap peas
- 1/2 cup fresh broccoli florets
- 1/2 cup pitted Greek olives
- 1 bottle (14 ounces) Greek vinaigrette
- 1/2 cup crumbled feta cheese

Slice mushrooms, peppers and zucchini; place in a large resealable plastic bag. Add the asparagus, onion, grape tomatoes, sugar snap peas, broccoli and olives. Pour the vinaigrette into the bag; seal the bag and turn to coat. Refrigerate for at least 30 minutes.

Drain the vegetables and discard marinade. Transfer vegetables to a grill wok or basket. Grill, uncovered, over medium heat for 8-12 minutes or until tender, stirring frequently. Place on a serving plate; sprinkle with feta cheese. **Yield:** 9 servings.

Editor's Note: If you do not have a grill wok or basket, use a disposable foil pan. Poke holes in the bottom of the pan with a meat fork to allow liquid to drain.

Olé, a Mexican Fiesta!

WHETHER it's Cinco de Mayo or another time of year, a south-of-the-border bash is always a crowd-pleasing party theme. To give your event plenty of spice, set out a spread of these mouthwatering dishes.

You can't go wrong with sensational main courses such as Terrific Turkey Enchiladas and Grilled Chipotle Shrimp. Cool palates with glasses of refreshing Topsy-Turvy Sangria, and please sweet tooths with generous slices of Dulce de Leche Cheesecake.

Don't forget to offer tortilla chips and salsa! With all of this fabulous Mexican fare, guests are sure to remember your bash for years to come.

Dulce de Leche Cheesecake

(Pictured at right)

PREP: 40 min. **BAKE:** 1 hour + chilling

I'm originally from Paraguay, and this cheesecake reminds me of my native land. If you can't find the dulce de leche, try caramel ice cream topping. —Sonia Lipham, Ranburne, Alabama

- 1-3/4 **cups crushed gingersnap cookies (about 35 cookies)**
- 1/4 **cup finely chopped walnuts**
- 1 **tablespoon sugar**
- 1/2 **teaspoon ground cinnamon**
- 6 **tablespoons butter, melted**

FILLING:
- 3 **packages (8 ounces *each*) cream cheese, softened**
- 1 **cup plus 2 tablespoons sugar**
- 1/4 **cup 2% milk**
- 2 **tablespoons all-purpose flour**
- 1 **teaspoon vanilla extract**
- 3 **eggs, lightly beaten**
- 1 **can (13.4 ounces) dulce de leche**
- 1 **cup (6 ounces) semisweet chocolate chips**
- 1-1/2 **teaspoons chili powder**

Place a greased 9-in. springform pan on a double thickness of heavy-duty foil (about 18 in. square). Securely wrap foil around pan. In a large bowl, combine the cookie crumbs, walnuts, sugar, cinnamon and butter. Press onto the bottom and 2 in. up the sides of prepared pan.

In a large bowl, beat the cream cheese and sugar until smooth. Beat in the milk, flour and vanilla. Add eggs; beat on low speed just until combined. Pour into crust.

Pour the dulce de leche into a microwave-safe bowl; microwave at 50% power until softened. Drop dulce de leche by tablespoonfuls over batter; cut through batter with a knife to swirl.

Place springform pan in a large baking pan; add 1 in. of hot water to larger pan. Bake at 350° for 60-70 minutes or until the center is just set and the top appears dull. Remove springform pan from water bath. Cool on a wire rack for 10 minutes. Carefully run a knife around the edge of the pan to loosen; cool 1 hour longer.

In a microwave, melt chocolate chips; stir until smooth. Stir in chili powder. Spread over cheesecake. Refrigerate overnight. Remove sides of pan. **Yield:** 16 servings.

Editor's Note: This recipe was tested with Nestle dulce de leche. Look for it in the international foods section.

Terrific Turkey Enchiladas

PREP: 35 min. **BAKE:** 35 min.

Enchiladas are a favorite dinner in my home. With ground turkey, this version is a tasty twist on the classic Southwestern dish.
—Jenn Tidwell, Fair Oaks, California

- 1-1/4 **cups frozen corn, thawed**
- 1 **can (4 ounces) chopped green chilies**
- 1 **cup fresh cilantro leaves**
- 1/3 **cup heavy whipping cream**
- 1/4 **teaspoon salt**
- 1/4 **teaspoon pepper**

ENCHILADAS:
- 3/4 **pound ground turkey**
- 1/3 **cup chopped onion**
- 1 **garlic clove, minced**
- 1 **tablespoon olive oil**
- 3/4 **cup salsa**
- 1 **tablespoon cornmeal**

2 teaspoons chili powder
1-1/2 teaspoons ground cumin
1 teaspoon dried oregano
1/8 teaspoon salt
1/8 teaspoon pepper
6 flour tortillas (8 inches), warmed
1-1/4 cups shredded Mexican cheese blend, *divided*
1/4 cup sliced ripe olives

Place the first six ingredients in a food processor; cover and pulse until blended.

In a large skillet, cook the turkey, onion and garlic in oil over medium heat until meat is no longer pink. Remove from the heat; stir in the salsa, cornmeal and seasonings.

Spoon 1/3 cup turkey mixture down the center of each tortilla; top with 2 tablespoons cheese. Roll up and place seam side down in a greased 11-in. x 7-in. baking dish. Spoon corn mixture over the top; sprinkle with olives and remaining cheese.

Cover and bake at 350° for 30 minutes. Uncover; bake 5-10 minutes longer or until the enchiladas are heated through. **Yield:** 3 servings.

Grilled Chipotle Shrimp

PREP: 25 min. + marinating **GRILL:** 10 min.

I created this for a Cinco de Mayo party, and my guests couldn't get enough. The creamy dipping sauce mellows out the shrimp's heat perfectly. —Mandy Rivers, Lexington, South Carolina

1/4 cup packed brown sugar
2 chipotle peppers in adobo sauce, chopped, plus 1/4 cup adobo sauce
6 garlic cloves, minced
2 tablespoons water
2 tablespoons lime juice
1 tablespoon olive oil
1/4 teaspoon salt
2 pounds uncooked large shrimp, peeled and deveined

CILANTRO CREAM SAUCE:
1 cup sour cream
1/3 cup minced fresh cilantro
2 garlic cloves, minced
1-1/2 teaspoons grated lime peel
1/4 teaspoon salt
1/4 teaspoon minced fresh mint

In a small saucepan, bring the brown sugar, chipotles, adobo sauce, garlic, water, lime juice, oil and salt to a boil. Reduce heat; cook and stir 2 minutes longer. Remove from the heat; cool completely.

Transfer mixture to a large resealable plastic bag. Add the shrimp; seal bag and turn to coat. Refrigerate for up to 2 hours.

Meanwhile, combine the cilantro sauce ingredients; chill until serving.

Drain and discard marinade. Thread shrimp onto metal or soaked wooden skewers. Moisten a paper towel with cooking oil; using long-handled tongs, lightly coat the grill rack.

Grill shrimp, covered, over medium heat or broil 4 in. from the heat for 6-8 minutes or until shrimp turn pink, turning once. Serve with sauce. **Yield:** about 5 dozen (1-1/4 cups sauce).

Topsy-Turvy Sangria

(Pictured below and on page 288)

PREP/TOTAL TIME: 10 min.

This refreshing drink is great for casual get-togethers. It's even better if you make it the night before and let the flavors steep. —Tracy Field, Bremerton, Washington

1 bottle (750 milliliters) merlot
1 cup sugar
1 cup orange liqueur
1/2 to 1 cup brandy
3 cups lemon-lime soda, chilled
1 cup sliced fresh strawberries
1 medium lemon, sliced
1 medium orange, sliced
1 medium peach, sliced
Ice cubes

In a pitcher, stir wine, sugar, orange liqueur and brandy until sugar is dissolved. Stir in soda and fruit. Serve over ice. **Yield:** 10 servings (3/4 cup each).

Favorites of France

DO CREPES seem synonymous with the haute cuisine perfected in the gourmet restaurants of Paris? The truth is, these super-thin treats are easy to make, versatile and fun to eat at a French-themed party.

Crepes lend themselves to many different fillings and can be made in advance and frozen. Just consider the scrumptious creations here, from sweet and fruity variations to savory entrees. (Use the Basic Crepes recipe below or ready-made crepes from your grocery store to fix the other recipes in this section.)

With these no-fail favorites, you'll transform your kitchen into a Parisian creperie in no time. Ooh, la la!

Basic Crepes

PREP: 10 min. + chilling **COOK:** 20 min.

From the experts in our Test Kitchen, this simple recipe creates delicious crepes that are perfect for sweet or savory fillings. Use it to make other recipes that call for prepared crepes...or enjoy the three taste–tempting variations included below.

- 1-1/2 cups 2% milk
- 4 eggs
- 1 cup all-purpose flour
- 1-1/2 teaspoons sugar
- 1/8 teaspoon salt
- 8 teaspoons butter

In a small bowl, whisk the milk and eggs. Combine the flour, sugar and salt; add to milk mixture and mix well. Refrigerate for 1 hour.

Melt 1 teaspoon butter in an 8-in. nonstick skillet over medium heat; pour 2 tablespoons batter into center of skillet. Lift and tilt pan to coat bottom evenly. Cook until the top appears dry; turn and cook 15-20 seconds longer. Remove to a wire rack.

Repeat with remaining batter, adding butter to skillet as needed. When cool, stack crepes with waxed paper or paper towels in between. **Yield:** 16 crepes.

Shrimp Crepes: In a large skillet, cook 4-1/2 cups chopped fresh broccoli, 6 chopped green onions, 2 teaspoons minced garlic, 1/2 teaspoon salt, 1/4 teaspoon pepper and 1/4 teaspoon Worcestershire sauce in 3 tablespoons melted butter for 7-9 minutes or until the broccoli is crisp-tender. Remove and set aside. In same skillet, saute 1 pound peeled deveined uncooked shrimp in 1/4 cup wine until shrimp turn pink. Return broccoli to skillet and combine. Spoon the filling down the center of crepes; roll up. Place in an ungreased 15-in. x 10-in. baking pan. Bake, uncovered, at 350° for 15-20 minutes or until heated through. Meanwhile, prepare 1 envelope bearnaise sauce according to package directions. Serve sauce over crepes. **Yield:** 8 servings.

Creamy Strawberry Crepes: In a large bowl, beat 1 package (8 ounces) softened cream cheese, 1-1/4 cups confectioners' sugar, 1 tablespoon lemon juice, 1 teaspoon grated lemon peel and 1/2 teaspoon vanilla extract until smooth. Fold in 2 cups sliced fresh strawberries and 2 cups whipped cream. Spoon about 1/3 cup filling down the center of 14 crepes; roll up. Garnish with additional sliced berries. **Yield:** 7 servings.

Banana Crepes: In a small skillet, bring 2/3 cup sugar, 2/3 cup orange juice, 1/2 cup butter and 4 teaspoons grated orange peel to a boil. Remove from the heat. Peel 6 medium firm bananas and cut in half lengthwise. Add to the orange sauce; cook over medium heat until heated through, about 1 minute. Place 1 banana half in the center of a crepe; roll up. Place crepes seam side down on a plate; drizzle with orange sauce. **Yield:** 6 servings.

Sweet-Tart Rhubarb Crepes

(Pictured below and on page 288)

PREP/TOTAL TIME: 25 min.

Sit down to a breakfast or brunch featuring these tongue–tingling delights. What a luscious way to use homegrown rhubarb!
—*Elizabeth King, Duluth, Minnesota*

- **5** cups finely chopped fresh *or* frozen rhubarb, thawed
- **3/4** cup sugar
- **2** tablespoons all-purpose flour
- **2** tablespoons orange juice
- **1** tablespoon butter
- **1** teaspoon grated orange peel
- **16** prepared crepes (9 inches)
- Confectioners' sugar and additional grated orange peel, optional

In a large saucepan, combine the first five ingredients. Cook, stirring occasionally, over medium heat for 15-18 minutes or until tender. Remove from the heat; stir in the grated orange peel.

Spread 2 tablespoons rhubarb filling down the center of each crepe; roll up. Sprinkle with the confectioners' sugar and additional grated orange peel if desired. **Yield:** 8 servings.

Editor's Note: If using frozen rhubarb, measure the rhubarb while still frozen, then thaw completely. Drain in a colander, but do not press liquid out.

Warm Banana Crepes

PREP/TOTAL TIME: 10 min.

This yummy dish from our Test Kitchen team is so fast to fix, what looks like a weekend-only treat can be served anytime. It's even speedier if you use ready-made crepes from the store (sold near the berries in the produce section) instead of making your own.

- **1/2** cup butter, cubed
- **1/2** cup packed brown sugar
- **4** medium ripe bananas, halved lengthwise
- **4** prepared crepes (9 inches)

In a large skillet, melt butter. Add brown sugar; heat and stir until sugar is dissolved. Add bananas; cook until light golden brown, turning once.

In an small ungreased skillet, heat crepes for 10 seconds on each side or until warm.

Place two banana halves in the center of each crepe. Fold the sides over filling and roll up; drizzle with brown sugar mixture. **Yield:** 4 servings.

Hubby's Favorite Crepes

(Pictured above right)

PREP: 30 min. **COOK:** 15 min.

Have leftover cooked chicken from last night's dinner? Here's a wonderful solution. The saucy, creamy main course brings a smile to my husband's face every time he sees it on the table.
—Joanne Sieg, River Hills, Manitoba

- **1/4** cup butter, cubed
- **1/2** pound sliced fresh mushrooms
- **1/4** cup finely chopped onion
- **1/4** cup all-purpose flour

- **2** cups 2% milk
- **2** teaspoons chicken bouillon granules
- **1/2** teaspoon Italian seasoning
- **1/4** teaspoon pepper
- **1/2** cup sour cream
- **3** tablespoons sherry *or* chicken broth
- **2** cups finely chopped cooked chicken
- **2** tablespoons minced fresh parsley, *divided*
- **15** prepared crepes (9 inches)
- Additional sour cream, optional

In a large skillet over medium-high heat, melt the butter. Add mushrooms and onion; saute until tender. Sprinkle with the flour; stir until blended. Gradually add the milk. Stir in the chicken bouillon granules, Italian seasoning and pepper.

Bring to a boil; cook and stir for 2 minutes or until thickened. Stir in sour cream and sherry. Remove 1 cup sauce; set aside. Stir chicken and 1 tablespoon parsley into remaining mixture; heat through.

Spread 3 tablespoons chicken filling down the center of each crepe; roll up. Drizzle reserved sauce over the top. Sprinkle with remaining parsley. Serve with additional sour cream if desired. **Yield:** 5 servings.

Festive Fun with Fondue

DUNK, swirl, eat, repeat…the directions for guests at a fondue party are just that simple but oh, so delicious! Why not dive right in by hosting your own fondue fun? Simply rely on the creative concoctions here.

You'll find plenty of savory choices flavored with ingredients such as beer, cheese, curry, barbecue sauce and mustard. They're sure to please the hearty appetites in the crowd. And don't forget dessert! Offer sweet treats featuring chocolate, caramel and almonds.

Just set out some fondue pots and let everyone take a dip. No matter which rave-winning recipes you choose, you'll be happy you took the plunge!

Golden Mustard Fondue

(Pictured at left in the photo above)

PREP/TOTAL TIME: 20 min.

Pretzels and rye bread take on the taste of a German Oktoberfest celebration when you dunk them into this sweet, tangy creation. Try serving it with chicken fingers and slices of sausage, too.
—Darlene Brenden, Salem, Oregon

1/2 cup sugar
 4 teaspoons all-purpose flour
1/4 teaspoon salt
 1 cup half-and-half cream, *divided*
1/4 cup Dijon mustard
 1 egg yolk, beaten
1/3 cup cider vinegar
Pretzels *or* cubed rye bread

In a small heavy saucepan, combine sugar, flour and salt. Stir in 3/4 cup half-and-half cream and Dijon mustard until smooth. Cook and stir over medium-high heat until the mixture is thickened and bubbly. Reduce heat; cook and stir 2 minutes longer.

Remove from heat. Combine egg yolk and remaining cream. Stir a small amount of hot mixture into egg yolk mixture; return all to the pan, stirring constantly. Bring to a gentle boil; cook and stir 2 minutes longer. Remove from the heat. Gently stir in vinegar. Keep warm. Serve with pretzels. **Yield:** 1-1/2 cups.

Sweet & Sassy Sauce

(Pictured at center in the photo at left)

PREP/TOTAL TIME: 10 min.

Are your friends and family big on barbecue? Then you'll want to make sure your get-together includes this tangy, lip-smacking fondue. It's easy to whip up with just six basic ingredients.
—*Nancy Mueller, Bloomington, Minnesota*

- 1/3 cup honey barbecue sauce
- 1/3 cup orange marmalade
- 1/4 cup orange juice
- 2 tablespoons soy sauce
- 1-1/2 teaspoons minced fresh gingerroot
- 1/4 teaspoon crushed red pepper flakes

In a small saucepan, heat all ingredients to allow the flavors to blend. Serve warm or at room temperature. **Yield:** 1 cup.

Curry Mayo Dipping Sauce

(Pictured at right in the photo at left)

PREP: 5 min. + chilling

Curry powder and a dash of hot sauce bring bold flavor and a nice amount of zip to this fantastic mayonnaise-based dip.
—*Joan Hallford, North Richland Hills, Texas*

- 1 cup mayonnaise
- 3 tablespoons 2% milk
- 5 teaspoons curry powder
- 1/4 teaspoon hot pepper sauce

In a small bowl, combine all ingredients. Refrigerate for at least 1 hour. **Yield:** about 1 cup.

Beer & Cheddar Fondue

(Pictured at right)

PREP/TOTAL TIME: 15 min.

This super snack is my mother's favorite, so I always fix it for her on her birthday. On the side, I serve everything from pretzels and sausage to apple slices, bread cubes and chunks of veggies.
—*Amanda Wentz, Virginia Beach, Virginia*

- 4 cups (16 ounces) shredded cheddar cheese
- 1 tablespoon all-purpose flour
- 1 cup beer *or* nonalcoholic beer
- 3 garlic cloves, minced
- 1-1/2 teaspoons ground mustard
- 1/4 teaspoon coarsely ground pepper
- **Pretzel dipping sticks and sliced smoked sausage**

In a large bowl, combine the cheese and flour. In a small saucepan, heat the beer, garlic, mustard and pepper over medium heat until bubbles form around sides of pan.

Reduce heat to medium-low; add a handful of cheese mixture. Stir constantly, using a figure-eight motion, until almost completely melted. Continue adding cheese, one handful at a time, allowing cheese to almost completely melt between additions. Keep warm. Serve with pretzels and sausage. **Yield:** 2 cups.

Almond Custard Fondue

(Pictured at left in the photo above)

PREP/TOTAL TIME: 25 min.

I've been whipping up this smooth, decadent dessert for nearly 40 years. It's a wonderful way to treat friends and family after dinner. Offer brownies, cake, mini waffles or cookies as dippers.
—*Patricia Swart, Galloway, New Jersey*

 1/2 **cup sugar**
   2 **tablespoons cornstarch**
 1/4 **teaspoon salt**
   2 **cups half-and-half cream**
   2 **egg yolks, beaten**
   1 **tablespoon butter**
 1-1/4 **teaspoons almond extract**
Cubed brownies, cake, miniature waffles *and/or* cream-filled chocolate sandwich cookies

In a large heavy saucepan, combine the sugar, cornstarch and salt. Stir in cream until smooth. Cook and stir over medium-high heat until thickened and bubbly. Reduce heat; cook and stir 2 minutes longer.

Remove mixture from the heat. Stir a small amount of the hot mixture into the egg yolks; return all to the pan, stirring constantly. Bring to a gentle boil; cook and stir 2 minutes longer.

Remove from the heat; stir in butter and extract. Keep warm. Serve with brownies, cake, waffles and/or cookies. **Yield:** 2 cups.

Cheese Lover's Fondue

(Pictured at center in the photo above)

PREP: 15 min. **COOK:** 20 min.

French bread cubes and sliced apples are perfect with this classic fondue made with two kinds of cheese and a dash of hot sauce.
—*Linda Vogel, Elgin, Illinois*

   4 **teaspoons cornstarch, *divided***
   1 **tablespoon plus 1 cup dry white wine, *divided***
 1-1/2 **cups (6 ounces) shredded Gruyere cheese**
 1-1/2 **cups (6 ounces) shredded Swiss cheese**
   1 **garlic clove, peeled and halved**
 1-1/2 **teaspoons lemon juice**
 1/8 **teaspoon garlic powder**
 1/8 **teaspoon dried oregano**
 1/8 **teaspoon Worcestershire sauce**
   3 **drops hot pepper sauce**
Cubed French bread *and/or* sliced apples

In a small bowl, combine 2 teaspoons cornstarch with 1 tablespoon wine; set aside. Combine the cheeses and remaining cornstarch; set aside.

Rub sides of a large saucepan with cut sides of garlic; discard garlic. Add remaining wine to the pan and heat over medium heat until bubbles form around sides of pan. Stir in lemon juice.

Reduce heat to medium-low; add a handful of cheese mixture. Stir constantly, using a figure-eight motion, until almost completely melted. Continue adding cheese, one handful at a time, allowing cheese to almost completely melt between additions.

Stir in garlic powder, oregano, Worcestershire sauce and hot pepper sauce. Stir cornstarch mixture; gradually add to the pan. Cook and stir until mixture is thickened and smooth. Keep warm. Serve with French bread cubes and/or sliced apples. **Yield:** 2 cups.

Heavenly Chocolate Marshmallow Fondue

(Pictured at right in the photo above)

PREP/TOTAL TIME: 15 min.

Guests won't be able to resist this rich, silky chocolate creation featuring butterscotch chips, marshmallow creme and coconut. Banana chunks are another yummy option for dipping.
—*Sarita Naegeli, Edmond, Oklahoma*

   1 **package (11 ounces) butterscotch chips**
   4 **ounces unsweetened chocolate, chopped**
   1 **can (14 ounces) sweetened condensed milk**
   1 **jar (7 ounces) marshmallow creme**
 1/4 **cup 2% milk**
 1/2 **cup flaked coconut**
   1 **teaspoon vanilla extract**
Fresh strawberries and cubed angel food cake

In a large microwave-safe bowl, melt butterscotch chips and chocolate; stir until smooth. Stir in condensed milk, marshmallow creme and milk. Microwave at 15-second intervals, stirring until smooth. Stir in the coconut and vanilla. Keep warm. Serve with strawberries and angel food cake. **Yield:** 5 cups.

Caramel Apple Fondue

(Pictured below and on page 288)

PREP/TOTAL TIME: 25 min.

I set out this warm caramel dip with apple slices while we're watching football games on Sundays. It really warms us up.
—Katie Koziolek, Hartland, Minnesota

- 1/2 **cup butter, cubed**
- 2 **cups packed brown sugar**
- 1 **can (14 ounces) sweetened condensed milk**
- 1 **cup light corn syrup**
- 2 **tablespoons water**
- 1 **teaspoon vanilla extract**

Apple slices

In a heavy 3-qt. saucepan, combine butter, brown sugar, milk, corn syrup and water; bring to a boil over medium heat. Cook and stir until a candy thermometer reads 230° (thread stage), about 8-10 minutes. Remove from the heat; stir in vanilla.

Transfer to a small fondue pot or 1-1/2-qt. slow cooker; keep warm. Serve with apple slices. **Yield:** 3-1/2 cups.

Editor's Note: We recommend that you test your candy thermometer before each use by bringing water to a boil; the thermometer should read 212°. Adjust your recipe temperature up or down based on your test.

Mexican Fondue

(Pictured above)

PREP: 15 min.   **COOK:** 1-1/2 hours

A handful of ingredients and a few moments of prep work are all you'll need for this festive blend. Not only does it take advantage of convenience items, but a slow cooker does most of the work.
—Nella Parker, Hersey, Michigan

- 1 **can (14-3/4 ounces) cream-style corn**
- 1 **can (14-1/2 ounces) diced tomatoes, drained**
- 3 **tablespoons chopped green chilies**
- 1 **teaspoon chili powder**
- 1 **package (16 ounces) process cheese (Velveeta), cubed**

French bread cubes

In a small bowl, combine corn, tomatoes, green chilies and chili powder. Stir in cheese. Pour mixture into a 1-1/2-qt. slow cooker coated with cooking spray.

Cover and cook on high for 1-1/2 hours, stirring every 30 minutes or until cheese is melted. Serve warm with bread cubes. **Yield:** 4-1/2 cups.

PARTY POINTERS. When hosting a fondue party, figure on one fondue pot for up to six people. Offer your guests a range of fun dippers that suit the types of fondue you're serving. Remember— never leave your fondue pots unattended.

Time for Tailgating!

WHEN your favorite sports team is playing the big game and you're heading to the stadium, it's time for a parking lot party featuring great food and camaraderie with fellow fans. For an unbeatable menu no one will soon forget, turn to the fresh-air fare here.

You'll score big points with your crowd when you serve Baja Chicken & Slaw Sliders, Fired-Up Polenta Shrimp Rounds, Steak Teriyaki Quesadillas and Mini Pear Crisps. Each delicious dish is easy to make for an outdoor get-together.

Just open your tailgate, start cooking these winning recipes and get ready to hear lots of cheers!

Baja Chicken & Slaw Sliders

(Pictured at right)

PREP: 30 min. **GRILL:** 10 min.

From the creamy lime sauce to the crunchy and colorful coleslaw, these handheld chicken sandwiches demand attention. They're guaranteed to satisfy even the hungriest of partygoers.
—*Janet Hynes, Racine, Wisconsin*

- 1/4 cup reduced-fat sour cream
- 1/2 teaspoon grated lime peel
- 1/4 teaspoon lime juice

SLAW:

- 1 cup broccoli coleslaw mix
- 2 tablespoons finely chopped sweet red pepper
- 2 tablespoons finely chopped sweet onion
- 2 tablespoons minced fresh cilantro
- 2 teaspoons finely chopped seeded jalapeno pepper
- 2 teaspoons lime juice
- 1 teaspoon sugar

SLIDERS:

- 4 boneless skinless chicken breast halves (4 ounces *each*)
- 1/2 teaspoon ground cumin
- 1/2 teaspoon chili powder
- 1/4 teaspoon salt
- 1/4 teaspoon coarsely ground pepper
- 8 Hawaiian sweet rolls, split
- 8 small lettuce leaves
- 8 slices tomato

In a small bowl, combine the sour cream, lime peel and lime juice. In another small bowl, combine the slaw ingredients. Chill the sauce and slaw until serving.

Cut each chicken breast in half widthwise; flatten to 1/2-in. thickness. Sprinkle with seasonings.

Moisten a paper towel with cooking oil; using long-handled tongs, lightly coat the grill rack. Grill chicken, covered, over medium heat or broil 4 in. from the heat for 4 to 7 minutes on each side or until no longer pink.

Grill the rolls, cut sides down, for 30-60 seconds or until toasted. Serve the chicken on rolls with lettuce, tomato,

sauce and slaw. **Yield:** 8 servings.

Editor's Note: We recommend wearing disposable gloves when cutting hot peppers. Avoid touching your face.

Steak Teriyaki Quesadillas

PREP: 20 min. + marinating **GRILL:** 15 min.

The slighly smoky flavor of these gently charred quesadillas really complements the sweet, tangy pineapple and savory steak.
—*Lisa Huff, Wilton, Connecticut*

- 1/3 cup reduced-sodium soy sauce
- 1/3 cup reduced-sodium chicken broth
- 1 tablespoon brown sugar
- 1 teaspoon minced fresh gingerroot
- 1/2 teaspoon onion powder
- 1 garlic clove, minced
- 1 beef top sirloin steak (1 inch thick and 3/4 pound)
- 1/2 cup finely chopped fresh pineapple

1/2 **cup finely chopped red onion**
1/2 **cup finely chopped green pepper**
2 **cups (8 ounces) shredded part-skim mozzarella cheese,** *divided*
6 **flour tortillas (8 inches)**

In a small bowl, combine the first six ingredients; set aside 3 tablespoons for filling. Pour remaining mixture into a large resealable plastic bag. Add the steak; seal bag and turn to coat. Refrigerate for 2 hours.

Drain the steak and discard the marinade. Grill steak, covered, over medium heat or broil 4 in. from the heat for 8-11 minutes on each side or until meat reaches desired doneness (for medium-rare, a meat thermometer should read 145°; medium, 160°; well-done, 170°).

Remove steak from the grill and cool slightly; cut into bite-size pieces. In a large bowl, combine the pineapple, red onion, green pepper and beef.

Sprinkle half of the cheese over three tortillas. Using a slotted spoon, top with beef mixture. Drizzle with the reserved soy mixture. Sprinkle with remaining cheese; top with remaining tortillas.

Grill over medium heat for 1-2 minutes on each side or until cheese is melted. Cut each into six wedges; serve immediately. **Yield:** 18 wedges.

Fired-Up Polenta Shrimp Rounds

PREP: 25 min. + marinating **GRILL:** 10 min.

I like to do more with my grill than just sear steaks and burgers. This recipe is a great way to expand your cookout horizons.
—*Jennifer Rodriguez, West Jordan, Utah*

1/4 **cup olive oil**
3 **garlic cloves, minced**
2 **teaspoons lime juice**
1 **teaspoon chopped seeded jalapeno pepper**
1/2 **teaspoon cayenne pepper**
1/4 **teaspoon pepper**
1 **pound uncooked medium shrimp, peeled and deveined**
SAUCE:
1/2 **cup mayonnaise**
1 **green onion, finely chopped**
1 **teaspoon chopped seeded jalapeno pepper**
1 **teaspoon hot pepper sauce**
1/2 **teaspoon cayenne pepper**
POLENTA:
1 **tube (1 pound) polenta, cut into 12 slices**
2 **tablespoons seafood seasoning**

In a large resealable plastic bag, combine the first six ingredients. Add the shrimp; seal bag and turn to coat. Refrigerate for up to 2 hours. In a small bowl, combine the sauce ingredients; chill until serving.

Sprinkle the polenta with seafood seasoning. Drain the shrimp and discard the marinade. Thread shrimp onto metal or soaked wooden skewers.

Moisten a paper towel with cooking oil; using long-handled tongs, lightly coat the grill rack. Grill the polenta and shrimp, covered, over medium heat for 5-8 minutes or until polenta is lightly browned and shrimp turn pink, turning once. Spoon the sauce over polenta; top with shrimp. **Yield:** 1 dozen.

Editor's Note: We recommend wearing disposable gloves when cutting hot peppers. Avoid touching your face.

Mini Pear Crisps

(Pictured below)

PREP: 25 min. **GRILL:** 20 min.

I put these fun desserts on the grill while everyone is enjoying my main dish and snacks. These yummy crisps are always a hit.
—*Joni Hilton, Rocklin, California*

1 **cup quick-cooking oats**
1 **cup packed brown sugar**
1/3 **cup all-purpose flour**
1 **teaspoon ground cinnamon**
1/2 **teaspoon ground nutmeg**
1/2 **cup cold butter**
1/2 **cup chopped pecans**
1/2 **cup raisins**
8 **medium pears, peeled and sliced**
Vanilla ice cream, optional

In a large bowl, combine the first five ingredients. Cut in butter until crumbly. Stir in pecans and raisins.

Divide pears among eight greased 4-1/2-in. disposable foil tart pans. Sprinkle with oat mixture.

Prepare grill for indirect heat. Grill the crisps, covered, over indirect medium heat for 15-20 minutes or until the pears are tender. Serve warm with ice cream if desired. **Yield:** 8 servings.

Substitutions & Equivalents

EQUIVALENT MEASURES

3 teaspoons	= 1 tablespoon	16 tablespoons	= 1 cup
4 tablespoons	= 1/4 cup	2 cups	= 1 pint
5-1/3 tablespoons	= 1/3 cup	4 cups	= 1 quart
8 tablespoons	= 1/2 cup	4 quarts	= 1 gallon

FOOD EQUIVALENTS

GRAINS

Macaroni	1 cup (3-1/2 ounces) uncooked	= 2-1/2 cups cooked
Noodles, Medium	3 cups (4 ounces) uncooked	= 4 cups cooked
Popcorn	1/3 to 1/2 cup unpopped	= 8 cups popped
Rice, Long Grain	1 cup uncooked	= 3 cups cooked
Rice, Quick-Cooking	1 cup uncooked	= 2 cups cooked
Spaghetti	8 ounces uncooked	= 4 cups cooked

CRUMBS

Bread	1 slice	= 3/4 cup soft crumbs, 1/4 cup fine dry crumbs
Graham Crackers	7 squares	= 1/2 cup finely crushed
Buttery Round Crackers	12 crackers	= 1/2 cup finely crushed
Saltine Crackers	14 crackers	= 1/2 cup finely crushed

FRUITS

Bananas	1 medium	= 1/3 cup mashed
Lemons	1 medium	= 3 tablespoons juice, 2 teaspoons grated peel
Limes	1 medium	= 2 tablespoons juice, 1-1/2 teaspoons grated peel
Oranges	1 medium	= 1/4 to 1/3 cup juice, 4 teaspoons grated peel

VEGETABLES

Cabbage	1 head	= 5 cups shredded	Green Pepper	1 large	= 1 cup chopped
Carrots	1 pound	= 3 cups shredded	Mushrooms	1/2 pound	= 3 cups sliced
Celery	1 rib	= 1/2 cup chopped	Onions	1 medium	= 1/2 cup chopped
Corn	1 ear fresh	= 2/3 cup kernels	Potatoes	3 medium	= 2 cups cubed

NUTS

Almonds	1 pound	= 3 cups chopped	Pecan Halves	1 pound	= 4-1/2 cups chopped
Ground Nuts	3-3/4 ounces	= 1 cup	Walnuts	1 pound	= 3-3/4 cups chopped

EASY SUBSTITUTIONS

When you need...		Use...
Baking Powder	1 teaspoon	1/2 teaspoon cream of tartar + 1/4 teaspoon baking soda
Buttermilk	1 cup	1 tablespoon lemon juice or vinegar + enough milk to measure 1 cup (let stand 5 minutes before using)
Cornstarch	1 tablespoon	2 tablespoons all-purpose flour
Honey	1 cup	1-1/4 cups sugar + 1/4 cup water
Half-and-Half Cream	1 cup	1 tablespoon melted butter + enough whole milk to measure 1 cup
Onion	1 small, chopped (1/3 cup)	1 teaspoon onion powder or 1 tablespoon dried minced onion
Tomato Juice	1 cup	1/2 cup tomato sauce + 1/2 cup water
Tomato Sauce	2 cups	3/4 cup tomato paste + 1 cup water
Unsweetened Chocolate	1 square (1 ounce)	3 tablespoons baking cocoa + 1 tablespoon shortening or oil
Whole Milk	1 cup	1/2 cup evaporated milk + 1/2 cup water

COOKING TERMS

Here's a quick reference for some of the cooking terms used in *Taste of Home* recipes:

BASTE To moisten food with melted butter, pan drippings, marinades or other liquid to add more flavor and juiciness.

BEAT A rapid movement to combine ingredients using a fork, spoon, wire whisk or electric mixer.

BLEND To combine ingredients until *just* mixed.

BOIL To heat liquids until bubbles form that cannot be "stirred down." In the case of water, the temperature will reach 212°.

BONE To remove all meat from the bone before cooking.

CREAM To beat ingredients together to a smooth consistency, usually in the case of butter and sugar for baking.

DASH A small amount of seasoning, less than 1/8 teaspoon. If using a shaker, a dash would comprise a quick flip of the container.

DREDGE To coat foods with flour or other dry ingredients. Most often done with pot roasts and stew meat before browning.

FOLD To incorporate several ingredients by careful and gentle turning with a spatula. Used generally with beaten egg whites or whipped cream when mixing into the rest of the ingredients to keep the batter light.

JULIENNE To cut foods into long thin strips much like matchsticks. Used most often for salads and stir-fry dishes.

MINCE To cut into very fine pieces. Used often for garlic or fresh herbs.

PARBOIL To cook partially, usually used in the case of chicken, sausages and vegetables.

PARTIALLY SET Describes the consistency of gelatin after it has been chilled for a short amount of time. Mixture should resemble the consistency of egg whites.

PUREE To process foods to a smooth mixture. Can be prepared in an electric blender, food processor, food mill or sieve.

SAUTE To fry quickly in a small amount of fat, stirring almost constantly. Most often done with onions, mushrooms and other chopped vegetables.

SCORE To cut slits partway through the outer surface of foods. Often used with ham or flank steak.

STIR-FRY To cook meats and/or vegetables with a constant stirring motion in a small amount of oil in a wok or skillet over high heat.

General Recipe Index

This handy index lists every recipe by food category, major ingredient and/or cooking method, so you can easily locate recipes to suit your needs.

✓ Recipe includes Nutrition Facts and Diabetic Exchanges

✓ Recipe includes Nutrition Facts and Diabetic Exchanges

✓ Recipe includes Nutrition Facts and Diabetic Exchanges

✓ Recipe includes Nutrition Facts and Diabetic Exchanges

✓ *Recipe includes Nutrition Facts and Diabetic Exchanges*

✓ *Recipe includes Nutrition Facts and Diabetic Exchanges*

✓ Recipe includes Nutrition Facts and Diabetic Exchanges

✓ *Recipe includes Nutrition Facts and Diabetic Exchanges*

✓ Recipe includes Nutrition Facts and Diabetic Exchanges

✓ Recipe includes Nutrition Facts and Diabetic Exchanges

Alphabetical Recipe Index
This handy index lists every recipe in alphabetical order so you can easily find your favorites.

✓ Recipe includes Nutrition Facts and Diabetic Exchanges

✓ Recipe includes Nutrition Facts and Diabetic Exchanges

✓ Recipe includes Nutrition Facts and Diabetic Exchanges

✓ Recipe includes Nutrition Facts and Diabetic Exchanges

✓ *Recipe includes Nutrition Facts and Diabetic Exchanges*